"In [the 2020] presidential election year, historian and journalist A. J. Baime has given America a winner."

—***St. Louis Post-Dispatch***

"*Dewey Defeats Truman*, A. J. Baime's lively and insightful account of the second-most shocking presidential upset in modern history, delivers the best-reasoned and most revealing examination to date of that memorable mid-century election."

—***New York Journal of Books***

"I thought the stakes had never been higher for Americans than [in November 2020]—until I read A. J. Baime's astonishing *Dewey Defeats Truman* . . . The parallels between 1948 and 2020 are staggering . . . This is a classic underdog story that works brilliantly regardless of any nods to the present day. And even though its end is known, Baime still manages to create superb tension as Truman takes his message to the American public . . . Someone buy those screen rights."

—***Haaretz* (Isreal)**

Dewey Defeats Truman

BOOKS BY A. J. BAIME

The Accidental President (2017)

The Arsenal of Democracy (2014)

Go Like Hell (2009)

Big Shots (2003)

Dewey Defeats Truman

The 1948 Election *and the* Battle for America's Soul

A. J. Baime

Mariner Books
Houghton Mifflin Harcourt
BOSTON NEW YORK

First Mariner Books edition 2021

hmhbooks.com

Library of Congress Cataloging-in-Publication Data
Names: Baime, A. J. (Albert J.), author.
Title: Dewey defeats Truman : the 1948 election and the battle for America's soul / A.J. Baime.
Other titles: 1948 election and the battle for America's soul
Description: Boston : Houghton Mifflin Harcourt, 2020. | Includes bibliographical references and index.
Identifiers: LCCN 2019042905 (print) | LCCN 2019042906 (ebook) | ISBN 9781328585066 (hardcover) | ISBN 9781328588593 (ebook) | ISBN 9780358522492 (trade paper)
Subjects: LCSH: Presidents—United States—Election—1948. | United States—Politics and government—1945–1953. | Truman, Harry S., 1884–1972. | Dewey, Thomas E. (Thomas Edmund), 1902–1971. | Wallace, Henry A. (Henry Agard), 1888–1965. | Thurmond, Strom, 1902–2003.
Classification: LCC E815 .B35 2020 (print) | LCC E815 (ebook) | DDC 324.973/0904—dc23
LC record available at https://lccn.loc.gov/2019042905
LC ebook record available at https://lccn.loc.gov/2019042906

Book design by Chloe Foster

Printed in the United States of America
DOC 10 9 8 7 6 5 4 3 2 1

Every vital question of state will be merged in the question, "Who will be the next President?"

—Alexander Hamilton

It is not just a battle between two parties. It is a fight for the very soul of the American government.

—Harry Truman, Chicago Stadium, October 25, 1948

Contents

Introduction ix

PART I: The Disintegration of the Democratic Party 1

PART II: The Surging GOP 45

PART III: The Conventions 131

PART IV: The Campaigns 167

PART V: Election Climax 261

Epilogue 350

Acknowledgments 355

Notes 357

Index 404

Introduction

A GROUNDSWELL OF WHITE NATIONALISM. Impeachment headlines. A president caught in a bitter public feud with his own Congress. A resurgence of populism. A game-changing new form of media. A chief executive aiming fake news accusations at the national press. War and terrorism in the Middle East. A booming economy, with historically low unemployment. The FBI on the trail of a major presidential candidate regarding a possible Russian conspiracy.

The year was 1948.

This book is about the first postwar presidential election, which was the first election to play out on the "television machine" and was the most shocking electoral upset in the history of the United States, at least up until 2016. In the years after 1948, it was commonly said that all Americans could remember exactly where they were on two occasions: when they heard the news of the Japanese attack on Pearl Harbor and when they learned the result of the 1948 presidential election. Harry S. Truman's campaign was called at the time "the most colorful and astonishing political campaign in modern American history," "a gigantic comedy," "the wildest campaign of the century."

The impetus for this book is another I wrote, *The Accidental President,* published in 2017; it covers the first four months of Truman's presidency, when an obscure vice president with relatively little formal education found himself suddenly in charge of a world war following the death of Franklin Roosevelt. (Readers who consumed that book may want to skim chapter three in this one, which covers Truman's history and thus some familiar details.) While researching that book, I realized that the challenges of peacetime, in the wake of a global conflict and the birth of the atomic age, could be equally staggering. In the run-up to his longshot bid to be elected in his own right, Truman faced the founding of Israel and the start of the 1948 Arab-Israeli War. He desegregated the military. He launched the Marshall Plan and the Berlin Airlift. The explosive Alger Hiss espionage charges set off the "Red Scare."

The year 1948 saw a brutal and at times deadly struggle in which black southerners sought to exercise their right to vote. It witnessed the beginning of a historic realignment of the Democratic "Solid South," which transformed states like Alabama, Mississippi, South Carolina, and Georgia into the Republican strongholds they remain today.

Documents of the time express startling fear on both sides of the aisle that Moscow would attempt to meddle in the American election. One campaign official wrote in a secret memo in 1947 that "the Kremlin will sponsor political disturbances everywhere it can throughout the next twelve months . . . It will try to influence the result of the 1948 election by every means conceivable."

The Operation Sandstone atomic-bomb tests, anxiety that World War III could break out at any moment—all of this formed the stage upon which the election campaigns unfolded. The shifts in the tides of power moved with ruthless force, creating the geopolitical world of the future, our world of today.

Dewey Defeats Truman will bring readers inside the situation rooms of four campaigns: Harry Truman's Democratic Party, Thomas Dewey's Republican Party, Henry Wallace's breakaway Progressive Party (which was largely controlled by a secret cell of Communists), and Strom Thurmond's States' Rights Democratic Party (the "Dixiecrats," a campaign of unapologetic white supremacy). While the election's victor is the ultimate focus of the book, my goal was not to favor one candidate's policies over another, but rather to state the facts and how they were perceived at the time. Although two of these candidates performed poorly in the end, their stories in retrospect are extraordinary. Oftentimes we can learn as much from election losers and charismatic political misfits as we can from the winners.

I have tried as often as possible to let original documentation unfold this narrative — to allow these historical characters to bring themselves to life through their own memorandums, diaries, and oral histories. The expectation I set for myself was this: If they could read this book today, they would find it fair, factual, and expressive of the almost desperate urgency that fueled their quests for the presidency. As the *New York Times* put it just before Election Day in 1948: "The fate of the nation and of civilization is at stake."

Truman believed that history repeats itself. "The history of the world," he wrote, "has moved in cycles and . . . very often we find ourselves in the midst of political circumstances which appear to be new but which might have existed in almost identical form at various times during the past six thousand years." My guess is that readers will find the election season of 1948 uncannily relevant today.

At the same time, I am hoping readers will find inspiration in this book. During 1947–48, the bipartisan discourse was mercilessly vitriolic — as it is today. Yet when faced with a national emergency, Democrats and Republicans came together to launch some of the most enduring policies in the country's history (the Truman Doctrine, the Marshall Plan). These leaders realized that their duty as public servants was not to their parties but to all Americans, in the vital struggle for the future.

A. J. BAIME

OCTOBER 30, 2019

PART I

The Disintegration of the Democratic Party

The loud outcry against President Truman exceeds anything we have heard in a long time. There is about it a savage quality.

— ***Washington Post,*** **October 11, 1946**

1

"Whither Harry S. Truman?"

"ALL IN," A SECRET SERVICE man said.

It was 7 p.m. on August 14, 1945. A White House usher closed the door to the Oval Office and Harry Truman stood from behind his desk, staring out at a crowd of some two hundred perspiring radio and newspaper reporters who had just pushed their way in. Klieg lights from newsreel cameras glared off the president's wire-rim spectacles. A row of cabinet officials stood behind him, and at the edge of the room, the First Lady, Bess Truman, was seated on a couch, her hands folded in a ball on her lap. Truman held up a statement in his right hand and began to read. All in the room knew what this address would communicate, but still, the words had the effect of an electric shock.

"I have received this afternoon a message from the Japanese Government," Truman said, "in reply to the message forwarded to that Government by the Secretary of State on August 11. I deem this reply a full acceptance of the Potsdam Declaration which specifies the unconditional surrender of Japan."

The president's full statement took a few minutes to read. His final words were, "That is all."

When the doors to the Oval Office opened, reporters holding notepads dashed out to spread the news around the globe. World War II — the most destructive conflagration ever, a war that had consumed some sixty million human lives — was over.

Within minutes the news hit the radio. Outside on the streets of the nation's capital, the doors of churches, offices, theaters, and bars burst open, pouring frantic Washingtonians into the hot August night. Impromptu jitterbug contests broke out on street corners. Drunks swung bottles while standing atop cars. At the White House gates, people began to amass, and within an hour of Truman's declaration, a crowd bigger than the capacity of Yankee Stadium — some seventy-five thousand people — stood out on Pennsylvania Avenue. They began to chant: "We want Harry! We want Harry!"

Inside the executive mansion, Truman was busy making phone calls. He called his ninety-three-year-old mother, at her home in Grandview, Missouri. ("That was Harry," Mamma Truman said after hanging up. "Harry's such a wonderful man . . . I knew he'd call.") He telephoned the former First Lady, Eleanor Roosevelt, who was still reeling from the death of her husband, Franklin, just four months earlier. "I told her," Truman later recalled, "that in this hour of triumph I wished that it had been President Roosevelt, and not I, who had given the message to our people."

Meanwhile, the "We want Harry!" chanting grew in decibels. The din became irresistible, and so Truman and his wife stepped out onto the White House lawn. Looking fit in a creased and buttoned double-breasted blue suit, the sixty-one-year-old president made a V sign with his fingers as Secret Service men hustled around him. A news photographer jumped forward and froze the moment in black-and-white celluloid. "[Truman] was on the White House lawn pumping his arms like an orchestra conductor at tens of thousands of cheering Americans who suddenly materialized in front of the mansion," recalled one person present in the crowd. It was "the wildest celebration this capital ever saw."

White House aides brought out a microphone and a loudspeaker and placed them in front of Truman. He had always been an awkward public speaker, but on this occasion, it did not matter. No one cared. When he began to speak, the crowds instantly hushed.

"This is a great day," Truman said, "the day we've been waiting for. This is the day for free governments in the world. This is the day that fascism and police government ceases in the world. This is the day for Democracy." He paused, taking in the moment. He had spent a lifetime reading history, studying the sagas of past presidents, never in his wildest dreams imagining that he would become one of them. He knew then that the challenges awaiting him in the near future were beyond anything any president had ever confronted before.

"We are faced with the greatest task with which we have ever been faced," Truman said into the microphone. That task was to bring freedom to humanity all over the world and cultivate peace and prosperity at home. "It is going to take the help of all of us," the president stated. "I know we are going to do it."

All around the globe on this night, chaos reigned.

In the Far East, the cities of Hiroshima and Nagasaki still smoldered under radioactive clouds from the atomic bombings on August 6 and 9. Two days before Truman announced Japan's unconditional surrender, the first aerial photos of Hiroshima post-detonation appeared on the front page of the *New York Times.* It was almost impossible to understand what this new weapon was, how it could harness the power of the universe, and what it would mean for the future. The secretary of commerce, Henry Wallace, put the situation in perspective, writing in his diary the day after the Hiroshima bombing, "Everyone seemed to feel that a new epoch in the world's history had been ushered in. The scramble for the control of this new power is going to be one of the most unusual struggles the world has ever seen."

In Europe, surviving populations clawed out of the rubble from nearly 2.7 million tons of bombs dropped by Allied airpower between 1940 and 1945. Huge numbers of people were without food and water. In France, according to the nation's Ministry of Public Health, more than half of the children living in industrial areas had rickets. A third of the children in Belgium were tubercular. The US State Department estimated that nine million displaced persons were homeless in Europe — many of them Jews who had survived Hitler's "Final Solution." Some of the most gruesome death camps — Auschwitz, Buchenwald, Ravensbrück — had only recently been liberated, revealing the true depth of Nazi madness. At Auschwitz, the liberating Red Army had discovered more than fourteen thousand pounds of human hair.

In June 1945 the State Department had sent a lawyer named Earl G. Harrison to investigate the concentration camps, and his now-famous report — delivered to Truman just days after the president announced the surrender of Japan — painted a picture of a desperate situation. The occupying Allied forces in Europe had little resources to help the hundreds of thousands of displaced Jews, who were still dying in large numbers, right before their eyes. "As matters now stand, we appear to be treating the Jews as the Nazis treated them except that we do not exterminate them," Harrison wrote.

In the Middle East, Soviet, French, British, and American troops occupied the homelands of increasingly bitter ethnic and sectarian tribes. China was on the brink of a Communist revolution. The British government was destitute and desperate for loans. The United States and Soviet Union, meanwhile, were emerging from the war as history's first two global superpowers, and relations between the two were declining profoundly.

"Secular history offers few, if any, parallels to the events of the past week," reported CBS radio news anchor Edward R. Murrow, at the time of Japan's surrender. "And seldom, if ever, has a war ended leaving the victors with such a sense of uncertainty and fear, with such a realization that the future is obscure and that survival is not assured."

In Washington, the nation's elite politicians and officials were set to confront a scintillating mystery. Truman was a new president, a vice president who had risen to the Oval Office just four months earlier upon the death of Franklin Roosevelt. His obscurity confounded the world. What exactly did he intend to do as president of the United States? The atomic bombs had ended the war so unexpectedly quickly, there had been no time to plan for the postwar future, and the American people knew little about their new president's politics.

How would the administration handle the staggering challenge of converting to a peacetime economy? What would be the administration's policy regarding the Soviets and the bomb? What was Truman going to do about the millions of American workers who would now be laid off from domestic wartime jobs and pushed out of factories? How many of the 12.2 million men in uniform would be allowed to come home and resume their lives, and when?

Many of Truman's friends on Capitol Hill were sure he would bring conservatism to a Democratic presidency, as so many had hoped for so long. Others were convinced he would maintain the path of FDR and embrace Roosevelt's liberal New Deal policies.

"Whither Harry S. Truman?" asked the columnist Edward T. Folliard in the *Washington Post,* days after the war ended. "Is he going to the left, the right, or down the middle of the road?"

Politically, Truman had to know: This was not going to go well for him. Roosevelt had held the White House for over 12 years, and there is a natural tendency in democratic societies for periodic change. Churchill was unceremoniously swept from power in London in July 1945. In all of America's 169-year history, only twice before had a vice president been elected following a two-term presidency. And in those years, the political environment was hardly as fraught as it was now, in the aftermath of World War II and at the dawn of the atomic age. "The President's task was reminiscent of that in the first chapter of Genesis," noted Undersecretary of State Dean Acheson, "to help the free world emerge from chaos without blowing the whole world apart in the process."

Even before the war ended, Truman had begun to confidentially lay out a political philosophy of his own, what he called "the foundation of my administration."

In July 1945—the month before the atomic bombings of Japan—he had ventured to the Potsdam Conference in Allied-occupied Germany for a series of talks with Winston Churchill and Joseph Stalin. It had been a grueling trip. When the conference was over, Truman flew in one of FDR's most revered speechwriters, Judge Samuel Rosenman, so the two could begin to sketch out Truman's postwar plans in language Americans could understand, while the men traveled back to the United States together aboard the navy cruiser USS *Augusta*.

FDR had nicknamed Rosenman "Sammy the Rose." The judge had helped fine-tune FDR's public voice over the years. (According to some, it had been Rosenman who had coined the term "New Deal.") Now Truman wanted Rosenman to do the same for him.

One evening in the president's cabin aboard the *Augusta,* as the two men huddled alone, Truman told Rosenman, "Sam, one of the things I want to do after we get home . . . is to get busy on my domestic program. I would like to submit most of it at the same time instead of on a piecemeal basis. Ordinarily that would be done in a State of the Union message next January, but I cannot wait that long."

"Fine," Rosenman said. "What in general are the things you would like to say?"

The judge leaned his bulky frame forward to reach for a pad and pencil, and he began taking notes while Truman spoke off the cuff on a variety of issues. There in the president's cabin, with the dull drone of the *Augusta*'s engines in the background, the Truman presidency began to take shape.

Rosenman's eyes widened as he outlined Truman's thoughts. "You know, Mr. President," he said, "this is the most exciting and pleasant surprise I have had in a long time."

"How is that?"

"Well," the judge said, "I suppose I have been listening too much to rumors about what you are going to do—rumors which come from some of your conservative friends . . . They say you are going to be quite a shock to those who followed Roosevelt—that the New Deal is as good as dead—that we are all going back to 'normalcy' and that a good part of the so-called 'Roosevelt nonsense' is now over. In other words, that the conservative wing of the [Democratic] party has now taken charge."

Roosevelt had launched hugely controversial, expensive, and interventionist policies to steer America out of the Great Depression and through the war. For the most part, they had worked, but in the process they had inspired bitterness and rivalry—between the White House and Congress, and between the Right and the Left. Now Truman was planning to embrace similar left-wing policies in the postwar world. This was a brave move, Rosenman said, and a dangerous one.

"It is one thing to vote for this kind of a program when you are following the head of your party," the judge said. "It is quite another to be the head of a party and recommend and fight for it."

Back in the White House, upon Truman's return from Potsdam, the West Wing resumed its usual pace of frenetic activity. During late nights and early mornings, bookending the long list of appointments that filled the president's daily calendar, Truman continued to craft a message to Congress. He consulted advisers and all the major officers of the executive branch, and created in the process a buzz that could be felt throughout the halls of the Capitol. He wanted his message to land with all the weight of "a combination of a first inaugural and a first State of the Union message," as he put it.

On September 6, three weeks after he announced the surrender of Japan, Truman held his regular weekly press conference at 4 p.m. in the Oval Office, where he evaded questions on everything from the proposed Saint Lawrence waterway to his pick for an open seat on the Supreme Court. Afterward, when the door to the Oval Office closed and he was once again alone, he released his domestic plan, titled the "Special Message to Congress Presenting a 21-Point Program for the Reconversion Period," via his press secretary, Charlie Ross. It was the longest message to Congress since Theodore Roosevelt's administration, measuring sixteen thousand words.

"The Congress reconvenes at a time of great emergency," the message read. "It is an emergency about which, however, we need have no undue fear if we exercise the same energy, foresight, and wisdom as we did in carrying the war and winning this victory."

Truman asked Congress to create new laws to expand Social Security and unemployment and veterans' benefits. He asked Congress to raise the minimum wage, currently forty cents per hour. He asked for programs to outlaw racial and religious discrimination in hiring, and for federal aid to farmers and small businesses. He wanted government spending on housing, funding for the conservation of natural resources, and financing of public works —highways, federal buildings, three thousand new airports, and a massive program of scientific research.

"The development of atomic energy is a clear-cut indication of what can be accomplished by our universities, industry, and Government working together," Truman's message read. "Vast scientific fields remain to be conquered in the same way."

Truman asked Congress to maintain a large military "in a world grown acutely sensitive to power," despite the cost. He even asked Congress to pass a law raising the salaries of its own members. The message ended with the following words:

"The Congress has played its full part in shaping the domestic and foreign policies which have . . . started us on the road to lasting peace. The Congress, I know, will continue to play its patriotic part in the difficult years ahead. We face the future together with confidence—that the job, the full job, can and will be done. Harry S. Truman."

On September 7, Americans awoke to the realization that their new president was a full-on New Deal Democrat. As the United States' chief executive, he would safeguard the welfare of the common man. As he once had said, "The President has to look out for the interests of the 150 million people who can't afford lobbyists in Washington."

Truman's 21-Point Program ignited a political firestorm. It was so vast, there was something in it to offend just about everyone, no matter their political sensibility. Most of all, Washington powerbrokers were shocked at the amount of federal spending recommended by the president. "Not even President Roosevelt asked for so much at one sitting," argued the House minority leader, Republican Joe Martin of Massachusetts. The *Washington Post* called Truman's domestic program "the most far-reaching collection of economic policies ever promulgated by a public authority in the United States in peacetime."

For years under Roosevelt, the political climate in Washington had been growing more hostile, the partisan tension mounting. By 1945, a Democrat had occupied the White House for nearly thirteen years. With the Depression subsided, the war over, and a new president deemed by many to be weak and inexperienced, Republicans believed that the nation was ripe for a return to conservatism. Truman's 21-Point Program rallied the cause. Congressman Charles Halleck of Indiana summed up Republican reaction, the day after Truman released his domestic agenda.

"This begins the campaign of 1946," Halleck said, referring to the upcoming midterm election. "The gloves would be off from here on out."

2

"The Buck Stops Here!"

ON THE MORNING OF SEPTEMBER 21—five weeks after Truman's announcement of Japan's surrender—the president arrived in the West Wing in a foul mood. The offices teemed with employees who, like their boss, were fairly new on the job. Here was the handsome thirty-seven-year-old Irish American Matthew Connelly manning the Oval Office door as the president's appointments secretary. Here was the president's secretary Roberta Barrows, with two incessantly jingling telephones on her desk, and press secretary Charlie Ross trailing an ever-present cloud of tobacco smoke.

The pressure of the job was getting to Truman. In his morning staff meeting, he erupted in anger. "[Truman] said . . . he was liable to come in some morning with a headful of decisions and tell them all to 'go to hell,'" assistant press secretary Eben Ayers wrote in his diary of this meeting. "He said he did not want 'this job'—the presidency—but he's got it and he's going to do it."

In the weeks after the president had announced Japan's unconditional surrender, every typewriter in every newsroom in America, it seemed, was firing off bad news at machine-gun speed—with Truman's name in the headline. At megacorporations like Ford Motor Company and Westinghouse Electric, strikes had crippled production. The United States was on the brink of the biggest labor crisis in its modern history. Prices of consumer goods were rapidly rising, and Congress had ignored the president's anti-inflation policy, which Truman had called "a declaration of war against this new enemy of the United States."

Rising unemployment.

An acute shortage of meat in grocery stores.

A housing crisis. In Chicago alone, it was reported, one hundred thousand military veterans were homeless, living on the streets.

The nation's economy was in the grips of unprecedented change. During the war, the entire country—government, free enterprise, military—had joined in what Roosevelt termed "the Arsenal of Democracy," united in the goal of defeating the Axis powers. It could be expected that a return to normalcy would be rocky, but the government now found itself in gridlock, the president at the intersection of conflicting advice. "Everybody wants something at the expense of everybody else," he wrote his mother and sister, "and nobody thinks much of the other fellow."

All the while, the foreign policy of the United States was being challenged as never before. The Soviets were aggressively expanding power and control across Eastern Europe, shamelessly flouting agreements they had made at the Yalta and Potsdam conferences. All over the globe, the war's destruction created power vacuums, and the United States and the USSR had become rivals in the effort to fill them—with the American brand of freedom and democracy or the Soviet brand of totalitarianism. Many in Washington were already predicting military conflict. One of the State Department's chief foreign policy experts, Joseph Grew, had come to the conclusion that "a future war with Soviet Russia is as certain as anything in this world."

What position was the Truman administration going to take?

At 2 p.m. on September 21, hours after Truman blew up at his morning staff meeting, he met with his cabinet to discuss the most explosive issue confronting his administration. The proposed agenda: "The atomic bomb, and the peacetime development of atomic energy." What was to be done with this revolutionary new science? The US State Department used the term *balance of power* to describe a recipe for peace between the two emerging superpowers. And yet nothing tipped the balance more than the bomb. The United

States had it; the Soviet Union did not. The science behind the weapon was still a closely held secret, but it was only a matter of time before the Soviets developed their own atomic technology.

In the Cabinet Room, just down the hall from the Oval Office, Truman sat in the president's customary chair, with windows behind him offering a view of the White House Rose Garden. He turned first to his secretary of war, Henry Stimson. It was Stimson's seventy-eighth birthday and a bittersweet day. He was the only Republican in Truman's cabinet, and a holdover from FDR's administration. His career in high-level federal government went back thirty-five years (he had been secretary of war under William H. Taft), and it was his final day of work before retirement. Stimson had headed up the Manhattan Project in the executive branch since the early days of its existence. Now he was called upon to recommend policy for atomic energy going forward.

Stimson had come to a controversial conclusion: He wanted the United States to partner with the Soviets, to share the secret of atomic energy—now, before it was too late. "We do not have a secret to give away," Stimson said, according to the meeting minutes. "The secret will give itself away. The problem is how to treat the secret with respect to the safety of the world." The bomb had made the Soviets deeply suspicious of America's aims. "If we fail to approach them now," Stimson argued in a separate memo to Truman dated days earlier, "and merely continue to negotiate with them, having this weapon rather ostentatiously on our hip, their suspicions and their distrust of our purposes and motives will increase."

Grave risk accompanied either option—to include the Soviets in US nuclear research, or to exclude them. But Stimson believed that sharing the technology involved *less* risk. The difference meant "some chance" of "saving civilization not for five or twenty years, but forever."

The bombs used on Japan—code-named Fat Man and Little Boy—shocked the world with their destructive capacity, Stimson said, but the bombs soon to be born would be infinitely more powerful. Scientists were concerned, Stimson explained, that future bombs would have the potential to ignite the earth's atmosphere and "put an end to the world."

Truman ruminated. He alone had ordered the atomic bombings of Japan; now, six weeks after the annihilation of Hiroshima and Nagasaki, the fallout continued to poison relations with the Soviets. Truman's advisers were sharply divided. Attorney General Tom Clark believed the bomb was the best leverage the Americans had in terms of negotiating with the Soviets. Clark thought the United States "should continue to carry a big stick," according to the meeting minutes.

Another participant at the table — Henry Wallace of Iowa, the secretary of commerce — was dubious, and it was Wallace who would soon voice the loudest dissent. Wallace agreed with Stimson. The Soviets would soon have the bomb. "Science," the commerce secretary said, "cannot be restrained." Why not share the secret now, and make the Soviets partners in the quest for future peace?

Wallace's words carried significant weight. The fifty-six-year-old former vice president was a hero among liberal Democrats. In the Cabinet Room, he was unnerved. Truman was not inclined to share nuclear secrets with the Soviets. For the time being, Wallace would keep his thoughts to himself. He believed Truman and his closest advisers were on the wrong path. As he wrote in his diary, "Their attitude will make for war eventually."

"The pressure here is becoming so great I hardly get my meals in," Truman wrote his mother on October 13, 1945. Three weeks after the bomb debate, he faced increasing hostility in Washington and a disintegrating approval rating. A new sign appeared on his desk — painted glass on a walnut base, measuring thirteen inches long and two and a half inches tall. On the side facing the president, it said, I'M FROM MISSOURI. On the side facing whomever walked into the Oval Office, it said, THE BUCK STOPS HERE!

Truman doubled down on increasingly controversial policies. He knew his ideas would spark fury from the Republicans and even conservative Democrats, but he felt that he was right. On October 23, he made what the popular columnist Roscoe Drummond called at the time his "boldest, most vigorous, most uncompromising speech" yet to demand that Congress enact a "Universal Military Training" plan, in which every American male between age eighteen and twenty-two would serve the nation for a year in some capacity. It was the only way, he declared, "to maintain the power with which to assist other peace-loving nations to enforce its authority."

America was sick of war and tired of service; millions of voters were repulsed by the idea. It was all but ignored by Congress.

On November 19, 1945, Truman called on Congress to pass a national compulsory health insurance program for all Americans "who work for a living," regardless of their ability to pay for health care. "Under the plan I suggest," Truman argued, "our people would continue to get medical and hospital services just as they do now — on the basis of their own voluntary decisions and choices. Our doctors and hospitals would continue to deal with disease with the same professional freedom as now. There would, however, be this all-important difference: whether or not patients get the services they need would not depend on how much they can afford to pay at the time."

Republicans pounced. Truman's plan was "socialized medicine," said Senator Robert Taft of Ohio — "Mr. Republican." The American Medical Association opposed the plan. So too did many Democrats. The initiative went nowhere.

Truman began to lose the confidence of those advisers he depended on most. In Moscow, Secretary of State James Byrnes was conducting meetings with the Soviets, and he released to news agencies a communiqué on the proceedings without first informing the president. Truman learned of the outcome of the negotiations by reading the newspaper. He was livid.

When Truman asked General Douglas MacArthur — the supreme commander of the Allied occupying forces in Japan — to make a trip to Washington for a meeting in the White House, MacArthur defied the president's request and refused to come home, citing "the extraordinarily dangerous situation in Japan." (Truman told staffers that he was "going to do something with that fellow.")

In February 1946 Congressman Adam Clayton Powell Jr. — an African American Democrat from Harlem — attacked the Truman family in an interview with newspaper reporters after Bess Truman attended an event at a segregated theater, closed to African Americans. "My mind is not made up on some things but there is one thing of which I am now certain," Congressman Powell declared. "I will not vote for Harry Truman for president in 1948."

That same month, Secretary of the Interior Harold Ickes—the self-styled "old curmudgeon," a highly respected Roosevelt holdover—resigned after a disagreement over Truman's choice of a new undersecretary of the navy. Ickes accused Truman of trying to appoint a political crony who had grave conflicts of interest. Ickes held a press conference and viciously rebuked the president. The *Los Angeles Times* called it "the biggest press conference in the history of Washington"; "the White House will be rocking on its foundations from the reverberations two years from now" (i.e., the next presidential election).

When railroad workers went on strike in the spring of 1946, paralyzing the nation's transportation system and threatening the safety of the economy, Truman came up with a plan to draft striking railroad workers into the army, to force them to work. He called Alexander Whitney, president of the Brotherhood of Railroad Trainmen and one of the nation's most powerful union leaders, "un-American" and an "enemy of the people." Union support was the Democrats' calling card. Truman's move was bold, but hardly wise for a president with an election on the horizon. Whitney shot back at Truman, "You can't make a President out of a ribbon clerk."

"If I live and have my health," Whitney said in a speech to union workers in Cleveland, "I'll be fighting the infamy of such work when Harry Truman is back in Missouri and forgotten."

The biggest story in Washington became the unraveling of the Truman administration. The president was the butt of jokes. "I'm just mild about Harry" punned off the popular song "I'm Just Wild About Harry." "To err is Truman" became a popular quip. The star New York entertainer Billy Rose suggested that the comedian W. C. Fields run for president in 1948: "If we're going to have a comedian in the White House, let's have a good one." Columnists poured on the vitriol, criticizing everything from Truman's choice of neckties to his plan to add a balcony to the White House. His advisers were hacks, the critics said—"a lot of second-rate guys trying to function in an atom bomb world," in the words of one administration official, speaking to reporters anonymously.

Republicans feasted on schadenfreude. "If Truman wanted to elect a Republican Congress," Senator Robert Taft joked in a letter to the Republican governor of New York, Thomas Dewey, "he could not be doing a better job."

At 11:45 a.m. on September 19, 1946, Truman arose from behind the Oval Office desk to greet a delegation of black activists led by Walter Francis White. Truman expected the meeting to be another of the usual affairs that crowded his office calendar. Few came to see the president unless they wanted something from him, and Truman cynically called these visitors his "customers," whether they were Democrats or Republicans, white or black.

Walter Francis White, however, was no ordinary customer.

White was the leader of the National Association for the Advancement of Colored People. This struck Truman as odd, because White did not appear to be colored. He was of mixed race, and with his light skin and blue eyes, he could easily pass as Caucasian, which, it turns out, he sometimes did.

He had been raised in Atlanta, had gone to a black college, and had become involved in race activism soon after, moving to Harlem during the Harlem Renaissance to work for a fledgling organization called the NAACP. During the 1920s, he had gone undercover as a white man to investigate lynchings of black men in the South, and his reports on these crimes in his writings had shocked the nation. He became head of the NAACP in 1931. During the war, the organization had grown considerably, and with it, the stature of Walter White.

Following the end of the war, a horrifying spate of violence against black men in the South had mobilized White and the NAACP to fight back. Some of the victims had been black soldiers recently discharged from the United States military. In the Oval Office, White began to tell harrowing stories as Truman sat in his chair with his arms folded in front of him.

There was the story of John C. Jones, a corporal recently honorably discharged from the army, who had returned to his home in Minden, Louisiana. Jones had been suspected of loitering in the backyard of a home where a white woman lived. In August 1946, just a month before White's meeting with Truman, Jones was brutally tortured with a blowtorch, and then lynched. "The undertaker described him to us later," White recalled, "as having been jet black in color though his skin had been light yellow." Even though the perpetrators were known in their community, they were never charged. With an all-white police force, an all-white courtroom jury, a white judge and white lawyers guiding the rule of law, the family of John Jones had no shot at justice.

Jones had served his country during wartime. His own countrymen had killed him and had gotten away with it.

In another incident—also in the summer of 1946—two black couples were murdered in rural Monroe, Georgia. "The facts discovered by our investigators revealed a sordid background of twisted, sadistic sexuality," White recorded. "One of the lynched Negroes had become involved in a fight with a white man over the attentions which the latter had been paying to the Negro's wife." Within hours, the black man, his wife, and another black couple were rounded up and slain by a white mob.

"We turned over to the FBI and the Georgia Bureau of Investigation the evidence gathered by our investigators," White recorded, "naming seven ringleaders of the lynching party." The accused were known to members of their community. However, "a reign of terror and fear swept over Walton County and effectively shut the mouths of both whites and Negroes," according to White. One man who testified before a federal grand jury was beaten nearly to death.

Truman grew increasingly uncomfortable as White arrived at the story of Isaac Woodard, an army veteran who had spent fifteen months serving his country in the jungles of the South Pacific. On February 12, 1946, just hours after Woodard had been honorably discharged from the army, he was riding a bus in South Carolina, eager to reunite with his wife and family. At a stop near a small town he got off to use a bathroom, and when he went to get back on, the bus driver complained that Woodard had taken too long. The driver had Woodard arrested for being drunk, and when Woodard protested that he did not drink, a police officer attacked him, gouging out Woodard's eyes with a blackjack. Woodard was still wearing his military uniform at the time. He was placed overnight in a jail cell without medical care.

The NAACP had taken up Woodard's case, paying for a team of lawyers. A police officer was indicted. However, no witnesses would come forward, and when the officer was acquitted, a crowded courtroom erupted in cheering.

Truman was appalled. "My God!" he said to White. "I had no idea it was as terrible as that! We've got to do something!"

The next day, the president wrote Attorney General Clark: "I had as callers yesterday some members of the National Association for the Advancement of Colored People." He was "alarmed at the increased racial feeling all over the country" and asked for a special federal commission to investigate lynchings and civil rights. Clark immediately launched an investigation into the Woodard case, and a new group called the President's Committee on Civil Rights was soon formed. Its goal would be to challenge states with a history of lynching—such as South Carolina, Louisiana, Georgia, Alabama, and Mississippi—to enforce the rule of law. Truman told his assistant David Niles, who advised the president on social issues, "I am very much in earnest on this thing and I'd like very much to have you push it with everything you have."

"The main difficulty with the South," Truman wrote in a letter to a friend, "is that they are living eighty years behind the times . . . I am not asking for social equality, because no such things exist, but I am asking for equality of opportunity for all human beings, and, as long as I stay here, I am going to continue that fight. When the mob gangs can take four people out and shoot them in the back, and everybody in the [local area] is acquainted with who did the shooting and nothing is done about it, that country is in a pretty bad fix from a law enforcement standpoint. When a Mayor and a City Marshal can take a negro Sergeant off a bus in South Carolina, beat him up and put out one of his eyes, and nothing is done about it by the State authorities, something is radically wrong with the system."

Long before most other white Americans, Truman could see that the nation was at a crossroads with respect to its racial identity. He came from a state in which segregation was still the norm. He had grown up with these traditions, thinking of them as a normal part of daily life. Some of his closest friends and political allies were powerful Democrats who hailed from southern states, who were highly entrenched in southern traditions of white supremacy. One of them, Senator Burnet Maybank of South Carolina, had confided in a friend while both he and Truman were aboard FDR's funeral train in 1945: "Everything's going to be all right—the new President knows how to handle the niggers."

Maybank was in for a surprise.

Over the same summer that a wave of lynchings terrorized blacks across the American South, terrorism threatened what little stability was left in the Middle East. On the morning of July 22, 1946, a few minutes before noon, the phone rang at the switchboard of the palatial King David Hotel, which looked out over the Old City of Jerusalem. The switchboard operator picked up to hear a female voice, warning that the hotel should be evacuated, that there was a bomb inside.

The warning was ignored.

The hotel served as headquarters for the British military command in Palestine and the United Kingdom's Criminal Investigation Commission, which had recently raided the headquarters of a militant Zionist organization called Irgun and seized a number of documents. Those documents were now inside the hotel, along with numerous British and Palestinian officials. Irgun was willing to use violence to push for a Jewish homeland. From the organization's point of view, there were few if any other options. Recent violence against Jews in Poland had continued to fuel the rage of Zionists, who were critical of laws preventing Jews from leaving Europe and immigrating to Palestine.

At roughly noon, an explosion ripped the pink limestone face off the hotel. Nearby trees were lifted from the soil and hurled like toothpicks. Windows of buildings throughout the neighborhood shattered.

A scramble for survivors began. By 9:30 that night, the local Palestinian authorities reported forty-one dead, a number that would reach ninety-one within the next two days, and included numerous high-level British officials. Irgun—led by Menachem Begin (a future prime minister of Israel)—took responsibility. The bombing of the King David Hotel put the world on notice: There was going to be war in the Middle East between Jews and Palestinians.

In Washington eight days later, Truman gathered his cabinet to discuss the Palestine problem. The situation was "loaded with political dynamite," one cabinet officer noted. Jews who had survived the Nazi Final Solution had been organizing an effort to establish a homeland in Palestine. American money was pouring into the effort, but opposition was fierce. Arab tribes had occupied these lands for fourteen hundred years. The region was governed by the British Mandate for Palestine, in which British officials ran the local governments and, in the process, gained access to cheap oil from the Arabs. The mandate reached back to the days after World War I, and part of the original British commitment to the region was the eventual establishment of a Jewish state in Palestine. That homeland had yet to materialize. Now, more than two decades later, the Jews were intent on making it happen.

In the White House, Truman showed members of his cabinet a file four inches thick—letters that had been sent to the White House in support of the Jews in their quest for a homeland. He was surprised when members of his cabinet pushed back, ferociously. If the United States supported a Jewish homeland, argued Secretary of the Navy James Forrestal, the Arabs would be incensed. America depended on Saudi Arabia for oil, and in fact for the first time in its history the United States was about to start importing more oil than it was pulling out of the ground in its own territory. In the event the nation went to war with the Soviet Union, the US military would need Saudi oil.

Besides, argued Forrestal, if the Jews attempted to create a homeland in Palestine, the Arabs would destroy them. "You just don't understand," Forrestal argued. "Forty million Arabs are going to push 400,000 Jews into the sea. And that's all there is to it. Oil—that is the side we ought to be on."

A Jewish homeland would likely require American troops to ensure its survival. A memo from the Joint Chiefs of Staff that summer to the heads of the State, Navy, and War Departments warned against the use of American troops in the region. "The Middle East could well fall into anarchy and become a breeding ground for world war," the Joint Chiefs' memo declared.

The main opposition to a Jewish homeland came from Truman's own State Department. The department's lead diplomat on Middle East matters, Loy Henderson, was virulently opposed to a Jewish state, and his voice was influential in the department. Truman summoned Henderson to the White House to grill him on his views. In the room at the time were two of Truman's closest advisers on the issue — David Niles and Clark Clifford, both of whom supported a Jewish homeland. When Henderson arrived at the White House to state his case, he quickly realized he was outnumbered.

"After I set forth my reasons [for opposing Zionism]," Henderson recalled, "I was cross-examined. What were the sources of my views? . . . It seemed to me that the group was trying to humiliate and break me down in the presence of the President." But Henderson held his ground. The Palestine problem "was one that would be sure to give rise to strife, hatreds, recriminations, intrigue, and political machinations on a domestic and international level for years to come," he recalled, "and I did not want it to be also our particular problem." He went on to explain that these were not his views alone, "but of all our legations and consular offices in the Middle East and of all the members of the Department of State who had responsibilities for that area."

Leaders of Arab states knew that the future of the region was likely to depend on the opinion of a single man — Harry S. Truman. Such was the power of the American presidency in this new postwar world. The Egyptian prime minister, Nokrashy Pasha, wrote Truman promising that his people would "resist at all costs" the establishment of a Jewish homeland in Palestine. Other Palestinian leaders warned that any Jewish homeland would result in immediate warfare.

A majority of American voters, however, stood behind a Jewish state. All the emerging 1948 presidential candidates — candidates not beholden to the wishes of the State Department — were happy to make promises of support to Jewish groups. On June 20, 1946, Truman received a petition backing the creation of a Jewish state from nine US senators. It pointed out that "in Hitler's concentration and extermination camps, 6,000,000 Jews were tortured, gassed or burned to death . . . The 1,500,000 Jews still left alive in Europe are largely destitute, unwanted or homeless with a well-grounded need and want to migrate to Palestine." Among the public figures speaking out in favor of the Jews were Eleanor Roosevelt, the film star Orson Welles, the labor leader David Dubinsky, and numerous liberal columnists such as the popular writer I. F. Stone.

Truman told his political aide Oscar Ewing, "I am in a tough spot. The Jews are bringing all kinds of pressure on me to support the partition of Palestine [into two states, one for Arabs] and the establishment of a Jewish state. On the other hand the State Department is adamantly opposed to this. I have two Jewish assistants on my staff, Dave Niles and Max Lowenthal. Whenever I try to talk to them about Palestine they soon burst into tears because they are so emotionally involved in the subject. So far I have not known what to do."

Truman heard again and again from fellow Democrats: Prominent Jewish campaign donors were asking for assurance that he would support a Jewish homeland. If not, these powerful constituents would turn to the Republicans. Jews made up roughly 4 percent of the national electorate, but they held considerable influence in critical states, including California, Ohio, Pennsylvania, Illinois, Maryland, and most notably New York, the nation's most populous state. Truman grew resentful of the pressure Jewish organizations were putting on him to move against the wishes of his own State Department.

"Those New York Jews!" the president reportedly said in conversation with the publisher of the *New York Post,* Ted Thackrey. "They're disloyal to their country. Disloyal!"

"Would you mind explaining a little further, Mr. President?" Thackrey demanded. "When you speak of New York Jews are you referring to such people as [the highly respected financier and statesman] Bernard Baruch? Or are you referring to such New York Jews as my wife?"

The Palestine problem was turning into a make-or-break issue in the 1948 election. At one point, Truman hosted four Middle Eastern diplomatic officials who told him that the prestige of the United States was declining rapidly in the oil-rich Arab world. Truman said, "I'm sorry, gentlemen, but I have to answer to hundreds of thousands who are anxious for the success of Zionism; I do not have hundreds of thousands of Arabs among my constituents."

Wherever he looked, Truman faced tough choices.

Should he support the Jews in a quest for a homeland, and please huge numbers of American voters in the process? Or should he side with his own State Department and the oil that was critical to national security?

Should he come out in support of black Americans and the NAACP for civil rights? Or should he side with the Democratic base in the South, led by powerful and popular white congressmen who would oppose any such notions, and without whom the future of the Democratic Party would be imperiled?

Should he support unions and workers in their right to strike and demand rights from big business? Or laws that curb the rights of strikers, in an effort to stabilize the economy during the critical period of reconversion to peacetime?

For American voters, the rising prices of consumer goods was the biggest problem of all, the one they felt with their wallets on a daily basis. Treasury officials, banking officials, the president, and Republican leaders in Congress were at war over the issue of whether to stabilize prices by law. Should the federal government have the power to set the costs of steaks and nylon stockings?

In all of these issues: What was the right thing to do? And what was the politically popular thing to do?

Stuck between opposing forces, Truman saw his presidency weaken. He was ridiculed in cartoons, lambasted in opinion pieces. "It was a cruel time to put inexperience in power," wrote the columnist Richard Rovere.

Truman alone held the key to the first nuclear arsenal. Never before had an American president controlled such awesome power. And yet, never before had one been so publicly emasculated. Meanwhile, prices of consumer goods continued to soar. The president's approval rating dropped to 37 percent from 87 percent in just one year, as the 1946 midterm elections approached.

The pressure on the president was becoming nearly unbearable. At one point, Drew Pearson, the nation's most popular political columnist, criticized Truman's wife and daughter in a radio broadcast for traveling on a private railcar when soldiers were left off the train because seats were scarce. The accusation was untrue. When Pearson showed up to a White House press conference, Truman angrily confronted him. Secret Service agent Henry Nicholson was standing nearby. He recalled Pearson turning pale as Truman poked a finger into his abdomen.

"God damn you," Truman said, "you call me what you want — thief, robber — but the next time you tell a falsehood about my wife I will punch you right in the nose, and don't think I wouldn't."

3

"Can He Swing the Job?"

MILLIONS OF AMERICANS WERE STILL baffled as to how Truman had become president in the first place. "Here was a man who came into the White House almost as though he had been picked at random off the street," recalled White House correspondent Robert Nixon. Truman had no college degree. He had never had the money to own his own home. He had never been the mayor of a city, never served as governor of a state. His presidency was the result of a chain of events so unlikely, only destiny could account for them. He himself would later say that he became the most powerful man in the world "by accident."

He was born in Lamar, Missouri, on May 8, 1884. His father was a farmer and mule trader; his mother was a crack shot with a rifle and remarkably educated for a farm woman reared in the nineteenth century. The Truman home had no plumbing. By the time Harry was in school, the family had moved to Independence, Missouri, to a home that had electricity, and Harry had two siblings — a brother named John Vivian and a sister named Mary Jane.

As a boy, he found three passions that would guide his personal and political future. The first was Elizabeth "Bess" Wallace. "When I was about six or seven years old," he would recollect, "my mother took me to Sunday School and I saw there the prettiest sweetheart little girl I'd ever seen . . . She had tanned skin, blond hair, golden as sunshine, and the most beautiful blue eyes."

For the rest of Truman's days, Bess would be the focus of his emotional life. It would take years of courting before the object of his devotion would pay any attention to Harry. Her family belonged to Independence's social elite, while the Trumans were farm people. A family friend would remember Bess's mother saying, "You don't want to marry that farm boy, he is not going to make it anywhere.'"

Truman's second passion was reading. Around the time he first laid eyes on his future bride, he contracted diphtheria. "He ended up being paralyzed for about a year," recalled Harry's sister, Mary Jane. "So, that's when he started reading so much. He couldn't do anything else and he couldn't get up without help, and so he'd lie on the floor and put books down on the floor in front of him and read the book that way." He became obsessed with history and the leaders who had shaped it, from Moses and Hannibal to Ulysses S. Grant and George Washington.

Truman's third passion was politics. As his daughter, Margaret, would later write, "You have to understand how profoundly the Trumans identify with the word Democrat."

The Truman family considered themselves "Rebel Democrats," tracing their political identities back to the Civil War. Both of Harry's parents came from slave-owning families who sided with the South. Truman's mother often told the story of how, when she was a child, Union loyalists known as Jayhawkers had raided her family's farm, killing the farm animals and burning the family home to the ground. For many families like the Trumans, in places like Missouri and to the south, the Union army and President Abraham Lincoln became inextricably linked to the Republican Party. The Trumans saw their party affiliation as an obsession born of a lost war. Their devotion to the Democratic Party was unquestioned, like the color of their skin.

"Democrats were not made by campaign promises and rational debate, in Independence," Margaret Truman later wrote. "They were born."

• • •

Were it not for a world war, Truman would probably never have left the farm, nor gotten married. Here is where destiny intervened for the first time in his life. In April 1917, when the United States entered World War I, he was thirty-three years old. On March 30, 1918, he sailed for France, a lieutenant in the US Army's 129th Field Artillery Regiment, Thirty-Fifth Division. By the time his group, Battery D (194 men), made it to the front lines, Truman had been elevated to captain, due largely to his age. It was his first shot at leadership.

Truman led his soldiers on horseback into the Argonne Forest for the largest American military operation in history up to that time—the Meuse-Argonne Offensive. Over twenty-six thousand American troops were killed. When the enemy surrendered and Truman's Battery D had fired the last shots on November 11, 1918, he took enormous pride in the fact that his unit had not lost a single man. Before Truman left Europe, he received a letter from Bess Wallace back in Missouri. "You may invite the entire 35th Division to your wedding if you want to," she wrote. "I guess it's going to be yours as well as mine."

Truman returned to Independence, married Bess, and moved into the Wallace house at 219 North Delaware Street, which would be his home for the rest of his life, outside of his years in the White House. In 1920 he opened a business with a wartime buddy, "my Jewish friend" Eddie Jacobson, on Twelfth Street in nearby Kansas City. Truman & Jacobson was a haberdashery with twenty feet of storefront, big glass windows, and a sign at the top: SHIRTS, COLLARS, HOSIERY, GLOVES, BELTS, HATS. After just two years, the recession of 1921–22 put Truman & Jacobson out of business, and left Harry in dire financial straits. "I am still paying on those debts," he would write in a diary, twelve years later.

At thirty-eight, he was lost and broke, living in his wife's family home, where his in-laws looked down their noses at him. Once again, destiny intervened.

During one of his last days at Truman & Jacobson, Harry was in the store behind the counter when a local political figure named Mike Pendergast stepped in off the street. Truman had served in the army with Pendergast's son Jim, and Mike had gotten to know Truman.

"How'd you like to be a county judge?" Mike Pendergast asked.

"I don't know," Truman said.

"If you would like, you can have it."

Truman needed a job. In Jackson County, judges were county commissioners — elected officials rather than arbiters of jurisprudence. Truman had no political experience, but he did have the one thing he needed to win an election: the backing of the Pendergast family, most importantly Tom Pendergast (Mike's brother), who controlled the Kansas City Democratic machine. Weighing over 250 pounds, Tom Pendergast was a legend in Missouri. He was a kingmaker — so powerful that he could pick candidates for political office and all but guarantee their victory. It was also well-known that, in Jackson County, Pendergast had his fingers in the rackets — gambling, liquor.

Truman won his first election in 1922 to become a Jackson County judge. From there, the "Big Boss" Tom Pendergast controlled his political career. As Truman's war buddy Harry Vaughan later put it, "Old Tom Pendergast wanted to have some window dressing. And Truman was really window dressing for him because he could say, 'Well, there's my boy Truman. Nobody can ever say anything about Truman. Everybody thinks he's okay.'"

In 1934 Pendergast was desperate for a Missouri candidate who could represent his political machine in the US Senate. When one of his underlings mentioned Truman's name, Pendergast shrugged. "Nobody knows him," he said. "He's an ordinary county judge and not known outside Jackson County." Then: "Do you mean seriously to tell me that you actually believe that Truman can be nominated and elected to the United States Senate?"

Having run out of potential candidates, Pendergast flexed his muscle and won fifty-year-old Harry Truman a job in Washington. The Missouri press was outraged. Truman was "Boss Pendergast's Errand Boy," "the Senator from Pendergast." Before leaving for Washington with his wife and daughter, Truman stopped in to see the Boss. Pendergast told him, "Work hard, keep your mouth shut, and answer your mail."

"If you had seen Harry Truman . . . in the freshman row in the Senate, you would hardly have picked him as a future leader," remembered the *Wash-*

ington Post's Marquis Childs. "He seemed to be one of those inconspicuous political accidents — a nice fellow cast up by the workings of machine politics." According to one *Post* story on freshman senators, Truman was "not considered brilliant, either as an orator or as a scholar."

Truman stayed under the radar, voting consistently along party lines, supporting Franklin Roosevelt and his New Deal. Nearing the end of his first term, he came into work one morning in 1939 to learn that Tom Pendergast had been indicted on tax-evasion charges. On May 29 of that year Boss Pendergast landed at Leavenworth. The news was an extreme blow to Truman's already shaky reputation. "The terrible things done by the high ups in K.C. will be a lead weight to me from now on," he wrote his wife.

By the time Truman gathered his friends to discuss his reelection plans in 1940, the Nazis had invaded Poland and World War II had begun in Europe. The Missouri senator's career was over, Truman's friends agreed. The popular Democratic governor Lloyd Stark was running for Truman's Senate seat. "We didn't give him a chance," recalled Truman's friend A. J. Granoff, a Kansas City lawyer. "We expected him to be beaten badly."

Truman dug in and ran one of the most storied campaigns in Missouri history. Along the way, the family finances grew so dire that a bank foreclosed on the home his mother and sister were living in, in Grandview. But once again, Truman's life took an inexplicable turn. Against all odds, he defeated Governor Stark to win the Democratic primary in the closest election the state had seen in almost two decades, then went on to win in November.

No one could point a finger at Boss Pendergast. Harry had done it on his own.

As Truman began his second Senate term, news of Nazi triumphs shocked the world. Early in 1941 President Roosevelt received $10.5 billion in appropriations for emergency defense purposes. Truman took a road trip in his Dodge on his own dime to inspect the army construction sites that were consuming much of that money. What he saw concerned him, and on February 10, 1941, he made a speech on the Senate floor.

"I am introducing a Resolution," Truman said to his fellow senators, "asking for an investigation of the National Defense Program." Truman's idea was to set up a Senate committee to police government military spending. Soon he was traveling the nation with a team of senators — five Democrats, two Republicans — uncovering inefficiencies and raw-material bottlenecks. When the Japanese attacked Pearl Harbor and the United States entered the war, Truman found himself in an extraordinary position. The so-called Truman Committee was poised to become vital to the war effort. When the committee released its first report in 1942, on cost overruns at military construction sites, the *Washington Post* commented: "To thousands, the first question after the shock of the Truman report must have been: Who in the world is Truman?"

Two years later, as an ailing FDR prepared for his fourth election campaign, his advisers convinced him to drop his vice president, Henry Wallace, from the 1944 ticket. Wallace had a following, but he had failed to ingratiate himself with many in Roosevelt's inner circle, and aides feared his far-left-leaning views and personal idiosyncrasies would be a liability in the campaign. FDR needed someone new. "Truman just dropped into the slot," recalled Ed Flynn, a powerful Bronx political leader who was in the White House with FDR on July 11, the night the decision was made.

Truman himself had no idea of the machinations that would land him on the 1944 ticket — not yet. As the party delegates readied to nominate a VP candidate at the Democratic National Convention in Chicago Stadium, Truman agreed to take a phone call from Roosevelt, who was in Washington. The Missourian ended up in a crowded suite at the Blackstone Hotel on July 22. The phone rang. A party official named Bob Hannegan picked up, and Roosevelt's voice came through so loud, others in the hotel suite could hear.

"Bob," FDR said, "have you got that fellow lined up yet?"

"No," said Hannegan, with Truman standing next to him. "He is the contrariest goddamn mule from Missouri I ever dealt with."

"Well, you tell that senator that if he wants to break up the Democratic party in the middle of a war, that's his responsibility."

Truman agreed to follow Roosevelt's lead, and was nominated by the party at a frenzied convention meeting that night. On election night — November

7, 1944 — FDR won a fourth term, and Harry Truman became America's vice president.

Eighty-two days after the beginning of his fourth term, FDR was dead of a cerebral hemorrhage, and the first thing that could be heard out of the mouths of many when they learned the news was: "Good God! Truman will be President!" Truman was a few weeks shy of his sixty-first birthday. He took the oath of office on April 12, 1945, with Bess and his only child, Margaret, standing beside him. "The gravest question mark in every American heart is about Truman," Michigan senator Arthur Vandenberg wrote in his diary the night Truman was sworn in. "Can he swing the job?"

Patriotism and victory were on Truman's side. Democrats and Republicans rallied behind the new president. The Allies won the war, and revealed the war's greatest secret — the atomic bomb. Truman's approval rating hit 87 percent after the Japanese surrender, higher than Roosevelt's had ever been. But in the weeks following, that number began to sink slowly and steadily, and with it, the hopes of the entire Democratic Party.

4

"I Was Amazed at How Calm He Seemed in the Face of Political Disaster"

ON JULY 9, 1946, ROUGHLY eleven months after Truman announced the surrender of Japan, he held a lunch at the White House unlike any that had ever occurred in the executive mansion. Administration officials gathered around a projection machine, and fresh footage of the latest atomic bomb test rolled. The test shot had gone off eight days earlier, on July 1, at a site in the Pacific. Film cameras captured the fury: A sudden white light blinded the camera lens momentarily, giving way to a ballooning fireball that resembled a new sun being born.

The president watched silently as the footage showed the shot from different camera angles. No one in the room felt the impact more than Truman. The death toll in Hiroshima and Nagasaki was so vast, the actual numbers would never be known, and Truman was haunted by the decision he had made to use the bomb. It was the most controversial decision any president had ever made, and Truman feared having to make it again.

Sitting near the president, Henry Wallace — now the secretary of commerce — said the explosion looked like a tremendous "blooming chrysanthemum." Wallace leaned over to Dean Acheson, an official from the State Department, and said that in fifteen or twenty years, "You will look toward

Washington and see these beautiful chrysanthemums arising one after another."

The latest bomb test was the culmination of a series of events over the past five months that made everyone watching the footage feel as if World War III was in the making. On February 9, 1946, Soviet dictator Joseph Stalin made a rare appearance on a speaker's platform, at the Bolshoi Theater in Moscow. An avoidance of future war "was impossible under the present capitalistic development of world economy," Stalin said in his speech. He announced a Five-Year Plan of preparation "to guarantee our country against any eventuality." His Five-Year Plan sounded suspiciously like the Four-Year Plan Adolf Hitler had announced in 1936, which in retrospect was an economic and industrial campaign to prepare for war. Clearly alluding to the atomic bomb, Stalin added a promise that Soviet scientists would "not only catch up with but also surpass those abroad."

Less than a month later, on a stage at Westminster College in Truman's home state of Missouri, former British prime minister Winston Churchill delivered his chilling "Iron Curtain" speech.

"From Stettin in the Baltic to Trieste in the Adriatic, an iron curtain has descended across the Continent," Churchill said, using the term *iron curtain* publicly for the first time. "Behind that line lie all the capitals of the ancient states of Central and Eastern Europe. Warsaw, Berlin, Prague, Vienna, Budapest, Belgrade, Bucharest and Sofia, all these famous cities and the populations around them lie in what I must call the Soviet sphere, and all are subject in one form or another, not only to Soviet influence but to a very high and, in many cases, increasing measure of control from Moscow."

Many historians would mark Churchill's Iron Curtain speech as the first public admittance that the Cold War had begun.

It was just four months after Churchill's speech that a B-29 Superfortress of the 509th Bombardment Group roared over a sapphire lagoon full of empty US Navy ships near Bikini Atoll in the Pacific. Aboard the decks of the ships were animals tied in place — pigs, goats, and thousands of rats, among others — so that scientists could study the effects of an atomic airburst on their bodies. Bombardiers let loose a bomb of the type used on Nagasaki; it had GILDA painted on it in slim black letters, and also a photograph of Rita Hayworth—star of the new film *Gilda*—from an *Esquire* magazine, pasted to its iron body. The Gilda shot was no secret; it made the covers of newspapers worldwide, and its fallout was politically radioactive, exacerbating tensions with Moscow.

This was the bomb that had provided the footage for Truman's lunch viewing in the White House.

Two weeks after the viewing, on July 23, Henry Wallace came to see Truman, wanting to talk about the bomb and the Russia situation. The timing was no coincidence; the following day, another atomic test was scheduled to take place. Wallace arrived at the White House just after noon and was shown in for a 12:30 p.m. meeting.

Ever since the 1944 Democratic National Convention in Chicago, when Wallace had been pushed off the ticket to make room for Truman as the VP candidate, the two men were terribly uncomfortable in each other's presence. Truman was embarrassed. Wallace was bitter. In the White House on the night of April 12, 1945, when Harry Truman spoke the thirty-five-word oath to assume the power of the presidency, Wallace was standing roughly ten feet away, his eyes like lasers pointed at Truman's hand as it rested on the Bible. From Wallace's point of view, it should have been him and not Truman sworn in that night. In the aftermath, Truman and Wallace did their best to contain their mistrust of each other.

That was about to change.

Wallace hand-delivered Truman a letter he had written to the president. "I have been increasingly disturbed about the trend of international affairs since the end of the war," the letter read, "and I am even more troubled by the apparently growing feeling among the American people that another war is coming and the only way that we can head it off is to arm ourselves to the teeth."

Wallace made cogent points: "Atomic warfare is cheap and easy compared with old-fashioned war. Within a very few years several countries can have atomic bombs and other atomic weapons."

"Having more bombs — even many more bombs — than the other fellow is no longer a decisive advantage."

"The very fact that several nations have atomic bombs will inevitably result in a neurotic, fear-ridden itching-trigger psychology in all the peoples of the world."

Wallace pleaded with Truman to change US policy toward Russia, "to find some way of living together." This would "reassert the forward-looking position of the Democratic Party in international affairs, and finally, would arrest the new trend toward isolationism and a disastrous atomic world war."

Truman was immediately suspicious. The next morning, he brought this letter to his staff meeting. "It looks as though Henry [Wallace] is going to pull an Ickes," Truman said, referring to former Interior secretary Harold Ickes, who had quit his post and publicly attacked the administration a few months earlier. Truman had every reason to be concerned.

At 11 a.m. on September 10, Wallace again visited the Oval Office, to talk over a speech he intended to give two days later at Madison Square Garden. Truman appeared distracted; he was weathering the fifth day of a nationwide maritime strike, as well as a truck drivers' strike in New York City. The Wallace meeting lasted only fifteen minutes, but its impact would imperil Truman's standing for years to come. According to Wallace's account, he pulled out his Madison Square Garden speech and began reading it, page by page. Truman nodded as Wallace read, uttering "That's right" and "Yes, that is what I believe."

Wallace wrote in his diary, "The President apparently saw no inconsistency between my speech and what [Secretary of State James] Byrnes was doing," referring to negotiations the secretary of state was holding with the Soviets and others, in Paris. According to Truman's version of the Wallace meeting, Truman had "no time to read the speech," but was pleased Wallace was "going to help the Democrats in New York by his appearance."

On the morning of September 12 Wallace released his speech to the press, before it was to be delivered that night. Truman held his weekly press conference at 4 p.m., unaware that the reporters present had already obtained the text of Wallace's address.

"Mr. President," one called out, "in a speech for delivery tonight, Secretary of State — I mean Commerce — Wallace — [laughter] — has this to say about the middle of it, 'When President' —"

Truman interrupted. "Well now, you say the speech is to be delivered?"

"It is, sir."

"Well, I . . . I can't answer questions on a speech that is to be delivered."

"It mentions you, which is the reason I ask, sir," the reporter continued. "In the middle of the speech are these words. 'When President Truman read these words [Wallace's speech], he said that they represented the policy of this administration.'"

"That is correct," Truman said. He went on to say that he "approved the whole speech."

Wallace delivered the speech that night. Just before he took the stage, one of his political advisers convinced him to excise certain sections, and Wallace obliged. The omitted passages served to make the speech more inflammatory. Wallace called for an about-face in the United States' relations with Moscow, and the speech came across as pro-Soviet. These two sentences in particular wounded the president: "I am neither anti-British, nor pro-Russian," Wallace announced. "And just two days ago, when President Truman read these words, he said that they represented the policy of his Administration."

All over the States and Europe the next day, newspapers carried stories that the Truman administration had suddenly and drastically altered its foreign policy — that the United States would break off close ties with Britain and end its opposition to Soviet expansion. In Paris, where Secretary of State Byrnes was busy negotiating with the Russians, the Wallace speech sparked anger and confusion. Byrnes sent Truman a furious note over the teletype machine, threatening to resign immediately. "You and I spent 15 months building a bipartisan policy . . . ," Byrnes wrote Truman. "Wallace destroyed it in a day." Senator Arthur Vandenberg, head of the Senate Foreign Relations Committee, was with Byrnes in Paris, and he released a statement criticizing the Truman administration, saying, "We can only cooperate with one Secretary of State at a time." Humiliated, Truman had to release his own statement that there "has been no change in the established foreign policy of our Government."

Editorials excoriated the president, and the timing could not have been worse for Truman, as it was just weeks before the 1946 midterm elections. It "grows worse as we go along," Truman wrote his sister and mother. "Never was there such a mess and it is partly my making."

On September 18 Wallace met with Truman to discuss the debacle. Truman said that he had been so disturbed by reaction to the speech, he was having sleepless nights. Wallace defended his address.

"The public is profoundly interested in peace," he said, as he recalled in his diary. "My own mail is running five to one in favor of my speech. Peace is going to be an issue in this campaign [the 1948 election, two years away]. The people are afraid that the 'get tough with Russia' policy is leading us to war. You, yourself, as Harry Truman, really believed in my speech."

The president was adamant: "I must ask you not to make any more speeches touching on foreign policy. We must present a united front abroad."

Outside, in the White House press gallery, packs of reporters awaited Wallace, smelling a scoop. "What shall I tell the press when I go out?" Wallace asked Truman. "There are a hundred or more hungry wolves out there."

Truman summoned his press secretary, Charlie Ross, and together they worded a benign statement that Wallace would refrain from making further speeches on foreign policy.

Less than a week later, a letter Wallace had written to the president in July was leaked to the press. In it, Wallace argued that the Truman administration's foreign policy could lead to a third world war, and that "there is a school of military thinking" that advocated a "preventive war" against the USSR, before the Soviets had their own bomb.

The Wallace letter was gas on an already smoldering fire. Truman was so upset by it, he sent Wallace a missive, telling him from the gut exactly what he thought. It was so acidic that, when Wallace read it, he called the president.

"You don't want this thing out [to the press]," he told Truman over the phone.

The president agreed and sent a messenger to retrieve the letter. It was subsequently destroyed; what it said exactly has never been known. Nevertheless, Truman fired Wallace on that day, September 20, 1946, by phone. "I called him and told him he ought to get out," Truman wrote Bess, who was in Independence at the time. "I believe he's a real Commy and a dangerous man."

Later that day, in his regular press conference, Truman said, "I have today asked Mr. Wallace to resign from the Cabinet."

Reporters were stunned. "There were audible gasps and a stir and a low whistle from one correspondent," assistant press secretary Eben Ayers wrote in his diary. When the room cleared, Truman spoke aloud, quoting Julius Caesar: "Well, the die is cast."

Henry Wallace was a former vice president. He was a hero of New Deal liberalism. He was adored by masses of left-wing voters. He was also a potential candidate for 1948, a man who had the power to tear the Democratic Party apart. His firing caused a sensation. "The Wallace thing is getting worse I believe," Truman wrote Bess, "and I'm getting worried."

That fall of 1946, in meetings with the Democratic National Committee chairman Robert Hannegan, the president expressed his concern over the 1946 elections. Truman found no solace when Hannegan asked him not to campaign for any of the Democrats running for Congress. The less voters saw of Truman, Hannegan said coldly, the better. Around this time Truman wrote a philosophical letter to his daughter, Margaret, in Missouri, which included the following observation:

> To be a good President, I fear a man can't be his own mentor. He can't live the Sermon on the Mount. He must be Machiavelli . . . a liar, double-crosser . . . to be successful. So I probably won't be, thanks be to God. But I'm having a lot of fun trying the opposite approach. Maybe it will win.

Truman left the White House at 3:30 p.m. on Halloween, bound for Missouri by train, so he could cast his vote in a midterm election he already knew would be devastating to his presidency. Republican congressional candidates nationwide were campaigning effectively with a three-syllable slogan: "Had enough?" Polls showed that Americans had indeed had enough of the Democrats, and that the Wallace mess in particular hurt the party. Truman had come down with a bad cold, and he arrived home in Independence feeling dejected and miserable.

At 9 a.m. on the day of the election, the president, accompanied by his daughter, arrived at Independence's Memorial Hall. Parting a crowd of hometown fans, he entered a voting booth at 9:03. He showed Margaret how to fill out the ballot, as it was her first time voting. When they were finished, they walked together out of the building. Facing the crowd, Truman said, "Well, the show's over."

That night, as Truman rode a train back to Washington, he sat down to enjoy his favorite activity: a game of poker. Also at the table was his press secretary, Charlie Ross, members of the White House press corps including Merriman Smith of the United Press and Tony Vaccaro of the Associated Press, and his aide Clark Clifford. As the voter returns rolled in over the radio, Truman remained composed. The train was nearing Cincinnati when the men learned that a Republican tide was washing over the country. "I was amazed at how calm he seemed in the face of political disaster," Clifford recorded. "The conventional political wisdom at that point was simple: Harry Truman was a caretaker President."

When Truman awoke on November 6, he had all the evidence he needed that the nation had lost faith in him. In a landslide, Republicans won majorities in both houses of Congress for the first time since 1928. In the House of Representatives, Republicans now outnumbered Democrats 246 to 188. The Republicans gained thirteen seats in the Senate, including one in Truman's home state. History had showed that midterm elections could often damage a new sitting president, but few midterms had demonstrated such a complete shift in the tides of power—in Washington and in state capitals from coast to coast. The election was noteworthy for another reason: New faces in Congress included Joseph McCarthy of Wisconsin, John F. Kennedy of Massachusetts, and Richard Nixon of California.

In New York, meanwhile, Republican governor Thomas Dewey was reelected by a margin of 680,000 votes—the biggest majority in state history.

The response in Washington was devastating to the Truman administration. Senator J. William Fulbright of Arkansas—a member of Truman's own Democratic Party—called on the president to appoint a Republican as secretary of state, second in line to the presidency, since there was no vice president (Truman had vacated that office when FDR died). Then the president should resign, so there would be a Republican president and unity in Washington.* "I am only suggesting that it would be the best thing for the country as a whole," Senator Fulbright said. "It probably would be the wisest thing for the President to do . . . It will place the responsibility of running the Government on one party and prevent a stalemate that is likely to occur."

Newspapers such as the *Chicago Sun* and the *Atlanta Constitution,* along with numerous Republican leaders, came out in favor of Fulbright's proposal. Truman laughed the idea off, calling Fulbright "Senator Halfbright." But the proposal was taken seriously enough that Charlie Ross had to put out a statement saying Truman would not resign.

Back in the White House, Truman wondered aloud to friends and staffers whether he would stand for election in 1948. He could not use the word *reelection,* because he had never been elected chief executive in the first place. He called the White House "the Great White Jail," and said he was looking forward to the end of what felt like a prison sentence.

Around this time, he began to notice something strange in the mansion at 1600 Pennsylvania Avenue. The walls and floors of the White House had begun to creak and moan. At one point Truman borrowed a stethoscope from his staff physician, Dr. Wallace Graham, pressing it up against a wall to

*This occurred before the Presidential Succession Act of 1947, which placed the Speaker of the House next in line for the presidency after the president and vice president. At the time, the secretary of state would have been next in line.

hear the building's unsettling sounds. "The damned place is haunted sure as shootin'," he told Bess.

Then one day the First Lady became alarmed when she noticed that the five-and-a-half-foot-tall chandelier in the White House Blue Room was trembling. Standing beneath it, she heard the faint jingle of the chandelier's crystals as they moved seemingly of their own volition. Professionals called in to give the White House a diagnosis found the building structurally unsound. The second floor was caving in. The White House, like the administration, was in a state of historic disintegration.

PART II

The Surging GOP

I will be president. It is written in the stars.

— Thomas Dewey

5

"You Are Getting as Much Publicity as Hitler"

THE WHITE HOUSE ASIDE, no building in the United States had been the setting for more presidential aspirations than the executive mansion in Albany, New York. Red brick with white trim, the Queen Anne–style residence at 138 Eagle Street was originally constructed in 1856 for a wealthy banker. Two decades later, Samuel Tilden became the first New York governor to move in. In 1876, in one of the closest elections in American history, Tilden lost his bid for the White House to Rutherford B. Hayes. Grover Cleveland lived in the mansion while he was governor, moving to the White House in 1885. During Theodore Roosevelt's term as New York governor, a gymnasium was added to the home. When Franklin Roosevelt moved in, he had an indoor swimming pool built. FDR served two terms in the residence before his move to the White House.

On the evening of November 4 in 1946 — the night before the midterm election — New York governor Thomas Dewey and his wife, Frances, entertained friends and campaign officials in the Albany executive mansion. Staff members scurried about, emptying ashtrays and passing out drinks. At 6:15, from inside the mansion, Dewey delivered a radio speech urging all voters to exercise their right to vote. He compared the "confusion and chaos" in Washington to the "team work Government" in Albany.

The following morning, Dewey and an entourage headed for New York City, where the governor cast his vote at a polling station on East Fifty-First Street. That night, at a Dewey rally, crowds chanted "Dewey for President!" By the time Dewey was back in Albany, he had won a second term as governor, beating the Democratic challenger James M. Mead by a historic margin.

Dewey was just forty-four years old. Relatively short in stature at five foot eight (he was known to occasionally stand on a dictionary while orating), he had a short stub-like nose, side-parted brown hair, and a mustache so fastidiously kept, it looked like each hair had received his personal attention. Since his childhood days selling newspapers in rural Michigan, accomplishment was Tom Dewey's sustenance, and the evening of the midterms was thus far the greatest night of his professional life. After his opponent conceded, Dewey took his baritone voice to the airwaves in a short radiocast from microphones set up in the mansion. His address sounded less like a victory message than a presidential State of the Union.

"What has happened today," Dewey said, "means much more than an ordinary election. It was not a mere matter of choosing between one man and another. In this election our people were making a choice between different kinds of government, involving two different political philosophies . . . A troubled world looks to us, not only for material help, but for spiritual inspiration, for a renewed devotion to the ideals of genuine liberty."

Over the next days, congratulatory mail swamped the Dewey family, who skipped the Army–Notre Dame football game at West Point in order to write thank-you notes. The Deweys had never experienced such adulation. The governor read in the newspapers that he was now a front-runner for the Republican ticket in 1948, and how Albany was to be "the Mecca" for Republican powerbrokers once again, as it had been during the halcyon days when Dewey's hero Theodore Roosevelt lived there. Dewey was "riding the very crest of the 1946 Republican wave," noted the *Christian Science Monitor.* "Today, the prospects of 1948 look like very much more than an illusion. They look like a positive hope."

On December 18, weeks after the election, Dewey met privately at 138 Eagle Street with Republican leaders, while reporters fingered cigarettes in the nearby pressroom, hoping for a major national story. Would he run in '48? When Dewey emerged from his meeting, the reporters swarmed.

"Governor," yelled one, "are you ready to announce your candidacy for President?"

"Certainly not," Dewey said coldly.

"Certainly not ready?"

"Certainly not, period."

When New York's new legislative session began, the governor did what he did best: He rolled up his sleeves and got to work. Along with his offices in Albany, he kept a suite at the Roosevelt Hotel at 45 East Forty-Fifth Street in New York City, and he spent most of his weekends at his working dairy farm in rural Pawling, New York. In Albany, he worked with the state's administration. In the city, he rubbed elbows with the Wall Street crowd and Republican Party officials who represented voters in the world's largest metropolis.

Dewey's youthful stamina impressed everyone but his wife, who often found herself lonesome in her upstairs suite in the Albany mansion and at the dinner table, where she dined with her two boys and an empty chair where her husband was supposed to be. Late nights for Dewey were the norm. Lunch was the same every day, eaten at his desk: a chicken sandwich, an apple, milk. Dewey was all business. He smoked but never more than a pack a day. He drank but never more than two highballs in a sitting. Meanwhile, he drove his staff hard. "This didn't make him popular with those people he had to deal with," recorded Republican National Committee chief Herbert Brownell Jr. "But it did make him effective."

The governor's desire for efficiency was as extreme as his phobia for germs. He knew how hard the job could be: "A good many people have the idea that politics is a sordid business, to be left to those who cannot make a living by anything else. Others have the idea that it is a simple business, in which anyone can become qualified as a sage overnight or with a brief space of speech-making or handshaking. The fact is that politics is the science of government. So far it has defeated all the best minds in the history of the world. At least I have not yet heard of the perfect government."

• • •

The country's surge toward the Republican Party was a long time in coming—the war had sustained Democratic rule beyond what it might have been in more normal times. In 1946 Republicans had been out of power in Washington for fourteen years. The entire political careers of national figures had come and gone during that time. The Democrats' hold on the White House through FDR and now Truman, plus the Democrats' majority in both houses of Congress, had demoralized the party of Lincoln. In terms of the presidency, it was the longest winning streak for a single party in a generation.

"The long tenure of the Democratic Party had poisoned the air we Republicans breathed," remembered Congressman Joe Martin of Massachusetts, who became Speaker of the House following the 1946 election. "Many of the experiments of the New Deal seemed to us certain to undermine and destroy this society . . . Roosevelt's philosophy [notably high federal spending on social programs] weakened our ideals of self-reliance, and we are poorer for it . . . I am sorry to say, it has encouraged too many people to depend on the government instead of themselves."

Now finally the Republicans were beginning to take control again, taking back both the House of Representatives and the Senate. Republicans unseated Democratic governors in Idaho, Ohio, and Massachusetts. "The greatest advantage I had in 1946," recalled Richard Nixon, who won his first House seat that year in California's Twelfth Congressional District, "was that the national trend that year was Republican." "Anyone seeking to unseat an incumbent needed only to point out all the things that had gone wrong and all the troubles of the war period and its aftermath," added Democrat Jerry Voorhis, who lost to Nixon that year. "Many of these things were intimate experiences in the everyday lives of the people."

Five weeks after the 1946 election, the nation's most respected pollster, George Gallup, wrote in the *Los Angeles Times,* "The public's reaction to last month's election is to sign over 1948 to the Republicans. People who think the Democrats will win the 1948 presidential election are almost as scarce as the proverbial hen's teeth."

The question became: Who would be the Republican nominee? When

Gallup released his first post-1946-election numbers, Dewey was the choice of 52 percent of Republican voters nationwide, far ahead of any competitor. Second was former Minnesota governor Harold Stassen — thirty-five points behind.

"The always efficient Gov. Thomas E. Dewey is quietly gaining ground," noted the syndicated political columnists Joseph and Stewart Alsop. "His successes are sending powerful chills of apprehension down the spines of his rivals."

Thomas Dewey had become a Republican even before he left his mother's womb, according to his father. He was born on March 24, 1902, in an apartment above the general store in the town of Owosso, Michigan. The town was proud of its three hotels, its tire factory, and its three miles of paved roads. Dewey's father, George, owned the local newspaper, and he was so dedicated to Republican politics that he listed the following announcement in his newspaper upon the birth of his only child: "A ten-pound Republican voter was born last evening to Mr. and Mrs. George M. Dewey. George says the young man arrived in time for registration for the April election." GOP ideology was woven so thickly into the fabric of this family, Thomas Dewey would later say that "it was one of those things we took for granted, as it was assumed that all good people were Republicans."

Young Tom was a natural leader. He was selling newspapers by age eleven, and by thirteen he had his own magazine-sales business. Rarely a family dinner would pass without talk of politics. Dewey's early memories romanticized the successes of Theodore Roosevelt. Dewey's father subscribed to the progressive Republicanism that Teddy Roosevelt championed — "Negro" rights, progressive tax reform, conservation of natural resources, internationalist foreign policy. George Dewey even nicknamed his son Ted, as those were Thomas E. Dewey's initials.

The powerful Republican Henry Stimson, who was then US attorney general for the Southern District of New York, defined the era's Republican liberalism in a letter to Theodore Roosevelt during this time: "To me it seems vitally important that the Republican party, which contains, generally speaking, the richer and more intelligent citizens of the country, should take the lead in reform." Though the Deweys were not rich, they agreed.

Dewey attended the University of Michigan, and he came of age during the Roaring Twenties, an era when post–World War I Republicanism dominated Washington. Warren G. Harding, then Calvin Coolidge, then Herbert Hoover — for twelve years a Republican ran the country.

During these years, the GOP evolved. Leaders redefined Republican values as a reaction to the horrors of World War I — a war that some prominent Republicans believed the United States should never have participated in. As if with a scalpel, liberalism was removed from the GOP's ideology. In the place of internationalism was isolationism; in the place of progressive change was "normalcy"; in the place of federal spending on social programs was small government that largely left taxation and spending to the states. The Republicans had renounced Theodore Roosevelt's liberalism, but the Deweys never did.

After graduating from college, Dewey moved to New York and became chairman of the New York Young Republican Club. He studied law at Columbia University, but his real love, surprisingly, was music. He took voice lessons, and on March 24, 1923, his twenty-first birthday, he gave his first recital in hopes of embarking on a singing career. Whether it was a case of laryngitis or stage fright on the performer's part, the concert was a disaster. Dewey gave up on that dream and immersed himself in the law, taking a job with the firm McNamara and Seymour.

When Wall Street crashed in 1929, ushering in the Depression, Dewey was living on Manhattan's Upper East Side with his wife, Frances, and in 1931, at an event for the Young Republican Club, he was introduced to Herbert Brownell Jr., an ambitious fellow attorney with the firm Lord Day & Lord. Originally from Nebraska, Brownell was a brilliant Yale man who, like Dewey, had been a Republican seemingly from birth. He wanted to run for the New York state legislature, and although Dewey had no experience, he agreed to manage Brownell's campaign.

Dewey delivered his first speeches from the back of trucks on Manhattan street corners. He distributed vinyl records of Brownell speeches — "a novel idea in those days," Dewey later remembered. He and Brownell were eager young rookies in a teeming metropolis where Republicans had always been outnumbered by Democrats. Brownell nevertheless won a seat in the New York State Assembly in 1932, notwithstanding a national surge away from the party of Hoover, as FDR won the White House for the first time. Dewey would remember Brownell's campaign as "chaos," but Brownell came to his own conclusions. If Brownell's campaign proved one thing, it was that Tom Dewey was going places. "He gave you the impression of having a goal, and getting there fast," Brownell recalled, "and if you were kind of a drag on it, or didn't quite follow what he was saying . . . he sort of didn't bother with you anymore."

Around the same time Dewey was first experimenting in the New York political scene, he was appointed as a special prosecutor to investigate corruption in the city. Two years later, he was made an assistant US attorney, and at just thirty-one years old, he was the youngest ever to take on the job in Manhattan's Southern District. At the time Dewey was sworn in, the Jewish gangster Waxey Gordon's sensational trial was already in progress, and Dewey was thrown into the heat of courtroom battle. Self-conscious about his height, he made up for it with swagger.

"Gentlemen," he told the courtroom his first week as a trial prosecutor, "there will be a lot of dead men mentioned during this case."

Dewey was instrumental in putting Gordon behind bars for ten years, on charges of income tax evasion. The case put Dewey on the map as a rising star in the Southern District.

The prosecutor's office suited Dewey. By the time he was thirty-five, he was running for attorney general of the state of New York, and he was already getting national publicity. Prohibition-era New York was the perfect petri dish for a prosecutor to grow into a national figure, if he had legal brilliance and fearless drive. This was the New York of Lucky Luciano, of Meyer Lansky, of Murder Inc. Even when Prohibition came to an end in 1933, there were plenty of criminal gangs to go after.

In 1935, during the depths of the Depression, anyone lacking a moral compass would do anything for a buck. "The mobs had a tremendous hold on the legitimate business life of the community," Dewey later recalled. "As a matter of fact you could feel it. It was almost as if you could touch it." Dewey opened a special-prosecutor's office on the fourteenth floor of the Woolworth Building on lower Broadway, a block from City Hall. He recruited seventy-five police officers to go undercover in New York's underbelly. "They did not look like cops," Dewey recorded. "They had small feet, alert minds, and tough, wiry frames . . . They were of many national extractions and spoke the languages of the countries of their fathers. This, then, was to be known as the grand jury squad."

Dewey installed an untappable phone in his office, and put twenty stenographers to work in one large room under constant supervision. Witnesses and turncoats were made to give testimony in rooms with blinds drawn. All scrap paper was burned in the building furnace. With a staff of twenty deputy assistant attorneys, ten investigators, ten accountants, two grand jury reporters, and four messengers under him, the special prosecutor began cracking some of the most shocking criminal cases the city of New York had ever seen. Dewey's men once raided two hundred brothels in a single day. But it was the case of Lucky Luciano — Manhattan's top mob boss — that made Dewey a national hero. Dewey's office indicted Luciano on April 3, 1936, and the ensuing case produced the most lurid newspaper headlines of the era.

"Gangsters Split Girls' Tongues."

"Girl Says Squealer's Feet Were Burned with Cigars."

"Torture Is Laid to Vice Bosses."

Using the testimony of call girls and their madams, Dewey won Luciano a thirty-to-fifty-year prison term.

Next on Dewey's docket: "Tootsie" Herbert, labeled "the meanest poultry racketeer of all time." Jacob "Gurrah" Shapiro, "the terror of New York City's garment industry." Louis "Lepke" Buchalter, who went to his death in the electric chair. "No man deserved it more," Dewey concluded. The special prosecutor got credit for putting all these figures behind bars.

Dewey's top prize was James J. Hines — the fedora-sporting, jowly-faced boss of New York's Tammany Hall. The trial against Hines drew tremendous attention. It was not just Hines on the stand, but Tammany Hall itself, the notoriously corrupt organization that had controlled Democratic power in New York City for generations. Dewey proved in a courtroom that Hines had illegal connections with the city's most high-profile gangsters, and Hines was convicted of thirteen counts of racketeering. It was the biggest blow to Tammany Hall since the trial of Boss Tweed in 1873. The morning after the trial ended, Dewey invited photographers into his office so they could snap pictures of him reading the morning paper, which ran a banner headline on the front page: "Hines Guilty."

At just thirty-seven, Thomas Dewey was a household name. He had achieved seventy-two convictions out of seventy-three prosecutions. People joked that Dewey could successfully prosecute God. The attorney's nickname, "Gangbuster," was used for a popular radio series. Hollywood pumped out movies inspired by Dewey's trials—*Marked Woman* in 1937, starring Humphrey Bogart as a Dewey-esque crime fighter, and *Racket Busters* in 1938, also starring Bogart.

Dewey ran for governor in New York in 1938 and lost by a slim margin to the Democrat Herbert Lehman. But the young prosecutor's campaign drew enough attention that it launched him into the rarified group of elite national Republicans.

"You made a glorious run and you demonstrated that you possess a deep measure of popular affection and confidence," Senator Arthur Vandenberg of Michigan—one of the most revered Republicans in the nation—wrote Dewey on November 11, 1938. "So far as the Republican party is concerned, you have irresistibly become one of its chief figures and one of its ranking leaders . . . We need the precise influence and viewpoint which you typify. The more active and more aggressive you are in our party councils, the happier many of us will be."

Franklin Roosevelt was ending his second term at the end of the 1930s, and the Republicans were desperate for a new man who could counter the Democrat's success. On December 1, 1939, in the newly opened "Dewey for President" headquarters in Midtown Manhattan, crowds pushed in to catch a glimpse of the young legal mastermind.

"I have confidence in the Republican party," Dewey said in the opening speech of his first presidential campaign. "It always has stood for good government and stable business. Today's responsibility is to reawaken hope and courage in a nation which has been driven almost to despair by incompetent government and unstable business."

In his delivery, Dewey lacked spark, that unnameable charisma that FDR exuded, but the youthful Republican made up for it with cold precision and endless ambition. So fresh-faced and boyish was he that FDR's secretary of the Interior, Harold Ickes, quipped that Dewey had "thrown his diaper into the ring."

"You are getting as much publicity as Hitler," a friend wrote Dewey during the 1940 presidential campaign. Dewey failed to win the nomination; the dark horse Wendell Willkie swooped in and won over the party faithful. However, Dewey won enough respect within the Republican ranks, it was said that it was not a matter of *if* he would be president, but *when.*

In 1942 Dewey won the governorship of New York—his first political executive office. He was the first Republican to win New York's top political office since 1920. The state was larger and more populated than many countries, and its political landscape was full of pitfalls. New York City was home to the most diverse population of any city on earth, with vast numbers of Irish, Italians, Jews, and Poles. The city voted largely Democrat. Upstate lay broad swaths of rural forests and farms populated by conservative whites who feared footing the bill for the big city. Meanwhile the nation was at war—a tricky time for an inexperienced politician to take over. Dewey moved into 138 Eagle Street and employed the brand of Republican liberalism that he had grown up with, the progressive politics of Theodore Roosevelt.

Dewey doubled state aid to education and raised the salaries of state workers while reducing the state's debt by millions. He increased scholarship funds for returning veterans, and moved hundreds of millions of dollars into a "Postwar Reconstruction" fund, which was instrumental in guiding the state out of the war with far less economic chaos than most other states. In a ceremony before popping camera flashes, he used twenty-two pens to sign a trailblazing desegregation law, which sought to eliminate racial and religious discrimination in hiring, and it made New York the most progressive state in the nation on race issues. Dewey's labor policy resulted in far more harmony between unions and big business than existed at the federal level.

In 1944 Dewey won the Republican Party's nomination and set off on his first presidential campaign. Few believed he had a chance of toppling Franklin Roosevelt, running for a fourth term, but the candidate proved a fearless fighter. Not everyone loved him. He was accused of being cold, lacking the social nimbleness that politics sometimes required. "Dewey would always take on a face-to-face political fight," recorded Herbert Brownell, who was now the head of the Republican National Committee, and the mastermind behind Dewey's campaign. "He didn't care if it ended up in a shouting match; he would usually dominate the scene." There was that mustache, and the stiff Dewey countenance. The author and politician Clare Boothe Luce famously said of him, "How can the Republican Party nominate a man who looks like the bridegroom on a wedding cake?"

As an underdog, Dewey ran an attack campaign. It would be most remembered for the September 25, 1944, Oklahoma City speech — called "one of the most vitriolic speeches ever made by a Presidential candidate" by one Washington correspondent present. Dewey decried FDR's record as "desperately bad," blamed the president for the loss of "countless American lives" in war, and accused Roosevelt of running a campaign of "mud-slinging" and "ridicule."

While Dewey lost the election, his attack strategy worked to some degree. He succeeded in coming closer to beating FDR in 1944 than Alf Landon did in 1936 or Wendell Willkie in 1940, defeating FDR in states including Ohio, Indiana, Wisconsin, and Iowa. When it was over, and Dewey conceded at 3:45 a.m. on November 8, 1944, FDR muttered, "I still think he's a son of a bitch."

In 1946, Dewey — like the rest of the nation — watched closely as Truman floundered in the White House. The tragedy, Dewey told a friend, privately, was that Truman had two more years until the end of his term, and there was no inclination things would get any better. On April 1 of that year Brownell intoned in a Republican National Committee report, "The Truman administration is . . . a failure . . . Harry Truman is the weakest President since Pierce."

Following Dewey's success in the gubernatorial reelection, he was a new man, friends and colleagues observed. He was a more personable leader than he had been in 1944, less of a prosecutor and more of a seasoned politician. "It has been wickedly said that when he entered politics he gave off all the human warmth of a porcelain plumbing fixture," noted the syndicated columnists Joseph and Stewart Alsop, "whereas today he has achieved the status of an electric toaster."

Whether or not the New York governor would run for president became the hottest gossip in Republican circles. Dewey knew what it felt like to lose a national election. Once, in a meeting with top Republican leaders including Brownell and Senator Arthur Vandenberg of Michigan, Dewey spoke philosophically about defeat. He mentioned two politicians in particular — Wendell Willkie (who lost to FDR in 1940) and Al Smith (the four-term New York Democratic governor who lost to Hoover in the 1928 presidential election). Both men had phenomenally successful careers. Both were pillars in the canon of American public servants. But future generations would remember them almost exclusively for one thing: *losing.* For a man of Dewey's ambition, the prospect of losing the presidency twice was not something he wanted to entertain.

"As long ago as Philadelphia, in 1940 [the Republican National Convention]," Dewey told his Republican colleagues, "I deliberately decided that I was not going to be one of those unhappy men who yearned for the Presidency and whose failure to get it scarred their lives."

6

"It Is a Total 'War of Nerves'"

> Our nation is faced today with problems, present and future, which equal in scope and significance any it has hitherto met in 171 years of existence . . . What America does today, what America plans for tomorrow, can decide the sort of world the generations after us will possess — whether it shall be governed by justice or enslaved by force.
>
> — **Dwight Eisenhower, August 29, 1947**

NO ONE COULD HAVE FORESEEN what would happen next. "I think it's one of the proudest moments in American history," recalled Clark Clifford, the president's special counsel and increasingly one of his closest advisers. "What happened during that period was that Harry Truman and the United States saved the free world."

The year 1947 opened ominously. The British government released a white paper concerning the country's finances. The war had left the United Kingdom destitute and His Majesty's government would no longer be able to fulfill its international financial commitments. The London *Times* labeled the white paper "the most disturbing statement ever made by a British government." Days later in Washington — on Friday, February 21 — Dean Acheson, the undersecretary of state, was in his office when an assistant came to him bearing two documents that had been delivered by messenger that morning from the British ambassador to the United States. "They were shockers," Acheson would later write.

The papers explained that the United Kingdom would no longer be able to deliver aid to Greece and Turkey, two nations that were on the brink of falling victim to Soviet-inspired Communist revolution. In a short period of time, all British economic aid to the countries would stop.

For some time, intelligence reports had warned that Soviet-backed Communist guerillas were gaining control of Greece and Turkey. British aid was all that was keeping the Kremlin from Sovietizing these nations, and if the Soviets could take Greece and Turkey, they would have an easy road into the Mediterranean and the Middle East.

On Monday, February 24, Acheson and his boss, the new secretary of state, General George C. Marshall, met with Truman in the White House. In Truman's eyes, no man deserved more respect than Marshall, who had served as army chief of staff during World War II and whose very countenance inspired trust and reverence. Marshall made the case that the United States had to take over the burden of aid to Greece and Turkey, to stop the Soviets from advancing. A Truman assistant, John Steelman, was in the room and recorded that the president was "very convinced . . . that there was only one way to deal with the Communists and that was to let them know straight from the shoulder where he [Truman] stood."

All the major players in Washington sensed that this was a crossroads. Secretary of the Navy James Forrestal wrote in a letter to a friend during this week, "The next eighteen months look to me to be about the most critical that this country has ever faced."

By this point Truman was well aware of the dark forces at hand. Months earlier, the State Department's top Russia expert, George Kennan, had made an analysis of Soviet psychology in a paper that had come to be known as the "Long Telegram." Kennan concluded that the Soviets believed their security could only result from a "patient but deadly struggle for total destruction of rival power."

More recently Truman had received a report written by two advisers, Clark Clifford and George Elsey, called "American Relations with the Soviet Union" (known as the Clifford-Elsey Report), which laid out in chilling terms what the Americans should understand about Stalinist power politics. The Soviets already controlled much of Eastern Europe. The Kremlin's goal was to dominate every nation it could. Italy, France, Korea, China, Greece, Turkey, Iran — all had been ravaged by war and were now balanced on a razor's edge, ready to fall to one side or the other. Economic hardship in these nations made them easy pickings for the Kremlin.

According to the Clifford-Elsey Report, "Development of atomic weapons, guided missiles, materials for biological warfare, a strategic air force, submarines of great cruising range, naval mines and minecraft . . . are extending the range of Soviet military power well into areas which the United States regards as vital to its security." (Truman was so unnerved by this report, he told Clifford, "If it leaked it would blow the roof off the White House, it would blow the roof off the Kremlin"; he confiscated all copies Clifford had produced, and the report would not surface again until historians got ahold of it, twenty-two years later.)

Now the State Department's two top officials — George Marshall and the dapper aristocrat Dean Acheson — were confronting Truman regarding aid to Greece and Turkey. It was time for decision. Marshall himself had just returned from a mission to save China from falling to Soviet-backed Communist leadership, a mission that had failed. China was on the brink. Would Western Europe and the Middle East be next?

Truman made a determination that was to define US foreign policy for decades to come. "This was, I believe, the turning point," he wrote in his memoirs. "Wherever aggression, direct or indirect, threatened the peace, the security of the United States was involved." The idea was to use money instead of soldiers to fight the Soviets. Economic aid was imperative if countries like Greece and Turkey were going to create stable democratic societies. Without financial aid, these nations had no chance.

The president knew support for Greece and Turkey would be highly controversial. It would require the Democratic administration to get the Republican-controlled Congress on board with an unprecedented program that would hand out hundreds of millions of taxpayer dollars to foreign governments, free of charge. This at a time when the Republicans were charging the Democrats and "High Tax Harry" with overspending, when Americans were anxious about their own volatile economy.

Truman explained the situation in a letter to Bess: If the United States did not commit to Greece and Turkey, "we prepare for war. It just must not happen. But here I am confronted with a violently opposition Congress whose committees with few exceptions are living in 1890; it is not representative of the country's thinking at all. But I've a job and it must be done — win, lose, or draw."

On February 27, 1947, Truman welcomed into the White House the nation's most influential figures in foreign policy. Here were Dean Acheson and General Marshall from the State Department. Six congressmen arrived, including Republicans Arthur Vandenberg of Michigan and Speaker of the House Joe Martin of Massachusetts. The president opened the discussion, then turned the floor over to the secretary of state. Marshall had a prepared statement with him. He spelled out in dire terms what would happen if the Soviets succeeded in sacking Greece and Turkey: "It is not alarmist to say that we are faced with the first crisis of a series which might extend Soviet domination to Europe, the Middle East and Asia."

Marshall made clear: No amount of American financial aid could guarantee success. "The choice," according to the secretary of state, "is between acting with energy or losing by default."

At the end of the presentation, Vandenberg — head of the Senate Foreign Relations Committee and at times a fierce Truman critic — said solemnly, "Mr. President, if you will say that to the Congress and the country, I will support you and I believe that most of its members will do the same."

Which is exactly what Truman planned to do — address the hostile Eightieth Congress in person. He began work on what many would consider the most important speech of his life thus far. An administration official named

Joseph M. Jones was tasked with writing the first drafts. "All . . . were aware," Jones recalled, "that a major turning point in American history was taking place. The convergence of massive historical trends upon that moment was so real as to be almost tangible."

The speech would not only attempt to win over an opposition Congress, it would also be a direct signal to Joseph Stalin that Truman was going to support nations in an effort to resist Soviet bullying. Truman worked over the final drafts himself. As his special counsel Clark Clifford put it at the time, the speech would be "the opening gun in a campaign to bring people up to [the] realization that the war isn't over by any means."

On March 12 Truman climbed to the rostrum in the Capitol before a phalanx of microphones. Behind him sat Vandenberg and Joe Martin, both of them Republicans. In front of Truman was the entire federal legislature. Millions more were listening over radio. The president began, laying out a philosophy that would come to be known as the Truman Doctrine.

"The gravity of the situation which confronts the world today necessitates my appearance before a joint session of the Congress," Truman began. "The foreign policy and the national security of this country are involved." Nowhere in this speech was the Soviet Union mentioned. Truman continued:

> At the present moment in world history nearly every nation must choose between alternative ways of life. The choice is too often not a free one. One way of life is based upon the will of the majority, and is distinguished by free institutions, representative government, free elections, guarantees of individual liberty, freedom of speech and religion, and freedom from political oppression. The second way of life is based upon the will of a minority forcibly imposed upon the majority. It relies upon terror and oppression, a controlled press and radio, fixed elections, and the suppression of personal freedoms. I believe that it must be the policy of the United States to support free peoples who are resisting attempted subjugation by armed minorities or by outside pressures.

For most Americans, Truman's address came across as just another presidential message. The gravity of the situation in Europe, and the demands of meeting that challenge, were not immediately appreciated by a populace wearied by war.

There was little time for interpretation or deliberation, however. Even before the president delivered his Truman Doctrine speech, Secretary of State Marshall took off for Moscow in hopes of negotiating directly with the Soviet dictator Joseph Stalin on the postwar future. The continent was emerging from a brutal winter, and what Marshall saw in Europe unnerved him. Entire national infrastructures were still in shambles. Mass starvation was imminent.

In the Kremlin, the secretary of state found Stalin unwilling to compromise on much of anything. Marshall would remember watching Stalin doodle pictures of wolves on paper and respond with shocking indifference to the human misery that was rampant in countries like Czechoslovakia, Italy, Germany, and France. Stalin was in no hurry to help.

"We may agree the next time, or if not, the time after," Stalin told Marshall.

It was clear to Marshall that the Soviets were content to see Europe starve. Weak nations were nations incapable of attacking the Soviet Union. As Marshall's official translator Charles Bohlen later described this situation, "Europe was recovering slowly from the war. Little had been done to rebuild damaged highways, railroads, and canals . . . Unemployment was widespread. Millions of people were short on rations. There was a danger of epidemics. This was the kind of crisis that Communism thrived on. All the way back to Washington, Marshall talked of the importance of finding some initiative to prevent the complete breakdown of Western Europe."

While Marshall was abroad, on April 16, 1947, the famous financier Bernard Baruch gave a speech in the United States in which he used the term *Cold War* to describe US-Soviet relations, and from that time forward, the term worked its way into the American lexicon.

On April 28 Marshall arrived back in the United States. The next day, he told a nationwide radio audience: "Disintegrating forces are becoming evident. The patient is sinking while the doctors deliberate." Marshall gathered the top analysts in the State Department and ordered them to begin thinking of a plan to save the continent, and to report to him "without delay."

"Avoid trivia," he told them.

On May 9, 1947, the day after Truman's sixty-third birthday, the House of Representatives voted to appropriate $400 million (roughly $4.6 billion in today's numbers) for aid to Greece and Turkey. The Truman Doctrine was so controversial, during the vote, dissidents in the House shouted that it was "a declaration of war on Russia." One week later, Truman took off in his presidential airplane, nicknamed the Sacred Cow, bound for Missouri, where his ninety-four-year-old mother lay dying. On May 22, in the presidential suite at the Muehlebach Hotel in Kansas City, he signed the Greek-Turkish aid bill into law.

Less than a month later, on June 5, George Marshall delivered an eleven-minute commencement speech at Harvard University. In the address, he voiced the ideas that became known as the Marshall Plan. "The entire fabric of European economy" had been destroyed by war, Marshall explained. The continent had no resources with which to recover.

"The truth of the matter," Marshall said, "is that Europe's requirements for the next three or four years of foreign food and other essential products—principally from America—are so much greater than her present ability to pay that she must have substantial additional help, or face economic, social and political deterioration of a very grave character."

What Marshall proposed was a program to use financial aid to fight "against hunger, poverty, desperation, and chaos." Without naming the Soviet Union, he said that "governments, political parties or groups which seek to perpetuate human misery in order to profit therefrom politically or otherwise will encounter the opposition of the United States."

The idea was a program to spend billions of dollars on rebuilding Europe, for only nations with viable infrastructure, commerce, food, and political stability would be able to resist the wave of Soviet expansion. Truman later explained, "Nations, if not continents, had to be raised from the wreckage. Unless the economic life of these nations could be restored, peace in the world could not be re-established."

Following Marshall's speech, the debate in Washington began. The conservative Congress had approved hundreds of millions of dollars for two small countries. But billions for Europe was a much tougher request. Behind the scenes, Truman had helped to envision the Marshall Plan, and he got behind it immediately. Vandenberg was daunted by the idea. "We now apparently confront the Moscow challenge on every front and on every issue," Vandenberg wrote to Senator Robert Taft. "It is a total 'war of nerves' . . . I am sure that Secretary Marshall is alive to this fact."

Taft, the conservative powerhouse in the Senate, wrote a friend saying he had "no confidence whatever in [Marshall's] policy." Conservative Republicans would dig in and fight against such massive federal spending, Taft was sure. "In my opinion," he wrote, "the policy of Secretary Marshall may well be the principal issue in the next election."

The president himself would later say that it could take decades before the world would know for sure if radical programs like the Truman Doctrine and the Marshall Plan would prove successful. To his surprise, however, powerful forces were already taking shape from within his own party to destroy them.

If a rogue politician wanted to make himself heard in 1947, Madison Square Garden was a good place to do it. Built by Tex Rickard for boxing matches in the heart of New York City at Eighth Avenue between Forty-Ninth and Fiftieth Streets,* MSG was known as "The House That Tex Built." It held nineteen thousand seats, and on the night of March 31, 1947, every one of them was taken, every seat paid for. American flags hung between four sprawling banners that read DON'T ARM TYRANNY; FEED PEOPLE, DON'T FIGHT THEM; WE DON'T WANT A CENTURY OF FEAR; and U.N.: THE HOPE FOR WORLD PEACE.

---

*Madison Square Garden later moved to its current location between Seventh and Eighth Avenues and Thirty-First and Thirty-Third Streets.

The crowd was noteworthy for the number of fresh young faces—youth at a political rally, not your usual crowd in 1947. But then nothing about this rally was usual. It was the birth of a new antiestablishment, and its hero was Henry Wallace of Iowa—whom Harry Truman had fired from his cabinet six months earlier.

Warm-up speakers had no trouble getting this crowd going. There was the late president's son Elliott Roosevelt, a US Army Air Forces officer; the astronomer Harlow Shapley, head of the Harvard College Observatory; and the actor and comedian Zero Mostel. One by one they came onstage to throw jabs at the Truman punching bag. When the keynote speaker appeared, fans went wild. Henry Wallace's eyes peered out from under his swoop of iron-gray hair. Wearing a rumpled suit jacket that hung from his tennis-player shoulders, the fifty-eight-year-old looked younger than his years. Wallace was going to fight Truman's new foreign policy plans with all the power he could summon. When he began his speech, an ABC radio hookup took him nationwide.

"Unconditional aid" to anti-Soviet nations, Wallace said, will "unite the world against America and divide America against itself." He called on the United Nations rather than the Truman administration to come to the aid of Greece and Turkey. The UN's budget was "less than the budget of the New York City Sanitation Department," Wallace railed. The way forward was to fund the UN, not to employ foreign policy measures that the Soviet Union would view as confrontational.

"In the name of crisis, America is asked to ignore the world tribunal of the United Nations and take upon herself the role of prosecutor, judge, jury—and sheriff—what a role!" (Roars from the crowd.) "In the name of crisis, facts are withheld, time is denied, hysteria is whipped up." (Woots! Hollers!) "The Congress is asked to rush through a momentous decision [on the Truman Doctrine and Marshall Plan] as if great armies are already on the march.

"I hear no armies marching," Wallace said. "I hear a world crying out for peace."

Soon after Wallace's New York City appearance, he embarked on a two-week speaking tour in Europe, to argue that the Truman administration was moving the United States toward war with the Soviet Union. "The world is devastated and hungry," Wallace said to a sizable crowd in London. "The world is crying out, not for American guns and tanks to spread more hunger but for American plows and machines to fulfill the promise of peace."

Washington powerbrokers were stunned. Not so long ago Henry Wallace was considered one of the most powerful New Deal Democrats, a man who nearly became president. Now he had gone abroad to attack his own country's political administration.

In a cabinet meeting with Truman in the White House, Attorney General Tom Clark weighed whether Wallace should be allowed to reenter the United States. On the floor of the House of Representatives, Democrats and Republicans argued about whether Wallace's passport should be revoked, and even the possibility of prosecuting him under the 1799 Logan Act, which forbade private citizens from corresponding with foreign governments without authorization. The chairman of the House Un-American Activities Committee, Republican J. Parnell Thomas of New Jersey, charged that the Logan Act "covers Wallace like a cloak."

When Vandenberg accused Wallace of making "treasonable utterances," the former vice president responded with equally flammable rhetoric.

"There is only one circumstance under which phrases like 'treasonable utterances' could be used to describe my speeches," Wallace told reporters in London. "That would be when we were at war . . . The fact that such words as 'treason' have been used in describing my trip [to Europe] indicates that, in the minds of the men who use these phrases, we actually are at war."

On April 10 Truman held his weekly press conference, and a reporter asked the president if Wallace was "in good standing of the Democratic Party."

"Certainly," Truman said.

"Would you like to have him campaign on the Democratic ticket next year, Mr. President?"

Truman said he thought Wallace "will probably campaign for the Democratic ticket."

From Britain, Wallace responded to Truman directly after reading of this conversation in the press. "I shall be campaigning in 1948 with all my power," Wallace said. "But I will be campaigning for the ideals of the free world and the men who best express these ideals. I hope, but I cannot guarantee, that they will be on the Democratic ticket."

Back in the United States, Wallace continued on the road, holding anti-Truman rallies. FBI agents began to prowl these events as rumors surfaced that Wallace's supporters included numerous individuals with Communist sympathies. In Cleveland on May 2, Wallace drew an audience of four thousand people, with another fifteen hundred outside unable to get tickets. In Minneapolis on May 12, six thousand people paid to hear Wallace speak. In Chicago on May 14, twenty thousand people paid from sixty cents to $2.40 to hear Wallace, "filling Chicago Stadium for the first time in political history," according to an account sent to the FBI's chief, J. Edgar Hoover. Five days later, Wallace spoke before twenty-seven thousand rally participants at Gilmore Stadium in Los Angeles.

Increasingly, Wallace drew a line between the Soviet and American ways of thinking, and while Americans were growing paranoid of Communists abroad and rumored secret Communist cells at home, Wallace became the only major public figure in the United States pointing blame for the Cold War not on the USSR but on America and its president. Wallace warned that the Truman Doctrine was no plan for peace but rather an attempt to insert American influence into affairs abroad where it did not belong. He warned that the Marshall Plan would lead down "a road to ruthless imperialism." He slammed Winston Churchill for his "hatred of Russia," calling Churchill "an imperialist."

Far-left liberals, mostly in California and on the East Coast, found a haven in Wallace's peace rallies. Others saw in them a strange threat; there was a whiff of pro-Sovietism to Wallace's message, which made many suspicious of his motivations. In April 1947 Churchill called Wallace a "crypto-Communist" who was part of a "vast system of Communist intrigue which radiates from Moscow." In June, the American Anti-Communist Association sought a court injunction to keep Wallace from speaking at the Watergate Amphitheater in Washington.

Was Wallace a conduit for Communist infiltration? Even a stooge for Stalin himself? Wallace confronted the issue head-on.

"If it is traitorous to believe in peace," he said at a conference in New York, "we are traitors. If it is communistic to believe in prosperity for all, we are communists. If it is red-baiting to fight for free speech and real freedom of the press, we are red-baiters. If it is un-American to believe in freedom from monopolistic dictation, we are un-American. I say that we are more American than the neo-Fascists who attack us. I say on with the fight!"

Days after Wallace uttered these words, in June 1947, the first organized "Wallace for President" group met in Fresno, California. The "Wallace in '48" movement was on.

7

“The Defeat Seemed like the End of the World”

ON THE AFTERNOON OF JUNE 29, 1947, as debate over the Marshall Plan raged in offices all over Washington and Henry Wallace was on tour battering the Truman administration, the Secret Service delivered the president to the Lincoln Memorial, to give a speech Truman knew could shatter what was left of his own party. The president was met by Walter White, head of the NAACP, and Eleanor Roosevelt. Together the three walked toward a stage set up at the base of the Lincoln Memorial, the lanky Mrs. Roosevelt awkwardly towering over both Truman and White.

For months, Truman’s stand on race matters had become a prickly mystery in Washington. Now Truman would solve that mystery, and accept the consequences. He was going to become the first president to address the NAACP.

All four major radio networks were set to broadcast the speech, in addition to networks overseas. Huge crowds of NAACP members were already on hand. They were young. They were old. They were in uniform. They were war veterans in wheelchairs. They made up the biggest gathering in the NAACP’s thirty-eight-year history.

White spoke first. “There are 100,000 people here today at the foot of

Abraham Lincoln in Washington," he began. "I am told that between 30 and 40 million other Americans may be listening to the radio at this hour. Countless others listen overseas . . ."

When it was Truman's moment, he looked out from the podium and saw a sea of brown faces. Behind the crowd, the Washington Monument stood erect against a blue sky. Truman's speech called for federal protection against violence and discrimination and equality in employment and education. It stressed the right to vote for every citizen as critical to the definition of Americanism. America had "reached a turning point in the long history of our country's efforts to guarantee freedom and equality to our citizens," Truman said.

"Every man," he continued, "should have the right to a decent home, the right to an education, the right to adequate medical care, the right to a worthwhile job, the right to an equal share in making the public decisions through the ballot, and the right to a fair trial in a fair court."

When Truman sat back down, he turned to Walter White and told him, "I said what I did because I mean every word of it—and I am going to prove that I do mean it."

The next day, newspapers hailed Truman's speech as one of the most significant moments in American civil rights history. Yet as Truman expected, the address infuriated white southern Democrats, who were incensed by what they perceived as a betrayal. Going back to the 1870s, southern politicians, though traditionally conservative, had aligned themselves with northern Democrats primarily for a single reason: race. Southerners voted Democratic, and in exchange, northerners would leave matters of race and law enforcement to state governments, even those with traditions of white supremacy and segregation going back generations.

Now the times were changing. The war was a race reboot in America. If black Americans could be drafted to go to war and fight and die for their country, activists like Walter White argued, they should be able to vote in every state, and sit next to a white person on a bus. If black Americans were to pay the same taxes as white Americans, then they should enjoy the same benefits. Truman's NAACP address recommended federal civil rights laws that threatened to destroy long-held southern traditions, and end the South's allegiance to the Democratic Party in the process.

Reaction played out in the press. The popular senator Harry Byrd of Virginia called Truman's speech a "devastating broadside at the dignity of Southern traditions and institutions," and warned of "disastrous results in racial hatred and bloodshed." A group of twenty-one Southern Democrats in Congress led by Senator Richard B. Russell of Georgia announced they would plan a filibuster to "stand guard" against any civil rights legislation.

During the weeks after Truman's NAACP speech, racial anxiety gripped the South, and a grassroots campaign of white power began to inject fear into local communities, where in many cases black residents far outnumbered whites. Cross burnings were reported. "Talmadge White Supremacy Clubs" popped up in Georgia, named for the late Eugene Talmadge, a three-term Georgia governor who for years had actively promoted segregation in the state. According to one newspaper account, the Talmadge Club's pledge card read in part that "the rule of our Government should be left entirely in the hands of white citizens."

Truman's stand on civil rights put him in a game of chicken against the southern power base of his own political party. Senators, congressmen, and governors from the South were sure that, if they put enough pressure on him, the president would back down.

"The world seems to be topsy-turvy," Truman wrote Bess, who was back home in Missouri. "I can't see why it was necessary for me to inherit all the difficulties and all the tribulations of the world—but I have them on hand and must work them out some way—I hope for the welfare of all concerned . . . All we can do is go ahead working for peace—and keep our powder dry."

In the spring of 1947 Truman and the Eightieth Congress clashed in their most fierce battle yet. "Mr. Republican" Robert Taft of Ohio and Fred Hartley Jr., a House Republican from New Jersey, introduced the Taft-Hartley bill, sweeping legislation aimed at pulling power away from labor unions. The bill proposed outlawing closed shops (workplaces allowing only union workers), restricting labor unions from making contributions to political campaigns, making certain kinds of labor strikes unlawful, and requiring union leaders to declare that they were not members of a Communist party.

The bill, Truman believed, unjustly favored big business and Wall Street, and labor union members agreed. Tens of thousands of workers took to the streets in protest. On June 4, nearly twenty thousand union workers jammed New York's Madison Square Garden to hear speakers denounce the bill; above the stage hung a sign saying, MR. PRESIDENT: VETO THE TAFT-HARTLEY SLAVE LABOR BILL. Six days later, another sixty thousand workers marched up Eighth Avenue in Manhattan. On June 17, ten thousand leather and shoe workers marched through Lynn, Massachusetts. More than 170,000 letters, 550,000 cards, and 27,000 telegrams flooded the White House mail room, mostly urging Truman to veto the bill—which he did.

Truman's veto message to the Eightieth Congress included words like *startling, dangerous, far-reaching, unprecedented, unworkable, burdensome, arbitrary, unnecessary, impossible, ineffective, discriminatory, clumsy, cumbersome, inequitable, backward, unfair, unwarranted, interfering, drastic,* and *troublesome.*

In June, the Senate voted to override Truman's veto, as Republicans joined with many Democrats including the president's close personal friend Tom Connally of Texas. In the House, more Democrats voted for the bill than against it. Taft-Hartley was enacted on June 23, 1947. "The defeat," recalled the Democratic National Committee's publicist Jack Redding, "seemed like the end of the world."

At the same time, Truman faced a furious backlash from liberal politicians over an executive order the White House released on March 21. Executive Order 9835 created a "loyalty board" that subjected federal employees to background checks to ensure that "maximum protection . . . be afforded the United States against infiltration of disloyal persons into the ranks of employees." Suddenly, the FBI had the power to look into people's private lives and root out those who had affiliations to organizations that were, or at least were believed to be, politically unacceptable. That is, Communist.

Executive Order 9835 was issued in response to Cold War jitters. A 1946 spy scandal in Ottawa, Canada, that resulted in the arrest of some three dozen suspected Soviet undercover agents shocked both Americans and Canadians, and "awakened the people of North America to the magnitude and danger of Soviet espionage," as the *New York Times* put it. Subsequent accusations that Communism was rife in federal agencies empowered Republicans to attack the Truman administration for being weak on Communism. Truman's decree sought to calm nerves, but in fact, for many, it had the opposite effect.

"It was a political problem," Clark Clifford explained. "Truman was going to run in '48, and that was it . . . The President didn't attach fundamental importance to the so-called Communist scare. He thought it was a lot of baloney. But political pressures were such that he had to recognize it."

Liberals were incensed. Henry Wallace called Truman's loyalty board "a campaign of terror unequaled in our history, reminiscent of the early days of Adolf Hitler." Recalled Truman's first press secretary, Jonathan Daniels: "Not even liberty seemed simple."

At the time, Truman was also overseeing the most momentous reorganization of the military and intelligence establishments in the country's history. The National Security Act of 1947, which Truman signed on July 26 of that year, created the new Central Intelligence Agency, the National Security Council, and the Air Force as its own branch of the military. The War and Navy Departments merged to create a single Department of Defense under one defense secretary. Truman appointed the former secretary of the navy, James Forrestal, as the first secretary of defense. The push to implement this military reorganization put so much pressure on Forrestal, he began showing signs of mental distress. (Forrestal would ultimately commit suicide, jumping from the sixteenth-floor window of the National Naval Medical Center in Bethesda, Maryland, in 1949.)

No problem, however, caused more of a headache for Truman in 1947 than the question of a Jewish homeland.

In the fall of 1947 the pressure on Truman to support a state for the Jews in Palestine had only increased, as had opposition from the US State Department. On October 3, 1947, Truman received a letter from one of his closest friends, Eddie Jacobson. It had been Eddie, "my Jewish friend," with whom Truman had opened his failed haberdashery, Truman & Jacobson, two decades earlier. Jacobson's letter was written on stationery from his new store, Eddie Jacobson's Westport Menswear in Kansas City.

"I think I am one of the few who actually knows and realizes what terrific heavy burdens you are carrying on your shoulders during these hectic days," Jacobson wrote. "I should, therefore, be the last man to add to them; but I feel you will forgive me for doing so, because tens of thousands of lives depend on words from your mouth and heart. Harry, my people need help and I am appealing to you to help them."

As Truman read this letter, the United Nations General Assembly was in the process of debating a solution for the Palestine conundrum, in Paris. Already Jews were immigrating to Palestine and smuggling in weapons, empowered by prophecies that they would return to the land they believed God had decreed as their own. Ultimately, on November 29, 1947, the UN adopted a resolution to partition Palestine into two states, one for the Jews and one for the Arabs. Subsequently, the British announced that they would end their mandate over the region, to take effect at midnight on May 14, 1948—which meant that twenty-six years of British rule over Palestine was about to end.

Now there was a deadline. If the British pulled out with no internationally supported policy to keep the peace, war would result—possibly world war, if the Soviets jumped in.

The United Nations' partition plan failed to assuage either the Jews or the Arabs. Each side thought it was getting less than it deserved. Public opinion in the United States supported the UN's partition plan; 65 percent of Americans favored it, according to a Gallup poll, compared with 10 percent who did not (the rest had no opinion).

Truman made up his mind: He would support the founding of a Jewish state. But in order to do so, he had to figure out a way to get his own State Department — and particularly the department's boss, George Marshall — on board. Truman summoned the young rising star of his administration, Clark Clifford. At forty-one, Clifford was in his third year working at the White House, and prior to coming to Washington, he had been a successful trial lawyer in Truman's home state of Missouri. When Clifford arrived in Truman's office, he could tell right away the president was troubled. Clifford took a seat in front of Truman's desk and listened closely.

"Clark, I am impressed with General Marshall's argument that we should not recognize the new [Jewish] state so fast," Truman said. Marshall was going to continue to take a "very strong position," the president believed. "When he does, I would like you to make the case in favor of recognition of the new state." Truman paused, and Clifford felt the gravity of the moment. "You know how I feel," Truman said. "I want you to present it just as though you were making an argument before the Supreme Court of the United States. Consider it carefully, Clark, organize it logically. I want you to be as persuasive as you possibly can be."

The 1948 election was a year away. From the time Truman had become an accidental president, on April 12, 1945, he told his staff he'd never wanted the job, that he was ready to move out of the "Great White Jail." But now his mind was made up. There was too much at stake not to run.

On November 12, he met in the White House with his secretary of defense, James Forrestal, and revealed his inner thinking on the upcoming national election. Truman told Forrestal how much he worried about his family, how difficult their lives had become because of his job. But he had no choice. He had to run.

"There is no question in my judgment as to the complete sincerity of the

President," Forrestal recorded in his diary, "that the only thing that holds him to this grinding job is a sense of obligation to the country and, secondarily, to his party."

Truman had no illusions about what it would take to launch his national campaign. All the odds were against him. The only way he could win would be to create a campaign strategy so unexpected, it would take the opposition by storm. There had always been rules in electioneering—some established by law, others by tradition. The only way to win would be by breaking the right ones and by risking his entire political reputation in the process.

8

"Dewey's Hat Is Tossed into Ring"

ON JUNE 12, 1947, GOVERNOR Dewey stepped off a train at the Mineola, Long Island, station. At a fund-raising luncheon at Jones Beach for five hundred Republican county officials, one of Dewey's closest advisers, J. Russell Sprague, introduced him.

"We are here to pledge our loyalty to him as a friend, as a great Governor, as a leader of our party, and as the next President of the United States."

The crowd went over the top as Dewey rose to his feet. New Yorkers loved the idea of having a New Yorker back in the White House again.

"That was a charming and overgenerous introduction," the governor said. "But I would like to assure Mr. Sprague again in public as I have in private that I am happy where I am. I like the company and my friends and I would not lightly give up those opportunities."

Who believed him? Not many. The next day's *New York Times* ran a front-page headline, "Dewey's Hat Is Tossed into Ring."

Over the next month, a "Dewey for President" campaign began to crystallize, without any fanfare or even any statement from the man himself. The incipient campaign was like a bullet in a chamber; the question was when to pull the trigger.

The governor's old friend Herb Brownell set up campaign headquarters in Midtown Manhattan to complement the Washington offices of the Republican National Committee, and Brownell began to recruit a team. There was Sprague, Long Island's most powerful Republican politico, and the strategist Edwin Jaeckle, former chair of the New York State Republican Committee and still a powerhouse in the state. Along with Brownell, Jaeckle had guided Dewey's gubernatorial campaigns. He would later describe his work with Dewey in these words: "I was like a trainer with a good horse."

Brownell started to rebuild the party from the ground up. "Reorganization of the national party machinery was long overdue," he recorded. He traveled by train from state to state to personally acquaint himself with local party leaders, so they would cooperate, in his words, "in building a new party structure." He aimed to consolidate power, to weave the various localities into a highly coordinated centralized juggernaut.

Brownell stepped down from his chairmanship of the Republican National Committee to manage Dewey's campaign. Yet the field of potentially strong candidates was growing crowded. Republicans believed they would take the White House, probably for the next eight years, but securing the nomination looked to be a harder fight than defeating Truman on November 2, 1948. Liberal and conservative factions were rivaling for control of the party. The conservative faction — in step with the Republican ideology of the 1920s and '30s as personified by Presidents Harding, Coolidge, and Hoover — wanted to curb governmental intervention in the economy, and abroad. The liberal faction of the party — as personified by Theodore Roosevelt, and now Thomas Dewey — embraced the power of the federal government and progressive domestic policies.

The conservatives were led by Senator Robert Taft of Ohio. Taft was a Cincinnati lawyer and Washington royalty — the son of the twenty-seventh president, William Howard Taft. The younger Taft had come of age in the White House. He was the product of the best schools in the nation, a Harvard Law man who had cemented himself at the center of the conservative coalition on Capitol Hill. Taft was a fighter and enormously respected. "For many voters, especially independents," according to Brownell, "'Republican' and 'Taft' were synonymous."

As a liberal Republican, Dewey supported the Marshall Plan and internationalist foreign policy. Taft threatened to create an "Anti-Marshall Plan Committee," arguing in a 1947 speech, "The solution of many of the European problems must rest with their own governments . . . Why should we make ourselves responsible for something entirely beyond our control?"

Dewey also supported Truman's Universal Military Training plan. Taft loathed the idea — too much government.

As governor of New York, Dewey had a proven record of spending on social programs. Those who mocked the idea of a "welfare state" were "very clumsy Republicans," Dewey said. "There has never been a responsible government which did not have the welfare of its people at heart," he had said. "Anybody who thinks that an attack on the fundamental idea of security and welfare is appealing to people generally is living in the Middle Ages." Taft fought for less federal spending at almost every turn, and blamed the current inflation crisis on High Tax Harry's spending.

The only major policies that both Dewey and Taft consistently supported were civil rights and desegregation, and a homeland for the Jews. In other words, Dewey agreed with Truman on many of the major issues.

Taft launched his campaign early, announcing his run at a press conference on October 24, 1947, in Columbus, Ohio. He was fifty-eight years old. Taft offered a short list of the issues that would be front and center in the 1948 election, and number one on his list echoed the conservative ideology of his father: "The general issue [is] between people who want more federal power and action and the people who want less." Taft, of course, wanted less.

"There will be violent differences of opinion," he warned of the months ahead.

By the time he announced his candidacy, his team had already booked nearly 160 hotel rooms in Philadelphia for the Republican National Convention, where the 1948 GOP candidate would be crowned.

Taft and Dewey were the heavyweights, but there were also dark horses in the making, including General Douglas MacArthur, the military commander of occupied Japan. Newspaper publisher William Randolph Hearst spoke for many when he wrote in a letter in 1948, "I think we are going to have war with Russia. I think MacArthur is the only President who could avert war with Russia and, if it could not be averted, I think MacArthur would be the only President who could win."

The most formidable dark horse, however, was Harold Stassen. At forty, Stassen was even younger than Dewey, and his politics put him in the middle, ideologically, between Dewey and Taft. He had been elected the Republican governor of Minnesota nine years earlier at just thirty-one, the youngest man ever elected governor of any American state. He had keynoted the 1940 Republican National Convention at just thirty-three, and had resigned as governor two years later to fight in World War II; he was awarded the Legion of Merit and became a war hero for his service with the US Navy in the Pacific Theater.

Holding no office when he returned home, Stassen announced a run for president before anyone, in 1946. Few took him seriously—until April 9, 1947, when Stassen went to Moscow and inexplicably got himself an in-person interview with the Soviet dictator Joseph Stalin. Upon his return to America, Stassen released a transcript of the meeting to the press. It quoted Stalin saying, "The USSR does not propose to" have war with the United States, and "if during war they [the United States and Soviet Union] could cooperate, why can't they today in peace?"

"The document was sensational," recorded Jack Redding, the publicist for the Democratic National Committee. "Here was a possible next President of the United States who was able to secure a face-to-face session with the Russian dictator."

"Among the rank and file of politicians," *Time* magazine stated in 1947, "the boys who know the ropes, no one laughs at Harold Stassen."

Herbert Brownell's candidate Tom Dewey was still the front-runner. But the quest for the nomination was going to be harder than either man thought. And the ideological landscape was growing increasingly diverse.

"From my point of view, we have a larger problem," Dewey wrote the Republican congressman from New York, John Taber, looking ahead to the 1948 Republican National Convention. Thus far a Democrat in the White House had been navigating the country through the postwar period. Now it appeared the Republicans would be taking over.

What would be the GOP policy toward the Soviets? Who would shape it?

"We are just beginning to win the cold war," Dewey wrote Taber. Dewey wanted to rally support for the Marshall Plan among Republicans. He believed that if "we win this cold war and can build a United States of Europe for a strong, free world," it would be worth the "grief" and the billions in Marshall Plan dollars "many times over."

"If we should lose the free world," he wrote ominously, "then isolated and alone, we would have a defense budget alone larger than our entire budget of today. That is, we should have it unless we too surrendered to the onward march of Communism."

One year before the election, on November 15, 1947, a Republican political operative wrote a scathing memo that landed on Dewey's desk (the signature on this memo is illegible). The document put into words a fear that was growing among both Democrats and Republicans — that the Soviets would attempt to influence the outcome of the 1948 presidential election. "The Kremlin will make no serious move in the direction of establishing peace in Europe and elsewhere before the 1948 election in the United States has been decided," the memo read. "In the meantime it will try to influence the result of the 1948 election by every means conceivable."

The document warned that the election was going to get unprecedentedly ugly. "When one considers, for instance, that including their families there are millions of people who directly and indirectly have spent almost half of their adult lives in drawing support from the payrolls of the Federal government [due to the liberal spending policies and social programs of the New Deal]; when one further realizes the degree of sheer desperation that will surely envelop these millions when faced with the threat of losing their regular income from this source, one need not wonder how vituperative and reckless will be the language and actions of this formidable contingent of Democrats."

What could make the difference, this writer implied, was Moscow. The

Kremlin was sure to prefer the Democrats in the White House: "Not that these men love the Democrats; they only hate the Republicans more or, what is more to the point, the men in the Kremlin are afraid of the Republicans more than they are of the tested Democrats.

"The United States of America is fair game for Moscow and has been for years," the memo concluded. "And, as far as anyone is willing to see, the year 1948 will be the year in which Soviet Russia will do everything in its power to influence the election here."

9

"Wall Street and the Military Have Taken Over"

WHILE THE REPUBLICANS JOCKEYED FOR position, Henry Wallace stunned the Democratic Party by declaring his candidacy for president. Wallace was going to run not as a Democrat but as the face of a new and highly controversial third party.

On December 29, 1947, Wallace assembled forty friends in ABC's radio studio in Chicago. His close advisers and his wife, Ilo, were there; they knew he was going to announce his run. However, Wallace had kept it a secret from all but those closest to him as to which party he would represent. All over the country, Americans heard Wallace's words, as he made the biggest leap of faith of his lifetime.

"Thousands of people all over the United States have asked me to engage in this great fight," Wallace said into the ABC microphone. "The people are on the march. We have assembled a Gideon's Army, small in number, powerful in conviction, ready for action." A vote for Wallace was a vote for peace, the candidate said. He declared himself the candidate of the new Progressive Party — a group that situated itself to the left of the Democrats, as the anti-Truman, antiwar choice for voters. Then he addressed the obvious conflict straight on: Would votes for Wallace, a liberal and a hero for New Deal Democrats, steal votes from Truman and the Democrats, and guarantee a GOP victory?

"The lukewarm liberals sitting on two chairs say, 'Why throw away your vote?'" Wallace asked rhetorically. "I say a vote for a new party in 1948 will be the most valuable vote you have ever cast or will ever cast. The bigger the peace vote in 1948, the more definitely the world will know that the United States is not behind the bipartisan reactionary war policy which is dividing the world into two armed camps and making inevitable the day when American soldiers will be lying in their arctic suits in the Russian snow."

Reaction to Wallace's announcement focused less on Wallace than on Truman. The following day, the *Washington Post*'s political columnist Edward Folliard described the political fallout: "Henry A. Wallace's hat-in-the-ring announcement last night met with scornful indifference at the White House, but evoked from Republicans a joyous cry of 'We're in in '48!'" Others saw in Wallace something far more dangerous. It was hardly a secret that Communists were supporting the Progressive Party, and following Wallace's campaign announcement, the story began to unfold in public. The liberal group Americans for Democratic Action put out a report stating, "New reinforcements — Communist-dominated unions and individuals well-known as CP [Communist Party] apologists — took their place at the front" of the Wallace movement.

"What do the Communists really want from Henry Wallace?" asked the Alsop brothers in their popular newspaper column right after Wallace announced his candidacy. "That is the question Wallace's third-party candidacy poses."

To the powerful elite of Washington, many of whom were caught up in Cold War fever, Wallace's seemingly obvious ties to Communist concerns were inexplicable. But Wallace had answers for his critics. Was America not a free country? Was it not legal for Americans to be Communists? Wasn't the whole nation founded on the idea of political and religious freedom? "If the Communists want to support me," Wallace told one crowd at a rally in Seattle, "they must do it on my terms. If the Communists are working for peace with Russia, God bless them. If they are working for the overthrow of the Government by force, they know I am against them."

The truth was more complicated. In the months leading up to Wallace's announcement, he had been working as editor of the small but influential magazine the *New Republic.* According to William Harlan Hale, one of the magazine's writers, Wallace was "seeing more and more of fewer and fewer people." These were men the *Washington Post* called Wallace's "stage managers," his "influential insiders" — the people shaping his campaign.

There was John Abt, a University of Chicago–trained lawyer who had for much of his career worked with labor unions. For years Abt had been a subject of interest for the FBI. He first came to the bureau's attention on May 10, 1945, during the secret testimony of a *Time* magazine editor named Whittaker Chambers, who was (according to the FBI's records) a "self-admitted espionage agent for the Soviet Union and [a] former member of the Communist Party." Chambers had admitted to being part of what the FBI called an "underground group" of Communists. Abt had been one of "the leaders of this group," which had in fact met at Abt's home at the time, on Fifteenth Street in Manhattan, according to Chambers.

Abt was a member of the Communist Party USA. (The FBI would later mark in his file that, according to informants, he had visited the USSR as recently as 1945 and "was reportedly in contact with various officials of Russia and satellite nations during the late 1940's.") Abt's sister Marion was public relations director for the Communist Party USA. Abt knew he was on the FBI's radar and he feared that his presence in the Wallace camp would cause problems. When he expressed these fears personally to Wallace, the candidate "brushed aside my concerns," Abt later recalled. "He urged me to become general counsel for the new party." Abt took on the role. It would be his job to use his legal expertise to get Wallace on the ballot in as many of the forty-eight states as he could.

There was Lee Pressman, a labor attorney who had studied at Harvard and Cornell and who had become politically active in left-wing groups. The same informant who had named Abt as a leader in an underground Communist movement had also named Pressman as a member.

Then there was Calvin Benham "Beanie" Baldwin, the slick-haired politico who was becoming the loudest voice in Henry Wallace's ear, and would in fact be Wallace's campaign manager. Baldwin had been Wallace's assistant when Wallace was secretary of agriculture, and had in 1947 helped to found the Progressive Citizens of America, a precursor to the new Progressive Party. The PCA, as it was called, had declared itself open to "all progressive men and women in our nation, regardless of race, creed, color, national origin, or political affiliation." By "regardless [of] political affiliation," the party was tacitly declaring itself open to those from the far-left flank — Communists and so-called fellow travelers.

"The facts . . . are," Abt later recalled, "that the Communist party was active at every level of the Progressive Party, most important in the state and local organizations."

The FBI knew this. "As you are undoubtedly aware," a field investigator wrote in a report to J. Edgar Hoover as early as June 3, 1947, "the Progressive Citizens of America is a new front organization which is propagating the Communists' political aims for 1948."

As for Wallace's own personal philosophy, he once told the head of the Communist Party USA, Eugene Dennis, personally what divided his thinking from Communist thinking. "All I said," remembered Wallace later, "was that there were two things I wanted him to understand — that the Communist Party doesn't believe in God, I do believe in God; the Communist Party doesn't believe in progressive capitalism, I do believe in progressive capitalism."

Henry Wallace knew, perhaps more than any other candidate, that someone declaring a run for the most high-powered office on the planet was putting himself at great personal risk. "I certainly told him before he made the decision," campaign manager Beanie Baldwin later remembered, "that it was going to be very rough going and a very rough campaign." Politicians, Wallace knew, were human beings, who are in essence made up of all the deeds they have ever done and all the things they have ever said. While a cloud of suspicion hung over Wallace already, he had more to worry about — a proverbial skeleton in his closet, an uncomfortable truth about his past that would be impossible to hide from the burning spotlight of a presidential campaign.

Wallace hailed from the conservative state of Iowa, born into a religious family that became, during his youth, highly influential in American farming communities. Leadership was part of the Wallace DNA. Wallace's father, Henry Cantwell Wallace, served as the secretary of agriculture under Warren Harding and Calvin Coolidge, and was a journalist and publisher as well. Young Henry Wallace grew up on a farm, graduated from Iowa State University in 1910, and began writing for his family's newspaper — *Wallaces' Farmer.*

In the early 1920s, shortly after his marriage to Ilo, Wallace began experimenting with hybrid corn seeds, and in 1926 he created Hi-Bred Corn. The seed spawned hearty stalks and high yields, and soon millions of rows of Wallace corn were reaching up to the sun across America and abroad. The company made Wallace fabulously rich, though he lived ascetically. During the Roaring Twenties — the Jazz Age — young Wallace remained a teetotaler.

His family background and success in farming brought Wallace to the attention of Franklin Roosevelt. Days after Roosevelt became the thirty-second president in 1933, he offered Wallace a cabinet post as secretary of agriculture, and from the early days of FDR's presidency, Henry Wallace was a rising star of the New Deal movement.

Wallace also earned a reputation as a first-rate eccentric. He dressed in dusty wrinkled suits, drank milk made out of soybeans, and was skilled in the art of throwing a boomerang. He was a font of seemingly far-fetched ideas, some of which would prove remarkably prescient. He imagined a day, for example, when people would wear wristbands that could both tell the time and deliver news, and a pill that would contain all the nutrients of a full meal. Long before many Americans had heard of tennis, Wallace had mastered a mean stroke. Once, while sparring in a boxing ring in a gym, he famously knocked out Senator Allen Ellender of Louisiana. But early on, Wallace's eccentricities served only to burnish his reputation.

One day in the early 1930s Wallace was visiting a museum dedicated to the work of the artist Nicholas Roerich, at 310 Riverside Drive in New York. There he met Roerich himself for the first time. Roerich was Russian born, and had come to the United States in 1920. By then he had gained fame for his explorations into untamed lands, his spiritual writings, and his art. With his wild, flowing goatee, he had the appearance of an aging mystic. Even by 1920s standards, when eccentricity was in vogue, Roerich took individuality to an extreme. Once in 1927, he disappeared in Asia for eight months. Newspapers chronicled the mystery, until he unexpectedly reappeared in Mongolia. On another occasion, officials in India refused to allow him to enter their country for fear he was a Russian spy.

Days into Henry Wallace's tenure as secretary of agriculture, he wrote Roerich, addressing him as "Dear Guru." "I have been thinking of you holding the casket — the sacred most precious casket," Wallace wrote. "And I have thought of the New Country going forth to meet the seven stars under the sign of the three stars. And I have thought of the admonition 'Await the Stone.'" He signed the letter, "In great haste of this strange maelstrom which is Washington."

A collection of letters to Roerich attributed to Wallace date from the 1930s, letters full of incomprehensible innuendos and hints of the occult. Washington figures were referred to in veiled terms: the "flaming one," the "sour one," the "wavering one." The letters spoke of "earth beat, the Indian rhythm of ancient America," and "fire from the heights." Only once in his life would Wallace ever comment on these missives, in an interview around 1950. The letters, he said, were "unsigned, undated notes, which I knew I never sent to Nicholas Roerich, but there were a few letters addressed to Nicholas Roerich signed by me and dated which were written in rather high-flown language."

In 1935 Wallace nominated Roerich for the Nobel Peace Prize and employed the artist-philosopher, sending him on a quixotic mission to Central Asia to search for plant life, on the payroll of the US Department of Agriculture. Roerich sped off with his wife and an entourage, and began to engage in activities that made local officials in Asia anxious. "The gist of the whole thing was that Roerich was playing international politics over there," Wallace later recalled. What made Roerich dangerous was his followers, Wallace believed. "When I use [the word] followers, I mean followers of the type of the most extreme Communists or most extreme Catholics or Fascists or Hitlerites — completely and utterly devoted fanatics."

Soon American diplomats in the region were reporting on Roerich's activities. Wallace became panicked. He ended funding for the trip and wrote Roerich, saying, "There must be no publicity whatever about [the] recent expedition. There must be no quoting of correspondence or other violation of Department publicity regulations."

Wallace never heard from Roerich again. The "guru letters" remained a secret, for the time being.

In 1940 FDR chose Wallace to run as his VP candidate, and the ticket breezed to victory. When the United States entered World War II, Wallace was one of the first in Washington to learn of the top secret Manhattan Project. It was during these early months of the war, when all appeared bleak in the wake of Nazi advances in Europe, that Wallace formed ideas that would fuel his postwar obsessions. Long before others did, he saw that the Soviet Union, the United States' most valued military ally against Hitler, would emerge from the war as an unprecedented power in the East. He foresaw the Cold War, years before most others did.

"It is highly essential that the United States and Russia understand each other better," Wallace wrote in his diary as early as 1942. "This means there must be better understanding among United States citizens concerning Russia and among Russian citizens concerning the United States . . . It means we must cooperate with Russia in the postwar period."

In 1942 Wallace distilled his thinking into a speech he called "The Century of the Common Man." "Some have spoken of the 'American Century,'" Wallace said. "I say that the century on which we are entering — the century that will come out of this war — can be and must be the century of the common man." The speech envisioned a future world peace, a world without racism, a world without greed, based on communal welfare. It was translated into more than a dozen languages and made Wallace an icon for left-wing intellectuals.

Wallace headed into 1944 believing he would remain on the Democratic ticket in the forthcoming election. According to a Gallup poll leading up to the Democratic National Convention, 65 percent of Democratic voters favored Wallace as the VP candidate to run with FDR in his historic fourth-term campaign. (Senator Alben Barkley of Kentucky ranked second at 17 percent; Harry Truman was way back in the pack, with 2 percent.) However, unbeknownst to Wallace, conspirators within the White House had created an almost Shakespearean plot to remove him from power. Wallace was just too weird, FDR's inner circle believed, and too liberal, even in the New Deal era. Democratic National Committee treasurer George Allen called him "the boomerang throwing mystic from the place where the tall corn grows."

At a wildly raucous 1944 Democratic National Convention in Chicago, Wallace was dumped in favor of the obscure senator from Missouri — Harry S. Truman. Wallace left Chicago devastated, the victim of brutal subterfuge. As a consolation, FDR told Wallace that there would be "a job for you in world economic affairs." Two weeks after the Chicago convention, Truman went to see Wallace in his office. The Missourian told Wallace how unhappy he was.

"You know," Truman said, "this whole matter is not one of my choosing. I went to Chicago to get out of being Vice President, not to become Vice President." Truman assured Wallace he had not involved himself in any "machinations" to knock Wallace off the 1944 ticket.

The important thing, Wallace said, was to look forward, not back. After Truman left, Wallace wrote of Truman in his diary: "He is a small opportunistic man, a man of good instincts but, therefore, probably all the more dangerous. As he moves out more in the public eye, he will get caught in the webs of his own making . . ."

In November, the FDR-Truman ticket won the election, and Wallace was appointed commerce secretary — a position he retained until Truman, now president, fired him from the cabinet in 1946.

Now in the winter of 1947, before any Democratic candidate had officially declared a run for president, Wallace began his campaign odyssey. He knew he could not win. But he also knew that he had an opportunity to change the national political landscape, perhaps even to steer the Cold War toward an end. "I had no illusions about being elected President . . . ," he later recalled, "and my reason for running was that I finally had to make good my bluff. When I threatened the Democratic party with either/or and they didn't come through on the either, I had to come through on the or . . . If the Democratic party was a war party, there was only one thing I could do, it seemed to me."

There was a giddiness about his run, a sense that the future of the country was wide open, and that a campaign about peace could enlighten people beyond the scope of a political power struggle. "We all had grandiose ideas of the possibilities of the Wallace campaign," recalled John Abt.

Wallace set up headquarters at 39 Park Avenue in New York City, a lavish four-story brownstone rented for $1,500 a month. Soon its rooms and offices were buzzing with publicity agents and party operatives and fund-raising experts. Well-known figures came out in support of Wallace: the writers Thomas Mann, Arthur Miller, Lillian Hellman, and Studs Terkel; the Pulitzer Prize–winning composer Aaron Copland; the architect Frank Lloyd Wright; the deaf-blind activist Helen Keller; even Franklin Roosevelt's son Elliott. Campaign donations came in from top-ranked writers like Norman Mailer and Clifford Odets. The famed artist Ben Shahn signed on to create campaign posters.

For a running mate, Wallace chose the forty-three-year-old US senator Glen H. Taylor of Idaho. Taylor added color to the ticket. He had grown up in a poor family, one of thirteen children, the son of an itinerant preacher. Taylor had joined the theater after the eighth grade and had been in the entertainment business as a country-and-western singer and a stage performer for years before he was elected to the Senate in 1944. He was known as the "singing cowboy." A tall, bald man who wore an obvious hairpiece of his own construction, Taylor had once ridden his horse, Nugget, up the steps of the US Capitol building.

In their first campaign event together, soon after Wallace announced his candidacy, Wallace and Taylor sat down in the CBS radio studio in New York. On a live national broadcast, Taylor boldly said, "I am going to cast my lot with Henry Wallace in his brave and gallant fight for peace."

When asked about the Communist controversy clouding their campaign, Taylor said he would be "glad to have their votes."

"I'm trying to get elected," Taylor said. "I'd be glad to have the votes of bank robbers too."

When asked why they were bolting the Democratic Party, Taylor answered for the two of them. "I am not leaving the Democratic Party," he said. "It left me. Wall Street and the military have taken over."

10

"There'll Be No Compromise"

> Never in our history have we been faced with such conditions — and a presidential campaign year. The campaign must go on, but remember the safety of the world and ourselves are inextricably tied together.
>
> — **Harry Truman, April 1948**

IN NOVEMBER 1947 — one year from the presidential election — a secret memo began circulating the White House entitled "The Politics of 1948." The document was written by a Democratic operative named James H. Rowe Jr. and had fallen into the hands of Clark Clifford. Clifford knew that Truman mistrusted Rowe, as they had had differences of opinion in the past, but the piece itself, Clifford thought, was brilliant. (Many years later the *Washington Post* would describe it as "one of this century's most famous political memorandums.") Clifford strengthened Rowe's polemics with the help of his assistant George Elsey, and delivered the memo to the president bearing his own byline, figuring that Truman would not take seriously a document authored by Rowe.

In remarkable detail, this memo dictated the road map for the Democrats'

1948 campaign, and for the next year it would remain in the president's desk drawer for easy reference.

"The basic premise of this memorandum — that the Democratic Party is an unhappy alliance of Southern conservatives, Western progressives and Big City labor — is very trite, but it is also very true," the Rowe-Clifford memo said on the first page. "And it is equally true that the success or failure of the Democratic leadership can be precisely measured by its ability to lead enough members of these three misfit groups to the polls on the first Tuesday after the first Monday of November, 1948."

The memo's conclusions:

1) The Democratic Party was "in profound collapse . . . The blunt facts seem to be that the Party has been so long in power it is fat, tired, and even a bit senile."
2) Although competition in the GOP was taut, Governor Thomas Dewey of New York would be the Republican nominee. "He will be a resourceful, intelligent and highly dangerous candidate."
3) Henry Wallace was also highly dangerous to Truman. "There is something almost messianic in his belief today that he is the Indispensable Man." Wallace's campaign was "motivated by the Communist Party line." The Communists "give him a disciplined hard-working organization and collect the money to run his campaign." Not only would Wallace get the backing of Communists and far-left-wingers, he could even win the support of the Soviet Union, the document noted. From the Soviet point of view, Wallace could not win, but he could pull enough votes from Truman to ensure that the Republicans won. The Soviet Union had strong reasons for wanting the Democrats to lose, the Rowe-Clifford memo claimed:

> Moscow is . . . convinced there is no longer any hope that the Truman administration will submit to the Russian program of world conquest and expansion [the memo read]. From the Communist long-range point of view, there is nothing to lose and much to gain if a Republican becomes the next President. The best way it can help achieve that re-

sult, and hasten the disintegration of the American economy, is to split the Independent and labor union vote between Truman and Wallace —and thus insure the Republican candidate's election.

Would the Soviets support Wallace's campaign? And if so, how?

4) To win in 1948, Truman had to court farmers (who traditionally voted Republican), laborers, Jews, and—perhaps most of all—black Americans. The story of the black vote in America was in one way rather simple. From the Civil War until the New Deal, blacks tended to vote Republican because of their devotion to Abraham Lincoln. In 1936, however, FDR won a majority of the African American vote (only 28 percent voted for the Republican candidate Alf Landon), and the Democrats had maintained strong black support since then.

Yet now it appeared that African Americans were veering back to the GOP. "The Negro bloc, which, certainly in Illinois and probably in New York and Ohio, does hold the balance of power, will go Republican," the document read. Thomas Dewey had been relentlessly and successfully courting the black vote in New York, and even the conservative faction of the GOP had done the same, while the "Southern Senators of the Democratic Party," the memo pointed out, were sure to make any real progress in any real civil liberties movement impossible under a Democratic administration.

Unless the administration were to make "a determined campaign to help the Negro (and everybody else) on the problems of high prices and housing —and capitalize politically on its efforts—the Negro vote is lost."

If the Democrats made such "a determined campaign" to go after the black vote, the white Southern Democrats with their Jim Crow traditions would be incensed. Still, the document's writers believed it was "inconceivable" that the South would "revolt" from the Democratic Party. Despite bitter resistance among Southern Democrats to Truman's civil rights position, "the South can be considered safely Democratic."

5) "The conflict between the President and the Congress will increase during the 1948 session." With the current Republican-controlled Congress, Truman had no chance of pushing through any of his major plans, and thus he had no

choice, the memo concluded, but to go all-out against his opposition Congress and engage in a political bare-fisted fight. "The strategy on the Taft-Hartley Bill — refusal to bargain with the Republicans and to accept any compromises — paid big political dividends. That strategy should be expanded in the next session to include all the domestic issues."

6) The stakes had never been so high. "The future of this country and the future of the world are linked inextricably with his [Truman's] reelection."

The map was drawn, the plan in place. Now Truman had to put it into action.

"It was clearly apparent to all of us in the White House staff," recalled adviser George Elsey, "certainly to the president himself, that the 1948 State of the Union message would be the opening gun." As Elsey wrote in a memorandum at the time, Truman's January 1948 State of the Union had to be "controversial as hell, must state the issues of the election, [and] must draw the line sharply between Republicans and Democrats. The Democratic Platform will stem from it, and the election will be fought on the issues it presents." David Lilienthal, head of the Atomic Energy Commission, wrote in his diary a few days before Truman's 1948 State of the Union speech, "This is the most important period in the history of the country . . . perhaps the most important in human history. So the message of the President will have extraordinary import."

In the Capitol on January 7, Truman climbed the stairs to the rostrum and stared out at a hostile Eightieth Congress. Robert Taft sat in the third row beside the outspoken Truman critic, Republican senator Homer Ferguson of Michigan. The secretary of state, General Marshall, was in the first row. Truman began his speech in his familiar drone — a flat voice with a distinct inability for emotional impact — and he delivered a message he knew would infuriate half the room. He wanted to raise spending on all kinds of benefits: unemployment compensation, old-age benefits, benefits for the surviving families of fallen soldiers.

Central to the message was civil rights. The president called "the essential human rights of our citizens" democracy's "first goal."

> The United States has always had a deep concern for human rights. Religious freedom, free speech, and freedom of thought are cherished realities in our land. Any denial of human rights is a denial of the basic beliefs of democracy and of our regard for the worth of each individual. Today, however, some of our citizens are still denied equal opportunity for education, for jobs and economic advancement, and for the expression of their views at the polls. Most serious of all, some are denied equal protection under laws. Whether discrimination is based on race, or creed, or color, or land of origin, it is utterly contrary to American ideals of democracy.

On seven occasions during his address, Truman paused in the expectation of applause, only to be met by deafening silence. Not even his own party, nor any of his close friends, offered any indication of support. One reporter present described "almost a half an hour of complete silence . . . Not even in the days of awful Congressional hostility to President Herbert Hoover . . . was there any such embarrassing reaction." When Truman's speech was over, his motorcade took him back to the White House. In the Oval Office, he pulled bottles of scotch and bourbon from a desk drawer and, with staffers gathered around his desk, toasted to "success in '48!"

But the response was devastating. In his GOP rebuttal, Senator Taft referred to Truman as "Santa Claus" for his spending policies, with "a rich present for every special group in the United States."

Truman doubled down. Soon rumors of another major speech began to spread through Washington. The impetus for this speech came from Truman adviser George Elsey, who argued that the president and the Democrats should push even further on civil rights. Elsey and others contributed to the speech, and Truman completed it with a few editorial markings. When staffers read the draft, they had mixed emotions.

"[Political adviser Charlie] Murphy and [press secretary Charlie] Ross were nervous," recalled Elsey. "They predicted a political firestorm from southern Democrats. Truman agreed with their forecast but was undeterred . . . It was time to lay it on the line in bold, clear terms. Thus, the landmark February 2, 1948, message to the Congress on civil rights."

Truman released the message to Congress via his press office, less than a month after his State of the Union and before he had made any official mention of a 1948 candidacy. The address read in part:

> The founders of the United States proclaimed to the world the American belief that all men are created equal, and that governments are instituted to secure the inalienable rights with which all men are endowed. In the Declaration of Independence and the Constitution of the United States, they eloquently expressed the aspirations of all mankind for equality and freedom.

Truman called for a ten-point plan that included passage of federal laws against lynching, a Fair Employment Practice Commission to prevent discrimination in the workplace, and laws protecting the right of minorities to vote, in all states, in every election.

As predicted, Truman's February 2 civil rights message blew the proverbial roof off governors' mansions in states across the South.

On February 7, a conference of southern-state governors drew large crowds and cameras to the small town of Wakulla Springs, Florida. A parade of white men and women clutching Confederate flags marched into a speaking hall. The hall's air grew heated as, one after the other, governors demanded action against Truman's civil rights proposals.

"We have been betrayed by the leadership of the Democratic Party," roared Governor Benjamin Travis Laney of Arkansas. "If these [laws] are to be imposed upon us, I for one would rather they come from a Republican than from the party for which I have given my allegiance."

Governor James Folsom of Alabama demanded that candidates pledge to uphold traditions of "white supremacy" at the Democratic National Convention.

The man emerging as the leader of this group was Strom Thurmond, the forty-five-year-old war hero who had been elected governor of South Carolina in 1946. Thurmond spoke with a heavy southern accent as he promised to lead a delegation to Washington to fight Truman's civil rights promises "in the strongest possible language." He could sum up his message in a sentence: "We may as well have a showdown once and for all."

Four days after Wakulla Springs, some four thousand rowdy politicians and their supporters gathered in Jackson, Mississippi, emitting rebel yells, waving Confederate flags, and adopting a resolution charging that Truman's civil rights plan "intrudes into the sacred rights of the state." On that same day, South Carolina's General Assembly adopted its own anti-Truman resolution, calling the civil rights proposals "un-American." Soon after, Alabama did the same. Then Virginia. Then Mississippi, where political leaders issued a resolution calling upon "all true white Jeffersonian Democrats" to stage a "fight to the last ditch" against Truman and his civil rights proposals.

Weeks earlier, Truman had read in the Rowe-Clifford memo that it was "inconceivable" Southern Democrats would "revolt." "The South can be considered safely Democratic," the document claimed. The assumption was wrong. A historic southern revolt was on.

On February 19 Truman appeared at the Mayflower Hotel in Washington, DC, addressing some twelve hundred people at the Jefferson-Jackson Day Dinner, an annual fund-raiser for the Democratic Party in honor of the party's two founders, Thomas Jefferson and Andrew Jackson — the namesake of Truman's own Jackson County, Missouri. A table directly in front of the speaker's platform remained empty; Senator Olin Johnston of South Carolina and his wife had bought tickets for the event but refused to attend because the Mayflower was not a segregated hotel and Mrs. Johnston was concerned that "she might be seated next to a Negro."

The move was a publicity stunt aimed at wounding Truman. It worked.

On the Monday after the Mayflower banquet, Strom Thurmond led a special committee of southern governors to Washington to meet in the offices of Senator J. Howard McGrath of Rhode Island, who was just taking over as chairman of the Democratic National Committee. The governors of Maryland, South Carolina, North Carolina, Arkansas, and Texas were led into McGrath's office at 2:30 p.m., followed by what the Democratic National Committee publicist Jack Redding recalled as "battalions of the press." The governors all took seats, with the exception of Thurmond, who proceeded to pace furiously, beads of sweat forming on his forehead.

"Will you now," Thurmond said, "at a time when national unity is so vital to the solution of the problem of peace in the world, use your influence as Chairman of the Democratic National Committee, to have the highly controversial civil-rights legislation, which tends to divide our people, withdrawn from consideration by Congress?"

McGrath answered in one syllable: "No."

Thurmond — a former lawyer — continued to fire questions, as if the senator was on the witness stand. But McGrath repeatedly answered no. Thurmond refused to relent. Chewing on a fat cigar, McGrath laid it on the line: "There'll be no compromise."

Just as some American politicos had feared could happen, the Soviets began to foment global political chaos right as the American election season got underway.

On February 25 Soviet-backed forces took control of Czechoslovakia in a bloodless coup d'état. The Czech coup, Truman said in a speech to Congress shortly after, "has sent a shock throughout the civilized world." The coup appeared to be in response to the Marshall Plan. Czech diplomat Jan Masaryk had publicly entertained the idea of accepting Marshall Plan dollars from the United States. The Soviets reacted. Communists took control of the country and, days later, Masaryk jumped — or was pushed — to his death from a third-story window.

Czechoslovakia was now firmly in the Kremlin's grasp, and American officials were forced to ask themselves: If the Soviets could take control of Czechoslovakia so easily, without a shot fired, which country was next?

Ten days after the Czech coup, General Lucius Clay — the man in charge of the American-occupied sector of Germany—wrote a memorandum to S. J. Chamberlin, director of army intelligence. The mood in Berlin, Clay wrote, had suddenly darkened. After the defeat of Hitler and the Nazis, the four Allied powers in Europe—the United States, Britain, the Soviet Union, and France—had taken control of Germany, and Germany had been carved into four occupation zones, one zone for each of these Allied powers. From the American point of view, reunification and a rebirth of Germany as a democratic nation was the ultimate goal. The United States was now learning that this goal was not shared by the Soviets, who controlled the eastern portion of Germany. The idea that the Soviets would ever willfully relinquish control of their German territory was a chimera, and so the Americans, French, and British had begun to coordinate their own zones into one unified state (soon to become West Germany), and were about to issue a new currency—the deutsche mark.

Berlin lay entirely within the Soviet zone—like an island in a Soviet sea—and the city was also partitioned into four occupation zones. In order for Americans to move people and supplies from the American-occupied sector of Germany into the American sector of Berlin, trains had to travel through Soviet-occupied territory and through Soviet checkpoints. The Soviet- and American-occupied sectors of Berlin bordered each other, putting the United States and USSR nose to nose in one of the most strategically important metropolises in Europe.

"For many months," General Clay wrote on March 5, "based on logical analysis, I have felt and held that war was unlikely for at least ten years. Within the last few weeks, I have felt a subtle change in Soviet attitude which I cannot define but which now gives me a feeling that it may come with dramatic suddenness."

The Soviets made no effort to hide their anger over the Truman Doctrine and the Marshall Plan. In a speech before the United Nations, Andrey Vyshinsky—the fierce Stalin loyalist and Soviet state attorney—attacked the American policies, calling the United States a "warmonger" that was using the atomic bomb as an intimidation tactic. Now the Soviets appeared to be making a move to take control of Berlin, to drive the United States out of the city. On March 25 the Soviets issued orders to restrict train traffic from the American sector into west Berlin. Truman was so unnerved, he wrote the former First Lady Eleanor Roosevelt: "It is the most serious situation we have faced since 1939. I shall face it with everything I have."

The reaction from the Truman administration was firm and swift. The president arranged to make his first Cold War address. On March 17, in the Capitol, Truman delivered a fighting speech in favor of the Marshall Plan. All over the country and abroad, people sat by their radios and heard, for the first time, the American president name the Soviet Union as an enemy of peace.

> Since the close of hostilities, the Soviet Union and its agents have destroyed the independence and democratic character of a whole series of nations in Eastern and Central Europe. It is this ruthless course of action, and the clear design to extend it to the remaining free nations of Europe, that have brought about the critical situation in Europe today . . . Now pressure is being brought to bear on Finland, to the hazard of the entire Scandinavian peninsula. Greece is under direct military attack from rebels actively supported by her Communist dominated neighbors. In Italy, a determined and aggressive effort is being made by a Communist minority to take control of that country. The methods vary, but the pattern is all too clear.

Two weeks later, on March 31, the US House of Representatives passed the European Recovery Program — the Marshall Plan — with a roll call of 329 to 74 (sixty-one of the seventy-four voting against were Republicans), authorizing $6.205 billion in foreign aid to countries that would use it to rebuild their infrastructures and resist Soviet infiltration. Again, the Kremlin reacted. On the same day the House passed the Marshall Plan, General Clay in Berlin cabled his boss, General Omar Bradley, the US Army's chief of staff in Washington, informing him of a Soviet announcement that all US military and civilian trains moving from the American sector of Germany into the city of Berlin would have to submit to inspections by Soviet military.

"It is undoubtedly the first of a series of restrictive measures designed to drive us from Berlin . . . ," Clay wrote. "It is my intent to instruct our guards to open fire if Soviet soldiers attempt to enter our trains."

Two days later, the Central Intelligence Agency issued a top secret intelligence report called "Possibility of Direct Soviet Military Action During 1948." "The possibility must be recognized that the USSR might resort to direct military action in 1948," it concluded, "particularly if the Kremlin should interpret some US move, or series of moves, as indicating an intention to attack the USSR or its satellites."

The Northern Hemisphere had divided into two opposing forces, and there seemed no turning back. Every presidential candidate was forced to consider the possibility of the election unfolding in a time of war.

As the Berlin standoff spread fear across the United States, violence was spreading across Palestine. On January 5, a truckload of bombs disguised as crates of oranges ripped apart an Arab office building in Jaffa, killing fourteen and wounding nearly a hundred others. A Jewish organization called the Stern Gang took credit. Six days later, gun battles broke out in sand dunes and orange groves along the coastal plain of Gaza, claiming twenty lives. On January 18, Arabs ambushed a group of Jews on a highway, killing roughly three dozen young men and women.

The United Kingdom was scheduled to withdraw from Palestine at midnight on May 14, but the British occupying forces had already lost control.

One morning in a February staff meeting in the Oval Office, Clark Clifford brought up Palestine. "People were blaming the United States for not acting," assistant press secretary Eben Ayers recalled Clifford saying in this meeting. "[Truman] said that there was nothing further he could do. He had done everything possible except to mobilize troops."

On March 6, 1948, Truman received an intelligence memo on the "Proposed Program on the Palestine Problem." "Unless immediate action is taken to preserve peace in Palestine," it began, "chaos and war will follow Great Britain's withdrawal on May 15th. Such a situation will seriously damage United States prestige and United States interests. It will surely be exploited by the Russians."

Truman still supported the United Nations proposal to partition Palestine into two states — one for the Jews and one for the Arabs — but the United Nations had made no progress. The Jews refused to embrace the plan. The Arabs refused to embrace the plan. And in the United States, the Palestine problem was highly politicized. Thomas Dewey was a popular governor in New York State, home of the city with the largest Jewish population in America by far. The Jews had been warm to Truman, but they would surely defect if they did not get what they wanted — Truman's promise to support a Jewish homeland in Palestine. All Truman had to do to be reminded of this fact was to reach into his Oval Office desk drawer and pull out the Clifford-Rowe memo, which pointed out that no candidate since 1876 had won the presidential election without capturing New York's electoral votes, except Woodrow Wilson in 1916. "Unless the Palestine matter is boldly and favorably handled [by Truman]," the Clifford-Rowe memo read, "there is bound to be some defection on their [the Jews'] part to Dewey."

Truman was hoping that somehow, the Palestine problem would solve itself, but as he waited, the whole affair blew up in his face. On Friday, March 19, the US ambassador to the United Nations, Warren Austin, informed the UN General Assembly that the United States was abandoning its support of the partition of Palestine into two states, in support of a UN "trusteeship" of the region. Austin's statement to the UN was in opposition to Truman's own position. Just the day before, Truman had met with Zionist leader Chaim Weizmann and had all but promised him that the United States would support a Jewish homeland. Now Austin was informing the UN that this was no longer the case.

When the story broke, Truman was stunned and worried. He wrote on his desk calendar, "The State Dept pulled the rug from under me today . . . The first I know about it is what I see in the papers! Isn't that hell? I am now in the position of a liar and a double-crosser. I've never felt so low in my life."

He called Clark Clifford at seven thirty the next morning: "Can you come right down? There's a story in the papers on Palestine and I don't understand what has happened."

When Clifford arrived, he found his boss "as disturbed as I have ever seen him." The backlash among Jewish organizations and politicians from states with Jewish constituents was furious, and the appearance of absolute ineptness was impossible to escape. As the *New York Times* political writer Arthur Krock commented, "At this time, the President's influence is weaker than any President's has been in modern history." Truman was left to pick up the pieces. Even his staff was stunned.

"All of this is causing complete lack of confidence in our foreign policy from one end of this country to the other end among all classes of our population," Clifford wrote to Truman. "This lack of confidence is shared by Democrats, Republicans, young people and old people. There is a definite feeling that we have no foreign policy, that we do not know where we are going, that the President and the State Department are bewildered, that the United States, instead of furnishing leadership in world affairs, is drifting helplessly. I believe all of this can be changed."

Truman and Clifford agreed: The time had come for the administration to make its move in support of the Jews. Both feared that if the United States did not do so, the Soviets would. And then there were the ethical considerations, the idea that so many millions of Jews had died at the hands of the Nazis, that justice was on their side. The British Mandate was to end, and at that time the Jews were going to declare a new state in Palestine. Without Truman's support, would the new nation have any chance of survival?

Earlier, Truman had ordered Clifford to prepare a case to argue the matter with Secretary of State George Marshall. The day had arrived. On May 12, Truman summoned his secretary of state to the White House. When Marshall arrived at 4 p.m. with the State Department's second-in-command, Robert Lovett (who had very recently replaced Dean Acheson in this position), they found Clark Clifford sitting in the Oval Office with the president. Clifford was nervous. "Of all the meetings I ever had with Presidents," he recalled, "this one remains the most vivid." Marshall was thought by many to be "the greatest living American," according to Clifford, and the young White House special counsel found himself "on a collision course over Mideast Policy" with the secretary of state.

Marshall was immediately suspect. When Clifford began his case in support of the Jews, he recalled, "I noticed thunderclouds gathering—Marshall's face getting redder and redder." When Clifford finished his argument, Marshall turned to Truman.

"Mr. President," said Marshall, "I thought this meeting was called to consider an important and complicated problem in foreign policy. I don't even know why Clifford is here. He is a domestic adviser, and this is a foreign policy matter."

Truman replied, "Well, General, he's here because I asked him to be here."

Marshall flatly accused Truman of making a decision that affected the future of the world based upon homespun politics. Lovett jumped in to agree.

"It is obviously designed to win the Jewish vote," Lovett said. "But in my opinion, it would lose more votes than it would gain."

As a former general, and even now as secretary of state, Marshall was committed to remaining above politics. He did not vote in elections, believing that doing so would compromise his independence. Now, he told Truman, "If in the election I was to vote, I would vote against you."

"Everyone in the room was stunned," Clifford recalled. "Marshall's statement fell short of an explicit threat to resign, but it came very close."

When it was clear no agreement could be reached, the meeting participants gathered up their papers and uncomfortably adjourned. As the deadline approached, Truman communicated his decision to General Marshall by messenger: The president would support the Jews in Palestine. Marshall had no choice. To oppose the president publicly would be to shatter the chain of command, and the general understood this fact. He responded that, while he did not agree with Truman's decision, he would not oppose it publicly. "That," Truman told Clifford, "is all we need."

Right up until the moment the British Mandate expired, Truman kept his decision to support a Jewish homeland a secret. In his May 13 press conference, a reporter asked, "Mr. President, will the United States recognize the new Palestine state?"

"I will cross that bridge when I get to it."

The mandate expired at midnight on May 14 in Palestine, which was

6 p.m. on May 14 Washington time. In Palestine, Jewish leaders declared the new nation of Israel and began to secure borders with a makeshift army. Eleven minutes later, Truman released a statement: "This Government has been informed that a Jewish state has been proclaimed in Palestine, and recognition has been requested by the provisional government thereof. The United States recognizes the provisional government as the de facto authority of the new State of Israel."

Truman was the first world leader to recognize the state of Israel. "The charge that domestic politics determined our policy on Palestine angered President Truman for the rest of his life," Clifford later wrote in his memoirs. "The President's policy rested on the realities of the situation in the region, on America's moral, ethical, and humanitarian values, on the costs and risks inherent in any other course, and — of course — America's national interests."

Meanwhile, the move did make for good politics. The night Truman recognized the new state of Israel, in Washington, the Israeli flag debuted at the Jewish Agency building on Massachusetts Avenue for a crowd of jubilant Zionists. In Palestine, the first shots of the 1948 Arab-Israeli War were soon fired, and violence and death began to spread across the region. Truman made a speech the night Israel was born, at Washington's Mayflower Hotel.

"I want to say to you that for the next four years there will be a Democrat in the White House," he announced. "And you're looking at him!"

11

"I Will Not Accept the Political Support of Henry Wallace and His Communists"

ON FRIDAY, JULY 4, 1947 —a date chosen for the obvious symbolism— Thomas Dewey left Albany by train with his wife and sons, headed west on a nine-state speaking tour. Dewey had yet to declare his candidacy, but the trip was clearly a test run for a national campaign. His first stop was Truman's home state of Missouri. Dewey moved through Oklahoma, Colorado, and Texas. At every stop, local politicians lined up to shake the hand of the man they believed would be the next president of the United States.

George Gallup's latest numbers hit the press while Dewey was in Texas; the New York governor remained the GOP front-runner. Dewey was polling at 51 percent, far ahead of Harold Stassen of Minnesota, who had surged ahead of Robert Taft, polling at 15 percent to Taft's 9 percent. In Salt Lake City, Dewey attended the National Governors Association conference, where he shopped around for a VP candidate, huddling for much of the time with Earl Warren, the progressive and popular young Republican governor of California. The trip was smooth sailing; the Dewey family's only contretemps was a skin rash from exposure to poison oak that made Mrs. Dewey miserable for days.

On January 16, 1948, at New York's executive mansion in Albany, a small group of Dewey insiders officially announced the launch of Dewey's historic run. Oswald Heck, Speaker of the New York State Assembly, told reporters, "The people have only to look at the record he has made at Albany in the last five years to gain assurance that he is the ideal man to successfully guide the nation through the perilous post-war years."

In Manhattan, Herbert Brownell fired up the Republican machine he had spent months building, hoping to propel Dewey into the White House. Brownell began a series of gatherings in New York with big donors, prying open wallets by means of ultralavish luncheons. The first occurred at the Waldorf-Astoria in New York on January 29, where the menu included "choice of cocktails, highballs and sherry," followed by an appetizer of smoked salmon, sturgeon, and anchovies, then lobster and crab Louis, then fumet of gumbo chervil with "tiny cornsticks," then hearts of celery with green olives and salted nuts, then filet mignon Henry IV with béarnaise sauce served with "a nest" of soufflé potatoes and new string beans, a dessert of Waldorf savarin au rhum with brandied cherries and golden sabayon, and a selection of cigars and cigarettes. Campaign donations flowed, as did the claret and bourbon.

The national committee hired one of the best advertising agencies in Manhattan, Albert Frank–Guenther Law, to manage publicity. The firm moved to make tactical plans in each state, along with a national ad blitz to run in general newspapers, religious newspapers, farm papers, university publications, business newspapers, and the foreign-language press. The committee commissioned a detailed "statistical analysis" of the 1946 elections, which revealed some remarkably encouraging facts about the national electorate. Statistics showed "further evidence as to the change in the colored vote from Democrat to Republican." Republicans had gained in 1946 in unexpected places, such as large industrial communities in traditionally Democratic strongholds like New York, Chicago, Philadelphia, Los Angeles, and Detroit.

"The outlook is exceedingly favorable," the analysis found, suggesting "a Republican trend which on the basis of historical precedent should almost inevitably bring about the election of a Republican President in the forth coming election."

Dewey ordered Brownell to assign a representative from the campaign to personally contact and woo the delegations that would be voting at the Republican National Convention from each of the forty-eight states. "The organizational job strikes me as being a staggering one but of the greatest importance," Dewey wrote Brownell. Every delegate to the national convention "may be of decisive importance."

Meanwhile, powerful global leaders began to arrive at the Albany executive mansion to curry favor with the man most likely to be in the White House come Inauguration Day in 1949. Former British prime minister Winston Churchill appeared at 138 Eagle Street for a nine-hour tête-à-tête with Dewey, as did Italian prime minister Alcide De Gasperi.

Eight states were scheduled to hold Republican primaries, and while the national convention would choose the 1948 ticket, the advance elections would spell out which candidate these eight states would be voting for in Philadelphia — a strong indicator of who would come out on top. The first primary was held in New Hampshire, and Dewey captured victory as expected. But when the spotlight moved to Wisconsin — a state where Dewey had beaten FDR in 1944 — things did not go as planned. Dewey found himself overwhelmed with work during a highly charged New York legislative session, and his advisers made the decision to leave the campaigning in the state to local politicos. Based on the 1944 stats, Dewey's team believed he had Wisconsin sewn up tight.

If the dark horse Harold Stassen had any chance of competing with Dewey nationally, he would have to charge out in front in the Midwest primaries. Stassen began to crisscross Wisconsin, where he was well known and liked, as he hailed from the neighboring state of Minnesota. Carloads of Stassen campaigners flooded Wisconsin's rural areas. On March 8, in a speech in Cleveland, Stassen grabbed headlines with a call to quash Communism in the United States.

"The Communist Party organization should be promptly outlawed in America," Stassen said, "and we should urge that it be outlawed in all liberty-loving countries in which there yet remains the authority in free men to do so."

Dewey arrived in Wisconsin just five days before primary day. When voters went to the polls, the governor was trounced. It was Stassen, then Douglas MacArthur, with Dewey coming in third.

In the coming weeks, Stassen — a towering figure physically, with a bald dome and a commanding speaking voice — surprised election observers by jumping out in front, winning Republican primaries in Nebraska and Pennsylvania. Suddenly the New York governor faced do-or-die in Oregon, where he was at a disadvantage — a big-city man in a rural farm state, a member of the eastern establishment out of his element in the Wild West.

Dewey was in trouble. "There isn't any use in deceiving you regarding the situation here in Oregon," a Republican delegate named F. N. Belgrano Jr., president of the First National Bank in Portland, wrote Brownell. "It is decidedly bad, and whether or not Stassen's lead can be whittled down and reversed will depend entirely on the personal efforts of the governor."

At the end of April, Dewey flew out of LaGuardia airfield bound for Oregon for a three-week fight. The national committee flooded Oregon's radio stations with programs such as "Dewey and Women's Rights" and "How Dewey Would Wage Peace." To court farmers, the campaign formed an "Oregon Farmers for Dewey" organization based in the Multnomah Hotel in Portland, which distributed 175,000 pieces of campaign literature to rural mailboxes highlighting Dewey's work on his upstate New York dairy farm, the candidate's "farm philosophy," and his ideas on how to fight cow mastitis. At one point, a reception with the Republican governor John H. Hall of Oregon was delayed because the bus carrying Dewey and his team ran over a dog. Dewey wired the owners his regrets and bought them a new cocker spaniel, which was subsequently named Dewey.

As the Oregon vote approached, Dewey and Stassen drew even in the race, and the contest attracted mobs of national press figures to a state that had never before found itself in the heat of the political spotlight. "The Governor is making rapid strides," recorded Clyde Lewis, a member of Dewey's campaign team, ten days into Dewey's boots-on-the-ground Oregon offensive. "I would say his chances as of today are at least equal to those of Stassen. Terrific enthusiasm is being generated and Oregon is agog at the attention it is receiving." The cost of Dewey's Oregon operation would add up to three times the record ever spent up to that point by a candidate in a primary in the state, some $250,000.

On the night Dewey arrived in Oregon, he had suggested to one of his aides the idea of challenging Stassen to a live debate. The next day, the aide wrote Dewey in a memo that such a debate could fill a thirty-thousand-seat stadium and "would be a *must* pick-up for the national networks." Nothing like such a debate had ever occurred in modern American history. Dewey's team broached the idea with Stassen's, and after haggling over the terms, Stassen agreed to debate "the little son of a bitch."

When Stassen accepted, Dewey aide Paul Lockwood approached the governor and said, "I think you can take the guy to pieces."

Dewey responded, "All right. God damn it, let's do it!"

The debate would tackle a single question—the controversial issue that Stassen himself had raised when he called for a new law making Communism illegal in the United States.

Should Communism be outlawed? Stassen believed yes; Dewey believed no.

The first-ever live-broadcast political debate during national election season was scheduled for the night of Monday, May 17—two days after the founding of Israel. It would take place in the studio of Portland radio station KEX with no live audience—Dewey's demand, since the diminutive candidate did not want to have to stand beside the six-foot-three-inch Stassen in front of a crowd. Fifty reporters were allowed to attend, and they sat with their backs to the wall in the studio, facing the candidates. Nearly a thousand local stations around the country would carry the event.

At 7 p.m. West Coast time, some forty million Americans tuned in. The two men arrived in the radio studio and shook hands—Dewey in a gray three-piece double-breasted pinstripe suit, Stassen in a two-piece suit of darker gray. The rules: twenty-minute speeches apiece, with Stassen going first, then each candidate would get an eight-minute rebuttal. The man speaking would stand at a lectern, while the one listening sat at a table ten feet away. Between the two, the debate's moderator, Donald Van Boskirk, head of the Multnomah County Republican Central Committee, would remain for the most part silent.

Van Boskirk welcomed listeners and introduced the candidates. Stassen then kicked off the debate, in a steady and confident tone.

"Chairman Van Boskirk," Stassen began, "your excellency Governor Dewey, and my fellow citizens: During the recent war I saw many young Americans killed. I watched ships explode and burn, planes crash in flames, men — our men, my friends — fall . . ."

It was a clever opening for Stassen — highlighting his war service, knowing that Dewey had never worn the uniform. However, as the hour moved on, Stassen realized he had made a drastic mistake. Dewey had spent much of his career arguing the most high-profile cases in courtrooms. He was cool, tactical, implacable, and brilliantly prepared. He ticked off twenty-seven laws already on the books that could be used to fight Communist plots in the United States, then argued that a law making Communism a crime could never work in a free society.

"The free world looks to us for hope, for leadership, and most of all for a demonstration of our invincible faith," Dewey said into the microphone while Stassen looked on. "The free way of life will triumph so long as we keep it free."

"Stripped to its naked essentials," Dewey concluded of Stassen's argument, "this is nothing but the method of Hitler and Stalin."

Dewey spoke last, and when he finished, radio listeners nationwide heard a few seconds of silence — dead air — before the moderator, Van Boskirk, jumped in to end the night. Dewey proved the clear winner. His team was ecstatic. "Herb," one supporter wrote Herbert Brownell afterward, "I feel that I can sense a great national tidal wave for Dewey that is cresting from Portland [Oregon] to Portland [Maine] and Hell to breakfast. That tidal wave started rolling in those few seconds of silence that you and I and a million of other guys felt when Dewey had finished that last eight minutes of the famous Dewey-Stassen debate."

Four days later, Dewey beat Stassen decisively in the Oregon primary.

Over the course of one live broadcast, Stassen had gone from a strong contender for president to all but out of the race.

While Dewey ascended, Henry Wallace fell. Wallace must have known that the guru letters were going to come back to haunt him. And indeed, around the time of the Dewey-Stassen debate, the letters fell into the hands of the country's most acidic political columnist, Westbrook Pegler, whose columns were syndicated in newspapers across the nation. *Time* magazine once stated of Pegler, "Mister Pegler's place as the great dissenter for the common man is unchallenged. Six days a week, for an estimated $65,000 a year, in 116 papers reaching nearly 6,000,000 readers, Mister Pegler is invariably irritated, inexhaustibly scornful. Unhampered by coordinated convictions of his own, Pegler applies himself to presidents and peanut vendors with equal zeal and skill. Dissension is his philosophy."

With guru letters in hand, Pegler took aim.

"We have had evidence," Pegler wrote, "that Mr. Wallace is not altogether one of us in his mental and religious or spiritual makeup." Pegler had experts compare Wallace's handwriting to that of the Roerich letters and found that the "screwball documents were written by the same person." Pegler quoted the letters extensively, such as this one, which ran in Pegler's March 9, 1948, column:

> The protecting shield of the great ones has been felt under very trying conditions. The Tigers are going through various tricks but with respect to them the man now in charge at the old house is excellent. The Flaming One is softhearted toward the Tigers and I fear has made commitments of some sort. The battle against the vermin is fierce . . .

Pegler wondered aloud before his millions of readers: "Is Wallace fit for power?"

One after the other, Pegler's columns raked Wallace's reputation. In the face of extreme embarrassment, however, Wallace kept his course, exhibiting an inner strength that only served to rally his hardcore followers.

All winter and into the spring of 1948, Wallace remained in the public eye. In highly charged testimony before the House Committee on Foreign Affairs on February 24, 1948, in the crowded caucus room in the Old House Office Building across from the Capitol, congressmen probed Wallace's intentions with biting questions. If he were president, and his secretaries of state and defense reported to him that Soviet aggression constituted the main threat to world peace, what would he do?

"I would tell them to get ready for war," Wallace said. Then he added quickly that such a scenario would be impossible, as he would never have such men in his cabinet. Wallace read an eleven-thousand-word statement condemning the Marshall Plan, and accusing Truman of "laying the foundations" for war with the Soviet Union. When asked why Wallace's condemnations of the Marshall Plan sounded markedly similar to those coming out of the Soviet Union — that the Marshall Plan was nothing but warmongering on the part of the United States — Wallace answered, "I'm not familiar with the Communist approach and am unable to discuss it."

A month later, Wallace appeared before the Senate Armed Forces Committee in another hearing packed with journalists and cameramen and gawkers who came to see the most controversial man in American politics. Wallace charged that the Truman administration had "deliberately created [a] crisis." Truman's Universal Military Training proposal would lead to a war that would result in "death and taxes for the many and very handsome profits for the few."

"Our country is in danger," Wallace said. "But the danger comes from our own policies which will bring war — unnecessary war — upon our country."

Back out on the road, Wallace's candidacy proved just how divided America had become. He could venture into large cities where numerous liberal intellectuals lived, and he could pack stadiums to the rafters with passionate followers. If the contest was to be held in March 1948 only among black youth in the South, Wallace would be elected president by a landslide. However, in white America far from the coasts and big cities — even in his home state of Iowa — his message seemed inexplicable and infuriating.

Wallace's tone conveyed such conviction and mistrust of the establishment, his presence was bound to incite violence. It was only a matter of time.

On April 6 Wallace arrived in Evansville, Indiana, for a rally at the Evansville Coliseum. As the sun set, he was in his hotel room preparing for his speech. A few miles away, a group numbering some twenty-five hundred — mostly angry white men — gathered at the event venue, pounding on doors and busting them open. Crowds of picketers swarmed into the coliseum's lobby. Police wielding nightsticks struggled to maintain control. All the while, the candidate was quietly practicing his speech, unaware of the maelstrom awaiting him.

Wallace's campaign manager, Beanie Baldwin, arrived at the venue ahead of the candidate. As Baldwin approached the coliseum entrance, picketers swarmed him; Baldwin was struck on the chin. More blows landed, and by the time the fracas ended, Baldwin's face swelled with bruises. Another Wallace campaign worker was bleeding from a cut over his eye. An usher working the event caught a shot to the face.

Minutes later, Wallace entered the coliseum through a side door. The protest had intimidated locals; only five hundred people were in the audience to hear Wallace speak. A local philosophy professor, George F. Parker, introduced the candidate. Professor Parker had been warned by Evansville College that his presence onstage at a Wallace event would be cause for his firing. Wallace defended Professor Parker: "Our country's heritage means nothing if it doesn't mean our freedom to express our political views without danger of losing our jobs." After the speech, Wallace required a police escort to get him to his car. Picketers surrounded the vehicle, and the candidate sat stone-faced for an hour, waiting for the protesters to disperse. Two days later, Professor Parker was fired.

Wallace headed west. In Albuquerque, he told a crowd, "According to newspapers I'm getting a lot of support from the Communists, and the Communist leaders seem to think they have to endorse me every day or so. There's no question that this sort of thing is a political liability. The Communists oppose my advocacy of progressive capitalism. They support me because I say that we can have peace with Russia. I will not repudiate any support which comes to me on the basis of interest in peace."

He was booed in response.

Wallace later remembered, "I was very much shocked at the extent to which hatred had been stirred up."

In Indianapolis, he and his team were denied hotel rooms. When he reached Iowa, officials at the University of Iowa barred him from speaking on campus. In Detroit, the union leader Walter Reuther was shot in his home by an unknown assailant, and Reuther's colleague, union man Pat Greathouse, accused Wallace followers of committing the crime (based on no apparent evidence). "It must be part of a communist plot," Greathouse told reporters. "[Reuther] has enemies among Wallace's followers."

In Birmingham, Alabama, on May 7, Wallace's running mate, Senator Taylor, was scheduled to speak to a black church congregation. When he attempted to enter through the front door, a white police officer stopped him.

"This is the colored entrance," the cop said. "The white entrance is on the side."

"I'll go through here anyway," Taylor said.

When he pushed forward, a scuffle broke out. Officers jumped on Taylor and his head hit the concrete sidewalk. "This is it," he was thinking. "They're going to beat me to death." He ended up in a jail cell, bleeding, booked for breach of the peace and disorderly conduct. In the cell a fellow prisoner said to Taylor, "They got me for pukin' on a sidewalk. What's your racket?"

"I am a United States Senator," Taylor said. "And they got me for trying to enter a meeting through a colored entrance."

When Wallace hit New York, Chicago, and Los Angeles, however, he was once again wildly embraced. After attending a Wallace rally, the political columnist Roscoe Drummond commented, "I have never seen a pre-convention campaign tour, even those of Wendell L. Willkie and Gov. Thomas E. Dewey, command even no-paying audiences of such size." A *Chicago Daily News* reporter who attended a Wallace event at Chicago Stadium wrote, "I'm here, I've seen it, and I still don't believe it."

The actress Katharine Hepburn warmed up the crowd at a Wallace event in Los Angeles. Charlie Chaplin and Edward G. Robinson contributed money to the campaign. Former Interior secretary Harold Ickes embraced Wallace ("Thousands of people believe that Mr. Wallace possesses the qualities they are looking for"), as did the black leader W.E.B. Du Bois ("Let the mass of American negroes, north, south, east, and west, cast their votes for Henry Wallace in 1948"). Frank Lloyd Wright wrote the candidate on June 1, 1948, in support of Wallace's campaign "to turn the rascals out."

Democratic Party operatives kept close tabs on the Wallace campaign. "The Third Party candidate has embarked way ahead of normal schedules, on a far-flung campaign which carries him into remote areas, unfrequented by other national campaigners," according to a report by the Americans for Democratic Action. "By April [1948] he had made over 26 major orations since announcing his candidacy . . . Wallace, according to any reasonable estimates, will have conducted the equivalent of nearly two full Presidential campaigns by the time the major parties and the third party hold their conventions."

Just how real was the Wallace threat? In February 1948 a young attorney named Leo Isacson answered that question. A political novice and supporter of Henry Wallace, Isacson ran in a special election to fill a US congressional seat in New York's Twenty-Fourth District—the Bronx—as the candidate of the far-left American Labor Party. Wallace endorsed Isacson, who was running against a Democrat, Karl Propper. The *New York Times* called the special election a "test of Truman-Wallace strength." Isacson stunned the establishment by winning. Suspected of being a Communist, he was so controversial that the State Department refused to issue him a passport, because officials believed his politics could make him a dangerous voice abroad. Never before had a member of the US Congress been denied an American passport.

The Isacson victory proved that Wallace was going to be a draw at the ballot box in places like New York City, but it further raised concern over the support Wallace was getting from Communists and fellow travelers. At a St. Patrick's Day address in 1948, a month after Isacson's win, Truman told a crowd in Manhattan: "I do not want and I will not accept the political support of Henry Wallace and his Communists. If joining them or permitting them to join me is the price of victory, I recommend defeat. These are days of high prices for everything, but any price for Wallace and his Communists is too much for me to pay. I'm not buying."

On April 14 and April 30, the United States detonated two more atomic test shots over the Pacific's Enewetak Atoll—code-named X-Ray and Yoke. X-Ray set a record for the highest yield of energy released during an atomic blast, until Yoke eclipsed it sixteen days later. Truman had authorized these operations as part of the Operation Sandstone tests. The effort to build these weapons and set them off had required more than ten thousand government personnel.

The bombs went off in secret but soon after made front-page headlines, sparking more debate on just how long it would take for the Soviets to develop a bomb, and what would happen to an American city should it be struck by an atomic weapon. The Army Medical Corps stoked the fear by releasing information gleaned from research these nuke tests provided, warning people to stay calm if atomic bombs began raining down on American cities, because hysteria would only cause more loss of life. "There is no known method of protecting those in the immediate neighborhood of an atomic bomb when it explodes," a Medical Corps spokesman told reporters, adding that "there is not much even a medical man can do" about radiation exposure.

Wallace saw these test shots as more US aggression toward the Soviet Union. They further fueled his campaign to stop what he saw as a march toward war.

On May 11, 1948, Wallace made his most controversial move yet: He released an open letter to Soviet leader Joseph Stalin. In it, he called for "definite, decisive steps" to end the "international crisis" that was coming to a head in Berlin. Wallace supported the "outlawing of all methods of mass destruction." He wrote that "peace is possible" and attacked critics who believed "the two nations cannot live at peace in the same world."

Even Wallace was shocked when, on May 17, Stalin responded. Wallace's ideas were in "need of improvement," Stalin said in a statement published around the globe. But they provided "a serious step forward," a "concrete program for the peaceful settlement of differences." Over the radio from San Francisco, a teary-eyed Henry Wallace declared himself "overwhelmed" by Stalin's statement. "I am humbled and grateful to be an instrument in this crisis," he said. "If I have done anything to further the cause of peace in the world, I shall have felt my whole campaign a tremendous success."

On May 18, the day after Stalin's response was made public, an FBI investigator informed bureau chief J. Edgar Hoover that Wallace's letter to Stalin "may be a possible violation of the Lane Act . . . an old statute passed around 1795 which prohibits a citizen in the United States from communicating with a foreign country concerning a matter bearing on diplomatic relations."* Hoover referred the matter to the attorney general that same day. Could Wallace have opened himself up to criminal prosecution?

No one was more suspicious and angry about Wallace's open letter to Stalin than the president. "We aren't dealing with Stalin through Wallace," Truman snapped.

---

*The investigator is likely referring to the Logan Act of 1799.

12

"For Better or Worse, the 1948 Fight Has Started"

ON THURSDAY, JUNE 3, 1948, a few minutes before 10 p.m., Washington's Union Station swelled with crowds who came to catch a glimpse of President Truman and his entourage. Truman was set for a cross-country trip the old-fashioned way: aboard a sixteen-car train, on the back of which was the *Ferdinand Magellan,* the 285,000-pound bulletproof luxury railcar that had been built for FDR a few years earlier. The *Ferdinand Magellan* would be home to the Truman family — Harry, Bess, and Margaret — for the next two weeks.

Truman was headed off on a speaking tour. The impetus for the trip was a memorandum written by the Democratic National Committee's publicist Jack Redding some months earlier, which outlined the idea of a national tour that would bring Truman into communities where Americans could experience the magic of the presidency and Truman's own personal charisma. It would be a trial run for the national campaign, which was set to kick off on Labor Day weekend. "If people see him in person," Redding's memo read, "they'll vote for him. His personality, his smile, his manner of approach, his sincerity all come through perfectly. People will trust him. Trusting him, they'll vote for him."

Soon after this memo was written, Truman received an invitation to deliver a commencement speech at the University of California at Berkeley. Campaign staff jumped on it as the perfect opportunity. The speech would allow the president to label the journey west "nonpolitical," meaning it could be paid for out of the president's discretionary travel fund. Truman was such an underdog, the Democratic National Committee was broke. Campaign donors had abandoned him. Why fund a lost cause? There was nothing nonpolitical about the president's tour, however. "The pretense that this is a 'non-political trip' disappeared almost as soon as the wheels of his 16-car special train started turning," one columnist aboard the train commented.

A dining car became a bullpen office space for the working staff, while another was transformed into a press car, with rows of desks lining either side and facing out the windows. The Army Signal Corps built a state-of-the-art communications setup aboard another train car, with radio and cryptographic equipment, so the president could be in contact with the White House at all times. At stops, telephone wires could be hooked into the communications room to receive calls, and Truman had his own telephone in the *Ferdinand Magellan.*

Teams of reporters boarded the train, carrying suitcases and typewriters and fingering smoldering cigarettes. The Democratic National Committee furnished two cases of liquor for the traveling press corps, to butter them up—one of scotch, one of bourbon. On the first night of the trip, columnist Richard Strout thumped out his lead while sitting in the press car: "Rolling across the United States with the biggest collection of news, radio, and cameramen in history, the Truman special train is a traveling question mark . . . For better or worse, the 1948 fight has started."

Truman was experimenting with impromptu speeches, a new strategy he had first tried out two months earlier in a White House talk to the American Society of Newspaper Editors. He had delivered "one of those deadly dull speeches" for which he had become known, recalled one person there that night, but after, "he began an entirely different, extemporaneous and off-the-record speech of his own, in his own vocabulary, out of his own humor and his own heart." David Lilienthal, head of the Atomic Energy Commission, heard the president speak that night. He wrote in his diary, "Why wasn't that on the record? That is what the whole country should hear."

Which is exactly what Truman aimed to do: Let the whole country hear him talk, off the cuff. Extemporaneous speeches were dangerous, however. Any gaffe would hit the newspapers as far off as London and Moscow, and embarrass the president to no end. In fact, that is exactly what the journalists on Truman's California trip expected would happen. "A large number of reporters went along," remembered Oscar Chapman, a political adviser and speechwriter on the train. "They were expecting to see a complete flop and they wanted to write about it."

Truman would not disappoint them.

On June 5 in Omaha, Truman marched out onto a speaker's platform at the Ak-Sar-Ben Coliseum, and looked out on a vast sea of empty seats. A scheduling error resulted in a near empty arena. (The error was made by Eddie McKim, one of Truman's poker buddies, an insurance man who lived in Omaha.) *Life* magazine published photos of the president speaking at a huge venue with almost no one in attendance. The *Chicago Daily Tribune* commented that "Truman in Omaha . . . was as flat as a platter of beer." The event was a debacle. "It was almost a death knell for the campaign," noted Truman appointments secretary Matthew Connelly, who was traveling with the president.

Two days later, in Carey, Idaho, Truman dedicated a new airport in honor of a fallen World War II soldier — or so he thought. "I am honored," he told a sprawling crowd of locals, "to dedicate this airport and present this wreath to the parents of the brave boy who died fighting for his country." Truman heard a loud gasp. A woman spoke up: "Mr. President, it wasn't my son, it was my daughter."

Truman composed himself, then said, "Well, I am even more honored to dedicate this airport to a young woman who bravely gave her life for our country."

It turned out, this young girl was no soldier; she had been joyriding in an airplane with her boyfriend and had crashed into a mountainside. "It wasn't anything to laugh at," recalled Truman aide Robert Dennison, who was present. "But it was awfully funny just the same."

At one point, Truman endorsed a Republican congressional candidate by mistake. On another occasion, during one of his extemporaneous speeches, he began talking about his meetings with Soviet dictator Joseph Stalin at the Potsdam Conference in the summer of 1945. "I like old Joe," Truman said. Remembered Clark Clifford: "The uproar caused by the remark was immediate, sustained, and understandable." From most Americans' point of view, Stalin was the major source of global war anxiety. This was a man who, during the 1930s political "purges" in the Soviet Union, had overseen the disappearance and murder of millions of his own countrymen.

After Truman's gaffe, Clifford approached the president with the press secretary Charlie Ross. "Mr. President," Ross said, "we just have to tell you, frankly, that your 'I like Old Joe' remark is not going over well. We are going to get hammered for it, we know you understand, and we know you will not want to repeat that phrase."

Truman paused reflectively. "Well, I guess I goofed," he said.

More trouble awaited in Berkeley. When Truman arrived, he was given a fanfare welcome and a motorcade through crowded city streets. His car was followed by a pair of army Jeeps carrying newsreel cameramen. The University of California president was a die-hard Republican, and when he introduced Truman at the commencement event, he punctuated his address with jokes about the president's incompetency. "I actually cringed," recalled speechwriter Charlie Murphy.

At another stop, Truman gave a speech that was meant for a different town, confusing listeners. "At this point," remembered speechwriter Murphy, "he decided that his staff work was not what it should be, and he called the staff in to meet with him around the table in the dining room on the train. He called the meeting, I'm sure, for the purpose of dressing the staff down." But when it came time, the president could see how hard everyone was working, and how exhausted they were. "He couldn't quite manage to scold us."

When the train reached Los Angeles, Truman came face-to-face in a hotel room with James Roosevelt II, the eldest son of FDR, who had been actively campaigning to have General Dwight Eisenhower take Truman's place on the 1948 Democratic ticket. Eisenhower had recently retired from the army and had taken a position as president of Columbia University in New York; he had declined to run for president of the United States, but politicos like James Roosevelt were still hounding him to save the Democratic Party from Harry Truman.

Truman poked his finger into Roosevelt's chest and said, "If your father knew what you were doing to me, he would turn over in his grave. But get this straight: Whether you like it or not, I'm going to be the next President of the United States. That will be all. Good day."

All along this two-week, 9,505-mile, seventy-three-speech trip, the pressmen aboard the train took potshots. "Not even the most charitable interpretation could describe the President's performance at Carey, Idaho, as other than monumental ineptitude," the *Washington Post* said of Truman's airport-dedication error. Columnist Henry McLemore, in the *Washington Evening Star*: "Governors are running like deer. State chairmen are deserting . . . Many are using starting blocks, so anxious are they to quit what they consider a lost cause."

Meanwhile, back in Washington, the Eightieth Congress completed its session and broke for recess after overriding three Truman vetoes in a single week — not one but three humiliations for the president. Among these overrides was a tax cut — the Revenue Act of 1948 — a bill Truman had called "the wrong tax cut at the wrong time." Truman argued that the measure was going to fan the flames of inflation. The Republican-controlled Congress pushed the legislation through, expecting to reap the rewards for cutting taxes come Election Day. Republican senator Eugene Millikin later commented that the tax cut "was deliberately contrived to attract votes."

The more astute staffers and reporters aboard Truman's train noticed that something was happening on this trip, apart from verbal missteps and congressional vetoes. "It wasn't until Butte, Montana, that he began to hit his stride," recalled White House correspondent Robert Nixon, who was traveling with the president. Truman began to draw larger crowds, and with his folksy style he connected with his audiences. "Truman began to just talk," recalled Nixon. "He began to talk, instead of orating. He used his Missouri dialect. He became natural in every way. His talks began to be highly effective and to go over."

Charlie Murphy recalled, "A typical reaction that you would hear from among people in the crowd was, 'Why, he's a nice man, I like him. He's not at all like what they say about him in the papers.' And you would hear this, time after time."

As for a campaign strategy, the Truman administration took an unexpected approach. Truman's speeches took aim at the Republican-controlled Eightieth Congress. In one city after another, this would be his beating drum. In Los Angeles, he blasted Congress for "inactivity" and for passage of "a rich man's tax law." In Olympia, he told another crowd, "If you want to continue the policies of the 80th Congress, that will be your funeral." Members of the press on tour with Truman were surprised by the president's aggression. "He is making his attack much more directly and militantly than had been expected," wrote columnist Richard Strout from aboard the Truman train. The president's Congress-bashing began to get under the skin of Republicans back in Washington. At one point Robert Taft made a speech denouncing Truman's tactics.

"The President is blackguarding the Congress at every whistle stop in the country," Taft barked.

The Democrats saw an opportunity. The national committee sent out a form telegram to mayors and the chambers of commerce of thirty-five cities, to conduct an informal poll: "Please wire the Democratic National Committee whether you agree with Senator Taft's description of your city as a quote whistle stop unquote."

The responses flooded in: Local city leaders—in Los Angeles; Seattle;

Idaho Falls; and Laramie, Wyoming; among other places — were indeed offended by Taft's reference to their towns as whistle-stops, a term denoting places so insignificant, trains stopped at them only when signaled.

The pique Taft's comment aroused out west worked to the president's advantage. Truman would use the term *whistle-stop* against his opponents for the next five months — right up to Election Day, November 2, 1948 — as he campaigned throughout America's heartland.

PART III

The Conventions

A stranger convention there never was . . . I've been seeing them now for close to a half-century but I've never seen one quite like this.

—Lowell Mellett, political writer, 1948

13

"We Have a Dreamboat of a Ticket"

ON JUNE 20, THOMAS DEWEY left New York by train for Philadelphia en route to the Republican National Convention, where the 1948 nominee would be crowned. In anticipation of a victorious Republican year, the City of Brotherly Love came alive with the GOP's elite and hangers-on. Dewey, his family, Herbert Brownell, and the rest of the team checked into twenty-five rooms on the eighth floor of the Bellevue-Stratford, which towered over the corner of South Broad and Walnut Streets downtown. Attendance was expected to be so high, the Republican National Committee had run out of hotel rooms. The committee rented out the Alpha Tau Omega fraternity house at the University of Pennsylvania to accommodate Republican delegates, charging six dollars per person per night.

By the time Dewey arrived at campaign headquarters in the Bellevue-Stratford's ballroom, the place was lavishly dressed in red, white, and blue bunting and decorated with Republican elephants. The ballroom was jammed shoulder-to-shoulder with Republicans gorging on free liquor. The campaign had ordered fifty thousand I'M ON THE DEWEY TEAM buttons, ten thousand Dewey cigarette holders, five thousand Dewey balloons, one hundred DEWEY IN '48 sashes, three hundred Dewey neckties, and twenty-five thousand handheld fans so attendees could keep themselves cool. The president of Life Savers candy had donated five thousand cartons of his product, while Pepsi executives kept the bar stocked with soda. A "Women's Committee" had done the heavy lifting in presenting the event. "The general idea of the Committee," noted a Dewey team memorandum, "is to make the Dewey headquarters *the* place in Philadelphia for visitors, and women particularly."

On the eve of the convention, news outlets clashed with conflicting predictions.

Pollster George Gallup had Dewey in front with 33 percent, with Stassen in second at 26 percent.

The *Chicago Daily Tribune* claimed that the contest would be between Taft and Dewey.

The *New York Times* reported that Stassen and Taft were joining forces in a "Stop Dewey" blitz.

Senator Arthur Vandenberg of Michigan was seen making the rounds, telling friends he had no interest in the nomination, all the while keeping a copy of an acceptance speech in his pocket, just in case. Speaker of the House Joe Martin of Massachusetts kept a "Martin for President" movement simmering while assuring friends he had no interest. Harold Stassen's team had set up headquarters in a different ballroom in the same hotel as Dewey's, the Bellevue-Stratford. Guests sipped on free coffee and sliced chunks off huge wheels of orange cheddar. "Cheese at Stassen's very good," commented a *New Yorker* correspondent.

Robert Taft's campaign set up headquarters in the Benjamin Franklin Hotel (a landmark that had gotten some publicity a year earlier for refusing to house the Brooklyn Dodgers, because the team had a rookie black player—Jackie Robinson). Taft showed up wearing a TAFT FOR PRESIDENT campaign button that was from his father's convention in 1908, the year William Howard Taft was elected. The younger Taft sat on a pink couch while a runt elephant named Little Eva—a Republican mascot—made its way through the crowd wearing a blanket over its back that read WIN WITH TAFT. When Little Eva approached Taft, a newsreel man aimed his camera at the senator. "Shake his trunk," he said. Taft picked up the elephant's dripping snout and gave it a shake.

"Shake it again," said the cameraman. "It's your baby."

As the front-runner, Dewey drew the biggest crowds. He pumped handshakes and smiled so hard, one present recalled, it looked like his mustache might fall off. Meanwhile the one politician who made the biggest splash in Philadelphia was not even present. "The great silent star of the political melodrama being unfolded here at Convention Hall is not a Republican but a Democrat," recorded the columnist Gladstone Williams. "He is Harry S. Truman, President of the United States. Mr. Truman is the inspiration of joy and jubilations of the thousands of Republican delegates."

On June 21, at the Philadelphia Convention Center, the first speakers took the stage. As was the tradition at party conventions, early on in the process the following words were spoken into the microphone: "We are assembled in this great city to nominate the next President of the United States." Congressman Martin of Massachusetts remembered the moment: "What was unique about Philadelphia in 1948 was that everyone from the permanent chairman to the man who fed hay to an elephant [mascot] we had installed in the basement believed this with all his heart when he heard it."

The political convention was a century-old institution, but this event was unlike any convention ever held before. In front of the stage, scaffolding had been set up to hold television cameras. The major national radio networks were on hand with their new TV equipment—ABC, NBC, and CBS. Five cameras beamed images of the proceedings into homes all over the East Coast (and only the East Coast, as that was as far as the broadcast could reach). Speakers onstage withered under the heat of 10,000-watt bulbs illuminating their faces for the cameras. It being summer, the hall felt like an oven.

"In a few minutes I began to wilt and go blind," recorded the political reporter H. L. Mencken, "so the rest of my observations had to be made from a distance and through a brown beer bottle." Speaker of the House Joe Martin had a different take: For the first time, "we were conducting our affairs in the living room of the U.S.A."

The first night's proceedings culminated in a fighting speech by Clare Boothe Luce—the playwright and former congresswoman from Connecticut. Harry Truman, she famously observed, was a "gone goose."

"Let's waste no time measuring the unfortunate man in the White House against our specifications. Mr. Truman's time is short; his situation is hopeless."

When the balloting began on the morning of Thursday, June 24, people packed the convention center for the roll call, while the major candidates remained in their hotel suites, following the action on TV. In his eighth-floor suite at the Bellevue-Stratford, Dewey sat in shirtsleeves, tensely gazing at a television set through trails of his own cigarette smoke. When the power suddenly went out on the TV, the candidate dashed down the hotel hallway to the room of one of his campaign aides, to watch the returns.

State after state cast its delegate votes, and when it was over Dewey topped the ballot, as expected. Yet he did not have enough votes to secure the majority needed for the Republican nomination. And so began a convention drama common to that era, before the reforms of the 1970s turned conventions into preordained theater. Behind the scenes, Brownell and his associates went to work to bring Dewey over the top. Brownell had been working for months to piece together this influential machinery, and now he flipped the switch. Orders went down the carefully constructed chains of command, reaching into the delegations of every state. Stassen was on the scene, his expansive forehead dripping with sweat. A delegate from Tennessee named B. Carroll Reece approached Stassen and told him how furiously the Brownell machinery was pushing to land Dewey's victory. Brownell was demanding that delegates vote for the New York governor.

"Harold," Reece told Stassen, "you have no idea of the pressure put on me. That Dewey machine is like a row of tanks."

Not until the third ballot did Dewey capture the nomination, grabbing a unanimous vote of all 1,094 delegates. Writing in his diary later that night, Senator Vandenberg recorded, "[Dewey's] 'blitz' was a thing of beauty."

At his hotel, Dewey showered, changed into a fresh suit, and made the drive with his wife to the convention hall in the back of a black limousine. It had been storming that night. As Dewey approached the arena, rain slowed to a stop and, as if on cue, a rainbow appeared, arcing over the City of Brotherly Love. Backstage in the convention hall, Dewey squirmed uncomfortably while makeup artists prepared him for the television broadcast. "I look just awful,"he commented. He could hear the crowds singing "Hail Hail, the Gang's All Here" while they waited for him.

When he stepped onstage with Mrs. Dewey, the masses gave him everything they had. The building's girders soaked up the vibrations from the roars and applause. Dewey stood, waving his arms like he was conducting an orchestra. His speech was just minutes long, but he hit the right notes for this crowd.

"It has been a difficult choice, in an honorable contest," Dewey said. (Applause!) There had been "spirited disagreement, hot argument." (Applause!) "But let no one be misled. You have given moving and dramatic proof of how Americans who honestly differ, close ranks and move forward, for the nation's well-being, shoulder to shoulder." (Applause!)

"For tonight," Dewey said, and he paused for effect. "Our peace, our prosperity, the very fate of freedom—hangs in a precarious balance."

After Dewey's acceptance speech, he headed to campaign headquarters at the Bellevue-Stratford to speak to his staff and his fans.

"Will you excuse me for being late?" he started. "I finally got through a call to my mother in Michigan and I had a chance to talk to her and give her my love . . ."

Dewey promised his audience that things were about to change. "I can assure you that we will have the finest housecleaning in Washington that ever there was in the history of our government," he said. Then he retired to his hotel suite, where the Dewey-ites had gathered to begin the next chapter of their campaign—the choice of a VP candidate. The man everyone believed would be the next secretary of state, John Foster Dulles, was in the room. Senator Vandenberg was there, as was Herbert Brownell. Conspicuously missing was Robert Taft, who had been invited but chose to nurse his wounded pride privately.

This hotel suite now represented the future of global power as far as everyone present was concerned. The leading candidate for VP was Charles A. Halleck, the conservative congressman from Indiana. (Since he was a candidate, Halleck was not invited to be present.) "We were all sworn to secrecy,"

Vandenberg wrote in his diary. "All of the following names were canvassed: Stassen, Warren [Earl Warren, governor of California], Green [Dwight Green, governor of Illinois], Knowland [Senator William Knowland of California], Bricker [Senator John Bricker of Ohio], Halleck [the aforementioned Indiana congressman], Hickenlooper [Senator Bourke Hickenlooper of Iowa], Ferguson [Senator Homer Ferguson of Michigan], and two or three easterners who were promptly dismissed for geographical reasons."

Somebody threw out Green's name.

"Let's not be mealy-mouthed about this," said Dewey. "We can't take him." Dewey thought for a moment. "We should have notes," he said. He turned to Dulles. "Why don't you take notes?"

Dulles grabbed a pad.

Brownell said, "Well, how about Charlie?"

Arthur Vandenberg and Joe Martin both said at the same time, "Charlie who?"

"Charlie Halleck."

Vandenberg shouted, "Oh, my God!"

"Halleck won't do," Dewey said. He was too conservative for Dewey's taste.

The group took a break for coffee and sandwiches at 2 a.m. By the time the meeting broke up at 4:30 in the morning, Dewey still had not made his choice. It was not until 11:30 the next day that Dewey associate J. Russell Sprague came barreling out, exclaiming to exhausted reporters: "It is the unanimous opinion of all of us that Governor Warren should be the candidate."

Earl Warren was not entirely surprised when the phone rang in his hotel room. Dewey offered the governor of California the VP slot and Warren accepted. Meanwhile, somebody had to break the news to Indiana congressman Charlie Halleck, who had been a front-runner and had been told he would get the nod. Dewey chose to do the job himself, and Halleck became emotional. His parting shot was significant. Dewey's platform and his choice of Earl Warren were decidedly liberal for the Republican Party, and not at all indicative of the mood in the current Republican-controlled Congress—as represented by Halleck, Bob Taft, Speaker of the House Martin, and others.

"You're running out on the 80th Congress, and you'll be sorry," Halleck told the candidate.

The Dewey-Warren ticket was the answer to the questions Republicans had been asking themselves for months. What was the way forward for the GOP in the postwar world? Dewey's brand of liberal Republicanism, the GOP ideology of Theodore Roosevelt? Or Taft's, a harking back to the conservative Republicanism of the 1920s?

Dewey won.

Already, the Republicans had made public the official plank that stated the party's policies. It embraced civil rights, recognition of Israel, admission of Alaska, Hawaii, and Puerto Rico as states, extension of Social Security benefits. But it also trumpeted more traditional GOP policies — reduction in public debt, more tax cuts, elimination of some federal bureaucracy. And of course: a crackdown on domestic Communism.

Dewey was thrilled with the platform, but the plank was a defeat for Taft and the leaders of the Eightieth Congress. Few realized at the time how problematic it could be to have a national party plank that the Republican presidential candidate embraced yet which made the party faithful in Congress uncomfortable. One who did realize it was Senator Vandenberg, who wrote in his diary after the convention, "If this is to be the policy of the next Republican Administration in the White House, it is desperately important to make it equally the policy of the Republicans in the next Congress."

Another of the few who noticed the discrepancy was Harry Truman.

Nevertheless, the ticket was set: two popular, young, energetic, and progressive GOP governors, from states that bookended the country. New York and California were two of the biggest states in the union, which between them counted for more than a quarter of the electoral votes needed to win in November. Dewey was vigorous and tough as nails, the first presidential candidate born in the twentieth century. Hugh Scott, the Pennsylvania congressman and new head of the Republican National Committee, spoke for many when he said, "We have a dreamboat of a ticket."

When Dewey arrived back at his mansion in Albany, his mailbox once again flooded with congratulatory letters and telegrams. "You will make a great president," wrote Dewey's longtime friend Tom Warren (no relation to Earl Warren). "I knew 28 years ago you would some day be president." Among the missives was one from the Republican senator B. B. Hickenlooper of Iowa. "Your victory," Hickenlooper wrote Dewey, "is practically assured."

Truman watched the first-ever televised national political convention from inside the White House, on the twelve-inch flickering RCA black-and-white TV set that had been placed in the Oval Office to the left of the president's desk. Yet on June 24, the night of Dewey's nomination, events in Europe tore the president's attention away from Dewey's moment in the spotlight. The Soviets had blockaded the border between the eastern and western sectors of Berlin. The western part of the city, controlled by American, British, and French occupation forces, was now sealed off, and completely surrounded by Soviet-occupied territory. Berliners in these sectors were suddenly cut off from supplies — food, coal, and some of their electric power.

That night, the streets in the western part of Berlin filled with frightened people who realized they were now in desperate straits — cogs in the Cold War standoff between the Americans and the Soviets, and dependent primarily on the US government to figure out a solution. One German leader in Berlin called on the world that night to help "in the decisive phase of the fight for freedom."

As Republicans were leaving their convention in Philadelphia, Truman was in the White House, focused on how to respond to the Berlin Blockade. Surely, he must have surmised, the timing of the Berlin Blockade was no coincidence; the Soviets seemed clearly to be attempting to create crisis at a time the Americans were focused on their electoral process. The day after the blockade began, on June 25, Truman gathered his cabinet. Secretary of Defense James Forrestal thought the blockade was "not as serious as indicated," according to the meeting's minutes. Secretary of the Army Kenneth Royall disagreed. "A very serious situation [is] developing," he said. Truman wondered whether it was time to evacuate American women and children from the US sector of Berlin.

The man in charge of the US forces in Berlin, General Lucius Clay, was making arrangements to use aircraft to bring supplies in. He had no other option. An aerial supply operation would require near-continuous flights. The airplanes had already begun to take off and land, crisscrossing each other in flight, moving from airports in western Germany into two airports in the blockaded part of Berlin. The logistics of such an operation in the long term would be staggering. Would it be possible to use airplanes to fly in food and supplies, day after day and night after night?

The day after Truman's cabinet meeting, on June 26, the president directed what he called an "improvised 'airlift'" to be put "on a full-scale organized basis and that every plane available to our European Command be impressed into service." The Berlin Airlift had begun.

14

"With God's Help, You Will Win"

ON JULY FOURTH WEEKEND, less than a week before the Democratic convention was to kick off, powerful members of the party panicked. James Roosevelt II — FDR's oldest son — made a move he hoped would save the Democrats from doom in 1948. Roosevelt had arranged for telegrams to be sent out to all 1,592 delegates who would be voting for the party nomination in Philadelphia, asking them to arrive in the city two days early for a special "Draft Eisenhower" caucus, in which the Democrats would make a high-profile plea to Dwight Eisenhower to run for president on the Democratic ticket. Eisenhower — the beloved army general who had commanded the Allied forces in the D-day landings in Normandy — was a mysterious figure, politically. Being a military man, he had spent his career above politics, and as far as anyone knew, he did not belong to any political party.

Over the next days, Democratic leaders came out in droves with Draft Eisenhower statements of their own: Senator Claude Pepper of Florida, former Interior secretary Harold Ickes, the powerful Democratic machine bosses Jacob Arvey of Chicago and Frank Hague of New Jersey, and more.

"Nothing quite so strange has occurred in a long time as the frantic clamor among discontented Democrats for Gen. Dwight D. Eisenhower to come and save them from Harry S. Truman," wrote the columnist Thomas

Stokes. If the Democrats failed to get Ike to run, commented the nation's most popular political columnist, Drew Pearson, "every seasoned political leader in the Democratic Party is convinced Harry Truman will suffer one of the worst election defeats in history." In pollster Elmo Roper's latest national study, Thomas Dewey was well ahead of Truman, 41.3 to 33.7 percent, but if Eisenhower ran as a Democrat, the public favored him over Dewey, 42.3 to 33.8 percent.

In the White House, Truman was humiliated by the Draft Eisenhower movement. "Doublecrossers all," he wrote in his diary. "But they'll get nowhere — a doubledealer never does." To Bess, he wrote, "This job gets worse every day. Look what . . . [the] Demorepublicans are trying to do to me now. But I'm going to lick 'em or go down fighting."

Ike himself responded politely but adamantly: He would not run.

All the while, the pressure in the White House mounted, as it seemed that war in Berlin could come at any moment. The same week that the Democratic convention began, Truman met with his military advisers to discuss the Soviet standoff in Berlin, again. "I've made my decision," he wrote in notes of this meeting. There would be no retreat. "We'll stay in Berlin — come what may."

On July 12, the first televised Democratic National Convention opened ceremonies in Philadelphia. From the get-go, the tone was one of irritability and despair. The heat in the city was unbearable. Hotel rooms were nonexistent. Across from the convention hall's front door, a man waved an EISENHOWER FOR PRESIDENT banner, even though Ike was not attending and would not be running. "The glum resignation of the leading Democrats has to be seen to be believed," wrote the columnists Joseph and Stewart Alsop. "There never has been anything like it in the major political history of the United States," wrote Erwin Canham, editor of the *Christian Science Monitor.*

In the White House, Truman watched on TV — the familiar calls to order, dull speakers failing to arouse attention. One thing seemed eminently clear: how much the world had changed in the four years since the 1944 convention. Atomic energy. The Iron Curtain. The Cold War. None of this terminology had held any meaning four short years earlier.

By this time Truman had picked a VP candidate — Alben Barkley of Kentucky. The president's first choice had been the popular Supreme Court justice William O. Douglas, but Douglas had declined, claiming lack of political experience. Truman believed the rumors, however, that Douglas did not want to be "a number two man to a number two man," as the president put it in his diary.

"I stuck my neck all the way out for Douglas," Truman told his staff, mixing his metaphors, "and he cut the limb out from under me."

On that first night of the convention, the president sat cross-legged in his bed wearing pajamas, watching Senator Barkley deliver the keynote. Truman was alone, as his wife and daughter were back home in Independence for the summer break. He held his chin in his hands, as if too tired to hold up his head. A friend was shown into the room and the two began to talk over the convention.

Truman reportedly said, "Why do they hate me so? I've tried to do the right thing. I've done everything I could. But they just don't seem to appreciate it."

From the president's point of view, his current approval rating — a miserable 36 percent — did not reflect the job he was doing. America was booming. Ever since the end of the war, economists had been sounding alarm bells. There was going to be another depression . . . There was going to be hardship and fear . . . But no depression had come. The labor force was strong, the incomes of average Americans in various sectors were strong, and people's standard of living in many parts of the country was high and rising. Despite high prices and a housing shortage, postwar America was on a tear. But no one was giving any credit to the Truman administration. Instead, the president was the picture of defeat.

Secretly, he had a plan.

Days earlier, a memo had appeared circulating in the White House, dated June 29, 1948, called, "Should the President Call Congress Back in Session?" The memo was unsigned, and the author of it would remain a mystery. It began: "This election can only be won by bold and daring steps, calculated to reverse the powerful trend now running against us. The boldest and most popular step the President could possibly take would be to call a special session of Congress in early August."

Congress had broken for recess, and was not scheduled to convene again until after the November election, which was more than three months away. Thus members of Congress who were running for reelection would have time to go home and campaign in their states. However, the president technically had the legal right to call an emergency session of Congress.

The Republicans at their convention had come up with a platform that exposed a schism within the GOP. The most influential Republicans in the Eightieth Congress were those on the farther right. They were out of step with the liberal Dewey-Warren ticket on many of the election's most important issues, such as housing reform and extension of Social Security benefits. Indeed, Dewey supported some of the same positions that the Truman administration did.

By calling the conservative-leaning Congress back into session and demanding that Congress enact legislation that reflected Dewey's own platform, Truman could drive a stake right through the Republican Party. If the conservative Eightieth Congress failed to enact Dewey's liberal legislation, Dewey would be embarrassed by his own party and an identity crisis within the Republican Party would be exposed. If Congress did pass the kinds of legislation the Dewey-Warren plank called for, the president would get the credit for it.

The idea was brilliant but controversial. Not since 1856 had a president called Congress back into an emergency session from recess during an election year.

Truman was scheduled to travel to Philadelphia on the convention's final night, July 14, to accept the nomination. Of the six vice presidents who had ascended to the Oval Office following the death of a president, only two had been renominated by their party to run for another four years — Calvin Coolidge and Theodore Roosevelt. The day before Truman left for Philadelphia, he arrived at his morning staff meeting full of anger and spewing epithets.

"He said he had made some outline of what he plans to say [at the convention] and added that he was going up there — to the convention — and if he can keep the swear words out of it, tell them just what he thinks," assistant press secretary Eben Ayers wrote in his diary. Truman broached the idea of calling a special session of Congress. "He said he was going to wind up by calling Congress back for a special session on July 19," recorded Ayers. "Putting in the swear words he expressed his attitude about calling them back, something like this: 'Now, you s-- of a b--, come on and do your g-- d--t.'"

When this staff meeting broke up, Truman told his team to get ready. Recalled Ayers: "As . . . we started to leave, the President commented we were going to have more fun in the next six months than we ever had in our lives."

Truman and his entourage arrived at Washington's Union Station at 7 p.m. on Wednesday, July 14, for the trip to Philadelphia. His wife and daughter had returned to the capital that morning, and they were by his side at the station. TV cameras followed Truman as he boarded the train. He wore a crisp cream-colored linen suit, with a dark tie and pocket square. When the train arrived in Philadelphia, rain was pounding the city.

A motorcade with police escort delivered Truman to the back door of Philadelphia Convention Hall, so the crowds would not see him. The convention speeches and resolutions were hours behind schedule, and the hall itself had no air-conditioning. The backstage room was so crowded "you couldn't have gotten a toothpick in that room, it was so jammed with people," recalled one of Truman's aides, General Louis H. Renfrow, who was present. Truman headed to a balcony outside where he could breathe. Soon the VP candidate Alben Barkley appeared and the two sat talking about old times under an awning to keep dry. As Barkley later recalled, they talked about "many things: politics, trivia, how to bring up daughters."

In the convention hall, alcohol and stifling heat had left the crowd in a daze. An electrical storm outside knocked out a fuse, causing further delay.

"It seemed like almost everything was going wrong," recalled White House correspondent Robert Nixon, who was covering the convention for the United Press.

The worst was yet to come.

During the final session of resolutions leading up to Truman's acceptance speech, protesters took control of the night. The Democrats had adopted a plank heavy on civil rights, supporting the right to equal opportunity in employment, equal treatment of all races in the military, and "security of person" (the lawful right not to be lynched). Southern Democrats were ready to make their protest against Truman's civil rights policies in front of television cameras. First, a delegate from Georgia named Charles J. Bloch came onstage and demanded to be heard.

"The south is no longer going to be the whipping boy of the Democratic party," Bloch yelled with a hoarse southern accent. "And you know that without the south you cannot elect a President of the United States." He called for the nomination of a new candidate to represent the Democratic Party, Senator Richard Russell of Georgia, adding, "You shall not crucify the south on the cross of civil rights."

A crowd of southern leaders paraded in front of the microphone. One yelled: "Mississippi has gone home!" Another voice, delegate Byrd Sims of Florida, came through: "He can't win. We must have new leadership." Governor Strom Thurmond of South Carolina stepped onto the stage. "Our fight is the fight of every American who does not want to be subjected to federal police control!" he yelled. Parts of the crowd booed Thurmond, who responded, "It's medicine you don't want to hear."

A large group of delegates from Mississippi and Alabama gathered in the aisle and walked out, waving Confederate flags on their way. The convention band started up with an impromptu version of "Dixie." Truman supporters blocked the aisles, forcing the southern protesters to push their way through. Grown men in suits were now jostling and shoving as if the arena floor was a school yard. The scene was descending into chaos. One reporter cataloged the moment: "A live donkey was led in and seemed properly astounded at the goings on. An Indian in full dress did a war dance in front of the speaker's rostrum . . . Firecrackers crackled, cowbells were banged, and over and over, and faster and faster, the band played 'Dixie.'"

The *Washington Post*'s Marquis Childs put the moment in perspective: "We may well be watching . . . the liquidation of one of the major parties."

Onstage, a convention organizer pounded a gavel before the microphone, attempting to regain control. By the time Governor Phil Donnelly of Missouri took the stage to introduce Truman, it was nearly 2 a.m.

The president marched up to the speaker's podium like a fighter entering a ring. The crowds stood for him and he smiled, picking up a glass of water off the podium and taking a sip. Behind him, Alben Barkley stood clapping his hands, his face grimly focused on the president. A brass band belted out an intro, and Truman said, "Thank you, thank you very much," just loud enough to be heard over the trombones.

He did not look like a president with a 36 percent approval rating. He looked like a man who knew in his heart he was going to win. But scanning the crowd, he saw a picture of defeat. "The delegates that evening were a tired, dispirited, soggy mass of beaten humanity," recalled David C. Bell, a Truman special assistant who was there that night. Truman's wife and daughter were in the crowd, on their feet but not clapping their hands. A scaffolding stood in front of the stage holding the TV cameras, but it was so late that the TV broadcasters had called it a night. Only the nationwide radio hookup was working. Truman struggled for a moment to adjust the phalanx of microphones in front of him. Then he began, his voice full of Missouri flavor.

"I can't tell you how much I appreciate the honor which you've just conferred upon me," he said. "I shall continue to try to deserve it." He paused for applause. "I accept the nomination." (More applause.) "And I want to thank this convention for its unanimous nomination of my good friend and colleague, Senator Barkley of Kentucky. He's a great man and a great public servant."

For months, rage had boiled in the president's gut. Now, all that anger came out as if a floodgate had opened. With a single sentence, Truman transformed the night.

"Senator Barkley and I will win this election and make these Republicans like it — don't you forget that!"

The crowd came alive instantly.

"We will do that because they are wrong and we are right," Truman said, "and I'm going to prove it to you in just a few minutes!"

In his memoirs, Truman recalled speaking this line. "I meant just that, and I said it as if I meant it. There could be no mistake. I intended to win."

Truman unleashed his fighting speech. He had tried to get the Eightieth Congress on board to enact his policies addressing high prices and the housing crisis, he said, but Congress had failed to pass these laws, and the American people were suffering. He denounced the Republican-controlled legislature as the "worst Congress in history." He called on farmers to vote for Democrats. Farmers — who traditionally voted Republican — had never been as well off as they were in 1948, following sixteen years of Democratic leadership, Truman said.

"Never in the world were the farmers of any republic or any kingdom or any country as prosperous as they are in the United States," he said. "And if they don't do their duty by the Democratic Party they are the most ungrateful people in the world!"

He called on the nation's workers, who were also seeing wages higher than they'd ever been before. "And I'll say to labor just what I said to the farmers. They are the most ungrateful people in the world if they pass the Democratic Party by this year!"

The crowds were on their feet. Tired eyes widened. "It was one of the most electrifying things that I had ever been present at," recalled Truman adviser Max Lowenthal. "He just had them on the ropes." Recalled Truman's Missouri friend Tom Evans: "I never in all my life got such a tremendous buildup in such a short time."

Truman took on the Southern Democrats who had just bolted the party in protest of his civil rights support.

"Everybody knows that I recommended to the Congress the civil rights program," Truman railed. "I did that because I believed it to be my duty under the Constitution. Some of the members of my own party disagree with me violently on this matter. But they stand up and do it openly! People can tell where they stand. But the Republicans all professed to be *for* these measures [as clearly stated in their platform]. But Congress failed to act."

Truman's speech reached its climax. "My duty as president requires that I use every means within my power to get the laws that people need on matters of such importance and urgency. I am therefore calling this Congress back into session on the 26th of July!"

The roar of approval was so loud it was a full thirty seconds before Truman could get another word in. "On the 26th day in July, which out in Missouri we call Turnip Day, I'm going to call that Congress back and I'm gonna ask 'em to pass laws halting rising prices, and to meet the housing crisis, which they say they are for in their platform. At the same time I shall ask them to act upon other vitally needed measures such as aid to education, which they say they are for. A national health program. Civil rights legislation, which they say they are for. And an increase in minimum wage—which I doubt very much they are for . . ."

Truman ended with a plea. "Now my friends, with the help of God and the wholehearted push which you can put behind this campaign, we can save this country from a continuation of the 80th Congress, and from misrule from now on. I must have your help. You must get in and push, and win this election."

The clamor was deafening. "Everybody jumped up. It was the wildest thing I've ever seen," remembered Frank Kelly, a journalist who was soon to join the Truman campaign staff. "Everybody was like zombies and all of a sudden they were alive. They were yelling. Truman amazed us all that night."

The convention's national committeewoman from Pennsylvania, Emma Guffey Miller, seized the moment. Convention workers helped her wheel onto the stage a five-foot replica of the Liberty Bell made out of eight thousand flowers, donated by the Allied Florists union of Greater Philadelphia. The floral Liberty Bell was a surprise to all. At Ms. Miller's signal, men with broomsticks started poking inside the bell, and from within it, forty-eight pigeons — one for every state — flew frantically into the hall.

Panicked pigeons swirled around the stage. Some flew toward the ceiling, where the metal blades of four thirty-six-inch fans whirled at high speed. Former Speaker of the House Sam Rayburn was on the stage, swatting at birds flapping desperately around his bald head. The national radio audience heard him yelling, "Get those goddamned pigeons out of here."

"I remember vividly all over the nationwide radio . . . you could hear the Speaker say, 'Shoo, shoo, shoo,'" recalled Neale Roach, the convention's director. Roach managed to flip the switch to the metal fans near the ceiling, turning them off. "All I could visualize was a bunch of blood and feathers being sprayed all over everybody."

By the time Truman's train was headed back to Washington, one of the most memorable national conventions of all time was over, and the empty hall in Philadelphia was littered with programs, newspaper balls, and a few feathers. As the train clattered over the tracks, news of Truman's "Turnip Day" emergency congressional session spread nationwide. Republican Speaker of the House Joe Martin would remember being woken up at three o'clock that morning, at his sister's house in North Attleborough, Massachusetts. His sister had picked up a ringing phone to find a reporter in Philadelphia yelling at her, wanting to talk to Speaker Martin.

"What do you want him for at this hour?" she inquired.

The reporter said, "Haven't you heard about *the President*?"

"Arrived in Washington at the White House at 5:30 a.m., my usual getting up time," Truman wrote in his diary the morning after the convention. By nine fifteen, he was in his upstairs study, surrounded by those familiar groaning White House walls. His door creaked open and the White House head butler Alonzo Fields peered in. Fields was surprised to see the president awake.

"Good morning, Fields," Truman said.

"Good morning, Mr. President. We did not hear from you and I was nosing around to see if you were up."

"Yes," Truman said. His wife and daughter were still asleep. "You send me a tray up here when it is ready."

"Sir," said Fields, "you had a rough night."

"Yes, I did," said Truman. "But, Fields, I am going to win this thing if there is a God in heaven."

"Yes sir," said Fields. "With God's help, you will win."

15

"What Is at Stake Here Is the Very Survival of Western Civilization"

AT 11:30 A.M. ON JULY 15—just six hours after Truman's return to the White House from Philadelphia—Secretary of Defense Forrestal and Secretary of the Army Kenneth Royall arrived at the Oval Office for a scheduled appointment with the president. Forrestal had requested the meeting to discuss the bomb. It was time to address the vexing questions surrounding history's most dangerous invention.

"The president was chipper and in very good form," Forrestal wrote in his diary, "and obviously pleased with the results of his speech at the Convention last night."

All over the country, Americans were reading in their newspapers about the most bizarre political convention that anyone could recall. Truman was not angry at the southern revolt, he told the secretary of defense: "I would have done the same thing myself if I were in their place and came from their states."

Forrestal brought with him a nervous energy that tended to put people on edge. He had a flattened nose, having taken a punch to the face as a young boxer in the military. He had earned a fortune on Wall Street before taking a job as undersecretary of the Navy under FDR in 1940, and although he did not need to work, he threw himself into his job so completely, he had become incapable of relaxing. On this morning, in discussing the bomb, he raised what he called the "serious question as to the wisdom of relying upon an agency other than the user of such a weapon, to assure the integrity and usability of such a weapon." In other words, he was asking the president to hand custody of the bomb over to the Defense Department.

Truman did not like what he was hearing. No one but the nation's chief executive should be able to make the decision to use an atomic weapon, he argued. He did not want, in his words, "to have some dashing lieutenant colonel decide when would be the proper time to drop one."

More than any other American, Truman understood the power of an atomic weapon — politically, psychologically, and practically. At one point in 1948, he told the head of the Atomic Energy Commission, David Lilienthal, "I don't think we ought to use this thing unless we absolutely have to. It is a terrible thing to order the use of something that" — he paused, bowing his head — "that is so terribly destructive, destructive beyond anything we have ever had. You have got to understand that this isn't a military weapon. It is used to wipe out women and children and unarmed people, and not for military uses. So we have got to treat this differently from rifles and cannon and ordinary things like that."

The United States had roughly fifty atomic bombs stockpiled. As of 1948, the Soviets had none. During the three Operation Sandstone nuclear tests in the Pacific that year, military scientists had designed a long-range detection system that could — if it worked — tip off US officials to an atomic-bomb detonation in other parts of the world, so the United States could monitor Soviet activities in this regard. If the Kremlin tested a bomb, Truman would know about it, and quickly. According to the latest estimates from the CIA — in a memo to the president dated July 6, 1948, two weeks before Truman's nomination in Philadelphia — "it is estimated that the earliest date by which it is remotely possible that the USSR may have completed its first atomic bomb is mid-1950, but the most probable date is believed to be mid-1953."*

*This estimate was overly optimistic. The Soviets would detonate their first atomic bomb roughly fourteen months from the time this memo was written, on August 29, 1949. The

For Truman, the whole discussion with regard to atomic bombs and how to stockpile them and when one might be used was a stiff reminder that he was going to have to conduct his election campaign under excruciating pressure. The tension from within Washington was growing. The threat to national security due to instability outside US borders was too. Violence was rampant in Palestine. The Israelis were clamoring for a $100 million loan from the United States, and for the US government to lift an embargo on the shipment of arms to the Middle East. Communism was spreading deep into the Far East. According to a US intelligence report from that month, "The position of the present [US-allied] National Government [in China] is so precarious that its fall may occur at any time."

On July 19 — four days after Truman's nomination — the president's cabinet convened again to discuss the standoff in Berlin. Secretary of State Marshall outlined the situation for the president. General Lucius Clay was recommending the deployment of armed convoys — specifically, convoys of two hundred trucks with an engineering battalion as an escort — to push through Soviet territory to the western sector of Berlin. There would be casualties, and the potential for all-out war. General Clay's bosses in Washington, headed by Army Chief of Staff General Omar Bradley, had countered Clay, preferring to continue the present airlift. Even as Truman sat talking with his cabinet, across the Atlantic in Berlin, thundering C-54 airplanes were landing and taking off in western Berlin, delivering hundreds of tons of food and supplies daily.

Secretary of Defense Forrestal pointed out to Truman that there was not enough manpower in the army to fight if the Soviets started a war in Berlin. Truman wrote in his diary, "We'll stay in Berlin . . . I don't pass the buck, nor do I alibi out of any decision I make."

The day after this cabinet meeting, on July 20, 1948, Truman issued Executive Order 9979 — a peacetime draft that would call for nearly ten million men to register for the military over the next two months, a draft that did not

---

United States' long-range detection system provided verification of the explosion, and the story broke around the world the following month.

make Harry Truman any more popular among war-weary voters. The draft executive order was tantamount to political suicide four months before an election, but Truman believed he had no choice.

Everywhere, there was talk of war. "The atmosphere in Washington is no longer a postwar atmosphere," the columnists Joseph and Stewart Alsop wrote. "It is, to put it bluntly, a prewar atmosphere . . . It is now universally admitted that war within the next few months is certainly possible."

In the days after the Democratic National Convention, Republicans reacted in shock to news that the president had called the Eightieth Congress back into an emergency session. They had followed the Democratic National Convention closely on radio and TV, but almost all were snoozing when Truman made his 2 a.m. acceptance speech.

By lunchtime the next day, the term *Turnip Day* was a national phenomenon — and a gauntlet. What were the Republicans going to do about the special session? With Congress in recess, many of these politicians had already left Washington to visit their families or head off on vacation.

In the Senate building in Washington, the congressional leaders of the GOP who were still in the city met to strategize — Senators Taft of Ohio, Vandenberg of Michigan, Eugene Millikin of Colorado, and the chairman of the Republican National Committee, Representative Hugh Scott of Pennsylvania, among others. As Scott remembered the scene, Vandenberg told his colleagues that the Eightieth Congress had to compromise and give in to Truman.

"Bob," Vandenberg said to Taft, "I think we ought to do something. We ought to do whatever we can to show that we are trying to use the two weeks [the emergency session] as best we can. Then we have a better case to take before the public."

Taft was livid. Scott would remember him saying, "We are not going to give that fellow anything," referring to Truman. Remembered Scott: "Anyone familiar with Bob Taft's method of ending a conversation will know that was the end of it."

Scott himself gave a statement to the press following this meeting: "It is the act of a desperate man [Truman] who is willing to destroy the unity and dignity of his country and his Government in a time of world crisis to obtain partisan advantage after he himself has lost the confidence of the people."

A few days later, on July 28, Taft went on national radio to fight back. "The Constitution says that the President may convene Congress in special session 'on extraordinary occasions,'" the senator began. "This call was announced by the President after two o'clock in the morning in the midst of a political speech to the Democratic Convention, solely as a political maneuver in the President's campaign for his own reelection. In the same speech he denounced the 80th Congress as the worst in history in spite of the magnificent cooperation he has received in every phase of foreign policy [the Truman Doctrine, the Marshall Plan]."

Taft urged his listeners to go to the polls. "The only way this fundamental difference can be resolved is by the vote of the people at the November election."

Governor Dewey chose to remain above the fray. "The Special Session is a nuisance [and] no more," he wrote his mother. His strategy was to divert attention from the special session, by reaching out to the one man who could do his campaign the most good. Reporters were notified by Dewey's staff that on July 24, the Republican nominee was expecting a special guest at his dairy farm in Pawling, New York. Members of the press took note.

Dwight and Mamie Eisenhower arrived at the Dewey farm in Pawling after a two-and-a-half-hour drive from New York City. The Eisenhowers and the Deweys lunched together on the side terrace of the candidate's white farmhouse. Afterward, the two men spoke privately about the face-off with the Russians in Berlin.

When reporters who had traveled to Pawling were invited to join in the conversation, Dewey faulted the Democrats for instigating the Berlin emergency. Democratic leadership had failed to ensure that Americans in western Germany would have legal rights to travel through Soviet-occupied Germany. A Republican administration could be relied upon to handle the situation in the future, Dewey argued, and the way to do that was with strength and firmness. It was time for the United States to stand up to the Kremlin, Dewey said.

"In Berlin we must not surrender our rights under duress," the candidate said, with Ike sitting beside him. "We stay in Berlin in defense of our rights and insist on every peaceable means of defending our rights."

Eisenhower added backbone to the candidate's sentiments. Here was "Iron Ike," World War II's greatest hero. His mere presence inspired confidence, dependability, patriotism. It also raised a scintillating question: If Ike was to enter politics, what party would he represent? Democrat or Republican? When asked, Eisenhower answered, "I have not identified myself with any political party. I think I reflect the Governor's views when I say we talked as two Americans." When asked if Eisenhower's visit was an endorsement of Dewey, the general remained coy.

"Let's not fool ourselves," he said. "Governor Dewey is a very significant person in the body politic."

Dewey and Ike sat closely enough that their elbows touched, the scene carefully choreographed so news photographers could capture their smiling faces up close in a single camera frame. Eisenhower appeared elated, his expression revealing his belief that he was sitting next to the man who would be the first Republican president since 1932.

Meanwhile, three days after the Democratic National Convention, six thousand rebel Democrats gathered in a redbrick armory in Birmingham, Alabama. They aimed high: to chart a new course for the political future of a vast section of the United States. This crowd was aroused and thirsty for vengeance. White men pumped Confederate flags in the air. A band thumped out "Camptown Races." Red, white, and blue bunting lined the walls. Delegates who had bolted the Democratic convention in Philadelphia now had their own convention, and a new political party: the Dixiecrats.

Not everyone was happy with the moniker; this group's emerging leader — Governor Strom Thurmond of South Carolina — particularly did not like it. But the name stuck. A Charlotte, North Carolina, newspaper editor had come up with the term for the breakaway Democrats as a play on words. Dixie, after all, was the nickname for southern states that had made up the Confederacy during the Civil War. Dixiecrat was also the name of a favorite breakfast dish at Cogburn's Grill in the capital city of Columbia, South Carolina—a greasy brown link sausage tucked into a folded slice of white bread.

The Dixiecrats' platform would focus on "racial integrity"; among the six thousand people in the Birmingham armory, there were no blacks. It was not just a southern affair, but it was southern-dominated. Delegations were gathered on the armory floor in clusters holding signs from their states: Florida, Georgia, Alabama, Louisiana, Texas, South Carolina, North Carolina, Oklahoma, Arkansas, Mississippi, Virginia, and Tennessee. Delegations came from as far away as Iowa.

All the major radio networks plus newsreel cameras were on hand for the keynote speaker—Governor Thurmond—who was escorted to the podium by men waving American and Confederate flags. The South Carolina governor wore a black suit and a thin black tie over a white shirt. He shook a pen in his right hand rhythmically while he spoke.

"I want to tell you, ladies and gentlemen, that there's not enough troops in the Army to force the Southern people to break down segregation and admit the Negro race into our theaters, into our swimming pools, into our homes, and into our churches," Thurmond snapped. "If the South should vote for Truman this year, we might as well petition the Government for colonial status . . . I can think of nothing worse for the South than to tuck its tail and vote for Truman. If we did we would be nothing worse than cowards. We are not going to do it."

As Thurmond spoke, he grew visibly angrier until his voice began to crack and his volume peaked. "These uncalled for and these damnable proposals he has recommended under the guise of so-called civil rights . . . I'll tell you . . . the American people . . . had better wake up and *oppose* such a program because the next thing will be a totalitarian state in these United States!"

The crowd responded. Thurmond was saying in plain words exactly what they wanted to hear. The governor then revealed the Dixiecrats' campaign strategy: If they could win enough electoral votes to prevent any candidate from achieving a majority needed to capture the presidency—according to the rules spelled out in the Constitution—the election would be decided by the House of Representatives in a vote. By that time, the theory went, the Democrats could possibly have regained control of the House, and the southerners could put their man—Thurmond—straight up against Truman, whose approval rating had been plummeting for months.

"If we throw the election into the House of Representatives, we will hold the balance of power," Thurmond shouted. "[The South has been] stabbed in the back by an accidental President with his desire to win the support of a minority bloc [black voters]."

After Thurmond spoke, Frank Dixon, the former Alabama governor, took the floor. "In Philadelphia," Dixon shouted, "a definite decision was made to enforce Truman's plan for a social revolution in the south. You heard the deliberate adoption of a program meant to destroy us." With Truman's plan, Dixon charged, blacks could go to white schools, and sit on white buses. Truman aimed to "reduce us to the status of a mongrel, inferior race, mixed in blood, our Anglo-Saxon heritage a mockery."

The South was mobilizing, and a new pro-segregation movement was born that day in Birmingham. One attendee called it "a riotous rebel convention." For the most part, the crowd was made up of ordinary southern white men along with a few women, people who considered themselves American patriots who wanted to defend the American traditions they had known all their lives, and their parents had known all of *their* lives. They saw no reason why outsiders from the North should force them to change. There were also some militant extremists in the crowd, a lineup of the country's most hardline white supremacists, including J. B. Stoner, who had been pushed out of the Ku Klux Klan for being too extreme and would later be quoted saying Hitler was "too moderate," and Gerald L. K. Smith, a hardline anti-Semite and racist. (Smith's extremist views got him banned from future Dixiecrat events.)

The Dixiecrats put forth a series of anti–civil rights and anti-Truman proposals — a "declaration of principles" to protect Americans "against the onward march of totalitarian government."

"We stand for the segregation of the races and the integrity of each race," the Dixiecrat platform stated.

Another conference was scheduled for August for the official nomination of a new presidential candidate — Thurmond, whose running mate would be Fielding Wright, governor of Mississippi. When critics suggested to Thurmond that the civil rights program embraced in the current Democratic platform was not much different from Roosevelt's platform in 1944, Thurmond responded, "I agree, but Truman really means it."

Officially, the Dixiecrats called themselves the States' Rights Democratic Party. The federal government, they claimed, had no right to dictate how states would police themselves, what their voting laws should be, and how their social traditions should play out. Thurmond himself claimed in a conference call from the governor's mansion in Columbia that the States' Rights Party was "not interested one whit in the question of 'white supremacy.'" It was federal encroachment on the states that fueled the southern revolt, he said. But this was a transparent fiction. Thurmond's rhetoric continued to focus on segregation. Democratic congressman Sam Rayburn of Texas — who had been a longtime Speaker of the House and was a close friend of Harry Truman's — summed up the whole controversy before a group of fellow Texas politicians. "All your high-flown political vocabulary boils down to just three words," Rayburn said. "Nigger, nigger, nigger!"

The political anxiety and anger among whites in the South was now aimed at one man. "The president has gone too far," Thurmond told members of the South Carolina Democratic State Committee. "As far as I am concerned, I'm through with him."

On July 23, a week after the Democratic National Convention, Henry Wallace arrived in Philadelphia for the first-ever Progressive Party convention, amid a political firestorm. The Progressives were gathering in the same hall where Truman and Dewey had been nominated. Before the first gavel pounded, conventioneers were on edge.

Two days earlier, the Justice Department had arrested twelve members of the Communist Party USA, charging them with a plot to overthrow the federal government. Among them were party leaders Eugene Dennis and William Z. Foster. One of the twelve was arrested in Detroit, most of the others in New York City. Progressive Party members were furious, as the timing was clearly aimed to vilify their movement. The Communist Party USA put out a statement saying the organization had been the subject of a "monstrous frame-up."

"The American people can now see to what desperate provocations Truman is driven in an effort to win the election, by hook or crook," the Communist Party's statement read. "The reported indictment of the Communists is neatly timed to embarrass the new people's party now holding its founding convention in Philadelphia."

On the Progressive Party convention's opening day, Wallace greeted reporters in the ballroom at the Bellevue-Stratford, unaware he was walking into a trap. Staring down two hundred reporters, the candidate began his press conference by announcing he would refuse to repudiate the support of Communists.

"So you can save your breath," he said.

Martin Hayden of the *Detroit News* stunned the crowd with a very different question: "Have you ever repudiated the authenticity of the Guru letters?"

"A tense, terrible silence seeped into the room," one attendee recalled. The cogs in Wallace's mind turned. He knew that most of the people in the room knew about the guru letters through the lurid columns of Westbrook Pegler, who had been writing about them relentlessly. Attempting to steer the conversation from the subject of the letters, Wallace said, "I never discuss Westbrook Pegler."

A tall man with greased-back gray hair then stood up and spoke. "My name is Westbrook Pegler," he said. Again, a hush fell over the crowd. Pegler reiterated the guru letters question.

"I never engage in any discussions with Westbrook Pegler," Wallace said.

Another reporter asked the same question. The tension in the room increased as two hundred reporters watched Wallace hanging on a pin. Wallace said, "Nor will I engage in a discussion with a stooge of Westbrook Pegler."

This time, H. L. Mencken stood up — Mencken, the literary lion, the "sage of Baltimore," one of the most famous political writers of his time. "Mr. Wallace," Mencken said, "do you call me a stooge of Pegler? If you won't answer the question as to whether you wrote those letters, tell us, at least, the reason you won't answer it."

"Because it is not important."

But it was. When the Progressive Party opened its first convention, the biggest story in the newspapers the next day was the guru letters. "The American press had one of its finest hours today," wrote the Associated Press's Relman Morin, "in an astonishing news conference with Henry Wallace."

The convention carried on. By this time the Progressive Party's campaign had taken on the nickname Wallace had given it when he announced his candidacy seven months earlier: Gideon's Army, referring to the biblical story of Gideon, who led a small army in a decisive victory over the oppressive Midianites thousands of years earlier. It was an apt allegory for Wallace for obvious reasons, and also because it reflected his deep religious thinking. Gideon's Army turned out in force for him. The crowds packed the hall, with more outside. Folk singer Pete Seeger sang songs and played his banjo. In the crowd were the writers Norman Mailer and Lillian Hellman, the future US senator and presidential candidate George McGovern, and large numbers of war veterans and union leaders.

For the first time in history, a black man gave a keynote speech at a national political convention. Charles P. Howard, publisher of a black newspaper in Iowa, addressed the teeming crowds on opening night, pleading with voters to support cooperation with the USSR, and charging the Truman administration with fomenting "corruption . . . betrayal . . . murder." It was "Wallace or war," Howard said.

"What is at stake here is the very survival of Western civilization," he told the crowd.

Over the next days, the crowds poured on the love for the Wallace movement. W.E.B. Du Bois spoke. VP candidate Glen Taylor brought out his wife and kids and played a number on his banjo. The black entertainer Paul Robeson spoke and sang. Wallace campaign manager Beanie Baldwin told reporters that the convention was not just some flash-in-the-pan movement; it was the "birth of a new party soon to be the first party." Outside the arena, "Peace Caravans" lined streets, where Gideon's Army members banged peace drums and slept in tents on Philadelphia's cement sidewalks.

On the final night, the whole convention moved to nearby Shibe Park, home to the city's baseball team, the Philadelphia Athletics. Wallace and his running mate Taylor accepted the new party's nominations. Wallace whipped a crowd of thirty thousand into a frenzy. Caucasians and African Americans mixed freely, as did union workers and intellectuals. Young women danced in sundresses. Wallace told them all that, if he had been president, the Berlin crisis would never have happened.

"Berlin did not happen," Wallace said. "Berlin was caused." He summed up what he perceived to be happening before everyone's eyes that night: "This convention is going to mark a great turning point not only in the history of the New Party, but also in the history of the world." The Wallace platform supported desegregation of public schools, a nationalized health insurance program, equal rights for women, minimum wages for workers who currently did not qualify under law (such as farmworkers), immigration reform, statehood for Alaska and Hawaii, support for Israel, and the rights of Communists to express their views.

"To make that dream come true," Wallace said, "we shall rise above the pettiness of those who preach hate and factionalism, of those who think of themselves rather than the great cause they serve. All you who are within the sound of my voice tonight have been called to serve mightily in fulfilling the dream of the prophets and the founders of the American system."

Wallace fans responded with "almost fanatical enthusiasm," *New York Times* reporter James Hagerty recorded. Crowds chanted "We want Wallace!" and "One, two, three, four, we don't want another war." An organist struck up "Battle Hymn of the Republic."

Before the night was over, a *Time* reporter asked Henry Wallace why the Progressive Party's platform so closely resembled that of the Communist

Party. "I'd say they have a good platform," Wallace answered. "I would say that the Communists are the closest things to the early Christian martyrs." At that press conference, Wallace's running mate was asked the same question. Senator Taylor responded that he had renounced Communism, but would not renounce Communist votes.

"Nobody can stop them from voting for us," Taylor said, "if they want."

Despite the Westbrook Pegler debacle, Wallace's convention was a rousing success. A new candidate, a new political party, a stadium packed to the rafters to participate in the party's very first election convention—all of it came together quickly and unexpectedly. "It will remain a thing of awe to professional politicians that people paid hard cash to see a man baptize his own party," the Associated Press columnist Hal Boyle commented. "This was something new."

The Wallace campaign was flush with cash. Days earlier, a single donor—the philanthropist Anita McCormick Blaine of Chicago, an heir to the McCormick Reaping Machine Works fortune—had agreed to donate hundreds of thousands of dollars. Wallace wrote to thank her, explaining that the money would go toward campaign literature and radio time and for party organizations in every state.

When Gideon's Army dispersed from Philadelphia, the stage was set for a historic election. Voters now had four major candidates to choose from. The Democrats were split on the right (by the Dixiecrats) and the left (by the Progressives). Truman and Dewey, meanwhile, held similar positions on many major issues, but not all. Four campaigns were out of the starting block, charging in different directions, fueled by the base support of masses of people convinced that they were in the right and that their foes were in the wrong. The nation was divided as it had never been before, and America's identity hung in the balance.

PART IV

July–September 1948

The Campaigns

It will be the greatest campaign any President ever made. Win, lose, or draw, people will know where I stand.

—Harry Truman to his sister, Mary Jane, October 5, 1948

16

"A Profound Sense of What's Right and What's Wrong"

FOR THE ROUGHLY 150 MILLION Americans in the summer of 1948, the first postwar presidential election was a landmark like none other. Anyone over the age of ten years old could vividly recall what life had been like during the Great Depression and during a war that had killed some 60 million human beings worldwide. Now, three years after the war's end, a vast majority of Americans were seeing signs of prosperity, despite high prices on many consumer goods, and new innovations that pointed to a future where anything seemed possible — but only if humanity could keep World War III from destroying it all.

The economy of the United States had arguably never been so strong. Unemployment was just 3.6 percent. The construction industry built $7.7 billion worth of new homes in the first half of 1948 — a record high. Since the beginning of World War II, stock prices of railroad companies, utilities, and industrials had roughly doubled on average. While inflation continued to worry everyday consumers ("The prices of food products have surged upward to the highest level in history," according to a July 1948 report from Truman's Council of Economic Advisers), the fact remained that the economy was robust and times were good.

For years, due to wartime rationing, consumer products of all kinds had been difficult to obtain. Now a new and uniquely American consumerism was emerging. Big supermarket chains like A&P and Safeway were opening superstores in cities and towns, while department stores like Marshall Field's and Macy's — the largest department store, which sold over $170 million worth of retail in 1947 — were reaping profits. The most popular whiskey was Seagram's, the most popular cigarette was Lucky Strike, and the most popular car brand was Chevrolet. The appetite for these products seemed insatiable.

Americans were particularly car crazy in the summer of 1948, and motorcycle crazy too. Ford unveiled the first all-new postwar model, the 1949 Ford, at the Waldorf-Astoria Hotel in New York on June 8, 1948. More than a hundred thousand orders came in during the next thirty days. Cadillac debuted the first tailfin on its 1948 line. A motorsport impresario by the name of "Big Bill" France founded a series of stock car races called NASCAR. In Southern California, a group of motorcycle fanatics founded a club called the Hells Angels.

The year 1948 saw the first flying machine to break the sound barrier, at an altitude of over seventy thousand feet — a jet called the Bell X-1 in the hands of test pilot Chuck Yeager. An inventor named Edwin H. Land had debuted the first instant camera — the Polaroid — which would go on sale later in 1948. Bell Laboratories unveiled the first transistor radios. The first bikini bathing suit appeared, named for the atomic tests at Bikini Atoll. The first national television nightly news program aired — *Camel Newsreel Theater,* named for its sponsor, Camel cigarettes, the nation's second-most-popular brand of smokes. Americans were fascinated with flying saucers. Babies were being born in record numbers. The professor of entomology and zoology Alfred Kinsey released his study *Sexual Behavior in the Human Male,* which "stirred up the greatest biological commotion in the U.S. since Darwin," noted the August 2 issue of *Life,* the nation's most popular magazine.

Offices were full of new inventions, like the Ediphone voice-recognition dictation device and the Remington Rand electric adding machine. Office buildings in some big cities had elevators that were no longer controlled by a man in a tie who stood inside the elevator car all day working the up/down lever, thanks to the Otis Electronic Signal Control. Explained *Business Week* in its July 10 issue: "You can now summon an elevator by simply *touching* a plastic arrow in the landing fixture."

The most exciting new technology was, of course, the television. The president of RCA, David Sarnoff, declared in the summer of 1948 that the television was going to change American life as much as Henry Ford's Model T had. "As television grows on an international scale," Sarnoff wrote that summer, "it will rove the globe for programs and literally make all the world a stage, as Shakespeare envisaged it." The applications of television cameras seemed limitless. Cameras could be mounted on the noses of "robot rockets," Sarnoff claimed. TV could also be the greatest educational tool ever known.

Television's first big test would be the 1948 election. For the first time, Americans would get to see their candidates in real time. They would be able to see famous political writers speaking, rather than just the words that thumped out of their typewriters, making the new media instantly and immeasurably powerful. Ultimately, television would be able to capture the human experience of political victory and defeat as Americans had never seen it before.

The Truman campaign began in earnest with a meeting on the night of July 22, at 8 p.m., in the State Dining Room of the White House. Funneling in was a motley crew of Truman friends—hardly a big hitter among them. As the former secretary of the Interior Harold Ickes described this bunch: "The political figures who surround the President . . . could all be blown out by one sure breath, as are candles on a birthday cake."

Here was Attorney General Tom Clark of Texas—a jowly, cigar-wielding Dallas lawman. Here were the young liberal political advisers Oscar Ewing and Oscar Chapman. And here was Matt Connelly of Massachusetts, Truman's appointments secretary. None of these men had ever held any major elected political office. The only man with any bona fide clout was Judge Sam Rosenman, the fedora-sporting New Dealer and speechwriter.

The first purpose of this meeting was the subject that drives all political campaigns: money. Who would lead the finance committee? Where would funding for the campaign come from? Truman's daughter would later recall, "The lack of money in the party war chest was literally terrifying." Five days before this July 22 meeting, the Republican National Committee had released a compendium of quotes from high-profile Democratic figures, who were all saying that Truman could not win, and this list was going to make raising money exceedingly difficult.

Former New Jersey governor Charles Edison: "Our governmental house is choked with litter and rubbish. It needs a thorough housecleaning from top to bottom." Leon Henderson, chairman of the Americans for Democratic Action: "To my second-hand knowledge he [Truman] has been advised by friends that he can't win and that he will be charged with the disintegration of the Democratic Party." Congressman Mendel Rivers of South Carolina: "Harry Truman is a dead bird." Every one of these quotes came from the lips of a Democrat and landed in the ears of potential donors. How could the party raise money if insiders and would-be donors felt that the candidate had no chance?

Even in Truman's own Jackson County, Missouri, voters had turned against him. "My brother Vivian . . . told me all about the situation politically in my home county," Truman recorded in his diary. "I don't see how it can be so bad—but it is." According to the latest numbers from pollster Elmo Roper, 64 percent of the American electorate believed Thomas Dewey would be the next president, compared with 27 percent for Truman.

In late June, one Democratic Party donor—Thomas Buchanan of the Buchanan, Wallover & Barrickman law firm in Beaver, Pennsylvania—had sent in a $100 check with a letter that put the Democrats' position into perspective. "I would like to take this opportunity to state that the party is in bad condition, particularly because we have a weak candidate and no clear policy which we can pursue . . . It is not easy to contribute to a campaign which under those circumstances has no possible chance of success."

In the White House on the night of July 22, the gloom was palpable. When asked who might serve as finance chairman, no one stepped forward. Truman knew morale among his staff was ebbing fast. It would be an uphill battle to establish his legitimacy, given that he had not been elected to the presidency in the first place. "The greatest ambition Harry Truman had was to get elected in his own right," Clark Clifford later recalled. "Every president who comes in as Vice President has this feeling. Truman felt it especially because he had been so criticized and deprecated."

The president decided it was time for a pep talk. "We are going to win," he told those assembled in the White House that night. "I expect to travel all over the country and talk at every whistle-stop"—alluding to his successful speaking tour back in June. "We are going to be on the road most of the time from Labor Day to the end of the campaign. It's going to be tough on everybody, but that's the way it's got to be. I know I can take it. I'm only afraid that I'll kill some of my staff—and I like you all very much and I don't want to do that."

Around this time, Truman met with members of the Democratic National Committee in the East Room of the White House, to talk over the campaign itinerary.

"The situation isn't as bad as the newspapers make it look," Truman said. "It is my intention to go into every county in the United States if possible. I want to see the people. This is the only way to answer the Republicans."

Outwardly, Truman was ever the optimist. But he knew the challenges he faced. "It's all so futile," he wrote his sister. "Dewey, Wallace, the cockeyed Southerners, and then if I win—which I'm afraid I will—I'll probably have a Russian war on my hands. Two wars are enough for anybody and I've had two [in the European and Pacific theaters of World War II]."

His goal was to see the people, to explore the places where candidates typically did not go, and to talk to voters face-to-face from the back of a train car. The more places he ventured, the more people he could attempt to woo, and in the process, he could share the magic of the American presidency with everyday Americans. "I'm going to make it a rip-snorting, back-platform campaign to what Taft calls all the whistle stops, but I call them the heart of America," he was quoted as saying in the summer of 1948. "When they count the whistle stops' votes, Taft may be in for a big surprise. I think the whistle stops will make the difference between victory and defeat."

• • •

Campaigns are about ideas — but also about the machinery to communicate them. Truman had surrounded himself with a ragtag group of advisers who came mostly from legal backgrounds and were like-minded in their desire to continue the legacy of FDR's New Deal. For months, these advisers had formed a think tank that met on Monday nights in the apartment of Oscar Ewing in the Wardman Park Hotel in Washington, DC. Ewing was a Harvard Law man and, until a year earlier, vice chairman of the Democratic National Committee, and his group consisted of seven or eight men, all with different areas of expertise, from civil rights to economics.

"We would meet at six o'clock for dinner," Ewing recalled. "My secretary would call all the members beforehand to find out if they were coming and what they would like for dinner." On most nights, steak and potatoes were on the menu. "I was their link with the President," recorded Clark Clifford, the rising star of the bunch.

In 1948 no one had the president's ear on political issues as much as Clifford, whose circuitous path to the White House was as surprising as Truman's. Clifford had been a trial lawyer in St. Louis when he joined the US Navy during the war. A friend of his, James K. Vardaman Jr., was a naval aide to Truman and was going on leave. Clifford ended up filling in for Vardaman at the end of the war, just in time to experience the atomic bombings of Japan from within the White House inner circle. Clifford had no political background but immediately emerged as a sharp thinker and a marvelous communicator, and with his handsome face and well-tailored pinstripe suits he was straight out of central casting. By 1947, newspapers were calling Clifford the "White House Wonder" and the "Capital's Golden Boy."

Within days of Truman's nomination, the Oscar Ewing group — via Clifford — began to funnel its ideas directly into the Oval Office. These ideas were intended to supplement the policies that Truman had been pushing since the end of World War II. The ultimate thrust would be FDR-driven progressive ideology, with the recognition that a reactionary return to 1920s conservatism would be disastrous in a country that had been newly reborn after the war.

As for organization, the Democratic National Committee moved into new headquarters in New York City a week after the Philadelphia convention. The Republicans had their headquarters in the capital city. The Democrats preferred New York — the biggest transportation hub, home to the advertising industry, and an important media base.

Starting Monday, July 26, movers hauled desks, telephones, typewriters, and teletype machines into a fifty-room office on the Biltmore Hotel's fourth floor, atop Grand Central Terminal on Forty-Second Street. Senator Howard McGrath of Rhode Island was a rookie boss of the Democratic National Committee, while the office would be managed by Neale Roach, who had been the chief organizer of the Democratic National Convention. From the get-go, Roach could see that spirit was lacking in the new headquarters. "Every morning when I would go into the office," he recalled, "I would notice that these girls on the reception desk looked like they didn't even have as much pep as somebody you would meet at a morgue. I got worried about it, because the impression was just one of defeat all the way through."

"The pressure was increasingly heavy," recalled the national committee's publicist Jack Redding, who would practically live among the thundering typewriters and telephones in the Biltmore offices in the months before the election. "Many days I didn't leave the building, eating my meals either in the [hotel] restaurant or at my desk . . . I began to lose weight, as well as sleep, and developed a fine set of dark circles under my eyes."

The Democratic National Committee's job was to map out the political territory, identify and cultivate influencers in every county in the country, and raise the funds necessary to conduct the candidate's national campaign. "Meetings were held at the White House at least once a week, sometimes three or four times a week," recalled Redding. "The White House meetings were concerned with campaign strategy."

One day at the Biltmore headquarters, Senator McGrath was speaking on the telephone while a potential campaign-finance chairman sat outside waiting to meet with him. This was Louis A. Johnson of Virginia — an attorney and former assistant secretary of war. By the time McGrath could finish his phone call and summon his guest, Johnson had grown ornery. He stormed in and halted in military style (he had served as a colonel in World War I).

"Young man," Johnson said to Senator McGrath, who was twelve years Johnson's junior, "I didn't come here to cool my heels waiting for you. I have important things to do. I came here to help the Democratic Party. I have nothing further to say to you. Good-bye!"

As Johnson headed for the door, McGrath yelled, "Come back! Come back here!" When Johnson paused, McGrath said, "I don't know what you're shouting about, Colonel, but if you think I insulted you, let me tell you something. I had Jake More, the state chairman of Iowa, on the telephone when you were announced. Ed Kelly [former Democratic mayor] of Chicago was waiting for me on another line. I don't know what you think, but in my opinion, I could not fail to complete those calls. I want you to know I'm working for the Democratic Party, too; and I'm not getting a salary to do it."

Johnson pivoted and took a seat. Soon it was settled: Johnson would be the new finance chairman for the Democratic National Committee. A staunch believer in Truman's approach to military expenditures — to keep the country strong while holding the line on spending, so federal funds would be available for other programs — Johnson had his own personal desire to see Truman succeed. He wanted to be the next secretary of defense. If he could help win Truman the election, he hoped the president would give him the job. Johnson's fund-raising would be crucial to the campaign's success, and to his own ambitions.

Along with organization and money, knowledge was key — knowledge of the communities where Truman would be campaigning, knowledge of how campaign issues affected localities across the country. Earlier in the year, the Oscar Ewing think tank came up with the idea to create a campaign research unit to unearth facts, figures, trends, and local issues that people cared about, in every town where the president would be speaking. One member of the Ewing group, David Morse, suggested an old friend named Bill Batt to head up the unit. Batt was in business in Philadelphia and was looking to get into government work, with an eye toward a future congressional run.

Bespectacled and brilliant, William Batt came to Washington, where he met with Senator McGrath and Clark Clifford. "They asked me to go up in a back room and work up a budget, which I did and it came to about eighty thousand dollars, if I remember correctly, to run an operation of the size they wanted for the . . . months between then and the election day."

Batt found office space on Dupont Circle near the Hamilton National Bank building. It was "miserably noisy," Batt recalled, as it was next to a construction site where the city was digging a roadway underpass. But it was affordable. Batt began recruiting. "We were looking for generalists," he recorded. "We were looking for exceedingly knowledgeable guys who knew the issues before the country and who were also good at research and were good at writing."

For a deputy, Batt hired Dr. Johannes Hoeber, a European-born political scientist who had been working for the city of Philadelphia. "We had been told right at the beginning that this Research Division was to operate in the strictest anonymity," noted Hoeber, "that even its existence should not be publicly known, mainly for reasons of security."

For living space, the researchers were given rooms at the national club of the American Veterans Committee on New Hampshire Avenue, around the corner from their office space. From July on, remembered Hoeber, "we lived, literally, a rather monastic life, locked up in this men's club on the third floor, almost dormitory style rooms . . . We were on tap 24 hours a day, and when we went from our office around the corner to the AVC club where we lived, to eat our dinner, the work just went on."

All of Truman's campaign advisers were thrilled with his performance at the Democratic National Convention. As Bill Batt put it in a July 22 memo to Clark Clifford, Truman had to show the American people "his courage, his coolness, his determination, his sincerity, and his fighting spirit — qualities he demonstrated in his magnificent acceptance speech at Philadelphia." That set a tone, they believed, that the president had to continue going forward — bold, fearless, and relentlessly aggressive.

• • •

Soon after the Philadelphia convention, Truman received a visit from Oscar Ewing. The Democrats had adopted a strong civil rights platform in Philadelphia, Ewing said. There was no turning back. He argued that Truman had to act now, to take the civil rights program to its logical next step. If he did not, Ewing intimated, voters would see him as waffling on the issue. If civil rights was to be an anchor of the Democratic platform, why wait?

Truman inquired exactly what Ewing was suggesting, and Ewing dropped a bombshell: The president should desegregate the military by executive order. If Truman asked the Eightieth Congress for legislation, he could lose, and that would be that. Nothing could make a statement about the future of race in America more than desegregation of the military. And by doing so by executive order, Truman could steer the black vote to the Democratic Party, perhaps for years to come.

The president considered the matter. It would be a dangerous move. The Southern Democrats had bolted the party, and this would be like slamming the door on them on their way out. How would America's military leaders respond? And the soldiers themselves? Yet it was the right thing to do, Truman believed. He decided to push forward, and he handed the mechanics of the job over to Clark Clifford, who handed it over to his assistant, George Elsey.

Normally, a White House staffer named Philleo Nash handled such matters, as Nash was the president's special assistant on minority affairs. Elsey went hunting through the executive mansion for Nash, only to find that he was on vacation.

"My gosh," Elsey told Clifford, "Nash is away and he's the only one that knows anything about this. This is his bailiwick — it's his department."

Deep in northern Wisconsin, Nash was on a fishing trip when he got a phone call at his hotel summoning him back to Washington. "[I] jumped on the night train," he recalled, "and was in Washington the next day." He arrived on a Friday, and by Sunday night, two executive orders were drafted and finalized. Truman was ready to pull the trigger.

On the morning of Monday, July 26, reporters were busy out in the field as the first day of the emergency special session of Congress began. But news of two executive orders quickly spread across Washington and beyond. Truman's Executive Order 9980 created a system of "fair employment practices" within the federal government, "without discrimination because of race, color, religion, or national origin." Simply stated: Any American who paid taxes would be as eligible for federal employment as any other, no matter the color of their skin.

The second executive order — 9981 — was the historic one. With the swipe of a pen, Truman desegregated the United States military. The move was entirely unexpected; it "caught almost everyone off guard," recalled Clark Clifford.

Soon after issuing the presidential decrees, Truman appeared before Congress to talk about his plan for civil rights legislation. He got a cool reception; some members of Congress refused to stand when he entered the Capitol. All he wanted to fight for, Truman said, was the ideals expressed in the US Constitution. "I believe that it is necessary to enact the laws that I have recommended in order to make the guarantees of the Constitution real and vital," he said.

The question on everyone's lips was about Truman's motivation. Was he a man on a moral crusade? Or was he after votes? Or both? The president knew how unlikely it was for him to be making such earthshaking decisions in the first place. He could easily recall his life before politics. Now he was the central figure of dramas that went to the core of what it meant to be an American. "I think he was motivated by a profound sense of what's right and what's wrong," observed Truman speechwriter Charlie Murphy, "and not by politics." Truman was from a family that sided with the Confederacy during the Civil War, from a family that had been slave owners, from a family where the word *nigger* could be spoken at the dinner table. "All I can say is that I'm sure this is what he thought was right," Murphy said of Executive Order 9981. "His views on the subject, as you may know, did not agree with those of other members of his family, including his mother."

Shock spread through the offices of members of Congress from the South, who immediately began planning a filibuster on the Senate floor. The talkathon began on July 29, with twenty-one southern senators, one after the next, teeing off on Harry Truman, beginning with John C. Stennis, a Jim Crow zealot from Mississippi. The filibuster got nowhere, but it proved that the Southern Democrats were going to continue to turn up the heat on Truman, right up until Election Day.

Roughly two weeks later, the Eightieth Congress's special "Turnip Day" session ended, with almost no new legislation on the books. Congress approved a $65 million loan to create a permanent home for the United Nations, in Manhattan. Two bills reached the president's desk—one on housing, one on inflation. While Truman called them inadequate, he signed them both, and the fight over the special session's legacy began. At the conclusion of the session, a reporter asked the president, "Would you say it was a do nothing session, Mr. President?"

"I think that's a good name for the 80th Congress."

The name stuck, and Truman would be hammering on the "do-nothing Congress" for the next three months.

Truman later admitted that he knew Congress would get almost nothing accomplished in the special session. "I felt justified in calling the Congress back to Washington to prove to the people whether the Republican platform really meant anything or not," he wrote in his memoirs. Republicans attacked the administration, saying the special session was a waste of money for American taxpayers. Republican senator Styles Bridges called Truman "a petulant Ajax from the Ozarks." One columnist, Fred Othman of the *Atlanta Constitution,* described the session as "the most expensive advertising campaign in the history of the vegetable business," as Americans were now desirous of turnips as never before.

"They sure are in a stew and mad as wet hens," Truman wrote Bess in Missouri, regarding the "'Hypercrits' known as Republicans." "If I can make them madder, maybe they'll do the job the old gods used to put on the Greeks and Romans . . . My best to everybody, kiss my baby [Margaret], lots of love to you, Harry."

17

"What Exciting Times You Are Having!"

THE MONTH OF JULY FOUND Thomas Dewey at Dapplemere, his fifty-two-cow dairy farm outside Pawling, New York. Dewey had owned this farm since 1938 (he'd put $3,000 down on the $30,000 property). He roamed the rolling hills with his two boys, making campfires and cooking eggs over open flames in a cast-iron skillet. "I am having a 'holiday' which consists of about two-thirds work at my farm," Dewey wrote one friend. Meanwhile his press team made the most of his vacation, putting out statements on the candidate's farming expertise, about the Dewey farm's "principal innovations in artificial insemination and pen stabling," on how the bacteria count in the milk at Dewey's farm was "the lowest of any of the dairy farms in the State." Dewey needed to keep farmers voting Republican, as they traditionally did.

At the same time, the candidate was experiencing a groundswell of support. Fan mail was pouring in; Dewey's team counted eleven thousand letters addressed directly to the candidate in the two weeks following the Republican National Convention. "What exciting times you are having!" wrote Winston Churchill, who sent Dewey a copy of his new book, *The Gathering Storm,* the first volume of his memoirs. Federal legislators hoping to curry favor in the new administration wrote the governor obsequious letters promising loyalty. But the real surge was coming from everyday Americans, eager to be part of Dewey's historic ascendancy.

The Metalart Corporation of Milwaukee sent Dewey a "Dewey broom" as a campaign prop suggestion ("Help sweep the nation clean with the new GOP victory broom"). The D. A. Pachter Company of Chicago offered to make a Dewey presidential coin ("We believe that it will offer tremendous excitement"). Small-time songwriters from all over the country sent the candidate campaign songs they had written: "Dewey Will Do It: Marching On to Victory," by Tom R. Hazard of Cine-Mart Music Publishers; "The Grand Old Party," by Perry Alexander and Woody Frisino of Dubonnet Music Publishing. There was "Tom Dewey for President" from the Eighth South Republican Club of West Forty-Eighth Street in New York City:

Here's a name which brings fame to the glory of All America and her cause
For Thomas Dewey is truly the symbol of great government and its laws.

As Dewey's vacation neared its end, he gathered his team at his farm to plan what they hoped to be the smartest, most data-rich presidential campaign that had ever been run. The team consisted mostly of the figures who had orchestrated Dewey's 1944 campaign: Herbert Brownell, Long Island Republican operative J. Russell Sprague, New York Republican state committee boss Edwin Jaeckle, and Elliott Bell, a former *New York Times* financial reporter and current New York State superintendent of banking, who had served as an economic adviser to the governor on numerous occasions.

In August, Dewey headed back to Albany, and on the eleventh, the Republican National Committee's chairman, Pennsylvania congressman Hugh Scott, arrived at the governor's mansion to report on a twenty-eight-state tour of the nation Scott had just completed. Scott had interviewed Republican officials and precinct bosses from all over and all had agreed, he reported, that Dewey should run the kind of tough-as-nails attack-dog campaign that he had run against Roosevelt four years earlier. He should gun for Truman the way he gunned for mob bosses like Lucky Luciano back in the day.

"Well," Dewey said, "this will come as news to you, then. That's not what we are going to do."

The way Dewey saw it, he had this election won; all he had to do was refrain from making mistakes or painting himself as reactionary. Dewey's closest advisers were recommending he run a careful campaign, and not rock the boat. They were of the opinion that the more commitments Dewey made as a candidate, the more his hands would be tied as president.

As committee chairman, Scott was alarmed. The party faithful, he said, expected Dewey to give the kind of ruthless attack speeches they believed had been most effective in 1944. Scott singled out Dewey's speech in Oklahoma City, in which the governor had gone after FDR in one of the most vitriolic addresses anyone could remember. Calling the president a blatant demagogue, Dewey had accused FDR of distortions of truth "which not even Goebbels would have attempted." This was a shocker — to compare the American president to Hitler's propaganda chief, in the midst of a murderous war. Four years had passed since that speech and Americans could still be heard talking about it.

"That's the worst speech I ever made," Dewey told Scott. "I will not get down into the gutter with that fellow" — meaning Truman.

Soon after Dewey's meeting with Scott, the conservative broadcaster Fulton Lewis Jr. brought up the same speech with the candidate.

"This campaign will be different from 1944," Dewey said.

"That Oklahoma City speech —"

"Exactly," Dewey said, interrupting Lewis. "It was all wrong. I was attacking the dignity of the office I was seeking."

"I didn't think so. I thought it was great. I thought you were attacking the dignity of the man who was seeking the office."

Dewey did not want to hear it. He had run an attack campaign for governor in 1938 and had lost. He had run an attack campaign for president in 1944 and had lost. His two campaigns for governor in 1942 and 1946 were different; Dewey had put forth an image of composed leadership and a focus on the job at hand. In those two campaigns, he had won. That was the kind of campaign he wanted to run in 1948, and his wife, Frances, strongly supported him on the matter. Polling data had confirmed the shrewdness of this strategy, revealing that, when Robert Taft and other Republican figures from the Eightieth Congress attacked Truman, the president only benefited. The public sympathized with him.

On the sixteenth and seventeenth of August, Dewey welcomed his campaign staff and VP candidate Earl Warren to the Albany mansion for two days of meetings to map out the strategy. Reporters were invited into jam-packed press conferences, throwing questions at the governor while Warren looked on quietly.

"Can you tell us when you start [the campaign]?" asked Earl Behrens of the *San Francisco Chronicle.*

"No definite date," Dewey said.

"How much of the Communist program at home and abroad will be brought up?" asked another reporter.

"I will tell you better on November 2nd," said Dewey.

The GOP candidate was no longer acting like a man running for president, but one who already *was* president.

In July Dewey held a press conference about the Berlin Blockade — how war could result from "the slightest mismanagement" of the crisis — and revealed that he was conducting daily phone conversations with his foreign affairs adviser John Foster Dulles, who was preparing to head to Paris to participate in United Nations negotiations on Palestine, Berlin, and more. It was as if Dewey was already running his own State Department. He had Senator Arthur Vandenberg, head of the Senate Foreign Relations Committee, give testimony on camera as to the New York governor's "thoroughly competent grasp of all our major foreign problems."

There was a focus on public appearances to make Dewey look presidential. In August he headed up a group of honorary pallbearers at the funeral of New York Yankees star Babe Ruth, before a crowd of seventy-five thousand standing in the rain outside St. Patrick's Cathedral in Manhattan. At the Albany governor's mansion, he invited motion-picture cameras to capture him in the mahogany-paneled Executive Chamber, speaking to his advisers. The footage could easily be mistaken for a man already in the Oval Office.

And always, there was the driving message of Dewey's success managing the Empire State, a state bigger than many countries, with a far more disparate populace than existed anywhere else on earth. State-built convalescent centers for wounded veterans, state-subsidized housing for more than sixty thousand people, a scholarly department set up at Cornell University to study labor-management relations in an effort to find solutions to labor strikes before they occurred—all of this was part of the Dewey legacy, a legacy his publicity managers were conveying to Americans via all manner of communications.

Behind the scenes his staff was busy setting up the itinerary for his cross-country campaign tour and delving into statistical algorithms in hopes of finding every advantage they could over Harry Truman. Dewey's campaign had identified that a total of seven voting districts in the 1946 midterm elections had swayed by the tiniest margin of 50 to 50.9 percent between Republican and Democrat, allowing them to funnel resources into those districts (two of them were in Truman's home state of Missouri). They knew that ten additional districts had been swayed by the slightly larger margin of 51 to 51.9 percent (there were also two in Missouri).

Dewey asked Brownell to begin courting celebrity figures from theater, literature, and the arts, the biggest names who could appear with Dewey when he arrived in Los Angeles to speak at the Hollywood Bowl in mid-September. "Why shouldn't we have some people, smart organizers, devote their full time to doing this and doing it well?" Dewey wrote Brownell on August 23. It was "a whale of an idea," Dewey noted.

An even bigger one, however, was *The Dewey Story*. Campaign staff came up with a plan to make Dewey a Hollywood star himself; they hired Louis de Rochemont—writer and producer for the popular newsreel series *The March of Time*—to produce a short movie on Dewey. The campaign budgeted production costs of $35,000, plus additional money to pay for prints. De Rochemont promised to finish *The Dewey Story* in time to show it in theaters before feature films during the final two weeks leading up to November 2.

At the same time, executives from the massive Madison Avenue advertising firm Batten, Barton, Durstine & Osborn reached out to all five major pollsters to interview them on their methods, as polls tended to get enormous publicity and were highly influential, especially to undecided voters. The Dewey team was creating the first-ever in-house polling unit. Four of these pollsters responded to questions about their process, and transcripts of these conversations were sent to Herbert Brownell at Dewey headquarters in Washington. Among the five major pollsters, only George Gallup refused to do the interview, but he did offer this statement: "Why does the Republican Committee want to spend any money? The results are a foregone conclusion."

Truman was set to begin his campaigning in Detroit over Labor Day weekend, with a speech that would court organized labor. Dewey's staff decided to wait and kick off the GOP campaign two weeks later. Instead of rebutting Truman himself in Detroit, Dewey was going to send a representative, and he chose Harold Stassen of Minnesota. When the phone call came in to Stassen from the Dewey campaign, Stassen was surprised.

"Why doesn't Dewey answer Truman?" he asked.

"The Governor doesn't want to start his campaign for another two weeks," a Dewey aide answered.

Later Stassen's aide Vic Johnston took a call from Dewey himself. Johnston reiterated the Stassen camp's surprise at the request to have Stassen make the rebuttal to Truman in Detroit. Wasn't there animosity between the Stassen and Dewey camps, following their clash in the primaries and at the national convention in Philadelphia?

"I'm the man who beat you in Wisconsin," Johnston said, as he had managed Stassen's Wisconsin primary campaign.

"That's exactly why I want you," Dewey answered.

18

"As for Me, I Intend to Fight!"

ON JULY 31, STROM THURMOND headed up the first official election-season States' Rights Democratic Party rally, at a watermelon festival in Cherryville, North Carolina. Some five thousand people turned out on an uncomfortably humid day. Tucked deep into a rural backwater, Cherryville was home to cotton mills, farms, and old-school southern sentiment, a climate in which Thurmond's message would hit home.

If the civil rights program of the president is enforced, Thurmond rallied his crowd, "the results in civil strife may be horrible beyond imagination. Lawlessness will be rampant. Chaos will prevail. Our streets will be unsafe. And there will be the greatest breakdown of law enforcement in the history of the nation. Let us tell them that in the South the intermingling of the races in our homes, in our schools and in our theaters is impractical and impossible . . . I did not risk my life on the beaches of Normandy to come back to this country, and sit idly by, while a bunch of hack politicians whittles away your heritage and mine. As for me, I intend to fight!"

Thurmond was determined to position his campaign as the last stand against a constitutional crisis. Federal encroachment on states' ability to make their own laws would cause "a virtual revolution in the Southern States," he said in Cherryville. As Thurmond put it in a letter to Governor Dewey: "The South's fight is not being waged on the theory of white supremacy but on

State sovereignty," an issue of "vital importance not only to the South but to the entire Nation." Still, it was the threat to segregation that drew a voracious response from Thurmond's listeners.

Many were asking: Who was this man, Strom Thurmond, who was so suddenly making a name for himself on the national scene? Americans came to recognize Thurmond, with his broad, toothy smile and his shiny bald head, from media coverage of the southern governor. Readers of newspapers and magazines learned that he was newly married to a former Miss South Carolina — Jean Crouch, who at twenty-two was roughly half his age. To prove his athletic prowess, he had posed standing on his head for a *Life* magazine photographer on his wedding day, less than a year earlier.

He became known in the inner sanctum of American intelligence too; the special agent in charge of the Savannah, Georgia, FBI office, E. D. Mason, described the governor's personality in detail in a 1948 memo to the FBI chief in Washington, J. Edgar Hoover. "Governor Thurmond is a thoroughly honest, reliable man," wrote the special agent. "He cannot be bought financially. He is slightly sluggish mentally . . . The Governor has admitted that he did not aspire to the leadership of the States Rights Party, but that it was virtually thrust upon him . . . His political future in the State of South Carolina seems somewhat assured as evidenced by almost unanimous acclamation of his States Rights Program, which seems to be a result of resentment on the part of South Carolinians to interference by outside interests in what they consider purely local problems."

The more Americans learned about Thurmond, the more it became clear that the history of segregation in the South could be illuminated through the family saga of this one man.

Thurmond was born the same year as Thomas Dewey — 1902. But he came from a place so far removed from the Michigan where Dewey grew up, it might as well have been a different country. Thurmond hailed from Edgefield, South Carolina, and his political story begins with his father, John Thurmond, who was three years old when the Civil War ended in 1865. The Republican president Abraham Lincoln and his Union army had won; slavery was to be abolished, and newly freed male slaves in the South were to be granted civil rights, including the right to vote. To ensure that these laws were respected in places like South Carolina, Union troops remained during the period of Reconstruction, led federally by a Republican administration.

In the 1870s, a paramilitary group called the Red Shirts, whose members were spread out across the southern United States, and especially in South Carolina and Mississippi, began a campaign to restore white supremacy, to destroy the Reconstruction, and to put the Democratic Party back in power. In Edgefield, a prominent Democrat and Red Shirt leader named Benjamin Tillman became a leader of a white supremacist movement. Like many white politicians in the South, Tillman—who had lost an eye to illness as a teenager—viewed the Republican Party as an instrument of northern oppression. Tillman's white supremacist views matched those of thousands of white people living in the South at the time, and his voice became their voice. "The struggle in which we were engaged meant more than life or death," he said of the Red Shirt campaign to reestablish white rule in 1876. "It involved everything we held dear, Anglo-Saxon civilization included."

Key to the traditions of white supremacy was the suppression of the black vote, and the black vote at the time was overwhelmingly for the Republican Party (the party of Lincoln). The paramilitary wing of the Democratic Party in South Carolina created a "Plan of the Campaign" to prevent blacks from exercising their right to vote. "Every Democrat must feel honor bound to control the vote of at least one negro," the plan read in part, "by intimidation, purchase, keeping him away or as each individual may determine how he may best accomplish it."

The year the Red Shirt movement crystallized, the nation saw one of its most controversial presidential elections, and one that would have a profound effect on the racial and political identity of both the South and the Thurmond family. The election was so close it became a matter of bitter dispute. The Republican Rutherford B. Hayes of Ohio trailed the Democrat Samuel J. Tilden of New York by nineteen electoral votes, but the results in Florida, Louisiana, and South Carolina were unclear. Both sides claimed victory, leading to a crisis in leadership. Congress created an electoral commission to solve the problem, made up of members of the Senate, the House, and the Supreme Court. Ultimately, a deal was struck: All of the disputed electoral votes from these three southern states were given to the Republican Hayes, who won the presidency 185–184, and in exchange, Hayes agreed to withdraw the federal troops occupying the South, thus ending the period of Reconstruction.

The so-called Compromise of 1877 had two major consequences: (1) White supremacy returned to the South, and (2) politically, the Democratic Party controlled the South. The South became a single-party system—the so-called Solid South, right up until 1948 and the Dixiecrat revolt. White politicians created laws that made it difficult or impossible for black Americans to vote in many southern states, and the federal government left lawmaking to the lawmakers in these states.

Meanwhile, riding on the coattails of the Compromise of 1877, "Pitchfork" Benjamin Tillman cemented his political power, ultimately becoming governor of South Carolina. His personal lawyer was Strom Thurmond's father, John Thurmond.

John Thurmond had designs on a political career himself. One day five years before Strom was born, John Thurmond got in an argument over a political appointment, and he shot and killed a man named Willie Harris. A jury acquitted him of murder, determining that he had acted in self-defense, and that the victim was raging drunk at the time. However, the killing derailed Thurmond's political career. Strom would grow up to achieve the political stardom that was denied his father. "He was my idol," Strom later said. "I tried to imitate him as much as I could."

Strom Thurmond was raised in a society in which segregation and white supremacy were the unquestioned norm. He was six years old when he experienced his first political handshake. His father took him via horse and buggy to meet Ben Tillman—who was by this time a sixty-one-year-old United States senator. When the Thurmonds reached Tillman's farm, the one-eyed senator greeted the boy.

"What do you want?" Tillman asked.

"I want to shake your hand," young Strom Thurmond said.

The senator reached out his hand and Strom grabbed it, then stood awkwardly holding hands with the old man.

"You said you wanted to shake," Tillman said. "Why the hell don't you shake?"

As Thurmond later recalled, "I shook and I shook, and I've been shaking ever since."

Thurmond attended Clemson College (now University) in his home state, then worked as a teacher and an athletic coach. He lived at home, and among the servants at the family's estate was a young black woman named Carrie Butler. Around the time that Butler, just sixteen years old, gave birth to a baby girl she named Essie Mae, Strom Thurmond left his post in Edgefield to work for a real estate firm in Virginia.

Essie Mae was, in fact, Thurmond's daughter, and she would remain a highly guarded secret for the rest of Thurmond's life.

By the time he returned to South Carolina, Essie Mae had been shuttled off to be raised by black relatives in Pennsylvania. Thurmond, meanwhile, began to climb in stature, becoming Edgefield County's superintendent of schools in 1928, then a state senator four years later. The year Thurmond was elected to the South Carolina legislature, FDR won 98 percent of the state's vote; such was the power of the Democratic Party's Solid South, of which Strom Thurmond was a member. The rules of white supremacy were well cemented in the state, and Strom followed the racial ideology of his father. Whites and blacks kept separate establishments, neighborhoods, and public schools. African Americans were prevented from voting.

When the Japanese attacked Pearl Harbor on December 7, 1941, Thurmond took a leave of absence to join the US Army. During the D-day landings in Normandy in 1944, he was aboard an invasion glider when fleets of these aircraft came whistling over the beaches of Normandy, crash-landing on French turf. Over the next year, he saw heavy combat, earning a Bronze Star and a Purple Heart. He witnessed the hell of Buchenwald. "Men were stacked up like cordwood," he recalled, "ten or twelve feet high. You couldn't tell whether they were living or dead . . . I had never seen such inhuman acts in my life. I couldn't dream of men treating men in such a manner."

When he returned to South Carolina, he was a war hero with substantial political experience for a man just forty-three years old, and perfectly situated to realize his father's dream — the governorship of South Carolina. But the South that Thurmond found waiting for him when he returned was different from the one he had known before. African Americans who had served in the military were emboldened by their own patriotism and a desire for justice. Blacks in northern states had organized into groups like the NAACP, which was well funded and staffed with highly trained lawyers. A new alignment of racial power was taking root. But the real shift occurred in the nation's judicial branch.

In 1944 a landmark Supreme Court decision in *Smith v. Allwright* challenged all-white elections in the South as never before. A black dentist named Lonnie E. Smith had sued an election official named S. S. Allwright for the right to vote in the Texas Democratic primary. The NAACP supplied the brilliant young lawyer Thurgood Marshall to argue the case, and the court had found Smith in the right.

"The United States is a constitutional democracy," the Supreme Court ruled. "Its organic law grants to all citizens a right to participate in the choice of elected officials without restriction by any state because of race."

The first full election cycle following *Smith v. Allwright* was in 1946, the year Strom Thurmond ran for governor. For the first time in generations, black people in the South were hoping to freely participate in the elections.

On August 13, 1946, a black man named George Elmore attempted to vote in a Democratic primary in Richland County in South Carolina. Since the South was a one-party system (the Solid South), the winner of the Democratic primary would be the winner of the office. Election officials refused to accept Elmore's ballot. With the help of lawyers from the newly empowered NAACP, Elmore sued. The outgoing South Carolina governor at the time, Olin D. Johnston, gave a speech to the state legislature in response to the Elmore case.

"We will have done everything within our power to guarantee white supremacy in our primaries and in our State in so far as legislation is concerned," Governor Johnston said. "Should this prove inadequate, we South Carolinians will use the necessary methods to retain white supremacy in our primaries and to safeguard the homes and happiness of our people. White supremacy will be maintained in our primaries. Let the chips fall where they may!" His audience understood what he meant by "necessary methods."

Yet a white judge in South Carolina decided the case in Elmore's favor. "For too many years," Judge J. Waties Waring ruled, "the people of this Country and perhaps particularly of this State have evaded realistic issues . . . Racial distinctions cannot exist in the machinery that selects the officers and law-makers of the United States; and all citizens of this State and Country are entitled to cast a free and untrammeled ballot in our elections."

By the time the ruling was issued, the 1946 South Carolina gubernatorial election was over. Strom Thurmond won the Democratic primary, and ran unopposed in the November general election. Thurmond was now one of the nation's youngest governors. But his white constituents knew they faced a battle over voting rights. Roughly 40 percent of the state's population was African American.

Throughout his adult life, Thurmond kept a secret relationship with his daughter Essie Mae. Her existence was highly dangerous to Thurmond the more he moved into the political spotlight. But he found ways to visit her regularly, and he helped her financially. She was a grown woman living in New York City when he became governor, and he convinced her to come back South to attend the all-black South Carolina State College. She would remember traveling out of New York on a nonsegregated train car, having to change trains in Washington, DC, and getting on a segregated car. Now back in the South, there were separate bathrooms, water fountains, waiting rooms—those for blacks and those for whites.

"Why I thought the world war might have changed things I'll never know," she later wrote in her memoirs. "I guess I felt that if our black soldiers could fight for America, America could fight for them, but that was not to be."

• • •

Shortly after Thurmond took office, on February 16, 1947, the phone rang in the Columbia governor's mansion. When Thurmond picked up the line he heard the nervous voice of the city editor of the *Greenville Piedmont,* a local newspaper serving a town one hundred miles northwest of South Carolina's capital. The editor told Thurmond a terrifying story: A black man named Willie Earle had been accused of the robbery and fatal stabbing of a white taxi driver. Earle had been arrested, but a white mob had taken him from the county jail by force. He'd then been stabbed, beaten, and shot through the head.

Police claimed to have substantial evidence that Earle was guilty of murdering the white taxi driver, Thomas W. Brown. But even if true, that did not condone the murder of Earle — not as far as the new governor Strom Thurmond was concerned. Thurmond knew he was on the spot. Would the rule of law hold up? The facts emerging were disturbing, and it was clear the case was going to get national attention.

Thurmond immediately ordered the FBI on the case, and brought in the strongest prosecutor he could find, Sam Watt of Spartanburg, who had successfully prosecuted 471 of 473 cases in the past year. Thurmond wanted to bring a murder case. Numerous witnesses were interviewed. The jailer, whose name was Gilstrap, told how a mob of some thirty white men had come to the jailhouse. "I knew they meant business," he told investigators. "They had a shotgun." The county physician said Earle had been stabbed five times, in the chest, stomach, forehead, neck, and thigh, before he was shot to death through the right temple. Numerous mob members named the man who pulled the trigger: R. Carlos Hurd Sr., a forty-five-year-old taxi dispatcher. Right before the victim was shot in the head, according to court testimony, he muttered his last words: "Lord, you done killed me."

This type of mob violence of white men against a black victim was not new. The South's darkest secret was one that stretched back decades. But in this case, unlike others, white men named a fellow white person as the triggerman in the lynching of a black American. Numerous newspapers, including the *New York Times,* called the case the biggest lynching trial in the history of the South. The courtroom was filled with reporters from national news outlets. A photo of the defendants being led into the courthouse ran in newspapers near and far. The governor faced fears that race riots could break out across the state, no matter which way the trial ended.

On May 27, 1947, predictably, an all-white jury found all the defendants not guilty. The *New York Times* and *Washington Post* ran editorials denouncing the verdict. "At least in that part of South Carolina, it's all right for a mob to take the law into its own hands and to commit murder—provided its victim is Negro," the *Post* stated. "That's the way they want it here. And they want no interference from the world outside." Governor Thurmond's role in the case left him unscathed. He was praised by outsiders for seeking justice, and excused by white constituents satisfied with the verdict.

Seven months later, Harry Truman gave his 1948 State of the Union address, his kickoff to the election season, calling for civil rights for all Americans. To white southerners like the Earle jury, it was a direct attack.

In the 1948 presidential contest, black Americans were hoping to vote in greater numbers than ever before. By the NAACP's estimate, the number of black voters registered in the South rose by 700,000 to 800,000 leading up to 1948. Harry Truman, Thomas Dewey, and Henry Wallace were fighting for the black vote. Strom Thurmond was fighting to hang on to the past. Thurmond's presidential run would be a historic litmus test—of federal versus state power, of black southerners' ability to exercise their right to vote, and of the Democratic Party's hold over the South.

19

"They Are Simply a 'Red Herring'"

ON JULY 31 TRUMAN LEFT the White House at 12:45 p.m., bound for National Airport, where he boarded the president's airplane — the Sacred Cow. He was flying to New York to dedicate the new Idlewild Airport. The event would give the US military the opportunity to showcase cutting-edge American aerial technology, before a crowd of some 215,000 people.

Everything about the ceremony was outsize. The navy flew in a group of Washington officials aboard a Lockheed Constellation — the largest air transporter in the world. Truman stood among political luminaries watching the largest display of airpower ever seen in peacetime, as the fastest airplanes streaked by at six hundred miles per hour, and the world's biggest bombers — the new B-36 and the B-50 — dove from the blue sky.

For the president, the scene was a reminder of the power of human curiosity and the speed of innovation. He had grown up in a horse-and-buggy world. He had fought in World War I when he was in his thirties, riding on horseback. Today he was watching some nine hundred airships thunder over an "airplane city" — Idlewild, now the largest public airport on earth.*

On a speaker's platform, Truman shook the hand of his Republican op-

---

*Idlewild is now John F. Kennedy International Airport, the largest airport servicing New York City.

ponent, Thomas Dewey. The president stood a couple of inches taller than the New York governor, and his white hair made him look old enough to be Dewey's father. It would be the only time during 1948 that Truman and Dewey would meet face-to-face. With their hands clasped, their noses just inches apart, they smiled, an offering of genuine political sportsmanship, as the camera flashes popped around them.

Truman leaned over and whispered in Dewey's ear, "Tom, when you get to the White House, for God's sake, do something about the plumbing."

At 4:05 p.m., Truman's plane took off from Idlewild, flew to Washington, dropped off some passengers, and departed seven minutes after landing, bound for Missouri, where the president was to vote in the state's Democratic primary — a formality, since he had already been nominated. While he was in flight, the most sensational domestic nonelection story of 1948 was breaking, in newspapers and over the radio.

On July 31, the day of Truman's appearance at Idlewild, in the hearing room of the House Un-American Activities Committee (HUAC) in Washington, DC, the committee chairman J. Parnell Thomas of New Jersey called a meeting to order at 10:15 a.m. The committee figures sat in a row at one end of the room, eight men in ties, including the freshman Republican congressman Richard Nixon of California and his colleague, Republican Karl Mundt of South Dakota.

The committee was conducting hearings on what these congressmen believed to be an underground Communist conspiracy that was infiltrating the ranks of American government. Chairman Thomas called for the first witness of the day: Elizabeth Bentley, a Connecticut woman who — in earlier testimony — had admitted to spying for the Soviet Union. Bentley, forty, walked to the front of the room and sat at a table just a few feet from the row of congressmen who would be questioning her. Crowds filled the room behind her, and directly to her right, a soundman wearing earphones sat hunched over recording equipment. Wearing a plain black dress and a bow in her hair, Bentley looked like any American woman who might have walked in off the street.

"Miss Bentley," Congressman Mundt said, "please stand and raise your right hand."

Once Bentley was sworn to oath, Senator John E. Rankin of Mississippi took the floor. He pointed out that leaders of the Communist Party of the United States, Eugene Dennis and William Z. Foster, had been arrested in July on charges of advocating for the overthrow of the American government.

"That has been known to President Truman and Governor Dewey of New York all this time," said Rankin. "It is about time that they got behind this committee and helped . . . drive these rats from the Federal, the State, and the municipal pay rolls."

Under questioning, Bentley began to unravel her story: she had been wooed into the Communist Party USA in the late 1930s as "an average run-of-the-mill member," she had cultivated relationships with people in government positions and had used them to "furnish information" to contacts within the Communist Party who were, she believed, Soviet agents.

"What kind of information?" asked Robert Stripling, the committee's chief investigator.

"All sorts of information," said Bentley. "Political, military, whatever they could lay their hands on."

Over the course of hours, Bentley named twenty-eight government officials and employees who had served as her informants, including Lauchlin Currie of Scarsdale, New York, who had been a close assistant to the late president Franklin Roosevelt, and Harry Dexter White, a former assistant secretary of the Treasury. (The shock of being named in this testimony was likely the cause of a heart attack that killed White, sixteen days later.) Currie, Bentley told the committee, "furnished inside information on this Government's attitude toward China, [and] toward other governments. He once relayed to us the information that the American Government was on the verge of breaking the Soviet [military] code."

When the questioning was over, reporters scrambled to get their stories out. Bentley had named two well-known American government officials as members of an underground Communist conspiracy. According to her testimony, this underground conspiracy had tentacles that reached all the way inside the White House. The Capitol Hill spy scare was only getting started.

Three days later, HUAC members heard the testimony of a disheveled *Time* magazine editor named Whittaker Chambers, who had been brought in to corroborate Bentley's testimony. Chambers had joined the Communist cause in New York City in 1924, when Communism in the United States was a fresh intellectual experiment in some circles. He said that he had been part of a group that aimed to infiltrate the ranks of American government, and that, when he decided to leave the Communist Party, he feared for his safety because of "the insidious evil . . . communism secures on its disciples." He lived for a year sleeping by day and "watching through the night with [a] gun or revolver within easy reach," because he had "sound reason that the Communists might try to kill me."

Chambers said, "The Communist Party exists for the specific purpose of overthrowing the Government, at the opportune time, by any and all means; and each of its members, by the fact that he is a member, is dedicated to this purpose."

When the congressional committee's chief investigator, Stripling, asked Chambers to name names, he offered a list including Lee Pressman and John Abt, two of the most powerful officials guiding the presidential campaign of Henry Wallace. Chambers also named one Alger Hiss.

"A ripple of surprise went through the room," remembered Richard Nixon, "because Hiss, who had not been mentioned in Miss Bentley's testimony, was a well-known and highly-respected figure in New York and Washington." Alger Hiss had ranked near the top of the State Department until recently, and had served as the secretary general at the San Francisco Conference, where the United Nations was founded in 1945. President Truman knew him well. According to Chambers's testimony, not only was Hiss a Communist, his wife and his brother were, too.

When the revelation appeared in the next day's papers, many simply refused to consider that the handsome and all-American-looking Alger

Hiss could be a Communist conspirator. Hiss was esteemed by high-ranking Democrats and Republicans. For his part, Hiss vociferously denied the charge.

Powerful people came to Hiss's defense. "Smearing good people like Lauchlin Currie, Alger Hiss and others is, I think, unforgivable," Eleanor Roosevelt wrote in her newspaper column. "Anyone knowing either Mr. Currie or Mr. Hiss, who . . . I happen to know fairly well, would not need any denial on their part to know they are not Communists. Their records prove it."

Two days after Chambers's testimony, the committee opened another hearing, and Alger Hiss appeared—tall, thin, and well-dressed. Hiss had contacted the committee, asking to testify to clear his name. In a voice so confident that, to some present, it came across as *too* confident, Hiss told the crowded committee room, "I am here at my own request to deny unqualifiedly various statements about me which were made before this committee by one Whittaker Chambers the day before yesterday."

Hiss lowered his voice dramatically. "I am not and never have been a member of the Communist Party," he said, and went on to refute everything Chambers had said about him, denying ever having laid eyes on his accuser.

One of these two men was lying, under oath. The ensuing drama became a national obsession.

At ten thirty on the morning that Hiss testified before the House Un-American Activities Committee, a White House usher opened the door to the Oval Office, and the Washington press corps pushed in. It was a Thursday, and the president had a particularly busy schedule—meetings with the secretary of state, the secretary of the Treasury, the attorney general, the director of the budget, and a dinner to discuss the upcoming election with officials from the Democratic National Committee.

Truman opened his weekly press conference by calling out the Eightieth Congress for failing to pass legislation he had proposed to curb inflation, which was becoming a hot campaign issue. ("High prices are not taking time off for the election," Truman had said.) The administration had come up with a plan that included wage and price controls and rationing, but Republicans had rejected it.

"There is still time for the Congress to fulfill its responsibilities to the American people," Truman said. "Our people will not be satisfied with the feeble compromises that apparently are being concocted."

When Truman opened the floor, reporters asked predictable questions about his upcoming campaign. One then asked, "Mr. President, do you think that the Capitol Hill spy scare is a 'red herring' to divert public attention from inflation?"

"Yes, I do," said Truman, "and I will read you another statement on that, since you brought it up." He picked a piece of paper up off his desk and spoke about the HUAC hearings, ending with the following: "The public hearings now under way are serving no useful purpose. On the contrary, they are doing irreparable harm to certain people, seriously impairing the morale of Federal employees, and undermining public confidence in the Government." He ad-libbed this last sentence: "And they are simply a 'red herring' to keep from doing what they [Congress] ought to do."

A reporter asked, "Don't you think the American public is entitled to this information?"

"What information?"

"That has been brought out in these investigations?"

"What useful purpose is it serving . . . ? They haven't revealed anything that everybody hasn't known all along, or hasn't been presented to the grand jury [a reference to the grand jury charging twelve members of the Communist Party USA with conspiracy to overthrow the government]. That is where it has to be taken, in the first place, if you are going to do anything about it. They are slandering a lot of people that don't deserve it."

"Mr. President," said one reporter, "could we use a part of the quote there, that last: they are simply a 'red herring,' etc.?"

"Using this as a 'red herring' to keep from doing what they ought to do," Truman said again, for emphasis.

It was a clever pun, but a politically dangerous one. The term *red herring* meant something that is misleading or distracting. "The President simply had acknowledged that this was a red herring," remembered the reporter Robert Nixon, who was in the room. "The meaning of the phrase 'red herring' was even ignored. It was made to appear that the President, in effect, was acknowledging that there was communism in Government and that some of the people in his administration and in the previous Roosevelt administration were traitors who had sold out their country to the Russian Government."

The next day, the words *red herring* made headlines on the front page of the *New York Times* and the *Washington Post*. GOP leaders used the story to berate the president. His "red herring" comment was "treasonable in spirit," said Congressman Kingsland Macy of New York. The columnist H. L. Mencken described Truman's "red herring" comment as "puerile whim-wham," and called on the House Un-American Activities Committee to "keep on until Truman is booted out of the White House." Dewey's campaign manager Herbert Brownell declared himself "shocked" by Truman's attitude, which was "seeming to cover up" the activities of Communists in government.

Republican senator Homer Ferguson of Michigan went even further. Ferguson pointed to Executive Order 9835, issued by the Truman administration in March 1947, which subjected federal employees to FBI oversight (the so-called loyalty board). Ferguson demanded that the administration start handing over the FBI files of government employees to congressional investigators. Ferguson's demand backed the president into a corner. If Truman handed over the files, he would be (to his mind) violating the privacy rights of American citizens whom he believed to be innocent. If he did not, he would open himself up to attacks by Republicans that he was weak on Communism, perhaps even participating in a cover-up of Communist infiltration in American government.

Truman flatly refused to turn over the FBI files of any federal employee, and Ferguson responded by demanding an impeachment inquiry. "The trend of presidential arrogance is becoming intolerable," Senator Ferguson said in a speech on the floor of the Senate, accusing Truman of abusing "executive immunity." The impeachment process went nowhere, but the headlines hurt Truman and inflamed the anger of conservative voters.

Meanwhile, the Alger Hiss investigation continued. In a private session, Chambers revealed to HUAC members detailed information about Hiss and his wife, supporting his claim that he knew Hiss personally. When Congressman Nixon asked Chambers if he would take a lie-detector test, Chambers said yes.

"You have that much confidence?" Nixon asked the witness.

"I am telling the truth," Chambers answered.

For many Americans at the time, the handsome, buttoned-up Hiss was more believable than the rumpled Chambers. For decades to come, the Hiss case would remain controversial. It would take years before the government revealed through declassified documents that it had decrypted many Soviet cables from the 1940s — and for most who have studied the matter, those cables and other supporting documents settle the matter: Hiss was lying; Chambers was telling the truth. Congressman Richard Nixon, in 1948, apparently had a winning hand to play.

What did it mean to be a Communist in the first place? In the summer of 1948, that depended on whom you asked. Yet the idea that the enemy could be "walking among us" — the person standing next to you online at the pharmacy, or the neighbor who kept to himself — caused the seed of fear to blossom. "Neither a man nor a crowd nor a nation can be trusted to act humanely or to think sanely under the influence of fear," the philosopher Bertrand Russell once wrote. For Americans, fear of Communism began to coalesce into panic. The Alger Hiss matter rooted this controversy deep in the collective American psychology.

In 1948 the National Security Council aimed to answer the question — what is Communism? — in a top secret memorandum called "Communism Is the Greatest Internal Security Threat at This Time." (This document was dated August 6, the day after Alger Hiss first testified before Congress.) "In different ages there have been different threats to the internal security of the United States," it read. "In this present age the threat is communism." Citing the Communist Party USA's sixty-eight thousand enrolled members, the document warned of a future in which the United States itself would cease to exist, leaving instead a "stateless, classless, Godless" society in which "there is no God, no soul, no immortality."

The Hiss case was a political hornet's nest for both Truman and Dewey. "If there turned out to be substance to Chambers's charges [regarding Alger Hiss]," recalled Richard Nixon, "Truman would be terribly embarrassed, and ordinarily this possibility alone might have spurred Republicans on in an election year. But special factors in the Hiss case favored a cautious approach [among Republicans]."

One of Dewey's closest advisers was John Foster Dulles, the world-renowned lawyer and diplomat who was widely believed to be Dewey's choice for secretary of state in the next administration. Dulles was a friend of Hiss's and had recommended Hiss for his current job as president of the Carnegie Foundation. And so the Hiss controversy had the power to stain Dewey's campaign as well as Truman's.

On August 11 Congressman Richard Nixon took a train to New York to visit the Dewey headquarters at the Roosevelt Hotel. Present was John Foster Dulles. Nixon had brought with him transcripts of hearings and private testimony in which Chambers revealed details about Hiss. Dulles read through the transcripts and began to pace in his office. He looked up at Nixon and said, "There's no question about it. It's almost impossible to believe, but Chambers knows Hiss."

The investigation had to continue. Where it would lead, none could say.

As the American press kept the story front and center, paranoia surrounding a Communist conspiracy grew. Americans were pressed to ask themselves: Which candidate in 1948 would more effectively expose Communists at home? Which would fight hardest to rid the nation of what appeared to be a sinister enemy? Candidates would now have to prove themselves on the issue. "Red Activity Looms Big in Campaign," the *Chicago Daily Tribune* declared in a front-page story. The Red Scare had begun.

• • •

Alger Hiss was not the only figure to pay a high price as a subject of the HUAC hearings. The proceedings brought renewed scrutiny to the presidential campaign of Henry Wallace.

Whittaker Chambers had publicly outted as members of an underground Communist ring John Abt and Lee Pressman — two of the most influential members of Wallace's Progressive Party. Photographs of Abt and Pressman appeared in newspapers nationwide. On August 19, 1948, the committee ordered the two men to testify the next day. When it was Abt's turn to speak, Congressman Nixon leaned over to a colleague and said, "Watch your step with this one. He's a smart cookie."

"It was clear that these were not regular, garden variety hearings," Abt later recalled. "Implicit was a threat of great danger. We had engaged in no illegal activity. But we were radicals."

Asked continuously to admit he was a Communist, Abt refused, pleading the Fifth Amendment so as not to incriminate himself. Lee Pressman did the same, and after the proceedings were over, he issued a statement, calling the hearing "a shameful circus," and the committee's leader, J. Parnell Thomas, "a Republican exhibitionist." He accused Thomas of "stale and lurid mouthings" that intended to steer attention away from the 1948 election's more important issues. Rather than comment on whether he was or was not a Communist, Pressman chose to catalog the Progressive Party platform: "civil rights, inflation, housing, justice for the heroic state of Israel, and the repeal of the Taft-Hartley Act."

Following Abt's and Pressman's testimony members of the press once again attacked Henry Wallace. A Georgia judge named Lee B. Wyatt told one reporter, "If I had my way about Wallace, I would say 'get the hell out and go back to Russia.' It makes my blood boil to hear Wallace and his Progressive Party presidential running mate say that we are provoking a war with Russia."

Nine days after Abt and Pressman pleaded the Fifth, Wallace headed south to begin a six-state campaign swing. He was going deep into Strom Thurmond territory. Wallace knew before he arrived that the potential for embarrassment and even violence was high. He had no support among whites from the South. Wallace's support of "Negroes" and civil rights, his highly publicized Communist connections, his call to appease the Soviets during this new Cold War — all of this made him a public enemy in the eyes of whites in the region who — though Democrats — were as conservative or more so than many Republicans.

As his campaign manager Beanie Baldwin later said, "I don't think any person in American political life ever demonstrated the sheer personal courage that Wallace did in that trip through the south."

Wallace arrived in Virginia on August 29, 1948. Before leaving, he made a statement that he would not speak to any crowd that segregated blacks from whites. He would not sleep in any building that segregated blacks from whites. He was traveling with a mixed-race campaign staff, and when he learned that certain hotels had canceled his reservations because they did not serve black Americans, he was not surprised. "This meant I had to stay in Negro homes everywhere I went," he recalled, "which was really slapping the southern tradition."

On his first day, Wallace addressed roughly a thousand people at a theater in a black neighborhood in Suffolk, Virginia. "We must learn from Jesus and Jefferson," he said. "The military strategies of history can give no answer to the problems of the atomic age." He proposed a billion-dollar-a-year federal subsidy for southern industry and agriculture. The Marshall Plan money pouring out of the United States to war-torn nations abroad could be better spent at home, he said, in towns like Suffolk. When Wallace left the hall, a dozen young white men heckled him.

"Hey, Joe Stalin is looking for you."

"Why don't you go to South Carolina?"

When Wallace reached Durham, North Carolina, protesters carried signs outside a state Progressive Party convention where he was scheduled to speak.

SEND WALLACE BACK TO RUSSIA, read one.

WALLACE — THE HITLER OF TODAY, read another.

"They continually shouted, 'Go back to Russia, you nigger lover,'" Wallace later recalled.

Inside the hall, Progressive Party supporters—black and white—intermingled. As Wallace made his way to the podium, escorted by an armed guard, a melee broke out outside and a Wallace supporter was repeatedly stabbed. The wounded man lay bleeding on the stairs leading to the hall while police tried to establish control. One officer fired a warning shot into the air to try to calm the tumult. As the stabbing victim was pulled from the ground and rushed to the hospital (he survived), inside the hall, Wallace gave his address, proposing a Marshall Plan that would send federal dollars not to Europe, but to the southern states. Boos and catcalls repeatedly interrupted him, causing the candidate to plead with his audience: "Please sit down! Please sit down!"

After the event, the members of the Wallace campaign team were unnerved. Beanie Baldwin asked Wallace, "Do you think we ought to go through with this?"

"Yes," Wallace answered, "we'll go through."

The next night, in Burlington, North Carolina, raw eggs, tomatoes, and an ice-cream cone rained down on Wallace's car as he arrived at a speaking event. An angry crowd of several hundred whites refused to let him enter the hall where members of Gideon's Army had gathered to hear him speak. He stood outside his car next to a police officer for fifteen minutes, incredulously staring out over a raucous assembly of hecklers.

"I would like to see some indication that I am in the United States!" he shouted. But the protest against him continued.

When Wallace did take the stage, boos greeted him, and another egg hit him. He tried to compose himself, beginning his speech with eggshell stuck in his hair and yolk running down his white shirt. When the candidate finished his speech and headed back to his car, a police guard followed closely, with one officer drawing his gun. Wallace headed for Mecklenburg, North Carolina, where a similar scene awaited. More eggs. More tomatoes. More signs: SELL YOUR JUNK IN MOSCOW, HENRY.

Wallace spoke at the courthouse in Mecklenburg because no hall or theater would rent the Progressive Party space. "I believe there are people in Mecklenburg County who still believe in human rights," he shouted over taunts.

In Dallas, Wallace was awoken after midnight by a Western Union messenger bearing a telegram that read, "Get out of town!" At another event, the window of a car containing two Wallace staffers — one white, one black — was smashed.

The national reaction to Wallace's trip South was a mix of outrage and apathy. By one reporter's account, the Wallace campaign had been targeted by twenty-seven eggs, thirty-seven tomatoes, six peaches, two lemons, an orange, and one ice-cream cone. But it had also shed light on a dark American truth. Wallace's chief treasurer, a Georgia-raised black man named Clark Foreman, who had once witnessed the lynching of a black man when he was in college, years earlier, called Wallace's southern odyssey "the greatest blow against slavery since the emancipation proclamation."

"As the direct result of Henry Wallace's trip through the South," wrote one journalist in the *New York Star*, "millions of Americans who were not aware of the meaning of discrimination in the South have suddenly been jolted. Segregation is no work of fiction, but a brutal fact. The conflict between American democracy and segregation hit home to millions."

Years later, looking back on this trip, Wallace would describe his encounter with "human hate in the raw." He had never experienced anything of the kind before, he said, and could not imagine doing so again.

COURTESY OF THE HARRY S. TRUMAN LIBRARY & MUSEUM

AP PHOTO

When Franklin Roosevelt died on April 12, 1945, the nation was shocked to witness an obscure vice president from Missouri become the most powerful man on earth. Harry S. Truman spoke the presidential oath that night (top) with his wife, Bess, and daughter, Margaret, next to him. For the rest of his term, Truman's approval rating tanked. When he was nominated to run for president at the 1948 Democratic National Convention in Philadelphia, few gave him any shot at victory. Truman's acceptance speech at 2 a.m. on July 15, 1948 (bottom), set the stage for a historic David-versus-Goliath battle in the first postwar presidential election.

PHOTO BY FRED MORGAN/NY DAILY NEWS ARCHIVE/GETTY IMAGES

AP PHOTO/BILL CHAPLIS

AP PHOTO

The night Thomas Dewey won the GOP nomination in Philadelphia on June 24, 1948 (top left), he laid down the gauntlet: "Our peace, our prosperity, the very fate of freedom hangs in precarious balance." Meanwhile, breakaway Democrat Henry Wallace (top right, campaigning in North Carolina on August 31) launched the Progressive Party with the help of an underground clique of Communists. Governor Strom Thurmond of South Carolina led a southern revolt from the Democrats, launching the anti-Truman, anti–civil rights States' Rights Democratic Party (the "Dixiecrats") at a July 17 convention in Birmingham, Alabama (bottom). Thurmond's message of white supremacy won him an immediate base across the South.

COURTESY OF THE HARRY S. TRUMAN LIBRARY & MUSEUM

BETTMANN/GETTY IMAGES

WALTER SANDERS/THE LIFE PICTURE COLLECTION/GETTY IMAGES

As election season opened in the spring of 1948, fear of a new apocalyptic war spread. The US military conducted atomic bomb tests in the Pacific (top left). The day before the final test shot, on May 15, the new nation of Israel declared its independence. That night, the new Israeli flag debuted in Washington (top right) and the first Arab-Israeli War began. A month later, on the night Thomas Dewey won the GOP nomination, the Soviets blockaded west Berlin. The Berlin Airlift began (bottom), and the Americans and Soviets stood nose to nose in the heart of Europe. "I have a terrible feeling . . ." Truman wrote in his diary, "that we are very close to war."

PHOTO BY ABBIE ROWE FOR THE NATIONAL PARK SERVICE. COURTESY OF THE HARRY S. TRUMAN LIBRARY & MUSEUM.

PHOTO12/UNIVERSAL IMAGES GROUP/GETTY IMAGES

The end of World War II saw a radical shift in race politics, resulting in Truman's historic civil rights programs and his desegregation of the military by executive order. On June 29, 1947, Truman became the first president to address the NAACP in a speech at the base of the Lincoln Memorial (top). Truman's civil rights program provoked furious pushback across the South. Prominent politicians and the Ku Klux Klan (bottom, at a 1948 cross burning) launched their own fight to keep their states segregated, to bar black Americans from voting, and to push Harry S. Truman out of office.

PHOTO BY BILL SITLER FOR UNITED STATES ARMY SIGNAL CORPS.
COURTESY OF THE HARRY S. TRUMAN LIBRARY & MUSEUM.

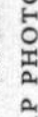
AP PHOTO

GEORGE SILK/THE LIFE PICTURE COLLECTION/GETTY IMAGES

Campaign season saw both continued prosperity and mass anxiety. On July 31, Truman and Dewey met in person for the only time during their campaigns (top left) at the dedication of Idlewild Airport in New York, while the largest-ever peacetime display of airpower thundered above. That same day, the sensational news broke that Communists had allegedly infiltrated American government; Alger Hiss, a former high-level State Department figure (top right, testifying before a congressional committee), became the story's central figure. Meanwhile, Henry Wallace claimed that Truman was leading the country to war with the Soviets. Wallace is pictured with folk singer Pete Seeger (bottom left). Running mate Senator Glen Taylor of Idaho appears in the photograph above Wallace's head.

COURTESY OF THE HARRY S. TRUMAN LIBRARY & MUSEUM

COURTESY OF THE HARRY S. TRUMAN LIBRARY & MUSEUM

DEAN CONGER/CORBIS/GETTY IMAGES

In the fall of 1948, the two major candidates crisscrossed the nation by train. Truman was considered all but out of the race, yet his "Give 'em Hell, Harry" speeches drew shockingly large crowds (top). All the major newspapers endorsed Dewey, and throughout Truman's campaign, his relationship with the press grew increasingly bitter (bottom left). Around the time the photo of Dewey was taken, in Laramie, Wyoming, *Newsweek* published an election survey: fifty political writers were asked which candidate they thought would win, and all fifty chose Dewey.

UNITED STATES INFORMATION AGENCY/PHOTOQUEST/GETTY IMAGES

PHOTO BY VERNON GALLOWAY. COURTESY OF THE HARRY S. TRUMAN LIBRARY & MUSEUM.

CBS/GETTY IMAGES

In the final climactic week of the 1948 election season, Truman and Dewey both visited Chicago, Cleveland, Boston, and New York, with Dewey following the president from city to city in a point-counterpoint political blowout. Both held final rallies at Madison Square Garden in New York (top, the scene before Truman's speech on October 28). On Election Day, the First Family cast their votes in their hometown of Independence, Missouri (bottom left). That night, Americans caught the first-ever election-night television broadcast as CBS's Quincy Howe reported on the returns (bottom right).

COURTESY OF THE HARRY S. TRUMAN LIBRARY & MUSEUM

LISA LARSEN/THE LIFE IMAGES COLLECTION/GETTY IMAGES

So assured was a Republican victory, news outlets across America and Europe reported on November 3, 1948, that Dewey had been elected. An early edition of the *Chicago Daily Tribune* declared "Dewey Defeats Truman" in a banner headline, and Truman famously held the newspaper up for photographers on November 4 while passing through St. Louis (top). Following the most significant political upset in American history up to that time came the most lavish Inauguration Day party, on January 20, 1949. Truman and new Vice President Alben Barkley of Kentucky were all smiles (bottom, Margaret Truman is at far left).

20

"There Is Great Danger Ahead"

THE EXECUTIVE MANSION WAS PHYSICALLY crumbling. "The White House Architect and Engineer have moved me into the . . . Lincoln Room — for safety — imagine that!" Truman wrote in his diary on August 3. He wrote his sister on the tenth of that month, "Margaret's sitting room floor broke in two but didn't fall through the family dining room ceiling. They propped it up and fixed it. Now my bathroom is about to fall into the red parlor. They won't let me sleep in my bedroom or use the bath."

The problem was kept a highly guarded secret. "Can you imagine what the press would have done with this story?" the president's daughter later wrote. "The whole mess would have been blamed on Harry Truman. The White House would have become a metaphor for his collapsing administration."

As engineers and architects hammered on walls and peeled back ceilings to reveal the building's old bones, staffers and the Democratic National Committee were working overtime piecing together an itinerary for Truman's campaign appearances. He was going to travel aboard the *Ferdinand Magellan* train car, as he had done in his "nonpolitical" trip two months earlier in June, crisscrossing the nation. He aimed to give more speeches and make more campaign appearances than any presidential candidate in history.

The tour would kick off Labor Day weekend in Detroit. To rest up beforehand, and to escape the structural problems of his current home, the president went on vacation. On August 20 Truman left the White House for a cruise aboard the presidential yacht — the USS *Williamsburg.* With a crew of advisers, poker buddies, a Secret Service detail of a half-dozen agents, and the White House physician, Dr. Wallace Graham, accompanying him, the *Williamsburg* left Pier 1 at the Navy base in Washington under the command of Captain Donald J. MacDonald.

For the next nine days Truman lounged on the ship's deck, paced its length in his bathing suit, and worked in his cabin as the party cruised Chesapeake Bay. At night, the group watched movies — *Key Largo* starring Humphrey Bogart and Lauren Bacall and *The Emperor Waltz* with Bing Crosby and Joan Fontaine. Truman loved boats. He could relax and be Harry instead of Mr. President. "In the intimacy of the ship," remembered George Elsey, "his language was unguarded." That said, Truman was so respectful of women, he never told what Elsey called "dirty stories." "He would laugh if others told them, but his repertoire was confined to political anecdotes, scatological only if they involved a politician."

It was a brief respite from a troubled world. In Palestine, the Arab-Israeli War had reached a temporary truce under the watchful eye of a United Nations mediator, Folke Bernadotte of Sweden. There was almost no hope that the truce would last. Jews in America were thrilled with the surprising strength of the fledgling Israeli army. At the same time, the State Department was alarmed. In the process of claiming territory, the Israelis had pushed some three hundred thousand Palestinians out of their homes and were refusing to allow them to return, creating a humanitarian crisis. "The situation is becoming daily more critical as cold weather sets in," a State Department official informed Truman.

In Moscow, Walter Bedell Smith, the American ambassador to the Soviet Union, was locked in direct negotiations with Joseph Stalin and his number two, the impossibly irascible Vyacheslav Molotov, over the standoff in Berlin. The talks were proving fruitless and the airlift in Berlin continued. American and British planes were landing three thousand tons of supplies in the western sector of Berlin each day.

On August 20, US officials in Berlin announced that the Soviets had raided the American sector of the city and had kidnapped seven German policemen at gunpoint. Three had apparently escaped but four were still missing and were feared dead. The next day, another report came out of Berlin that the Soviets had once again raided the US sector and had beaten and stabbed German police officers.

Days later, the Communist party in power in the Soviet sector of Berlin stormed city hall, demanding a liquidation of the Berlin city council. That night thirty thousand Berliners in the western sectors gathered in the hot night to protest. The city's elected mayor, Professor Ernst Reuter — whose administration the Soviets refused to recognize — demanded justice.

"We have said 'no' and we shall say 'no' again until liberty and democracy have been regained for Berlin," he announced. "We Berliners have said no to communism and we will fight it with all our might as long as there is a breath in us . . . The struggle for Berlin is a struggle for the freedom of the world."

In Washington, the Joint Chiefs of Staff and Secretary of Defense James Forrestal felt the pressure from across the ocean. They were attempting to clarify guidelines for the use of the atomic bomb. They created one document for "immediate use," while another was to take precedence "in the event of war." Forrestal's continued effort to have custody of the atomic stockpile placed in the military's hands was getting nowhere with Truman. No matter how much work the Defense Department put into creating guidelines for the bomb, any decision to use it remained with the president.

Back in the White House at the end of August, Truman prepared to begin his campaign trip while the Democratic National Committee made a frantic push to raise money. They needed $10,000 for Truman's nationwide Labor Day radio broadcast from Detroit, $10,000 for Truman-Barkley campaign posters, $17,000 for two Barkley broadcasts, etc.

Truman packed his bags for what would turn out to be one of the most unusual trips any president had ever made. Around this time, he received a visit from an old friend, Leslie Biffle, the secretary of the Senate. Biffle was from a small town in Arkansas. For a summer vacation, he had traveled undercover as a chicken farmer, driving through farming towns in the Midwest to gauge the grassroots sentiments of America, regarding the upcoming election. He told Truman that his impressions of voters defied everything he was reading about in the newspapers. Truman, Biffle said, could win.

"Do you think so?" Truman asked. "Do you really think so?"

Just after lunch on September 5, 1948, Truman and his daughter, Margaret, climbed aboard the *Ferdinand Magellan,* the rear car on a seventeen-car train parked at Union Station. Truman sported a gray fedora atop a blue suit, while Margaret wore a blue silk dress, a cocoa-brown hat, and a thick layer of red lipstick. At 2:30 p.m., with a jarring lurch, the train's steel wheels began to turn. Bess was on vacation visiting family in Denver. She would join the campaign soon. This would be the Truman family home for the foreseeable future — an adventure covering nearly thirty-five thousand miles.

The latest numbers by pollster Elmo Roper made Dewey's lead seem insurmountable. Roper had the GOP candidate running 46.3 percent to Truman's 31.5 percent, with Wallace at just 3 percent and "other candidates" at 2.4 percent. "I'd be much better off personally if we lose the election," Truman wrote his sister just before taking off, "but I fear that the country would go to hell and I have to try to prevent that." The reporters aboard had given the train carrying the president a nickname: the Truman Special.

The *Ferdinand Magellan* was the only train car ever built especially for presidential travel. Entering through the *Magellan*'s front door (which had a vault-like lock on it for privacy), the first thing one saw was a galley and pantry where cooks worked, followed by servants' quarters, then an oak-paneled dining space that featured a table covered in a white tablecloth and eight chairs upholstered with thin gold-and-green stripes. In the back of the train car, on one side, a lounge offered a row of comfortable chairs, behind which were two windows — three-inch-thick bulletproof glass. Atop those windows was the round presidential seal. Also mounted on a wall in this lounge was a speedometer, so the president could see how fast the train was moving.

A back door opened onto an outdoor speaker's platform at the rear of the train. When the train pulled into a "whistle-stop," staffers would set up a microphone with three loudspeakers, while Secret Service agents installed a rope to keep crowds at a safe distance from the president and his family.

Directly adjacent to the lounge were four staterooms marked A, B, C, and D. The two middle rooms made up the presidential suite, one for Harry and one for Bess. They were joined by a shared bath and shower room. Each stateroom had a bed, a dresser, and a telephone that could be hooked up when the train pulled into a station. The car was cooled using a blower system and some three tons of ice that needed to be continuously replaced.

In the dining and bar car, crowds lined up for a sendoff highball. Political reporters rubbed elbows with photographers and newsreel camera crews, Truman staff, Secret Service agents, Army Signal Corps engineers working in the communications room, and teams of railroad workers.

Another train traveled a few miles ahead of the Truman Special for safety reasons, as did an advance man, White House staffer Oscar Chapman, whose job it was to drum up interest in every town at which the president stopped, so that when Truman got onto the *Ferdinand Magellan*'s back platform to speak, everything was in order and crowds would be on hand, lured by a well-oiled advertising campaign coordinated and paid for by the Democratic National Committee and local Democratic organizations.

Campaign staffers had worked out what they'd hoped would be a smooth-running assembly line of facts, figures, and ideas for the president. Truman had Clark Clifford on board to handle the big speeches. "I lived in a little tiny stateroom where I slept and ate and wrote," Clifford remembered. "My big task in the campaign was to do the writing for the President." Clifford's assistant George Elsey would handle the shorter whistle-stop addresses. Truman would give these talks impromptu, using note cards full of relevant facts supplied by Elsey and his team. Elsey remembered, "I was armed with briefcases filled with notes and outlines for the first few days with the promise that the daily pouch flown from Washington to wherever we might be would have more from Batt"—Bill Batt at the secret research unit in Washington.

Truman staffer Charlie Murphy would write rough drafts of bigger speeches from his office in the White House, to send to Clifford for rewrites. "I worked at it night and day, every day," recalled Murphy of the campaign. "The pattern that evolved was that we would send a draft of a speech from here [the White House] at night, it would be flown by courier plane that would land wherever that train was before day in the morning." The speech would make its way into the hands of Clifford, who would work on it personally with Truman.

Everyone on board and at the White House — apart from Truman — believed that his chances at victory were near null. The only shot he had was to put on a campaign so surprising, it would take the nation by storm. "He was on his own five-yard line," Clifford recalled, "there were only three minutes left, and the only thing that could win the game for him was a touchdown. Now, why would he just go ahead and run plays through the line? He had to try any sort of innovative, surprising, startling kind of tactic that might work because he had everything to gain and nothing to lose."

On the first night aboard the Truman Special en route to Detroit, Truman had his whole staff to dinner. At a quarter after eight the next morning, the train pulled into Grand Rapids, where the president was set to give his first whistle-stop speech. Truman stepped out onto the *Magellan*'s back platform. He would remember the sight for the rest of his life.

It was pouring. Grand Rapids was a Republican stronghold. Still, some twenty-five thousand people were huddled under umbrellas and out in the elements. Rows of state police officers stood drenched in their uniforms. These were the first words in Truman's first official campaign-tour speech of 1948: "My, what a wonderful crowd at 8:15 in the morning," he said into his microphone. "It is a great day for me. It is a great day for you. I am just starting on a campaign tour that is going to be a record for the President of the United States."

What the people of Grand Rapids saw was not the man they thought they would. This was no stiff oratory, no FDR-like prose. There was nothing formal about it.

"The record proves conclusively that the Republican Party is controlled by special privilege; and that the Democratic Party is responsive to the needs of the people," Truman said. "Now the necessity that faces us is one of voting on November 2d. You must register, you must vote, if you expect to get a square deal in this great Nation. Doesn't do any good to talk about voting, if you are not on the books. Doesn't do any good to talk about voting, if you sit around on election day, too lazy to turn out. The interests of this great Nation are such that every man and woman of voting age in this country ought to turn out and vote on November 2d."

After his talk, Truman was ushered into a special train car designed for guests. Nearly four dozen local officials were there expecting a handshake — the heads of over a dozen auto union divisions, of the carpenters union, the plasterers union, the sheet-metal workers union, the financial secretaries typographical union. There was the head of the Democratic County Club, the former mayor of Lansing, the head of the Eleanor Roosevelt League, plus candidates for county clerk, state senator, and the US Congress. Labor Day Queen Miss Elayne Balance was on hand to present a bouquet to the First Daughter.

The train was on a strict schedule. All of this — the extemporaneous speech, the meet-and-greet — had to occur in fifteen minutes. Somehow, Truman managed to shake all the hands and the train moved on.

Meanwhile, unbeknownst to the president, the campaign had reached what Margaret Truman called "the first major crisis." The advance man, Chapman, was in Detroit, where Truman was scheduled to make his first major speech downtown in Cadillac Square that afternoon. The speech was set to go live nationwide on radio, but radio executives told Chapman they would need the $25,000 fee for the broadcast up front, or they would be forced to cancel. Chapman frantically contacted union leaders, but no one had that kind of cash on hand. A Truman aide happened to run into the wealthy Democratic governor of Oklahoma, Roy J. Turner, at a cocktail party at the Statler Hotel in Washington that day, and pleaded with Turner for help.

"Well, that broadcast is going to be made," Turner said. He got out his checkbook and wrote a check. "That broadcast goes on," he said.

When the train reached Detroit at 1:40 p.m., Truman and his entourage funneled into a row of limousines and rode downtown for the day's main event. Thousands lined the roads along the route. In Cadillac Square, 125,000 people stood awaiting the president. A nationwide radio audience listened in. Detroit was the spiritual home of the American labor union—not just ground zero for the votes of working Americans but also for the union leaders themselves, who had the power and funds to organize voter-registration drives and door-to-door canvassing. Big urban areas typically formed Democratic Party strongholds, but Detroit in particular—these were Truman people. And with this crowd, Truman had an ace up his sleeve: the Taft-Hartley Act of 1947, the federal law that had restricted the power and activities of labor unions, which Truman had vetoed and the Eightieth Congress had passed, over his protest. Taft-Hartley had proven the most controversial labor law in years, one that workers believed tipped the scales in favor of big business and Wall Street, over the rights of the common workingman and -woman.

"As you know," Truman said from the speaker's platform, "I speak plainly sometimes. In fact, I speak bluntly sometimes. I am going to speak plainly and bluntly today." The crowd roared. "These are critical times for labor and for all who work," Truman said. "There is great danger ahead." Citing Taft-Hartley he warned voters of "the boom and bust" that lay ahead if Thomas Dewey was elected president. "The 'boom' is on for them, and the 'bust' has begun for you." He warned of the predatory businessman with "a calculating machine where his heart ought to be . . . Labor has always had to fight for its gains. Now you are fighting for the whole future of the labor movement . . . I know that we are going to win this crusade for the right!"

After the Detroit speech, Truman sat with Margaret and motored in the back of a limo north out of the city, followed by cars holding camera crews from all three television networks. Along the trip, police estimated, a half million people stood on the sides of the roads.

The president's appointments secretary Matthew Connelly recalled the ride: "Along the highway from Detroit to Pontiac I'd see people alongside the highway. This was not organized and there were a lot of them out there . . . This tells me what I want to know." Others saw the turnout through a lens of colder logic. "A President can always bring people out," recalled Jack Bell, the top political reporter for the Associated Press, who was traveling with the Truman campaign. "Even if they are not going to vote for him, even if they hate him, people want to see the President in person you know . . . Most of them never saw a President."

In Pontiac, fifteen thousand people heard Truman speak. In Flint—"Vehicle City," where General Motors, the largest corporation on earth, was originally founded—an audience of thirty-five thousand turned out. Then it was back to the train to head south to Toledo, Ohio, where eighty-six local officials—from the city mayor to union representatives to journalists from the local newspapers and radio stations—were waiting to shake Truman's hand. By the end of the first night of campaigning, the train was full of weary people who wished they could take showers.

Truman was sixty-four years old, vigorous and in good health. Still, the staff questioned whether any man his age—healthy or not—could continue at this pace up until November 2.

21

"The All-Time Georgia Champion of 'White Supremacy'"

ON THE EVENING OF SEPTEMBER 7, the day after Truman's Detroit speech, Thomas Dewey gathered several of his advisers in the governor's mansion in Albany and switched on the radio. Five hundred miles due west, at the Masonic Temple on Temple Avenue in Detroit that night, the former governor of Minnesota and current president of the University of Pennsylvania — Harold Stassen — officially kicked off the GOP campaign with a blistering rebuttal to Truman.

"Yesterday in Detroit," Stassen began, "the American people were given an additional reason why there should be a change in the White House and Governor Thomas E. Dewey should be elected in November as the next President of our country." Truman's speech in Detroit, Stassen told a packed house, was "an extreme demagogic appeal to set class against class."

Stassen blamed Truman for the nation's high prices, for setting off "the inflationary spiral from which this country is still suffering." He blamed Truman for the housing crisis, which was acute in Detroit, where the poorest neighborhoods were among the most overcrowded in the country. He blamed Truman for "an all-time high record of strikes and work stoppages" that caused workers to lose over a billion dollars in wages. He told his audience that the surprisingly big crowds that had turned out to see Harry

Truman only did so because union bosses had threatened people with a "$3 fine for nonattendance."

"With a record of little judgment and less faith," said Stassen, "he [Truman] once again sets himself up as a prophet and attempts to arouse in America an unreasoning, nameless fear of future depression, unemployment and chaos if he is not retained in office." Truman, said Stassen, was "a colossal failure."

When Stassen walked off the stage, he took a phone call from Dewey. "He said he listened to the speech, liked it, and thanked me for it," Stassen recorded. This was no surprise; Dewey had read and approved every word of it ahead of time.

The day after Stassen's rebuttal speech, the nation's political spotlight shifted to an unlikely place — Georgia, where the Democratic primary race for the state's governorship was heating up. Traditionally, Republicans had no shot at winning a big election in Georgia, and the Democratic primary would in fact choose the next governor. This year the party faced a crisis, and Strom Thurmond's Dixiecrats were a looming threat.

The state's political crisis had begun in 1946. The governor-elect that year, Eugene Talmadge, died before he could take office. The state constitution had no apparatus to name a successor, and three men laid claim to the position. Since none of them could point to any precedent or law that would make such a claim stand, Georgia's secretary of state, Benjamin Fortson, paralyzed from the waist down, hid the governor's office state seal under his wheelchair cushion until the controversy could be cleared up, which took two years. The September 8 Democratic primary would decide the matter, which had by this time gained national attention.

Two candidates were now in the running. There was Herman Talmadge, son of the late governor-elect Eugene Talmadge, a legend in Georgia politics who had served three terms as governor and was a pillar in the region's white supremacist political structure. The *New York Times* once called him "the all-time Georgia champion of 'white supremacy.'"

"Wise Negroes," Talmadge had said before the 1946 midterm elections, "will stay away from white folks' ballot boxes."

Herman Talmadge was hoping to walk in his father's footsteps into the Atlanta governor's mansion, and to continue pressing for the segregationist laws he had known all his life. At a rally in Fort Valley, Georgia, in August 1948, Talmadge had told a crowd, "We're going to have white supremacy in Georgia, by peaceful means if possible, by force if necessary."

His opponent was Melvin E. Thompson, who had come up as an educator and had served in a previous governor's administration. Thompson publicly supported Truman's civil rights campaign and the Supreme Court's *Smith v. Allwright* ruling.

Leading up to the primary, racial angst spread through the state. Georgia's Ku Klux Klan chapters pledged support for Talmadge. The KKK's local grand dragon, Samuel Green, publicly announced he would turn out a hundred thousand Klan votes for Talmadge, who was polling a three-to-one advantage in the race. On the night before the primary, just after Melvin Thompson gave his final campaign address, thirty robed and hooded Klansmen gathered in the black section of the town of Valdosta and burned a cross in front of a group of a hundred blacks and a phalanx of police officers. Two other cross burnings, clear threats to African Americans who aimed to cast a ballot in the election, were reported that night.

The following morning, September 8, Georgians nervously went to the polls. A black man named Isaiah Nixon, who lived on a farm in Alston, Georgia, went to his local polling station to cast his ballot. Like many other black men in Georgia, he had registered to vote with the help of the local chapter of the NAACP. Nixon was strongly advised by election officials not to vote, but he cast his ballot anyway.

Later that day, Nixon was at home on his farm with his family. His wife was on bed rest, as she had recently given birth. A car pulled up and out stepped two white men whom Nixon knew: two brothers named Johnson. One was carrying a shotgun, the other a pistol. They yelled for Nixon to come outside, and both Nixon and his wife emerged from their home. When the Johnson brothers asked Nixon whom he had voted for, Nixon reportedly said, "I guess I voted for Mr. Thompson."

According to subsequent investigations, the Johnson brothers demanded that Nixon get in their car, and he refused. According to the defense lawyer who later represented the Johnson brothers, Nixon charged at them with a knife, though this version of the story was disputed. One Johnson brother fired a shot into Nixon's abdomen. When Nixon remained standing, his wife screamed, "Fall, Isaiah, fall!"

Herman Talmadge won the governor's race by a huge margin. Georgia's most widely read newspaper, the *Atlanta Constitution,* noted: "Herman Talmadge's victory in the gubernatorial Democratic primary . . . today may give the States' Rights Democrats a boost in their presidential campaign." Talmadge went on to become a popular governor, and then to serve twenty-four years as US senator. Two days after Talmadge's primary win, Isaiah Nixon died in a local all-black hospital. The Johnson brothers were charged with murder, but would ultimately be found not guilty by an all-white jury, on the grounds of self-defense.

Days after the Georgia gubernatorial primary, in a black school not far from the Georgia State Capitol, a teacher asked her third-grade students whether their parents were going to vote in the upcoming presidential election in November. A male student responded, "My mama ain't going nowhere and get shot voting."

On September 10, two days after the Georgia primary, Henry Wallace surged again to the top of the political news cycle. Following his trip through the Deep South, Wallace made a triumphant return to his strongest base, in the city of New York. Some forty-eight thousand people moved through turnstiles at Yankee Stadium, illuminating the striking cultural and political divide between the new conservatism building in the American South and the new liberal movement in New York, as personified by Gideon's Army. Promoters of this rally were claiming it was the largest political rally for which admission was charged in the history of the United States, and the largest political rally ever held in New York City.

The scene was, in the words of one man present, "a weird combination of the old-fashioned open-air church revival meeting, of chanting and songfest and evangelical fervor in mass." Banners hung from around the stage, reading SAFEGUARD FREEDOM, KEEP AMERICA FREE, FIGHT JIM CROW, and NO ISRAEL EMBARGO — the latter banner a protest against the weapons embargo that was keeping the Truman administration from sending arms to the Israelis. The speaker's platform was set up over the baseball field's second base. The black actor, singer, and activist Paul Robeson sang "Let My People Go" and "Old Man River." Folk singer Pete Seeger shouted into the microphone a description of his experience touring the South with Henry Wallace the previous week.

"I can tell you a lot of things the newspapers didn't tell you," Seeger said of Wallace's trip through Virginia, North Carolina, and Tennessee. "They were wonderful things. In Memphis, in Birmingham, in Durham, where white men and Negroes had never sat side by side before, they sat together and they sang and cheered Wallace — but the newspapers didn't tell you that."

More warm-up speakers took the stage. There was Wallace campaign officer Lee Pressman, who just weeks earlier had been accused of being a Communist conspirator by Whittaker Chambers during the Alger Hiss hearings, and Vito Marcantonio, US congressman representing the east side of Harlem, widely known for his support of Communist causes.

"They can call us Reds and call us pinks," Marcantonio announced. "But we never double-crossed anybody and nobody can call us yellow."

Wallace took the stage at 11:30 p.m. to thunderous applause. "This is a great American meeting," he said. "It is a meeting in the best American tradition — a meeting of men and women of all races, of all creeds." Wallace told his fans of the ugliness he had seen in the South, how the eggs and tomatoes had rained on him, how the faces of white Americans were "contorted with hate." But the trip exemplified "our American rights to freely assemble and freely speak," he said. "Fear is a product of inactivity and the greatest remedy for fear is to stand up and fight for your rights."

"We must work," he said in conclusion. "We will work so that on November 2, Americans can clearly choose."

22

“We’re Going to Give ’Em Hell”

AFTER HIS DETROIT SPEECH ON Labor Day weekend, Truman returned to Washington on September 13, before his campaign train headed west for California and all stops in between.

At 1 p.m., Truman welcomed Secretary of Defense James Forrestal and Secretary of the Army General Kenneth Royall to the Oval Office to discuss Berlin and the bomb. Forrestal bluntly asked Truman if he was prepared to push the proverbial button, in the event of war. According to Forrestal, Truman answered “that he prayed that he would never have to make such a decision, but that if it became necessary, no one need have a misgiving but what he would do so . . .”

“The situation in Berlin is bad,” the Atomic Energy Commission chief David Lilienthal wrote in his diary on this same day. “The Russians seem prepared to kick us in the teeth on every issue. Their planes are in the air corridor today, and anything could happen . . . The President is being pushed hard by Forrestal to decide that atomic bombs will be used . . . The President has always been optimistic about peace. But he is blue now, mighty blue. It is very hard on him, coming right now particularly.”

Later that night of September 13, Truman’s campaign-finance chief Louis Johnson held a fund-raising event at the White House. Johnson arranged to have some thirty wealthy potential donors gather for a tea in the Red Room.

After the staff served drinks on silver trays, Truman stood up on a chair and asked for the group's attention. He said his campaign was so desperate for money that, if donors did not come through with $25,000, the Truman Special, which was about to embark on a cross-country campaign trip, would not get beyond Pittsburgh.

"I am appealing to you for help," he said, "help to carry my message to the American people. We just haven't got the money to buy radio time. In Detroit on Labor Day we had to cut one of the most important parts of my speech because we didn't have the money to stay on air."

"Mr. Truman looked pathetic and alone," Drew Pearson wrote of this moment, in the *Washington Post.* (Pearson was presumably in the room.) "Some of the [Democratic National] committee's operations have been so amateurish they are unbelievable."

Still, two men wrote checks for $10,000 apiece.

At the end of this hectic day, Truman wrote in his diary: "I have a terrible feeling . . . that we are very close to war. I hope not . . . My staff is in a turmoil. Clifford has gone prima donna on me. So has Howard McGrath. It's hell but a part of the game. Have had to force McGrath to behave and Clifford too . . . I get a headache over it. But a good night's sleep will cure it."

Four days later, Truman left the White House again with Margaret. Bess was still in Denver visiting family. On track 16 at Union Station, the Truman Special was ready for departure. Vice presidential candidate Alben Barkley arrived at the track siding to see Truman off.

"I think I am going to mow 'em down," Truman said.

"Are you going to carry the fight to them, Mr. President?"

Truman smiled. "We're going to give 'em hell."

The president's twenty-four-year-old daughter leaned in and said, "Daddy, you shouldn't say 'hell.'"

Truman and Barkley grasped each other's hands, and then the president climbed into the *Ferdinand Magellan.* He was suffering a cold, which would serve to compound the discomfort of rail travel. That afternoon, he spoke in Pittsburgh, then in Crestline, Ohio. The train rolled into the small farming community of Rock Island, Illinois, at sunrise the next morning. Truman stepped out onto the *Ferdinand Magellan*'s back platform at 5:45 a.m. To his surprise, there were four thousand people waiting to hear him.

"I don't think I have ever seen so many farmers in town in all my life," he told the crowd. "I had no idea that there would be anybody else in a town the size of Rock Island at this time of day."

After his talk, he stood staring out at the scene with a staffer named William Bray, who remarked that this was a good beginning to this next leg of the trip. Truman asked why.

"Well, those people had to get up maybe at 4:30 in the morning to be here and if such a crowd is willing to come out to hear you it looks like a good omen," Bray said. "Maybe in spite of the polls, there are a lot of people who have not made up their minds and are willing to listen. And," Bray concluded, "that's all we can hope for."

On the morning of September 17, the Truman Special crossed into enemy territory. Like most heavily agricultural states, Iowa was firmly Republican. The state had gone to the GOP in all but three presidential elections dating back to 1856, and had landed squarely in Thomas Dewey's column over FDR four years earlier. Iowa had a Republican governor, and all eight congressmen and both senators were Republicans. Still, in each town where Truman stopped, he found a crowd awaiting him to hear his "rip-snorting" impromptu speeches.

The president waved peeled ears of golden corn at farmers. Local marching bands honked out crowd favorites. Swarms of motorcycle police sporting American flags revved their engines. So soon after the war, patriotism was palpable at these rallies, and the hours moved by in a montage of red, white, and blue. "It is fascinating," Margaret wrote in her diary on this day. "We made about six stops altogether, and we eat in between." At the station in Des Moines, the Truman Special picked up the First Lady. Porters helped Mrs. Truman get her luggage aboard; Bess settled in for what would be her first and only national presidential campaign tour.

By the end of the first week, the reality of life aboard a traveling train began to set in. "Going across the country, I imagine we were the laughing stock of the nation," recalled one Democratic Party official, John P. McEnery. "It was like a traveling circus," according to columnist Richard Strout, who was aboard. "Nothing in the world is remotely like the atmosphere on one of these transcontinental campaign caravans," the columnist Marquis Childs wrote of the Truman Special. "It is a perpetual public affairs forum, a gossipy smalltown sewing circle, a traveling rodeo, the mixture being unique and completely and unmistakably American."

The Union Pacific railroad kitchen offered surprisingly tasty fare. The menu included an à la carte breakfast: bacon and eggs ($1.25), griddle cakes with syrup ($0.50), fillet of salt mackerel, club style ($1.85). At lunch and dinner, martini and Manhattan cocktails ($0.60) and beer ($0.40) accompanied chicken à la King ($2.05) or pan-fried fillet of fish with tartar sauce ($1.80), while the gem on the dessert menu was ice cream with caramel sauce ($0.30).

The Truman family and the president's aides fell into a routine — as much as was possible, given that the schedule called for numerous whistle-stops at different times each day, from sunrise to well into the night. "The most important function was to take part in the daily policy meetings that took place to set the policy in the campaign," recorded Clifford. "We met every day around the dining room table on his car sometimes at breakfast, sometimes at lunch, and sometimes off and on during the day."

The advance team led by Oscar Chapman would be out in front of Truman's train by a day or two, and this team would funnel back information via telephone or messenger. "As an advance man," noted Chapman, "you first try to find out from your friends or whomever you've got the closest contacts with, the leaders from a different state or community, just what the situation is, what's the President's standing around there, what they feel about him, and what are the issues which they disagree with him on . . . Within a short time, you've pretty much got them catalogued into two or three groups of their likes or dislikes and their reasons."

Data was constantly flying in from Bill Batt's research division, working day and night in the Dupont Circle office in Washington. "They worked like dogs and they ground out an incredible amount of material," recalled presidential aide George Elsey, whose job it was to organize this material for Truman. "All kinds of historical, literary, political, economic data flowed from them, and the news clippings, photostats of useful documents, anything that would give a spark and vitality and originality and vigor to President Truman's campaign effort."

"When [Truman] would come into Chicken Bristle, Iowa, or some such place like that . . . ," noted Clark Clifford, "he would congratulate the town on their having a new sausage factory. That would be based on material that had just come in a few days earlier from the advance team." While Truman would have notes to help him aim his talk at the specifics of his location, he had to wing these speeches. "He didn't have time between stops to sit and think about what he would say at the next stop, because between stops, he had to do other things," recalled speechwriter Charlie Murphy. "So in this sense, I suppose he did more in writing his own whistle stop speeches than anyone else."

After a week of traveling, "we developed a pattern for the typical stop," recorded Clifford. "The President would emerge at the back of his car, make a few nice remarks about the town he was in, and then launch into an attack on the 'do nothing' Eightieth Congress. He would ask the crowd, 'How would you like to meet my family?' and wait with his head cocked for the response. Then he would introduce Bess Truman, always referring to her as 'the Boss.' After that he would present his daughter Margaret . . . 'who bosses the boss.' Then, as the train started to pull away, Margaret would toss a red rose to someone in the crowd."

Standing inside the train just behind a curtain, a few feet behind the president's back, an aide named Jack Romagna would be taking down in shorthand what Truman was saying during his impromptu speeches, so there would be a record of each whistle-stop talk.* At the same time, armed Secret Service agents would ensure the president's security. "We'd bring the rope up and let these people come right up to the back of the train, maybe 15, 20

*This is why Truman's hundreds of whistle-stop speeches are available today in the Truman archives.

feet away from the train," recalled Floyd Boring,* Truman's driver and bodyguard on the Truman Special. "We'd have control that way."

When the opportunity presented itself, Truman would be up before sunrise to take a "constitutional" walk, 120 steps per minute. A farcical retinue of Secret Service agents and members of the press would hustle after him. At one point, on his way back to the train after one such walk, Truman shook his fist at a group of photographers.

"You guys let me down," he said.

The photographers expressed their confusion at the president's remark. "Come on, boys," Truman said, "you have photographed me in every possible situation. I stopped back there at that gas station to use the men's room, and there wasn't one photographer to take my picture in that place." Roars of laughter followed.

The Truman family was a curiosity for Americans. They were so different from previous First Families — the aristocratic Roosevelts, the wealthy Hoovers. Mrs. Truman stood five foot four, with gray hair cropped short. She appeared well-tailored and matronly in conservative midwestern style, in a new wardrobe she had purchased at the dress shop Agasta Gowns on Connecticut Avenue in Washington. The staff kept a respectable distance, but liked her. Photographers knew to keep their camera lenses pointed elsewhere, and news scribes understood that whatever she said was off the record. "Despite Mrs. Truman's reserve in public," recalled George Elsey, "she was warmly human to those she knew."

Harry's favorite time of day was his bourbon cocktail with Bess. Privately, they talked through the issues the president faced, the speeches he was going to make, the policy decisions. But in public, Bess Truman formed her persona as the antithesis of Eleanor Roosevelt, who had used the position of First Lady to create her own political influence. Once, two years earlier, Bess was asked, "If it had been left to your choice, would you have gone into the White House in the first place?" She answered, "Most definitely would not

*Floyd Boring later took part in a gunfight during an assassination attempt on Truman in 1950 in Washington, which left one shooter and a Secret Service man dead.

have." Would she want Margaret to become a First Lady? "No." Did she think there would ever be a female president? "No." Had living in the White House changed her view of politics and people? "No comment."

The First Lady "wasn't trying to run the world," remembered Truman speechwriter Oscar Chapman. On the train in 1948, "she was just trying to help Harry. And I'm telling you, that went through that crowd [on the train], and you'll never understand the feeling that a man has when you catch that so clearly, that this whole group was, 'We're going to help this man . . . because she's out here trying to help him, and we're going to help him too.' You'd be amazed at the sincerity and the depth with which that particular group [Truman's staff] felt towards Mrs. Truman."

The Trumans' only child, Margaret, had her own unique iconography. Society columnists were riveted by her. She had been twenty-one years old at the time her father became president. Now twenty-four, she was set on blazing a nontraditional path. A profile of her in the *New York Times* in 1946, "Margaret Truman, Career Girl," summed up her story:

"The interest the public takes in Margaret Truman, as a young unmarried White House daughter, is wholly in the American tradition. In one notable respect, however, Miss Truman herself is not at all in the tradition of Presidential daughters of debutante age . . . [She is] earnestly working toward a career that no other Presidential daughter seems even to have thought of. The career would be in opera, as a coloratura soprano."

Margaret had grown up listening to her father playing the piano, and would often sing while he played. Voice lessons led to her first professional appearance, on March 9, 1947, on a live broadcast of ABC's *Sunday Evening Hour.* "Now don't get scared," her father wrote her before that night. "You can do it! And if anyone says you can't, I'll bust him in the snoot."

Two days before Christmas in 1947, Margaret sang on a professional stage in front of a crowd that included the president of the United States, for the first time, at Constitution Hall in Washington. Some critics hailed her skill and courage; others thought her ability to lure crowds stemmed solely from her role as First Daughter. The *Washington Post*'s music critic Paul Hume said she needed to find a new instructor. Nevertheless, by 1948, "Margie," as her father called her (with a hard *g*), was getting offers to appear onstage at Carnegie Hall, as a guest on the TV show *Pepsodent Hour with Bob Hope,* and from Cecil B. DeMille Productions in Hollywood.

Aboard the Truman Special, Margaret was, in her father's words, "my greatest asset," and the pride the president took in his daughter was a genuine, humanizing force. On the *Ferdinand Magellan*'s back platform at whistle-stops, crowds would yell for her.

"Where is Margaret?"

"How about a song?"

Still, there was no question of who was commanding this steel-wheeled adventure. It was, in the words of Truman's first press secretary, Jonathan Daniels, "the Odyssey of the 'everyday' American through our times. Truman was that 'everyday man'; he remains his greatest symbol."

Never had there been a president who looked and talked so much like the average voter. Truman had lived most of his life in obscurity—as a farmer, a soldier, a failed businessman, before destiny had intervened and placed him at the helm of the most powerful nation in the history of the world. "Hardly any other President has so personally shared all the vicissitudes of all the people," according to Daniels. Truman walked among them, as one of them. He was fallible, he was blunt, and he exemplified humility. "Judging by his appearance," recalled the reporter Robert Donovan, "he might have been an insurance salesman paying a call, or the family physician. As he drew nearer, the image changed from bland to crisp. The man who was nondescript from afar exuded a glow of vitality at closer range. The backs of his hands were covered with fine dark hairs, and when he shook hands his grip was strong."

"He had a tremendous veneration and respect for the institution of the Presidency," recalled George Elsey. "He didn't demand any respect at all for Harry S. Truman; he demanded respect for the President of the United States . . . He was without any guile or any pretense. He was a politician. He was proud of his being a politician. He thought it was an honorable word."

As the train chugged west, the president's campaign strategy began to emerge. "You know the issues in this campaign are not hard to define," he told an audience in Rock Island, Illinois. "The issue is the people against the special interests, and if you need any proof of that, all you need to do is to review the record of this Republican 80th Congress."

In Truman's speeches, Thomas Dewey was never mentioned. Truman aimed to run not against the Republican candidate, but against the Republican Congress, the Congress elected two years earlier, led by conservatives Robert Taft of Ohio, Joe Martin of Massachusetts, and Charles Halleck of Indiana. The line between the policies of Truman and the policies of the more liberal Republicans Thomas Dewey and Earl Warren was a gray one; in many ways — Palestine, civil rights, an increase in Social Security benefits — the two platforms resembled each other. The line between Truman and the Eightieth Congress, however, was stark and clear.

"While I knew that the southern dissenters [from the Democratic Party] and the Wallace-ites would cost some Democratic votes, my opponent was the Republican Party," Truman later wrote in his memoirs. "The campaign was built on one issue — the interests of the people, as represented by the Democrats, against the special interests, as represented by the Republicans and the record of the Eightieth Congress. I staked the race for the presidency on that one issue."

When the Truman Special pulled into Dexter, Iowa, at 11:15 a.m., on September 18, Truman and his entourage filed into cars while maintenance men with the Pennsylvania Railroad climbed aboard to service the train. "This was another blistering hot day," recalled one journalist present. The sun beat down on the president, who had already made six whistle-stop speeches that day. Truman was scheduled to speak to farmers at the National Plowing Contest, held at the private farm of Mrs. T. R. Agg, the widow of the dean of Iowa State College. When the president arrived, he was stunned to see that ninety thousand people were on hand, and if tradition were to hold up, a vast majority of these farming people were going to vote Republican.

In one field, rows of glistening luxury cars were parked, many sparkling new Cadillacs among them. In another field, a surprising number of private airplanes formed their own rows; event organizers were wandering around complaining that all these private aircraft had been parked in the wrong place. A correspondent from London's BBC, Leonard Miall, saw these airplanes and drew a conclusion. "You know farmers tend to vote their pocketbooks," he recalled. "The moment that I saw the number of private aircraft illegally parked in the wrong parking place for the plowing match I began to wonder whether the farmer's vote was going to be so solidly Republican in the '48 election as it was expected to be."

When Truman climbed up onto the speaker's platform, he stood under a huge sign reading WELCOME TO IOWA and looked out at a vast audience. He knew that he was addressing some very wealthy Americans. The Depression had ravaged this part of the nation, but farming communities like these had bounced back. Since 1940, the purchasing power of farmers had risen 70 percent, compared with 50 percent for the rest of the country. Bank deposits and currency among farmers had quadrupled during that time. Farmers in 1948 were enjoying a prosperity they had never known. One Iowa farmer told a reporter on this day, "I have my own airplane; my son has his own airplane. We both own Cadillacs . . . The depression hit the farmer first and hit him hard . . . [But] today, I have more money than I know what to do with or even count myself."

Toward the end of his speech, Truman raised the issue of the Commodity Credit Corporation. He knew that this crowd would catch on fast to the importance of the CCC, but he did not know that he was about to hit on a point that would have a major impact on the outcome of the election. The CCC was a government-controlled bank of sorts that stabilized farm income and farm commodity prices. In June the Eightieth Congress had passed a law that rewrote the charter. An obscure provision did away with storage bins that the government had previously used to help farmers with especially large harvests. Without these bins, farmers would have no way to store their grains if the harvest turned out to be surprisingly good; they would have to sell them all at once, and prices would thus drop precipitously. Truman noted:

> Now the farmers need such bins again. But when the Republican Congress rewrote the charter of the Commodity Credit Corporation

> this year, there were certain lobbyists in Washington representing the speculative grain trade . . . These big-business lobbyists and speculators persuaded the Congress not to provide the storage bins for the farmers. They tied the hands of the administration. They are preventing us from setting up storage bins that you will need . . . When the farmers have to sell their wheat below the support price, because they have no place to store it, they can thank this same Republican 80th Congress that gave the speculative grain trade a rake-off at your expense.

The crowds showed Truman little enthusiasm — a smattering of applause and that was it. The significance of his remarks was not yet apparent. Within weeks, however, during the harvest, the prescience of Truman's speech would become brutally obvious to farming communities across the country.

When he was done, he stepped into the crowd to perform a publicity stunt. Using mules and a plow, he demonstrated his farming prowess gained from years on his own farm as a young man in Missouri, by plowing a perfectly straight line. Then it was back to the train. Two Secret Service agents — James J. Rowley and Henry J. Nicholson — were on the train, gauging the dim response to the president's Dexter speech when Truman boarded.

Nicholson said, "There was not much of a demonstration there, Mr. President."

"Nick, don't worry about that," Truman said, as the Secret Service man later recalled. "I know these people. The fact is that they were there; I have no worry at all."

23

"The Presidency of the United States Is Not for Sale!"

THE DAY AFTER TRUMAN'S SPEECH in Dexter, Iowa, on the other side of the country, Thomas Dewey and his wife, Frances, boarded the "Dewey Victory Special" at Albany's Union Station and departed westward on a misty afternoon, on a trip Tom Dewey believed would end in the White House in January. Herbert Brownell gave a statement to the press saying Dewey's campaign would be "the most intensive in the modern history of the Republican party."

The train left track 8 at 4:15 p.m. Dewey had no Secret Service contingent, as he was not an elected federal official, but six New York State police officers aboard comprised his security detail. If elected, he would rank with Ulysses S. Grant as the second-youngest man ever to become an American president, at forty-six. (Theodore Roosevelt moved into the White House at forty-two.) Not including Dewey's speechwriters and top advisers, the staff comprised six research experts, two research secretaries, two press secretaries, a newsreel assistant, a radio assistant, a stenographer, a mimeograph operator, and two physicians. Dewey also had some help from an unlikely source.

"The FBI helped Dewey during the campaign itself by giving him everything we had that could hurt Truman, though there wasn't much," an assistant to FBI chief J. Edgar Hoover later told Truman biographer David McCullough. Hoover had designs on the attorney general job, in a new Republican administration.

Also on board the seventeen-car Dewey campaign train were eighty-one pressmen and -women — the A-team of the journalism world — who had elected to travel with the Republican nominee. The Alsop brothers, Robert Albright of the *Washington Post*, Jack Bell of the Associated Press, Leo Egan of the *New York Times*, and Richard Rovere of *The New Yorker* were among them. There were radio commentators aboard, picture artists, photographers, and enough photography equipment to start a Hollywood studio. Dewey was set to become "the most news-covered, radio-covered, still- and motion-picture covered Republican presidential candidate in political history," wrote Roscoe Drummond from aboard the Dewey train.

At 12:10 p.m. the next day, the train pulled into Rock Island, Illinois, where the candidate made his first appearance. Ten thousand people turned out to see him. That night, Dewey gave his first major speech, at Drake University in Des Moines, Iowa. Sheets of rain had swamped the football stadium in the afternoon, and the night's event was moved to the university's field house. Dewey spoke soberly of the problems the next administration would inevitably face, obstacles "as momentous as any which have ever confronted this nation," and he warned foreign nations expecting to capitalize on America's difficulties that no such benefits would be forthcoming.

He "spoke with special seriousness and special effect," recalled one attendee. "The glitter of success, the air of super-efficiency which marked his whole appearance here, may have been a little putting off. But this defect of too much perfection was compensated for by the impression that Dewey undeniably gave, of sensing the magnitude, the complexity, the difficulty of the task that is ahead of him." Commented another in the crowd that night: "Caravans from out in the state were organized to swell the audience. All that could be done by bunting, noise-makers, good radio and loudspeaker arrangements, careful seating and good crowd management was done with efficiency. The result was a meeting with such a strong smell of success about it that the observer was inclined to propose calling off the whole campaign as an unnecessary expense."

Like Truman, Dewey's itinerary had him making back-platform speeches at train stations in small towns, with big rallies scheduled along the way. Over the next days, the main thrust of his strategy came into focus for the American public. He was going to ignore the right wing of his party, and he was going to speak in poetic platitudes rather than make concrete commitments to any future policy. Thus, he believed, he would have a free hand to do what he wanted when he moved into 1600 Pennsylvania Avenue. The Dewey campaign could be summed up in a single word: *unity.*

In Des Moines, Dewey told a sprawling audience: "Tonight we enter upon a campaign to unite America," adding later, "we will rediscover the essential unity of our people." The next night in Denver, he spoke of "the unity that binds us together," and how "this strength and unity can be increased in the years ahead." The next night in Albuquerque, New Mexico, he stumped for a renewed "unity among our people." (There in Albuquerque, Dewey also made a rare campaign policy commitment that was in opposition to Truman's platform: more tax cuts for the American people.)

He would not be wearing Indian headdresses or ten-gallon hats. No gimmickry, no wisecracks, no policy bashing. Just unity.

Many of the journalists traveling with Dewey had also ridden aboard the Truman train, and they were struck by the contrast between the two campaigns. At overnight stops on the Dewey train, riders were invited to leave their laundry in marked bags in the train hallway. It was picked up by porters and delivered clean the next morning. No such luck aboard the Truman Special. Dewey speeches were mimeographed and distributed to the press well in advance, and the candidate did not deviate from them; most of Truman's speeches were impromptu.

Dewey strove to be high-toned and dignified in his public presentations, his speeches a mix of Lincolnesque rhetoric and Madison Avenue slickness. Truman, noted one journalist, "spoke the language of Robespierre in the mild tones of the Kiwanis Club of Independence, Mo." Dewey's appearances were perfectly choreographed, and held generally only after 9 a.m. Truman was not above speaking in his pajamas, sometimes in the rain at sunrise.

On Truman's train, it was whiskey and poker. On Dewey's, martinis and bridge. Truman's inner circle liked to crack jokes at Dewey's expense (a common quip was, "You really have to get to know Dewey to dislike him"). On Dewey's train, the name *Truman* was rarely spoken at all.

"The Truman show was threadbare and visibly unsuccessful, getting hardly more response than politeness demanded," columnist Joseph Alsop wrote from aboard the Dewey Victory Special. "The Dewey show was opulent. It was organized down to the last noise-making device. It exuded confidence. And it got a big hand. The contest was really too uneven . . . One felt a certain sympathy for the obstinately laboring President."

On both campaign trains, however, riders were inevitably vexed by the endless miles, the galaxies of faces at each stop, the shrill whistles of train porters, the uncomfortable humidity of the train cars. Aboard Dewey's train, Frank McNaughton of *Time* magazine captured the experience in a cable he sent out at one stop in Wyoming.

> Life begins at nine o'clock with a five-minute layover at some Tank-town . . . There are about a hundred out to see the candidate . . . The loudspeaker just broadcast, 'All interested in seeing Governor Dewey please walk to the rear of the train.' You listen to the cut and dried back platform speech on the wonders of the country, the future of the west, unity, and all the stock phrases until at each stop you are ready to scream for mercy. Thus it goes all day long. At night stops, you hustle into a hotel room . . . and try along with a hundred others to get a crack at a shower bath, a bit of dinner, a bit of battery fluid for your dynamo, before covering the major show. You wave and flirt with the girls along the parade route, but your heart isn't in it. Anything to relieve the boredom . . .

Winslow, Arizona. Flagstaff, Ash Fork, Prescott, Phoenix. Dewey stumped for Republican members of Congress, touching on issues without making commitments, always ending with: "And now, I want to introduce you to Mrs. Dewey." The crowds seemed perfectly satisfied. The Republican National Committee's Barak Mattingly summed up the Dewey campaign with five simple words: "Things are looking good everywhere."

In mid-September, from the statehouse in Columbia, South Carolina, Strom Thurmond announced the Dixiecrats' campaign itinerary. There would be no trip to California, no visit to Chicago or Boston, no appearance anyplace that would not welcome Thurmond's pro-segregation message. Thurmond was headed back to the nation's capital, then to Baltimore, followed by a tobacco festival in La Plata, Maryland, then on to Virginia and North Carolina.

From his office, Thurmond read a statement for reporters, admonishing Truman for not campaigning in South Carolina. "I had hoped," Thurmond said, "that he would come to our State and explain to our people why he saw fit to betray the principles of Jefferson and abandon the historic position of the Democratic Party on States' Rights by sending his so-called civil rights message to Congress."

Thurmond's campaign still stood on a single-issue platform: the ability of states to make their own laws regarding race and segregation. He took no stance on the Berlin crisis, nor on inflation, the Taft-Hartley law, or housing or tax reform. He had huge support in his home state, where George Gallup had him running at 52 percent of the vote as of mid-September, with Truman in second at 26 percent. Numerous newspapers had embraced Thurmond, papers like the *Charleston News and Courier* in South Carolina, which defended "the white man's party," and the *Nashville Banner* of Tennessee, which stated in an editorial, "The Democratic South finally is moving to cleanse the party temple. As did Hercules, at work on the Augean stables, it can be done in a day. That day is November 2."

Thus far, the polls outside of Thurmond's base showed little enthusiasm for him. In Texas, where he had hoped his campaign would gain traction, Gallup had him with only 6 percent of the vote. In Kentucky — another state where Thurmond was hoping to do well — Gallup gauged him at only 5 percent. In North Carolina, he was running at 13 percent. The numbers were far below what the Dixiecrats had hoped. Only in South Carolina, Alabama, Mississippi, Louisiana, Georgia, and potentially Florida was the Thurmond phenomenon catching on.

For Democrats, however, Thurmond represented a threat that went beyond the electoral votes in 1948. What would be the ultimate consequences of the southern revolt?

For the first time in well over half a century, the GOP was seeing real opportunity in these southern states. One document that began to circulate among Truman operatives in September was a memo called "Analysis of the Southern Democratic Revolt." It predicted that the Dixiecrats were going to cost Truman a sum of thirty-two electoral votes, from Mississippi, Alabama, Florida, and South Carolina. Beyond 1948, however, it appeared that Republican candidates could gain a foothold in these states.

In North Carolina, which the GOP had carried only once going back to 1872, "the Republicans [have] an excellent chance to capture 14 electoral votes," the analysis concluded. In Florida the election was "considered fertile territory for a Republican campaign." The entire region — what had been the Solid South of the Democratic Party — could present a new conservative GOP alignment going forward. The analysis concluded:

> A grass roots sentiment against Truman and the National Democratic Party exists. A part of the sentiment is based on the racial issue . . . The situation indicates both a regional party and a fight by the Republicans to gain a permanent foothold. The day calls for bold action. Alabama and Mississippi Democrats have broken a tradition of 80 years. If the Republican party campaigns in North Carolina, Tennessee and Florida, there may well be the commencement of new party alignments in the United States.

(That realignment would eventually happen, but not until the 1960s and '70s. No evidence exists that Thurmond understood the irony of his campaign: He wasn't creating a lasting new party; he was setting up a new power base for Republicans — and would eventually become one, himself, in 1964.)

Thurmond arrived in Washington, DC, by train with his wife, Jean, on the final day of September. Trailed by a noticeably small group of reporters, he lunched at the Mayflower Hotel a few blocks from the White House, then made a symbolic visit to the Alexandria, Virginia, home of the Confederate general Robert E. Lee. Thurmond next visited Gunston Hall, the home of the founding father George Mason. The next day, he hit Baltimore, where only about a thousand people were present in a theater that could accommodate twenty-seven hundred. He accused all three of his opposing candidates of promulgating a false message that was "spreading like wildfire," of "dishonest bargaining" for votes.

"In their traitorous bids for power, the three candidates — Dewey, Truman and Wallace — have endorsed force bills which they falsely call 'civil rights,'" Thurmond said. "We hereby put those three politicians on notice. American democracy cannot be bartered away like piece goods, and the Presidency of the United States is not for sale!"

"All agree that the Russians appear anxious to settle the real issues between us," Henry Wallace told an audience from atop a stage in Rochester, New York, on September 17. "I regretfully predict that the present negotiations between the United States and Russia will be interrupted by another war scare, unless the American people say 'no' in such uncertain terms that the negotiations will not dare to fail." The sponsors of World War III were "few," said Wallace, "but they are in the seats of power."

While Truman and Dewey both headed toward California, and Thurmond appeared in the nation's capital, Wallace took his message to New England and then to the Pacific Northwest, in an attempt to ratchet up publicity. But he faced surprising amounts of vitriol in places where he did not expect to find it. In Boston, a parade of marchers turned out carrying signs reading WHY NOT CONDEMN RUSSIAN IMPERIALISM TOO? The taunts of "Go back to Russia!" continued. Due to the threat of another outbreak of violence, Wallace required forty bodyguards when he attended a Boston Braves game against the Pittsburgh Pirates. Sitting in the stands, he could hear the fans booing and hissing at him.

The crowds attending his rallies were beginning to thin, and Wallace's tone began to change. He was nearing the end of one of the longest presidential campaigns any candidate had ever run, and he was growing exhausted. The people working against him were no longer just his opponents. They were his "enemies," he said. His message became less about policy and more about imminent calamity. The banks, the major corporations, the major political parties, all the powers that be were bullying the American public into war with the Soviet Union, and getting away with it, he believed.

"Their real intention is to surrender this country," he told a crowd in Portland, Oregon, "its resources — its people — our earnings — our children — to a chosen few who will march us either to slavery or to war — or to both."

Wallace's rhetoric was laced with an increasingly spiteful tone toward Truman — the man who had usurped Wallace's vice presidency during the 1944 election, the president who in 1946 had fired Wallace from the cabinet. Truman would "live in history as the worst defeated Democratic candidate who ever sought the Presidency," Wallace said.

The people working with Wallace were becoming more in tune with his idiosyncratic thought processes. He could steer from political policy into the metaphysical and back again seamlessly, though not always with convincing effect. "Wallace did not come without his own problems," remembered John Abt. "He was, quite literally, a mystic, and it was often impossible to appeal to his practical sense." One campaign staffer recalled Wallace talking about some issue and interrupting himself "to talk about the emanations he was receiving from the sky." When this staffer approached campaign manager Beanie Baldwin about the conversation, Baldwin said, "Of course. Didn't you know that about Wallace?"

As the election drew closer, the most uncomfortable truth about Wallace's campaign continued to play out before the American public. Wallace had said over and over again that he was not a Communist, and that he had no designs to inject Soviet influence into American policy. But the evidence linking his campaign to Communist causes had become blatantly obvious. At one point the *New York Times* ran the Communist Party USA's 1948 political platform and Wallace's Progressive Party platform side by side, to illustrate their striking similarities. Commented the writer William Henry Chamberlin: "It could reasonably be suspected that the same brain trust composed both."

"There was no secret about Communist support," Abt later said. "It can be said that the Communists did the bulk of the nitty-gritty work in the campaign and that, without them, there would have been no campaign to speak of . . . Wallace and [his running mate Glen] Taylor knew this, never tried to hide it and couldn't if they wanted to."

Abt, like many in the organization, looked at the matter almost patriotically. "Why shouldn't the Communists have every right — the same as all other U.S. citizens — to participate openly in a political campaign? Communists throughout Europe and Japan and Latin America were a legitimate part of the political landscape, winning seats in parliament and holding offices in city halls around the world."

Not a single person of public renown had gone on record saying that Wallace could win. His candidacy had become one not of hope but of protest. His staff was struggling to get his name on state ballots. Wallace was expecting his best results in New York, California, and Illinois, the states with the largest cities (and largest concentration of Communists and far-left-wing voters). But in Illinois, a state electoral board had voted to strike his name from the ballot. Abt had filed a lawsuit that, within a month, would reach all the way to the US Supreme Court (Wallace would lose in a 6–3 vote).

Wallace soldiered on, but he was becoming increasingly isolated. Even his wife refused to remain by his side on the campaign trail. She remained secluded at their farm in South Salem, New York. "She has always been very violently anti-communist," Wallace explained, "and I suppose she picks up gossip from her lady friends who are usually quite conservative." Added Abt: "Mrs. Wallace was particularly suspicious of Beanie Baldwin and myself."

Westbrook Pegler continued to print acidic attacks on Wallace. On September 21, Pegler claimed in his column to have obtained two more of the guru letters that Wallace had allegedly penned to Nicholas Roerich years earlier. "I am now ready," Pegler wrote, "to take care of Wallace any time he dares to deny that he wrote this historic nonsense." Pegler quoted these humiliating letters copiously, including this line: "I have hard fighting ahead which I can survive only by keeping close to the great ones." By this time Wallace was close to almost no one. All the powerful figures of his past—from Eleanor Roosevelt to the powerhouses of the New Deal to Harry Truman himself—had abandoned him.

24

"You Will Be Choosing a Way of Life for Years to Come"

ONE NIGHT ABOARD THE *Ferdinand Magellan* after another grueling day of whistle-stops, Truman sat reading over a speech he would be making in Denver the following day — a speech that would be aired nationwide on radio. The clatter of rail wheels formed a background drumbeat. Bess was in the train car's galley talking over the menu for the next day's meals (she was on a low-salt diet).

"It was a typical Truman family evening," recalled Margaret, who was sitting across from her father, "unchanged by the admittedly unique circumstances surrounding it. We were hurtling into the climax of the wildest presidential campaign in history. My father was fighting for his political life, and for something even more important — his political self-respect as a man and President. Yet the atmosphere in the *Ferdinand Magellan* was calm, tranquil to the point of serenity."

The train would be stopping at 11:05 p.m. in Junction City, Kansas, where Truman would make another whistle-stop speech. Sitting quietly in his chair — probably clutching a bourbon and water — his eyes rose from the page he was reading to the speedometer mounted on the wall right above Margaret's head.

"Take a look at that thing," Truman said.

Margaret turned and looked. The speedometer read 105 mph. "Wow," she said, concern clouding her face. She moved over to the window to look out at the blur of darkness — the vast Kansas prairie at night — rushing by.

Truman said, "Do you know what would happen if that engineer had to make a sudden stop?" He paused. "If he had to stop suddenly, we would mash those sixteen cars between us and the [locomotive] engine into junk. Don't say a word to your mother. I don't want her to get upset."

The door opened and press secretary Charlie Ross walked in. Truman had known Ross since grade school; Charlie had in fact been valedictorian of Truman's graduating class at Independence High School in 1901. Now, forty-seven years later, Ross was one of Truman's most trustworthy advisers. He wanted to know how the president was doing with the Denver speech. Truman said it was fine, then he said, "Charlie, send someone to tell that engineer there's no need to get us to Denver at this rate of speed. Eighty miles an hour is good enough for me."

The next morning, the Trumans awoke and looked out their windows to see stunning views of the Rocky Mountains. "We arrived in Denver at 8:50 a.m.," Margaret wrote in her diary. "Dad made a speech to about 25,000 people after a parade with thousands of people on the street." On the following night, in a national radio speech from within Colorado's State Capitol building, Truman threw his campaign into the next gear. From here on out, there would be more anger, more sarcasm, more all-out attack on the "do nothing" Eightieth Congress.

"Election day this year, your choice will not be merely between political parties," he said, with Colorado governor William Lee Knous standing beside him. "You will be choosing a way of life for years to come. This is a fateful election. On it will depend your standard of living and the economic independence of your community." The Republicans were "puppets of big business," "the same breed that gave you the worst depression in history."

"Today," he told his crowd, "I want to talk to you about what the Republican Congress has been doing to you, and to your families, and to your country." Over and over, he accused the Republican Congress of selling out the American people to the "profiteers." Six times, Truman denounced Wall

Street. If the Republican Congress was not stopped, he said, it was going to turn the western part of the country into "an economic colony of Wall Street." If the Republican Congress was not stopped, he said, it would destroy the West's natural resources — its forests, its water.

His message in Denver aimed to incite anger and perhaps stoke fear. "We shall have to fight the undercover Republican sabotage of the West," Truman railed.

With five weeks to Election Day, Truman was making no progress, if the newspapers were to be believed, and his increasingly populist tone left the pontificators surprised — even angry. "It is difficult to see how you could put a campaign on a lower plane," the columnist Frank R. Kent declared in the *Los Angeles Times* the day after Truman's Denver speech. "The most blatant demagoguery . . . in politics has piled higher than ever before."

One of the nation's two most respected pollsters, Elmo Roper, wrote in his newspaper column that he was finished with polling for the rest of the campaigns; there was no longer any point, because "Thomas E. Dewey is almost as good as elected to the Presidency of the United States." The *Atlanta Constitution* stated on its editorial page: "Nowhere is there any enthusiasm for Harry S. Truman. Even those who support him do so largely because they have less enthusiasm for Tom Dewey."

The only real base Truman seemed to have in his corner was made up of labor unions. James A. Hagerty declared on the front page of the *New York Times* in early October, "President Harry S. Truman will get a larger share of votes of organized labor than any other Presidential candidate, but this will not be sufficient to enable him to carry any of the more populous industrial states with large numbers of electoral votes."

With the presidential election all but decided, according to overwhelming public opinion, attention turned to the heated battle to capture control of the Eighty-First Congress. The Republicans held a 245 to 185 lead in the House, and a 51 to 45 lead in the Senate. "One can reasonably deduce that the makeup of the House should not be altered greatly by Dewey's election, although here and there seats will change hands," concluded the Alsop brothers in their syndicated column in mid-September. As far as most could see, however, the battle for the Senate was on. Democrats were campaigning hard to capture Senate seats in Illinois, West Virginia, Oklahoma, Kentucky, and Minnesota, hoping to narrowly regain control.

The Truman Special rolled on, through the Colorado Rockies and into Utah, where the president spoke to a crowd of twelve thousand people at the Mormon Tabernacle. Then it was on to Reno, Nevada, the "famous divorce city," as Margaret wrote in her diary. That night, the train crossed the border into California and the pine and juniper forests of the Sierra Nevada, into the high-elevation town of Truckee. Truman was scheduled to travel the entire length of California in a desperate fight for the state's twenty-five electoral votes. The polls showed him far behind Dewey in California, but gaining.

By the time Truman arrived on the West Coast, fatigue had begun to chip away at the staff's morale. Clark Clifford had broken out in a severe skin rash. "I was besieged by an attack of boils," he recalled. "It was a nightmare. For years afterwards I'd sometimes wake up at night in a cold perspiration thinking I was back on that terrible train. It was a *real ordeal.* I don't know quite how I got through it except I was young at the time and strong and vigorous."

Any time the train stopped for more than a few minutes, Truman campaigners and reporters would dash for laundromats in hopes of washing the stale odor out of their clothes, and to find some soap and a shower. The only shower on the train was in the president's suite in the *Ferdinand Magellan*. Deodorant was a rare find in stores (a new "stick form" version called Bar-It had just come to market that summer, for a dollar, plus tax). "What weeks of travel can do to your looks!" Margaret recalled. "I had a strong inclination to burn all my clothes." "When to get our laundry done became something of an obsession," recalled Clifford.

In the swaying *Ferdinand Magellan*, the First Lady and the First Daughter had fallen into the habit of incessant bickering. "My mother and I love to argue," Margaret later wrote of life aboard the Truman Special, "and one of the great frustrations of our life as a family has been my father's constant refusal to join us in our favorite sport." Meanwhile the men played cards. "The thing I remember most clearly," noted Jack Bell of the Associated Press, "was that there was a poker game going at the end of the press car twenty-four hours a day, with a two dollar limit game, seven card hi-lo stud, low hole card wild."

Newsmen could hear Truman's speeches from inside the press room on the train, so they grew lazy and stopped going outside to do any reporting. The most exercise their legs would get was during trips to the bathroom and bar car. The press corps believed they were covering a loser, and it showed. "Many of the reporters who traveled on our train had been condescending," remembered Margaret. "Contempt was lying around in hunks. But the people came to listen. What they heard came straight from my father's heart."

Around the time Truman entered California, something began to happen on the campaign trail, although the reporters traveling with the president failed to notice. In town after town, the whistle-stop speeches continued to draw surprising turnouts, and Truman's speeches were connecting more and more with audiences, who saw him as a fearless underdog fighting for survival on the biggest public stage on earth. The crowds began to feel his energy, and to pull for him, as if they wanted him to succeed. People would yell, "Give 'em Hell, Harry!" And he would shout back, "I'm just telling the truth about them [the Republicans] and they think it's Hell!"

"We had tremendous crowds everywhere," Truman wrote his sister from aboard the train. "From 6:30 a.m. in the morning until midnight the turnout was phenomenal. The news jerks didn't know what to make of it — so they just lied about it!"

"I never saw anything in my life like the enthusiasm with which the President was greeted at some of these what we called 'whistle stops,'" recalled aide Robert Dennison. "There were more people there than the population of the whole damn county. They came for miles, sometimes at the most ungodly hours, 5:30 a.m., 6 a.m. . . . And you could tell that they loved the President and loved his family." "Even after twenty-five years," recalled reporter Robert Nixon, "I can still see in my mind actual scenes of what happened. I can see the President . . . standing on the rear platform at his whistle stop speeches and the crowds at certain little towns and hamlets. I can remember the words he spoke and the things he did."

To his staffers, and to his family, Truman was unwavering in his confidence. "He fought, and fought, and fought," recalled Clifford. "He worked like a dog. He worked sixteen hours a day, day after day, week after week, and month after month. And at no times during the whole campaign did I ever hear him utter *a word* which indicated that he had the *slightest* doubt that he was going to win."

It was common knowledge aboard the train that not even the president's wife believed he could achieve his goal. One day, Truman was having breakfast with Bess and the executive director of the women's division of the Democratic National Committee, India Edwards, on the *Ferdinand Magellan.* Bess and India had known each other for years and were stark opposites in style and persona, which made moments like this ever so slightly awkward.

"You know, sometimes India," Truman said to Edwards as Bess looked on, "I think there are only two people in the United States who really think I'm going to be elected President . . . They're both sitting at this table and one of them is not my wife."

The battle for the Golden State was critical; only three states held more than California's twenty-five electoral college votes (New York, forty-seven; Pennsylvania, thirty-five; Illinois, twenty-eight). This fight would climax with a group of successive rallies in the nation's fifth-largest city—Los Angeles, with its growing movie industry. Truman was scheduled to host his biggest rally yet at Gilmore Stadium—which until recently had been the home of the Los Angeles Bulldogs, the city's professional football team—on September 23. Dewey was set to appear the following night, at the Hollywood Bowl.

All forecasts had Dewey and Warren carrying California, but by less than was expected. Earl Warren posed a peculiar problem for Truman. The Republican VP candidate from San Francisco had won the California governorship in 1942, and when he campaigned for reelection in 1946, he won both the Democratic and Republican primaries. California was split between a liberal majority along the coast and a more conservative populace in the farm belt that ran through the entire interior. Both embraced Warren, and his record showed that he and Truman agreed on most major issues.

"It will be extremely difficult to attack Mr. Warren on his record or generally on his stand on issues of the day," according to a Truman campaign memo, "since in the majority of the instances he is in accord with the Democratic program."

A bigger problem for Truman was that his campaign had once again run out of money. When the Truman Special hit San Francisco on September 22, there was no hall for the president to use for his first major West Coast speech, because so much of the budget had been reserved for his appearance in Los Angeles, the following day. The Democratic National Committee had arranged for Truman to speak for free on the steps of San Francisco's City Hall. The head of California's central party committee, Howard I. McGrath (no relation to J. Howard McGrath), had to pony up $400 of his own money so that lighting equipment could be rented to allow television cameras to broadcast Truman's speech, which was set for 8 p.m. West Coast time.

"We were startled when the crowd assembled at the City Hall," recalled McGrath. "With absolute conservative estimates, we had over 35,000 people standing in the dark in the air in the park in front of the City Hall." Then it was off over the Bay Bridge to Oakland, where Truman ripped into the Republican Congress, blaming it for high prices, the housing shortage, and poor education in schools.

"The most significant thing about the failures of this Republican Congress is that they show so clearly the attitude of the special interests who dominate the national Republican Party. Their actions set a definite, clear pattern. And that means a lot to your future," Truman told twenty-two thousand audience members in Oakland. "Big business interests in the East . . . control the Republican party."

Truman was opening himself up to criticism that he was trying to create class conflict to benefit his campaign. The argument was hard to refute, but still, the president seemed to wholly believe everything he was saying.

Thanks to campaign-finance man Louis Johnson, money trickled in, enabling the train to roll on. The day after Truman's Bay Area appearances, he headed south through the farm belt, turning up the heat on the GOP. In Fresno, he personally attacked the district's Republican congressman Bertrand W. Gearhart: "You have got a terrible congressman here in this district. He is one of the worst . . . He has done everything he possibly could to cut the throats of the farmer and the laboring man. If you send him back, that will be your fault if you get your own throat cut." In Bakersfield, Truman railed the Republican Congress for sabotaging the Democrats' farm program.

In Los Angeles, after nightfall, he was late for his speech due to street traffic. Some one hundred thousand people lined the streets to see his car roll by. Billboards trumping the Dewey-Warren ticket were everywhere. As the motorcade pulled toward the stadium's north gate, Truman could see the beams of forty searchlights in the night sky, reminding him that he was in the transplanted capital of the global movie business (New York City had been its home until recently). The stadium was filled to capacity; "you couldn't put any more in with a shoehorn," recalled California state senator Judge Oliver J. Carter. On a stage festooned with American flags, the master of ceremonies, actor George Jessel, stood at the microphone making idle remarks to kill time, while sitting in chairs onstage were Humphrey Bogart and Lauren Bacall, whose hit movie *Key Largo* was playing in theaters. The crowd grew restless, and audience members started yelling out: "We want Bogey!" "Let Margaret sing!" "You tell 'em, Harry!"

Finally, Truman arrived, and the crowd came alive. "This is a championship fight," Truman said, and the crowd responded as if it actually was.

In the hardest-hitting speech on Communism of his entire campaign, Truman launched a seething attack on Henry Wallace. Here in Los Angeles, the Red Scare was a major story. Less than a year earlier, ten Hollywood screenwriters had been charged by the US Justice Department with contempt of Congress for refusing to answer questions in front of the House Un-American Activities Committee, and in 1948 the "Hollywood Ten" were imprisoned. Truman's speech was careful not to fan those particular flames.

He focused instead on Wallace. Along with New York, California was a state where Wallace could steal enough votes from Truman to make a difference in the outcome. Truman went for the jugular.

"The fact that the Communists are guiding and using the third party shows that this party does not represent American ideas," he told the assembled crowd at Gilmore Stadium. "The simple fact is that the third party cannot achieve peace because it is powerless. It cannot achieve better conditions here at home because it is powerless."

Once again, Truman found his audience enthusiastic and receptive. Afterward, his motorcade headed for San Diego, where the president packed another stadium. "I just have never seen anything like it," recalled state senator Carter. "I don't think it will ever be repeated."

"It was at that point," recalled Howard I. McGrath, "when people decided that maybe this man did have a chance to carry California."

The Dewey Victory Special rolled into Los Angeles at 3:50 p.m. the next day. The goal was to outdo the Democrats in the power of the candidate's message, in crowd numbers, in Hollywood star power — in everything. For the second day in a row, Californians lined sidewalks to get a glimpse of a presidential candidate. Confetti strewn along the route made it look like snow was falling on the palm trees.

The Dewey campaign's efforts to recruit figures from the silver screen had paid off. Making appearances at the rally that night were Jeanette MacDonald, star of that summer's hit movie *Three Daring Daughters;* she would lead the crowd in "The Star-Spangled Banner." Walt Disney was on hand, along with Ginger Rogers, Randolph Scott, Lionel Barrymore, Barbara Stanwyck, and John Wayne, whose Howard Hawks–directed western *Red River* was currently playing in theaters. The rally was carefully choreographed by Warner Brothers director and dance choreographer LeRoy Prinz.

Onstage, Dewey came through in a perfectly measured cadence, his delivery as precise as a ticking clock. Like Truman, he chose Los Angeles to deliver his big anti-Communism speech.

"A grim, new struggle is on in the world," Dewey said. "It is a struggle between two exactly opposite ways of life for the mind and soul — the very future of mankind." Without mentioning Truman's name, Dewey called out the administration for having "bungled and quarreled . . . telling the world that ours is a blundering, bungling system." He skewered the president for his "red herring" comment; Truman was "shutting his eyes to the rampant evil" of Communism, while "Communists and fellow travelers have risen to positions of trust in our government." The Republican candidate continued:

> I propose that, next January 20 [Inauguration Day], we start a mighty world-wide counteroffensive, a counteroffensive not of aggressive acts but of truth, a counteroffensive of hope. I propose that we begin to tell our story — the American story — so well, so truthfully and with such meaning that the world will never again be in any doubt as to the choice between our way of life and theirs.

Dewey finished with a pledge to bring "a new unity for all America." For the audience, the speech was expeditious, poetic, climactic, and focused.

When it was all over, the street cleaners had their work cut out for them. "It would be foolish to make flat predictions about California at this stage," wrote the columnist Roscoe Drummond. "But the consensus still is widely on the Dewey-Warren side."

25

"The Democratic Party Was Down to Its Last Cent"

THE DAY AFTER HIS LOS ANGELES rally, Truman held whistle-stops in Yuma, Arizona, then Lordsburg and Deming, New Mexico, places where, historically, residents might have had more luck seeing a UFO than an American president. When the train crossed the Texas border, Truman entered Dixiecrat territory for the first time. While Strom Thurmond was not polling well in Texas, pockets of the state adamantly opposed federal civil rights laws, and Harry Truman.

Over a dozen whistle-stops were scheduled in the state, in tiny towns like Sierra Blanca and Valentine. Three major addresses were also planned. By this time, the speechwriters in charge of crafting the formal addresses were desperately far behind. Three days before the train crossed the Texas border, White House staffer Albert Carr wrote Matthew Connelly, the president's appointments secretary, "It is surprising to me that these speeches were not conceived, drafted and polished weeks ago, so that they did not have to be whipped into shape on the midnight before mailing."

The first major stop was El Paso. "The railroad station was at the end of a long street that had another street coming in at an angle," recalled White House staffer Donald Dawson, who had just recently joined the campaign train. "The President spoke from the back platform of the train. When he arrived, both of those streets were filled with crowds backed up for two city blocks trying to see the President and wanting to hear him speak. From that point on, it was a succession of personal triumphs."

The campaign had gathered more political muscle for the Texas trip. Congressman Lyndon B. Johnson, who was running for a Senate seat, came aboard looking disheveled and bewildered; Texans had just voted in the primary and Johnson did not know yet how the tally had come out. "He hadn't had any sleep or time to shave for three days," remembered Truman's first press secretary, Jonathan Daniels, who also boarded the train in Texas. The former Speaker of the House and current Texas congressman Sam Rayburn got on board, as did Truman's attorney general, Tom Clark.

Whistle-stops brought the train into small towns that looked like scenes from an old western movie. "I remember we stopped at one little place," recalled Donald Dawson. "There must have been 200 or 300 people there . . . A cowboy was on a bucking horse showing off for the crowd and trying to act smart." Truman finished his impromptu talk, climbed off the train platform, and approached the man. Holding the horse by the head, he opened its mouth, as only a seasoned farmer would be able to do.

"Your horse is eight years old and he's not a very good horse," the president joked.

The crowd roared with laughter as the man sheepishly turned and rode away.

Truman did not mention civil rights in Texas, but his integrated audiences spoke for him. Small numbers of black Americans showed up to hear him speak. At one whistle-stop, Truman shook the hand of a black woman, ignoring the boos from hostile whites. "In some towns," remembered Dawson, "they didn't even want the black voters to come down to the train. We just told them they were going to come. The President wanted them there."

On Sunday, September 26, John Nance Garner—former vice president under FDR—hosted the Truman campaign in tiny Uvalde, Texas. When Truman arrived, a marching band played for him and four thousand citizens turned out—at 5 a.m. "Cactus Jack" Garner hosted what Margaret called "the most tremendous breakfast in the history of the Truman family." There was white-winged dove, bacon, ham, fried chicken, scrambled eggs, rice in gravy, hot biscuits, local honey, and peach preserves. Truman gave Garner a bottle of Kentucky bourbon. "Medicine," the president said, "only to be used in case of snakebites."

In Bonham, Texas, the hometown of Sam Rayburn, the congressman and former Speaker of the House arranged a reception with the current Texas governor, Beauford Jester, who had courageously come out in support of Truman's civil rights efforts. In between handshakes and another parade, Truman met aboard the train with the ambassador to the Soviet Union, Walter Bedell Smith, who had flown in to confer with the president about the emergency in Berlin. When asked if there was going to be war, Smith answered, "That question is too deep for me to answer." By the time Truman made it to the stage that night in the hamlet of Bonham, twenty-five thousand people were out in the streets to hear Truman blast the Dewey campaign for serving up "unity" speeches without defining what he meant by the term.

"If we did have unity," Truman asked, "what kind would it be?" He answered his own question: "It would be unity in giving tax relief to the rich at the expense of the poor . . . Unity in refusing to give aid to our schools . . . Unity in letting prices go sky high in order to protect excessive profits . . . Unity in whittling away all the benefits of the New Deal."

By the time the Truman Special crossed the Oklahoma border, Truman had given twenty-two speeches in Texas, most of them extemporaneously. The Texas visit had been riotously successful and the campaign was depending on the state's twenty-three electoral votes, but once again, news came in that the money had run out. "We were headed for Oklahoma City," recorded correspondent Robert Nixon. "There was a lot of oil wealth aboard. The Democratic Party was down to its last cent . . . Word got around that we were going to have to call off the campaign trip. The train would be broken up, and we would have to make our way back to Washington on our own. That's how desperate it was."

The socialite Perle Mesta, known as "the hostess with the mostest" for the parties she threw in Washington, DC, was aboard. She went into the bar car where the wealthy oil men were drinking cocktails and made an announcement: The campaign was running out of cash. Mesta waved a check of her own. "And to keep this from happening," she said, "here's my check for $5,000."

Donors pulled out their checkbooks. The train was able to continue forward. But for how long, no one could say.

In Oklahoma City — the last major stop of this cross-country trip — Truman arrived late for his speech. "The President and everybody else piled off of the train into cars at the station," recalled one of the newspapermen on board. "We had motorcycle police and we went roaring through downtown Oklahoma City at 80 miles an hour, sirens screaming. Why somebody wasn't killed you often wonder. We roared into the fair grounds with dust flying, brakes screeching, and tires skidding." Onstage, Truman took aim at his opponents again. The Republicans had attacked him relentlessly for his "red herring" comment, claiming that he was responsible for Communists who had infiltrated American government.

> I should like the American people to consider the damage that is being done to our national security by irresponsible persons who place their own political interests above the security of the Nation. I regret to say that there are some people in the Republican Party who are trying to create the false impression that communism is a powerful force in American life. These Republicans know that this is not true. The time has come when we should take a frank and earnest look at the record about communism and our national security . . .
>
> Our Government is not endangered by Communist infiltration . . . The FBI and our other security forces are capable, informed, and alert . . . The Republicans ought to realize that their failure to deal with the big practical issues of American life, such as housing, price control, and education, is too plain to be hidden by any smoke screen.

> They ought to realize that their reckless tactics are not helping our national security; they are hurting our national security. I am forced to the conclusion that Republican leaders are thinking more about the November election than about the welfare of this great country.

Eighteen times, Truman was interrupted by applause from an audience of roughly twenty thousand people. When it was over, he headed back to his train. But the Truman Special was going nowhere. The Democratic National Committee had spent the campaign's last funds on the Oklahoma City radio broadcast. "We ran out of money, and we didn't have enough to get the train out of the station," Truman later explained. "I had to get on the phone and raise the money to get out of there."

Consternation spread through the train cars as the president of the United States made phone calls. His staff joined in. It was not only money that was short. The staffers were out of energy also. Clark Clifford called the head of the Atomic Energy Commission, David Lilienthal, from Oklahoma City, saying that he was "ready to crawl into a hole and die, but working on a second wind." On the final night aboard the train on this campaign swing, Clifford's assistant George Elsey wrote that he was "more dead than alive."

The Truman Special finally pulled into Union Station in the nation's capital at 10 a.m. on October 2. Another marching band. Another parade. Truman's campaign swing had made for endless newsprint, but few believed it had done the candidate any good. On the day the president returned to Washington, the nation's most influential newspaper—the *New York Times*—came out in favor of Dewey. The *Times* had endorsed only three Republicans in the past seventeen presidential elections and had gone against Dewey four years earlier. On this same day, the betting commissioner in Truman's home state of Missouri, James J. Carroll, set the odds of Truman winning at 15 to 1.

When the First Family arrived at the White House—then under construction and filled with scaffolding—the British ambassador to the United States, Sir Oliver Franks, was waiting for the president, wanting to debate solutions for the Berlin emergency. For Truman there would be no rest. The First Lady and the First Daughter went to their rooms and collapsed. They had just a few days to rest before their final campaign trip aboard the *Ferdinand Magellan* — this time across the northern United States.

"It's all over," Margaret wrote in her diary. "Until next week!"

PART V

Election Climax

For six to eight weeks the voters had been increasingly aware that something out of the ordinary was going on . . . It was so far from the ordinary that every rule in the lexicon was violated, political contradictions became the order of the day, and all laws of human nature blew sky high.

—Robert C. Albright, *Washington Post,* October 31, 1948

26

"This Was the Worst Mistake of the Truman Campaign"

THE GLAMOUR OF POLITICAL SPARRING in Los Angeles, Truman's thrill ride through Texas, the sense that the Republicans were about to take power for the first time in sixteen years — the nation was in the grips of election fever as never before. "Beyond any election in the nation's history, the verdict . . . will monopolize the interest of the world," wrote columnist John G. Harris in the *Boston Daily Globe*. "Many nations feel their destiny, too, is involved."

The 1948 campaign featured some historic firsts. There was the surging power of the pollster. The newly born television pundit. One in eight US families now owned a TV. Radio was ubiquitous as never before, even in rural backwaters. Circulation of daily weekday newspapers was well over fifty-two million, the highest in the history of any nation. Madison Avenue advertising agencies were richer and more powerful than ever. Never had candidates for major office had so many weapons at their disposal, so many ways to spread their truths and falsehoods and to spin the words of their opponents.

Both major parties were in the process of painful rebirth — Dewey leading the charge to liberalize the GOP, and Truman leading his own charge to keep the Democratic Party from coming undone. The fate of the Jews in the

Middle East, the fate of African Americans in the South, the fate of helpless war refugees in Palestine and all over Europe, the emergency in Berlin, the new Cold War, fear of Communism abroad, fear of Communism at home, the threat of atomic bombs — all of it seemed wrapped up in the '48 election.

The irony remained that — as fiercely dedicated as both major candidates were to their fight against the other — their platforms remained similar. They clashed on tax cuts and the Taft-Hartley labor law. But they agreed on increased government spending for Social Security and education. Both supported the Truman Doctrine and the Marshall Plan — the overriding internationalist concept that the United States had a duty to provide world economic and moral leadership. Both supported a strong stand against the Soviet Union and a bipartisan foreign policy. Both supported programs to root out Communist conspirators at home without employing "thought police" tactics and the outlawing of political beliefs in a free society. Both wanted to raise the minimum wage, to use federal funds to confront the housing crisis and clear urban slums, and to develop hydroelectric power.

Both Truman and Dewey supported the partition of Palestine and the formation of a Jewish state. Both supported immigration reform — the admission into the United States of "displaced persons," refugees of war and from politically unstable nations. Both supported civil rights programs.

In terms of policy, the Eightieth Congress clashed with many of these ideas. But for the two candidates, the most obvious thing that separated them was that one was considered a shoo-in and one, by public opinion, had no chance. The choice for voters was, in large part, in the fabric of the man, and which party was going to control the Eighty-First Congress.

Dewey's first major campaign swing seemed to uphold his commanding lead, and he had stayed true to his strategy. He would make few commitments and keep his campaign on a high plane.

Truman, on the other hand, was doing something wholly unexpected. He was painting a portrait for the public of a David-versus-Goliath fight, and of himself as a leader who had come from common folk. His language was the language of the common man — stripped bare of "two-dollar words," in Truman's parlance. He was out to protect the hundreds of millions of Americans powerless against the forces of greed that unrestricted capitalism could sometimes foster, to keep power in America where he believed it belonged: in the hands of the people. In doing so he was becoming more than a political candidate. He was becoming an American folk hero, and he was incessantly warning voters that the stakes of a presidential election had never been higher.

At one rally in San Antonio, Texas, Truman told a crowd gathered in the Gunter Hotel:

> Our government is made up of the people. You are the government. I am only your hired servant. I am the Chief Executive of the greatest nation in the world, the highest honor that can ever come to a man on earth. But I am the servant of the people of the United States. They are not my servants . . .
>
> I believe that if we ourselves try to live as we should, and if we continue to work for peace in this world, and as the old Puritan said, 'Keep your bullets bright and your powder dry,' eventually we will get peace in this world, because that is the only way we can survive with the modern inventions under which we live.
>
> We have got to harness these inventions for the welfare of man, instead of his destruction. That is what I am interested in. That is what I am working for. That is much more important than whether I am President of the United States.

The day Truman arrived back at the White House in early October, he found out that he and his family were going to move out whether he won the election or not. Two days earlier, the White House architect Lorenzo Winslow had announced that the entire second floor of the building — the space in which the president lived with his family — would have to be rebuilt. The "structural nerves" were in alarming decay, Winslow said. How long the Trumans needed to vacate, Winslow could not say. The work would cost somewhere between $750,000 and $1,250,000.

The president was home for just four days. Democratic leaders came to greet him in the White House, and the first question they asked the sixty-four-year-old was about his health and his stamina.

"Vitamin C stands for campaigning as far as I'm concerned," Truman said. "When I left town on this trip I had a cold and a sore throat. Now I'm rid of both and I gained 10 pounds while making 120 speeches."

"What do you think of those Texans tossing eggs at Henry Wallace?" asked Al Wheeler, the head of the Democratic Committee in the District of Columbia.

"I was sorry to hear about that—I really was," Truman said. "I guess the incident was building up for a long time. Some of those Texans have never liked Wallace . . . Add to that Wallace's Commie connections and you get some idea why those eggs were thrown. Those Texans couldn't hold out any longer. But I don't like that kind of a demonstration in a democratic country, regardless of the circumstances behind it."

Truman hosted the Democratic National Committee's research division at the White House, which officially ended its work on October 1. There was no more money to pay the team. Truman wanted to thank these dozen or so individuals personally. At roughly nine o'clock on a warm autumn night in the White House Rose Garden, Truman went from one campaign worker to the next to shake each hand personally.

"On election day," he said over and over, "we'll all celebrate together."

Dr. Johannes Hoeber, who had served as number two under Bill Batt in the division, remembered the moment the president shook his hand, and the confidence Truman displayed in his expression. Truman, Hoeber realized, truly believed he was going to win. "I remember catching the expression on Mrs. Truman's face at that moment, which was quite clear, that she herself didn't think this would happen," Hoeber recalled. "And on Margaret's face there was the same thing." But Truman seemed utterly sure. "There was no doubt in the President's mind," Hoeber recalled. "This is a memory which will stay with me always."

On Sunday, October 3, Truman met with campaign officials to discuss strategy. "What was most urgently needed, I felt, was a totally new approach,"

Truman later wrote in his memoirs. "We were pretty desperate," added Jonathan Daniels, Truman's first press secretary, who was at the White House that day. "We wanted something that would be a dramatic gesture of the President's effort for peace and security in the world."

Truman had the idea of sending an emissary to meet with Joseph Stalin in person, in a grand gesture of peace. Something had to be done to iron out the differences between the United States and the USSR, before it was too late, and a diplomatic effort would generate positive publicity, Truman believed. Back in 1945, he had tried a similar approach with Harry Hopkins, who had been one of Roosevelt's most trusted advisers before FDR had died. Hopkins had spent a week with Stalin in the Kremlin; Truman had asked Hopkins "to use diplomatic language or a baseball bat." The results had been good, and the American people were pleased. Truman thought now was the time to try again.

Hopkins, however, had since died of cancer. In a meeting with Truman's advisers, the president suggested sending the chief justice of the Supreme Court, Fred Vinson, to Moscow. Clark Clifford and his assistant George Elsey argued against the idea but Truman could not be swayed. He telephoned Vinson and asked him to come to the White House immediately. When Vinson arrived at the Oval Office, he had no idea why he had been summoned.

"I outlined to him what I had in mind," Truman later wrote. The president wanted the chief justice to go to Moscow on a special mission in an attempt to negotiate an end to the Cold War. "I asked Vinson to point out to Stalin that the folly and tragedy of another war would amount to an act of national suicide and that no sane leader of any major power could ever again even contemplate war except in defense. Surely the next war — an atomic war — could have no victors, and the total annihilation of vast areas was unthinkable." The president wanted "to go to any practical lengths to insure the future survival of the world," as he put it. The political reality — that Truman thought such a mission would be good for his campaign — was likely left unsaid.

Vinson sat listening quietly to the president's pitch. He had a face that registered little emotion, somber eyes unmoved under a pair of bushy gray eyebrows. The Kentucky-born justice was a towering figure and highly trusted by the president; Vinson had served as secretary of the Treasury before Truman had appointed him chief justice of the Supreme Court, and he had a calm, agreeable disposition. If anyone could talk sense into Stalin, Truman figured, Vinson would be a good choice.

"Mr. President," Vinson finally said, "as Chief Justice I must decline to undertake this mission to Moscow. But if you make it as a presidential request, I shall have a clear duty to comply."

"I am sorry, Fred, to do this to you," Truman came back. "But in the interest of the country and the peace of the world I am compelled to request you to go."

Vinson answered, "I'll be ready in a few days."

"I intend to discuss the purpose of this mission and mean to have the full agreement of our allies before you leave for Moscow," Truman told Vinson. "I will also tell our own people. But first, everyone who is concerned will be duly informed before any public announcement is made. We must be careful in all respects, or this could misfire and be misunderstood."

That afternoon, Truman met with his press secretary Charlie Ross and ordered him to notify the radio networks that the president would need a half hour for what he called "a public statement of major importance"—not campaign-oriented, and thus free of charge. Two days later, at 8 p.m., he had two senators—Democrat Tom Connally of Texas and Republican Arthur Vandenberg of Michigan—up to his second-floor study in the White House for an informal meeting. Connally and Vandenberg were the two most influential members of the Senate Foreign Relations Committee. Much to Truman's surprise, both senators opposed the Vinson mission. Truman wondered aloud if he should go to Moscow himself and meet with Stalin privately.

"You don't know any Russian and he doesn't know any English," said Connally. "Besides there's the question of authenticity. After you finish talking, what will you have? No witnesses or documents. And there's no possible way of telling about commitments agreed upon or promises made regarding the future."

After the meeting, Vandenberg told Connally privately, "He must be feeling desperate about the campaign."

When Truman called Secretary of State George Marshall to brief him on the upcoming Vinson mission, Marshall was alarmed. He was in Paris for United Nations negotiations with the Soviets and others. Marshall told Truman he felt the proposed Vinson mission was a mistake; it would make the Paris negotiations more difficult, and it might be construed as undermining the United Nations. After the call, Truman met in the Cabinet Room with advisers and the debate about the Vinson mission continued. Some were in favor; others not.

"I have heard enough," Truman said. "We won't do it."

Jonathan Daniels, who was in the room, recalled, "[Truman] got up and went out of the glass-paned door to the terrace by the rose garden and walked alone — very much alone that day — back [from the West Wing] toward the White House itself . . . The next time we saw him he was laughing with the reporters, the politicians and the police as he got back on that long train which everyone seemed so sure was taking him nowhere."

The story of the Vinson mission was far from over.

On October 8 Truman was in Schenectady, in upstate New York, when he got ahold of the morning papers. The news was bad. The story of the proposed Vinson mission had leaked and the reaction was furious. The press attacked Truman for using foreign policy as a campaign tool, even though Truman had called off the mission before it had gone anywhere.

The *Hartford Courant:* "The capital was alive with reports . . . that President Truman has been planning a sensational move in American relations with Russia which he originally intended to announce to the nation and the world in a radio broadcast last Tuesday night." The *Los Angeles Times:* "It is dangerous to the peace of the world to have a bumbler like Harry S. Truman handling any part of any international negotiations." The *Wall Street Journal* called the Vinson mission "a resounding blunder in Mr. Truman's conduct of foreign affairs. It is not his first mistake of this kind; but in view of the approach of November 2, it may well be his last."

Even Strom Thurmond had choice words on the proposed Vinson mission, calling it "further confirmation of the incompetency of Truman."

"This was the worst mistake of the Truman campaign," Clark Clifford recalled.

Aboard the *Ferdinand Magellan,* the president sat with press secretary Charlie Ross, trying to figure out how to mitigate the damage. Ultimately the administration put out a long statement on the doomed Vinson mission. "But the damage was done," Truman noted.

The day after the news broke, Truman awoke early as usual as the campaign train steamed through Ohio. In Akron, one hundred thousand people lined the streets to see the president cruise by in a motorcade to the Akron Armory. Akron was the unofficial rubber capital of the country, and on hand were well-dressed executives from Firestone, General Tire, B. F. Goodrich, and Goodyear.

"The Republicans have the propaganda and the money," Truman told this crowd. "But we have the people, and the people have the votes."

While in Akron, Clark Clifford slipped off the train and headed for a newsstand. A widely anticipated survey had been printed in the latest issue of *Newsweek* magazine, and it was expected to land on newsstands that day; campaigners aboard the Truman train had been talking about it for some time. Fifty political experts had been polled on the election outcome. When Clifford saw the story's headline, it hit him like a kick in the gut: "Election Forecast: 50 Political Experts Predict a GOP Sweep." "That Dewey would be favored hardly surprised me," Clifford recalled, "but the shocker was the vote: fifty to *nothing.*"

Clifford passed through the *Ferdinand Magellan* shortly after. Truman was sitting on a couch next to Margaret, reading a newspaper. Clifford tucked the magazine into his jacket.

"What have you got under your coat, Clark?" Truman asked.

"Nothing, Mr. President."

"Clark. I saw you get off the train just now and I think that you went in there to see if they had a newsstand with a copy of *Newsweek.* And I think maybe you have it under your coat."

Clifford reached into his jacket and handed over the issue. Margaret watched her father: "Dad stared at the magazine for a moment and then grinned."

"Don't worry about that poll, Clark," he said. "I know every one of those fifty fellows, and not one of them has enough sense to pound sand into a rat hole."

When Dewey arrived back in Albany for a short break before his final campaign swing, he found his mailbox filled with letters from angry voters. Truman's populism was getting to these Republicans. Why wasn't Dewey fighting back? How could he let Truman say all those things about the Republican Party? This was not the Thomas Dewey many voters expected. This was not the fearless and irascible Dewey of 1944, the attack dog whom FDR had labeled "a son of a bitch."

"The greatest danger that could exist would be for too many people to feel that we have a 'push-over,'" wrote J. E. Broyhill of the Broyhill furniture factories in Lenoir, North Carolina.

"If you don't open up on the one hundred and one iniquities of the Truman administration, the New Deal termites will win by default!" wrote one Earle S. Clayton of Greenfield, Ohio. "Strike while the iron is HOT!"

The Vinson-mission fiasco offered a golden opportunity for Dewey to go on the attack. He debated the matter with advisers in person and by phone. "No, I won't do it," the candidate reportedly said. "I'd rather lose the election than add to the damage this country has already suffered from this unhappy incident."

Dewey had a different plan. The perception was that Truman had somehow changed his thinking on US foreign policy, and so Dewey aimed to reassure the world that the United States had not changed course, that UN negotiations in Paris would continue, and that soon enough there would be a more steady hand on the wheel. Dewey was going to make a statement as if he was already the president, in an attempt to heal the wound that Truman's bungling error had created. On October 10, two days after the Vinson mission leaked to the newspapers, Dewey invited fifty reporters to the Executive

Chamber in Albany, where he read aloud a short statement. Britain, France, and other nations west of the Iron Curtain—"our friends of the free world," Dewey said—should be reassured that Americans "are in fact united in their foreign policy."

"The people of America wholeheartedly and vigorously support the labors of our bipartisan delegation at Paris and specifically its insistence on a prompt lifting of the blockade of Berlin," he said.

In the crowd in Dewey's office that day was the *Washington Post*'s political reporter Edward T. Folliard, who called Dewey's move "perhaps without precedent in American history." A presidential candidate was attempting to counteract the damage done by the acting president, in terms of the nation's foreign relations, in the middle of a presidential campaign.

One reporter asked Dewey if he was going to keep his foreign affairs adviser John Foster Dulles at the UN meetings in Paris, or whether he would call Dulles back to the United States. Implicit in the question was that Dewey would soon be the one to be shaping foreign policy, after he was elected, and that Dulles was about to become Dewey's secretary of state. Dewey answered, "Certainly." He would keep Dulles in Paris when he took command in Washington.

Six hours later, the governor and his wife were back aboard the Dewey Victory Special, blasting out of Albany for points west on a nine-state campaign swing, which would end with a climactic pre-election weekend extravaganza in New York City. Dewey was headed for the Midwest, where he would find friendly crowds. Gallup's latest numbers, released three days before the Republican candidate left Albany, had him ahead in Illinois (49 to 40 percent over Truman), in Michigan (52 to 41 percent), Indiana (52 to 40 percent), and Ohio (51 to 42 percent).

Still, at the headquarters of the Republican National Committee in Washington, GOP officials had noticed some unnerving trends. They were hearing the same stories as everyone else, about the size of the crowds that the president was drawing. They also noticed that the Republicans' bank account was starting to run low. While Dewey's campaign had a list of donors that included some of the oldest moneyed families in the country—Mellon,

Vanderbilt, Rockefeller—plus industrialists Alfred Sloan (chairman of the world's largest corporation, General Motors) and Walter Chrysler, the donations were not coming in from farmers and from other places where the Republicans had expected. Complacency and overconfidence had caused donors to keep their checkbooks in their pockets. Why donate to a campaign that has effectively already won?

For the first time, GOP officials started to believe that this election might be closer than anyone thought—maybe not in the electoral college, where they felt entirely confident, but in the Senate and in the presidential popular vote. In mid-October, the head of the Republican National Committee, Hugh Scott of Pennsylvania, attended a meeting of the United Republican Finance Committee of Greater New York at the Ritz-Carlton Hotel in Manhattan, to make a plea.

"We need the money and we need it early," he asserted. "I have been all around the country, have traveled 22,000 miles and have been in 32 states," he said. "The polls indicate a heavy electoral vote for Dewey and Warren, but that the popular vote is going to be rather close. Of course," he added, smiling, "we expect that President Truman is going to continue to help us all he can."

27

"Could We Be Wrong?"

ON OCTOBER 10, THE SAME day Dewey made his statement regarding the Vinson mission, Strom Thurmond sent the president of the United States a telegram. "Again renew my challenge to debate you face to face on the same platform, on your 'so-called civil rights program,'" Thurmond's telegram read. "Suggest we debate it in Virginia, Texas, or Missouri . . . You name the time and place."

The telegram was ignored.

Thurmond's Dixiecrat ticket, like the Progressive campaign, had long since begun to deflate, especially outside Thurmond's base in the Southeast. Not only was there little new material to keep reporters' typewriters crackling, polls showed Thurmond's numbers at just 2 percent nationally, behind even Henry Wallace, who was polling 4 percent. The only major financial support the States' Rights Democratic Party was getting came from the oil industry. Under the Truman administration, the federal government and private oil concerns were in a feud over who owned the rights to tidelands off the US coast, where inestimable amounts of oil lay pocketed under a shallow sea. Oil drillers in the Gulf states — such as Texas, Louisiana, and Mississippi — wanted the rights to drill, and wealthy oil executives saw in the States' Rights movement an opportunity to leverage power over the tidelands away from the federal government and back into the hands of local lawmakers and business organizations. But even this source of support was drying up.

"The oil men's generous enthusiasm for the Dixiecrats is now said to be waning," noted the Alsop brothers in their syndicated column on October 20.

Thurmond's campaign was further injured by an unfortunate incident. As a publicity stunt, his staff mailed out letters to all the governors across the country, inviting them to visit South Carolina and stay in the governor's mansion in Columbia. One of those letters went to William Hastie, the governor of the US Virgin Islands. Hastie had been appointed by Harry Truman as the first African American governor in the United States. Thurmond had no idea that Hastie was African American, and when Hastie politely declined the invitation, in mid-October, Thurmond's letter was leaked to the press. Only then did Thurmond learn of Hastie's race.

Humiliated, Thurmond issued a statement to the press claiming that the letter to Hastie was an "understandable mistake," the result of a clerical error. Thurmond's statement attacked "pro-Truman" newspaper columnists for publishing it. Then he blamed the incident on Harry Truman. Thurmond said he "did not know that Harry Truman, in his all-out bid for Negro votes, had gone so far as to take the unprecedented action of appointing a Negro governor of the Virgin Islands . . .

"I would not have written him if I knew he was a Negro," Thurmond went on. "Of course, it would have been ridiculous to invite him . . . Gov. Hastie knows that neither he nor any other Negro will ever be a guest at the Governor's house in Columbia as long as I am Governor or as long as the Democratic Party of South Carolina continues to elect Governors of my State."

Thurmond continued to tour through Kentucky and Tennessee. At a Memphis rally, he called Truman "an inefficient and confused little man," and Dewey "a pennyweight glamor boy." His barbs got rises out of his crowds but were unlikely to have any effect on his election prospects.

One American who was closely following Thurmond's campaign was

Governor Thurmond's mixed-race daughter, Essie Mae. She celebrated her twenty-third birthday on October 12, 1948. She had recently married Julius Williams, a black man who had served in the US military in World War II. One night they were watching the news on television in a hotel in North Carolina, where they had gotten jobs, and she saw her father on the TV. "His endless attacks on President Truman had made him so popular below the Mason-Dixon line," she later recalled.

Essie Mae's identity was so secret, not even her husband knew that she was Strom Thurmond's daughter, and as they watched Thurmond speak, she felt consumed by despair. She remembered hearing him say these words: "On the question of social intermingling of our races, our people draw the line. All the laws of Washington and all the bayonets of the Army cannot force the Negro race into our theaters, our swimming pools, our schools, our churches, our homes."

"I don't like that man," Essie Mae's husband said as they watched Thurmond talking on the screen. "I fought Hitler to end up with *that?* What's the difference?"

Essie Mae's father had always been kind and gentle with her, but now, he had been "brainwashed," she recorded, "if not by the Ku Klux Klan, then by the ghost of Pitchfork Ben Tillman."

"If the South had been stabbed in the back by Harry Truman," she wrote in her memoirs many years later, "my mother and I, and the blacks of South Carolina, had been stabbed in the back by Strom Thurmond."

"We went through Illinois and Indiana," the reporter Robert Nixon recalled of riding aboard the Truman Special in early October. "Indiana was normally a Republican state, but in towns where you knew the population was 20,000, in several instances, there would be a hundred thousand to see Truman. They would be jammed in for blocks around where loud speakers would have been set up. They had come from towns in the whole surrounding countryside, maybe as far away as a hundred miles . . . You didn't have to be very smart to say, 'Look here, something is going on.'"

Assistant press secretary Eben Ayers took a break from the White House to ride the Truman campaign train through the Midwest in early October. He returned to Washington and told his wife, "There is something happening. I think something's going to happen." Remembered Richard Strout, one of the most widely read political writers: "The Truman crowds had just changed in that last three weeks. They had changed enormously."

All the data still pointed to a Dewey landslide. Pundits had predicted that the Republicans would easily maintain a House majority but that the Senate was too close to call. Now even the Senate appeared to be leaning back toward the GOP. Columnist Joseph Alsop, on October 15: "This correspondent's inquiries have led to the view that the Republicans will not lose the Senate after all." Drew Pearson in the *Washington Post* claimed on October 14 that "about 75 percent of the newspapers have announced for Dewey . . . Dewey is certain to win, and it's only natural to want to be on the side of the winner."

Truman saw the numbers differently. The day before Pearson made this claim, he sat with his aide George Elsey, on the way from Duluth, Minnesota, toward the Twin Cities. Elsey was focused on facts and figures to prepare Truman for the upcoming whistle-stops, but Truman interrupted him and told him to start writing down some notes.

The president rattled off each of the forty-eight states, knowing by heart how many electoral votes came with a win in each. Elsey scribbled in pencil as the train swayed back and forth. In the corner of the page, Elsey jotted: "13 Oct 1948 between Duluth + St. Paul Minn." When Truman was done listing states and their respective electoral college votes, he said, "George, how many do I have?"

"Three-hundred-forty, Mr. President."

Truman smiled; that was more than enough to win. Elsey later remembered the moment: "The fact is, I thought Truman would lose."

At Democratic National Committee headquarters in New York's Biltmore Hotel, campaigners were desperately manning phones to find donations, and pulling all-nighters attempting to dream up out-of-the-box ideas. The committee had come up with novel strategies to spread the Truman message, but they cost money.

In mid-October, the committee released a comic-book version of a Harry Truman biography — sixteen pages of colorful drawings with captions. *The Story of Harry S. Truman* had a tagline on the bottom of the cover: "Farm boy, Soldier, Statesman, President!" Demand for the publication stunned committee officials. Over 3.3 million copies were printed. "Workers at the precinct level reported it as the most effective piece of campaign material they had," noted the committee's publicist, Jack Redding, who had a hand in writing the book's copy.

The committee had created a women's division with a budget of $50,000, to be headed up by India Edwards, later to become vice chair of the Democratic National Committee. The women's division was tasked with creating the first-ever political radio program aimed specifically at women voters. The show would be called *Democratic Record*, and it would air three times a week starting October 11, on ABC, nationwide, at 3:45 p.m. on the East Coast, when it was believed the largest audience of women would be at home with their radios on.

Each episode opened and closed with "The Missouri Waltz," in honor of Truman's home state, and it featured radio broadcaster Galen Drake interviewing women on important issues, with plenty of music and wisecracking woven in. Truman was campaigning through the Midwest when the first episode ran. The show was an instant hit. *Variety,* which covered the entertainment industry, reported on its success: "The 'Democratic Record' show is the best election pitch ever made on radio."

At one point, publicist Jack Redding called Eleanor Roosevelt, who was in Paris in negotiations with the Soviets, as a member of the US delegation to the United Nations. Mrs. Roosevelt had thus far remained silent on the election.

"I think, Mrs. Roosevelt, that you are the key to the situation," Redding told her over the phone. "I think your influence in America could elect President Truman. Without you . . . we may fail."

The former First Lady replied without hesitation. "I have been reluctant to be part of this campaign because of my United Nations responsibilities. You know that?"

Surely Redding figured that Mrs. Roosevelt was making an excuse; she was reluctant to get behind a losing cause. "Yes, ma'am," he said.

"But if it's as close as you say, and if you think I can help, I'll do it. But how?" The Democratic National Committee drummed up an idea to have Mrs. Roosevelt give a speech over ABC radio on the night of October 31, two days before Election Day. ABC officials, however, demanded a hefty fee: $25,721. The scramble for the money began.

The Republican campaign's short film, *The Dewey Story*, was set to debut on movie screens before feature films three days before Election Day. When the DNC staff heard about it, a committee official made a desperate call to the Universal Newsreel company. Universal had plenty of existing film capturing Harry Truman in various important scenes, for its newsreels over the past years, so a deal was struck to make a ten-minute Truman documentary. The Dewey team had shot its own movie with a $35,000 budget; Truman's film would have to use already-existing footage, and the Universal Newsreel company agreed to produce it for free. It would be released right before the election — if Universal could get it done in time.

Meanwhile, Truman himself moved from town to town, speaking extemporaneously, attempting to make personal connections with as many voters as possible. On October 13, at 7:55 a.m. in Adams, Wisconsin, Truman spoke to a group of children who were given permission to show up late for school so they could see the president on the back platform of his train. "The country is going to be in your hands in the next generation," he said, "and you ought to inform yourselves on all the things that affect your country, and the world, because the United States has assumed the leadership in the world unequaled in the history of the world, and we have got to assume that responsibility."

"On November 2," Truman said two hours later, in Spooner, Wisconsin, "you are going to make the most important decision that has been made in a generation, and that will be made for another generation, as to how this country shall be run."

In nearly every town, the crowd was bigger than expected. What did it all mean? On the night of October 16, from aboard the Truman train, the *Washington Post*'s Robert C. Albright typed four prophetic words onto a sheet of paper, as the train rolled through West Virginia: "Could we be wrong?"

28

"The Campaign Special Train Stopped with a Jerk"

THUS FAR, DEWEY HAD EXECUTED his plan perfectly. He appeared the apotheosis of composure. All he had to do to get elected, he believed, was to not make any mistakes. On October 13, however, he made a major one.

Dewey was speaking on the back platform of his train in the farming town of Beaucoup, Illinois, when, inexplicably, the train lurched backward straight toward the crowd of spectators. Dewey braced himself as frightened shouts came from the crowd, from spectators who thought for a moment that they might get crushed by a campaign train car weighing hundreds of tons. Dewey's temper got the better of him.

"That's the first lunatic I've had for an engineer," he said into his microphone. "He probably ought to be shot at sunrise, but I guess we can let him off because nobody was hurt."

The next day's newspapers recounted the event. One pun slipped past the news-desk editors: "The campaign special train stopped with a jerk." The train's engineer, a thirty-year-old war veteran named Lee Tindle, was not happy about being called a "lunatic" by the Republican nominee for president of the United States. He said he was not going to vote for Dewey anyway. "I think as much of Dewey as I did before," he said.

What seemed like a minor moment blew up into something bigger. Dewey's comment was interpreted as cold and uncaring toward working people, an accusation the Republicans had heard before. Dewey had in fact offended the biggest block of voters in the country: unionized labor. Truman saw an easy opportunity to rally railroad unions to his cause, accusing Dewey of insensitivity toward the plight of workers. From the back platform of the *Ferdinand Magellan,* in the town of Logansport, Indiana, the president praised his own "wonderful train crews" that had carried the campaign all around the country. "They've been just as kind to us as they could possibly be." Railroad workers painted LUNATICS FOR TRUMAN on the side of boxcars.

Dewey tried to ignore the barbs. But he was also seeing the newspaper stories about the spectacular crowds turning out for his opponent. He too sensed that something amazingly unlikely might be happening. On October 18, five days after the train-jerk debacle, Dewey's train pulled into Buffalo. He sought out a campaign aide named John Burton.

"Johnny," Dewey said, "we are slipping, aren't we?"

Burton agreed; there was cause for worry. He explained that Truman had recently lured a crowd of ten thousand people soon after sunrise in a pouring squall, in Albany of all places—practically in the backyard of the New York governor's mansion.

One thing that had become clear on the campaign trail: No matter how hard the candidate tried, Dewey could not turn on the charisma the way Truman could, the way Roosevelt had. "He didn't really like handshaking," remembered Herbert Brownell. "He wasn't good at it . . . He worked harder, studied longer than anyone else . . . He organized people. He was a really good fighter." But the handshaking? The ability to create human connection? "He just could not do."

Even so, all the data continued to show Dewey way out in front. The *New York Times* polled twenty correspondents in twenty states, and published the results on October 4. Dewey, it was predicted, would carry fourteen of those states, many of them by wide margins, including the big prizes of California, Illinois, and Pennsylvania. The latest Gallup poll of sixteen states showed Dewey ahead in all but one, while another survey of New England states showed Dewey carrying all of them but Rhode Island. The day after the train-jerk incident, the columnist Richard Strout wrote that Dewey's election was "as certain as anything can be in the course of American politics."

Dewey continued onward, pounding away on his unity theme. He campaigned through Minnesota for GOP senator Joseph H. Ball, who was locked in a critical race against the thirty-seven-year-old Democratic mayor of Minneapolis, Hubert H. Humphrey (later to serve as vice president in Lyndon Johnson's administration). In Indiana, Dewey visited with the Republican leader of the House of Representatives, Charles Halleck. Dewey was beginning to court the powerful right-wing faction of the GOP in Congress, of which Halleck was a pillar, in hopes that he would have friends on Capitol Hill, once he became president.

But Dewey's staff was getting jittery. Letters continued to flood into the Albany mansion and campaign headquarters in Washington, urging the candidate to change his course. "I am worried," wrote Helen Brigham of Hollywood, California. "Truman, with his barnstorming, name calling, and harping on one string — the 80th Congress — is winning friends from the largest class he appeals to. So I should like to ask why Mr. Dewey and Mr. Warren don't reply to him."

"Don't float in, fight your way in by slugging (as well as the Democrats are doing)," wrote Grace Burdick of San Diego, California, on October 21. "For heaven sakes fight!!"

It was still not too late for Dewey to change course, and finish out the campaign with an all-out attack. But he thus far refused to do it, and his wife, Frances, supported him in that decision.

Dewey's team announced the final itinerary of the campaign's climactic weekend before Election Day. The governor would speak in Chicago, Cleveland, Boston, and New York, in that order. His final campaign push followed a path identical to Truman's; Dewey would be close on Truman's heels in each of those four cities.

Henry Wallace refused to let up. His whole campaign had become about increasing the pressure on Truman. "I tell you," Wallace told a crowd in Reading, Pennsylvania, on October 19, "Harry S. Truman has abdicated . . .

He still sleeps in the White House, and that's about all." Wallace demanded that General George C. Marshall—one of the world's most respected men—be fired from his post as secretary of state. The Marshall Plan was "one of the most sinister and dangerous proposals to come out of this or any other country," he said. "It is a step toward war." The next night in Wilkes-Barre, Pennsylvania, Wallace said of Truman, "He's going to take the worst licking any Democratic candidate has ever taken . . . We're going to take our country back from the bankers and the generals and give it back to the people where it belongs."

The state where Wallace had the most traction was New York, where he was expected to earn 11 percent of the vote, a number that most analysts believed would guarantee Dewey's victory. Without Wallace on the ballot, those 11 percent of mostly liberal voters could have been expected to cast their votes for Truman. Which meant that Wallace was likely to cause Truman's defeat in one of the most critical states. The Wallace campaign still mattered—a lot.

Nevertheless, outside of New York, Los Angeles, and Chicago, Wallace was now all but ignored. At one point, he reached St. Louis and entered a room to find an audience of only a hundred people to hear him speak. The chairman of this event, Reverend Charles G. Wilson, was on hand to introduce Wallace. The mood was dark.

"I see a lot of faces that aren't here, faces of people who were with us a year ago," Wilson said. The reverend openly called himself "a tired liberal" and "confused." He told his small audience that he was ready to "sit this one out" and "crawl into a hole."

It was hardly the introduction Wallace desired. When he spoke, he tried to blow life into the room. "I'm not tired," he said. "I'm not confused, and I'm very happy to be here." He waited for applause, but very little of it came.

Wallace admitted that supporters were abandoning him. "I can't help feeling that their chief governing motive is that they hate Henry Wallace," he told his audience. "I don't know why they hate me. I'm still holding the door open for them. I used to say they'd come along after Truman was nominated.

But they didn't come flocking to us the way I hoped." Again, he refused to repudiate the Communists who supported him—especially in the fight against segregation. "If they want to help us out on some of these problems, why, God bless them, let them come along."

Wallace called on his Gideon's Army to keep on marching. But so few marchers were left. The following week, Gallup's latest numbers showed Wallace polling at just 3.5 percent of the national vote, half of what it had been at the beginning of 1948.

On October 18, with two weeks to go until Election Day, Truman's airplane landed in Miami. It was as close as he would come to Strom Thurmond's base movement. Truman would avoid entirely the four states where Thurmond was now expected to win—South Carolina, Alabama, Mississippi, and Louisiana. The First Family was set to attend the thirtieth National Convention of the American Legion, so Truman could write off the trip as nonpolitical and pay for it out of the president's travel fund, as the campaign coffers were once again running on empty.

"There was a parade through Miami and Miami Beach to the Roney Plaza Hotel, which is really gorgeous, all mirrors and antique white furniture," Margaret wrote in her diary. Along the route, roughly two hundred thousand Floridians came out. In an airplane hangar with twelve thousand Legionnaires on hand, Truman tried to put into perspective what it was like to be an American president, facing the possibility of yet another war, feeling the responsibility for the lives of American soldiers and so much more.

> Let me say here again, and as plainly as I can, that the Government of this country, like the American people as a whole, detests the thought of war. We are shocked by its brutality and sickened by its waste of life and wealth . . . The use of atomic weapons and bacteriological warfare, in particular, might unleash new forces of destruction which would spare no nation . . . We shall spare no effort to achieve the peace on which the entire destiny of the human race may depend.

Nowhere in Florida did Truman mention civil rights. Below the Mason-Dixon line, stumping for civil rights would have come across as tone-deaf. For over a year now, the influential Democratic politicos from the South had pressured Truman to drop his stance on civil rights, and among them was Florida's governor, Millard F. Caldwell. Yet it was clear that Truman was going to push this issue as far as it would go. Even if he did not campaign for civil rights in Florida, the people knew where he stood.

At one point during the campaign, Truman got a letter from an old friend named Ernest Roberts, who was close enough to the president to address him as Harry, and whose missive put the civil rights issue into a perspective that many Americans, and especially southerners, at this time embraced.

"You can win the south without the [civil rights program]," Roberts wrote Truman, "but you cannot win the south with it. Just why?? Well, you, Bess and Margaret, and shall I say, myself, are all Southerners and we have been raised with the Negroes and we know the term 'Equal Rights.' Harry, let us let the South take care of the Niggers, which they have done, and if the Niggers do not like the Southern treatment, let them come to Mrs. Roosevelt.

"Harry," Roberts continued, "you are a Southerner and a D— good one so listen to me. I can see, you do not talk domestic problems over with Bess??? You put equal rights in Independence and Bess will not live with you."

Truman wrote back, listing recent lynchings that had occurred in the South in which no justice was ever served. "I can't approve of such goings on and I shall never approve it, as long as I am here, as I told you before," Truman wrote. "I am going to try to remedy it and if that ends up in my failure to be reelected, that failure will be in a good cause."

After his trip to Florida—and a brief stop in North Carolina—Truman headed back to the White House. With every day leading up to the election, it seemed, the superpowers were moving closer to war, and one could only wonder if this was by the Kremlin's design.

At 11 a.m. on October 21, eleven days before Election Day, General Lucius Clay arrived in the Oval Office along with Secretary of Defense Forrestal and Secretary of the Army Kenneth Royall. Clay was in Washington for only twenty-four hours; the threat of war with the Soviets was so real, he needed to get back to Germany. He had crossed the Atlantic to speak to Truman.

The airlift was carrying five thousand tons of supplies into Berlin daily in good weather, and three thousand tons under poor conditions, Clay reported. Winter weather would soon put the pilots flying the supply missions at greater risk. No progress had been made with Soviet negotiations to end the blockade. Undersecretary of the Army William H. Draper Jr. was in the room during this meeting. He later described the hostile environment in which the airlift was being conducted: "At almost any point in Berlin, you could see three planes in the air, two on their way in and one or two on the way out . . . The Russians were buzzing the planes. They didn't shoot any down, but they came right near us. It's a wonder there weren't any accidents, and so starting a war, because that would have probably done it."

Following this meeting, Truman ordered the National Security Council to add sixty-six more C-54s to the supply operation, and to secure aviation fuel for "the extraordinary demands of the air lift as well as stockpile for emergency purposes."

On this same day, news broke of violence on the Korean peninsula, raising concerns that the US military and the Soviets might come nose to nose, in yet another part of the world. A Communist uprising on the peninsula's southern coast hinted at a possible bigger rebellion in the making. It was a story that had been developing slowly since the end of World War II. In the summer of 1945, Japanese forces had surrendered to the Soviets north of the 38th parallel and to the United States south of the 38th parallel. That latitudinal dividing line had since morphed into a national border between the Soviet-controlled north and the US-backed south.

For months, American intelligence sources had warned of increasing instability on the peninsula. In the south, the Republic of Korea had established a government in August 1948, headed by the US-backed president Syngman Rhee, who spoke English and had earned a PhD in the United States at Princeton University many years earlier. But in September, the Soviets established a rival government based in the city of Pyongyang in the north. According to recent reports from the Central Intelligence Agency, the

Soviets had some forty-five thousand occupation troops in North Korea. The same week that violence broke out on the Korean peninsula, the CIA issued a top secret document concluding, "It must be assumed that the USSR will not be satisfied with its present hold on North Korea and will exert continuing efforts to establish eventual control over all Korea."

Truman later recalled, "Rhee's government would be in grave danger if the military units of North Korea were to start a full-scale attack."

At the same time, the pressure on the Truman administration to figure out some solution to the Arab-Israeli war continued to tighten. The casualties were mounting in the Middle East, and included many civilians. The United Nations mediator in Palestine, Folke Bernadotte of Sweden, had come up with a two-state proposal, known as the Bernadotte Plan, which (among other things) called on the Israelis to allow Arabs to return to their homes in what was now Israeli territory. On September 17, while Truman was campaigning in Ohio, Bernadotte was assassinated—shot dead in broad daylight in Jerusalem by the Jewish extremist group the Stern Gang.

On October 17 a State Department official named John McDonald cabled Truman from Jerusalem. "Arab refugee tragedy is rapidly reaching catastrophic proportions and should be treated as a disaster," McDonald wrote. He concluded that, with approximately 400,000 refugees, the "approaching winter with cold heavy rains will, it is estimated, kill more than 100,000 old men, women and children who are shelterless and have little or no food."

The Palestine situation was inextricably linked with the American election. On the day Israel was founded, Truman had extended de facto recognition to the new Jewish state. It was provisional recognition, while full legal and diplomatic recognition was expected to follow, once Israel had held democratic elections. Now Truman was under extreme pressure to grant de jure recognition, in order to court the Jewish vote in America, most notably in New York. But Israel had not yet held democratic elections, and critics within the State Department were horrified by the treatment of the Arab refugees. The United Nations, the US State Department, Harry Truman, the

Jews, the Arabs—no entity could come forth with a plan that the others could agree upon. So any position Truman took had the potential for disastrous results.

The Democratic platform adopted in Philadelphia in July had promised "full recognition" of Israel, a rethinking of the arms embargo that prevented the United States from sending arms to Israel, and no modifications to the borders of Israel that were not "fully acceptable to the State of Israel." Truman was under intense pressure from Jewish groups in the United States to come through on all these promises, but thus far he had been unable. The Democratic candidate for governor of Connecticut, Chester Bowles, had written Clark Clifford: "Like you and everyone else who is concerned about November 2nd, I am worried about the Jewish situation. We have an ardent group of Zionists here in the State and they have been urging me strongly to send a telegram to the President urging him to extend *de jure* recognition to Israel."

The president ultimately tried to take the issue off the table—to avoid making commitments until after Election Day. He advised his State Department to use "any parliamentary procedures available" and to "use every effort to avoid having U.S. delegation [to the United Nations] drawn into the debate." Truman subsequently told the undersecretary of state, Robert Lovett, that "every effort [should] be made to avoid taking position on Palestine prior to" the election.

On October 22, Dewey forced the Zionist issue onto the front pages. He gave an address in New York promising to bring "unity to our country to meet the great problems ahead." Then his campaign made public a letter the governor had written to the American Christian Palestine Committee of New York, in which he attacked "the vacillation of the Democratic administration" on the Palestine issue. He stated that a Republican administration would give "wholehearted" support to Israel and welcome Israel "into the family of nations."

Dewey was tacitly promising that he would grant immediate de jure recognition, or so it seemed. What was Truman going to do about it?

That night, the Truman Special pulled out of Washington for the final weeklong campaign frenzy. Clark Clifford stayed behind to strategize a response to Dewey's letter. Clifford tapped out a memo to Truman, to be forwarded to him on the train. "I am working on a statement on Israel now and will have it ready to submit to you on Sunday morning," Clifford wrote. "I consider Dewey's action a serious error on his part and the best thing that has happened to us to date. Affectionate regards."

The next night — Saturday, October 23, at 10:00 — Truman delivered what his daughter, Margaret, would later call her favorite speech of the campaign, in Pittsburgh. At the city's Armory Hall, with one hundred thousand people on hand and a national radio audience tuned in, Truman put on an unexpected comedy routine. It was a surprising moment of levity, given the pressure weighing on him. Dewey, Truman said, was acting like "some kind of doctor with a magic cure for all the ills of mankind."

Twirling an imaginary mustache, pretending to be a doctor, Truman asked the crowd: "You been bothered much by issues lately?"

Then he became the patient. "Of course, we've had a few," Truman said. "We've had the issue of high prices, and housing, and education, and social security, and a few others."

He switched to the doctor again. "That's too bad," he said. "What you need is my brand of soothing syrup — I call it unity."

The crowd erupted in cackles and applause. Truman then ran through a litany of "symptoms" that the American people were suffering — the Taft-Hartley law, inadequate funding of Social Security, a stagnant minimum wage, etc. His administration had come up with policies to confront all of these issues, but had passed little in the way of legislation, due to the Eightieth Congress's refusal to come aboard. Dewey's claim that he was a magic cure-all was a sham, Truman said. "He opened his mouth and closed his eyes and swallowed the terrible record of the good-for-nothing 80th Congress."

The next morning, as Truman headed east to Cleveland, Clifford's proposed statement on Israel arrived aboard the train. Truman released the statement at 9:10 that morning.

> The Republican candidate for President has seen fit to release a statement with reference to Palestine. This statement is in the form of a letter dated October 22, 1948, ten days before the election. I had hope our foreign affairs could continue to be handled on a nonpartisan basis without being injected into the presidential campaign. The Republican's statement, however, makes it necessary for me to reiterate my own position with respect to Palestine.

The statement then reprinted what was in the Democratic platform, released back in July at the Democratic National Convention, most notably: "We pledge full recognition of Israel." For Americans who had been paying attention, it was equivocation at its best. Truman's party had pledged "full recognition" but none had come. He merely repeated what he had said three months earlier, and criticized Dewey for violating the bipartisan spirit of American foreign relations. Meanwhile Truman's State Department had to remain mute on the subject, to restrict any communications on the matter until after November 2. Undersecretary of State Robert Lovett wrote his boss George Marshall, "Am told removal of restrictions on normal procedures may be expected . . . when silly season terminates."

29

"We Are Engaged in a Great Crusade"

THE FINAL WEEK OF CAMPAIGNING saw the two major candidates in a point-counterpoint showdown, as Truman and Dewey followed the same route — Chicago, Cleveland, Boston, New York.

Truman began the battle with his most vituperative attack yet, in Chicago on October 25. Prior to his arrival, he spoke in whistle-stops en route to the Windy City. When he reached his main destination of the day, three hundred thousand people stood in the streets. "A parade a mile long," Margaret wrote in her diary. "Huge fireworks and displays, too much noise." Before a jammed crowd at Chicago Stadium, Truman walked onstage along with Bess, Margaret, and Ed Kelly, Chicago's mayor. The president was going to push hard, in an effort to draw Dewey into a rhetorical brawl.

Truman began by warning against the reactionary forces of an "extreme right wing" that, he said, would put Wall Street's needs over those of the common man.

"Do you want that kind of future?" he asked.

A crowd of some twenty-five thousand roared, "No!"

He then compared the rise of Thomas Dewey to the rise of Adolf Hitler, and accused Republican leaders of using the same tactics Hitler did for "stupefying the German people" in order to take advantage of them.

"This evil force must be defeated," he shouted. "I shall continue the fight. And I pledge to you that I shall never surrender . . .

"It is not just a battle between two parties," Truman said of this election. "It is a fight for the very soul of the American government."

"So emotional was Mr. Truman that he stumbled over words at times," recalled the *Chicago Daily Tribune*'s Willard Edwards. The *New York Times*'s front page the next day ran a banner headline: "President Likens Dewey to Hitler as Fascist Tool." The speech was the most inflammatory of any of the campaign's, and one of its writers, David Noyes, later acknowledged that it was partly crafted to lure the GOP opponent into an open slug match.

Dewey heard Truman's speech over the radio while aboard the Dewey Victory Special, which left Albany that night, bound for Chicago. Listening to Truman compare him to Hitler, Dewey's face contorted with rage. He had finally had enough. Sitting across from him were his advisers—pressman James Hagerty, Edwin Jaeckle, and advertising maven Paul Lockwood. Dewey held a draft of the speech he was scheduled to deliver in Chicago the night after Truman's Windy City rally. It was another "high-minded" address on unity. Dewey said he wanted to "tear it to shreds."

He took a poll of the room and every one of his aides disagreed. Dewey should stick to the plan, they said. His wife was in the train car and she said, "If I have to stay up all night to see that you don't tear up that speech, I will."

The Dewey Victory Special pulled into Chicago's LaSalle Street Station at 4 p.m. the next day. A reception committee and motorcade was on hand to transport the Dewey party around downtown, where 125,000 people greeted him on the streets. That night, on the same stage where Truman spoke the night before, Dewey received an ovation lasting two minutes and forty seconds. ABC television cameras were rolling, while NBC was taking the speech nationwide via radio. He started in—"Thank you so much for this glorious welcome"—and was immediately interrupted again by applause. Dewey then defied his team and unleashed the first attack speech of his campaign.

> The purpose of this campaign is clear. It's to bring something better to our country than the confusion, inconsistencies, weakness and bitterness that we now have in Washington . . . We all know the sad record of the present administration. More than three years have passed since the end of the war. It has failed tragically to win the peace. Instead, millions upon millions of people have been delivered into Soviet slavery while our own administration has tried appeasement one day and blustered the next.

Dewey berated his opponent for his "weakness" and "incompetence," for the administration's "grave problems and troubles." Truman had reached a "new low in mud-slinging." The Democratic party was a "failure, with their party split in all directions . . . Its candidates have spread fantastic fears among our people . . . scattered reckless abuse . . . attempted to promote antagonism and prejudice."

Forty times, Dewey had to pause for applause. This is what most of his fans had wanted all along: a fighting spirit, a response to the populism that was infuriating countless Republican voters. Dewey had finally delivered.

The night of Dewey's Chicago speech, Truman arrived in Cleveland, where he had a special message he had been saving for just the right moment. The message was for the newspapermen and the pollsters who had been reporting on his perceived failures through the entire campaign and for most of his presidency.

By Truman's estimation, 90 percent of the daily newspapers were against him. The *New York Times*, the *Los Angeles Times*, the *Wall Street Journal*, the *Washington Star*, the two biggest papers in his home state of Missouri — the *St. Louis Post-Dispatch* and the *Kansas City Star* — all had endorsed Dewey. Over the past few months, newspaper columnists had leveled every insult imaginable at the president. That very week, the *Los Angeles Times* would call Truman "the most complete fumbler and blunderer this nation has seen in high office in a long time." Also that very week, the *Chicago Daily Tribune* would call him "an incompetent" and worse. The columnist Westbrook

Pegler had called Truman "a sorry and pathetic squirt," "the little squealer who broke the rules," and "a tacky county commissioner in a scene of historic humiliation."

As Truman saw it, the newspapers and radio stations were "operated, or subsidized by the same private interests that always benefited from Republican economic policies," he later wrote. He resented "the commonplace practice of distorted editorials and slanted headlines in the press and of outright misrepresentation in the daily offerings of the columnists and commentators. The worst offense of all was the editing and distorting of the facts in the news."

Truman saw the inner workings of the media as a conspiracy to favor one candidate over another using what amounted to fake news. It was the pollsters who had done the most damage, and it was the pollsters whom Truman attacked on the night of October 27, before a packed Cleveland Municipal Auditorium:

> Now, these Republican polls are no accident. They are part of a design to prevent a big vote, to keep you at home on November 2nd, by convincing you that it makes no difference whether you vote or not. They want to do this because they know in their hearts that a big vote spells their defeat. They know that a big vote means a Democratic victory, because the Democratic Party stands for the greatest good for the greatest number of the people. The special interests now running the Republican Party can't stand a big vote — they are afraid of the people. My friends, we are going to win this election.

The next night, the Dewey Victory Special rolled in for a gala event in the same hall. It was packed, and the crowd stood for an ovation lasting three minutes and twenty seconds. Dewey attacked Truman for using divisiveness for his own political gain. The Dewey-Warren campaign, the Republican candidate said, had "not been guilty of using our high responsibility to rip our country apart or to arouse fear or prejudice. We will win this campaign and we will win it by clean and decent methods."

Dewey then blamed the administration's foreign policy failures for the Cold War. "In a little more than three years," he said, "the Soviet Union has extended its sway nearly half way around the world and now rules more than five hundred million human beings."

By almost all accounts, Dewey's speech was a hit. Senator Arthur Vandenberg gushed in a letter to the candidate the next day: "Your Cleveland speech was one of the greatest of our time."

Six days left. "I remember coming into Pittsfield, Massachusetts, about 6 o'clock on a very frosty morning," recalled John Franklin Carter, a speechwriter on board the Truman Special. "Pittsfield has a population of something like thirty thousand people and there were fifty thousand people waiting to see the train. And then I realized that something really phenomenal was happening." In Hartford, Connecticut, on this same day, a police-estimated one hundred thousand people came out to see "Give 'Em Hell" Harry—"a human sea," the *Hartford Courant* described the scene.

Clark Clifford recalled the excitement generated by the campaign in its final push. "That last month you could actually feel it," Clifford said. "The last ten days of the campaign were something of a triumph. Now we were all indoctrinated with the fact that he had a real long shot on our hands; but that last ten days, that last five days even, you could sense there was something going on. I remember thinking, 'Well, I don't know whether we're going to make it or not, but, by god, I bet if we had another week we would surely make it.'"

The advance man Oscar Chapman noticed too. Arriving a day or two ahead of time in the towns Truman was set to speak in, Chapman could sense the shift in the attitude of the people. "The month of October absolutely confirmed my conviction that he was going to be elected," he recalled.

Now late in the game, a surprising list of Truman supporters had come to the candidate's aid. Eleanor Roosevelt finally went public urging voters to choose Truman, in a radio address (DNC officials had scrambled to raise the $25,721 fee to ABC for the radio time, delivering it in cash in a brown paper bag). Twenty-seven leading writers endorsed Truman, including Nobel Prize winner Sinclair Lewis and Pulitzer Prize winners Conrad Aiken and Archibald MacLeish. Truman Capote and Carson McCullers endorsed Truman. Thirty-six FDR associates came out in support of the president, including Harold Ickes, who had been Truman's most outspoken critic a year earlier. The new president of the Screen Actors Guild, Ronald Reagan, came out for Truman, saying he was "more than a little impatient with those promises the Republicans made before they got control of congress a couple of years ago."

Press reports told an entirely different story from the one the Truman campaigners were seeing. The day before Truman reached Massachusetts, the *Boston Daily Globe* printed a front-page story that Dewey "has a safe lead over President Harry S. Truman in Massachusetts," and that the state would tip to the GOP for the first time in twenty-four years. That same day, the *New York Times* published a front-page story that read: "Thomas E. Dewey and Earl Warren, Republican nominees for President and Vice President, respectively, appear certain to defeat President Harry S. Truman and Senator Alben W. Barkley, their Democratic opponents, by a large plurality in the Electoral College."

Robert Nixon of the White House press corps remembered filing a pre-election story with the New York office of the United Press Service at the end of October. "The tenor of this story," he recalled, "was that there was a snowballing tide of public opinion for Truman that indicated very strongly that he would be the winner in a great political upset. My New York office was part of the Hearst organization, which blatantly opposed any and all Democrats. They had hated Roosevelt with a passion, and they despised Truman because they considered him a very inept man." The upshot: "They never used my story. They never put it on the wire. They thought I was crazy."

In Boston, the Truman party checked into the Statler Hotel. The reception was near pandemonium. "I've never seen such a mob in a lobby," recalled campaign staffer and speechwriter Frank Kelly. "They had to fight to get him [Truman] through, and people were just cheering madly." Kelly looked over at an anxious police officer.

"How does this crowd compare with what Roosevelt drew when he came through Boston?" Kelly asked.

"Roosevelt never drew a crowd half as big as this in Boston," the officer replied. "We like Harry better up here."

Truman and his family were escorted via a private elevator to his thirteenth-floor quarters in the Statler. Then it was off to Mechanics Hall, where he delivered his Boston speech — a scathing attack on his "red herring" critics, and a shot across the bow of Communists who, Truman said, were trying to influence the outcome of the election.

"Get this straight now," the president barked. "I hate Communism. I have fought it at home. I have fought it abroad. I shall continue to fight it with all my strength. I shall never surrender. The fact is, the Communists are doing all they can to defeat me and help my Republican opponent," he said. "I'll tell you why. The Communists don't want me to be President because this country, under a Democratic administration, has rallied the forces of all the democracies of the world to safeguard freedom and to save free people everywhere from Communist slavery."

Truman finished with a plea: "We are engaged in a great crusade . . . This is Roosevelt's fight. And now it is my fight. More than that, it is *your* fight. We are going to win."

The applause lasted for several minutes. The evening was notable for another reason: "Biggest applause of the evening outside of that given the Truman family was for Congressman John F. Kennedy [serving his first term]," noted the *Boston Daily Globe* writer Elizabeth Watts, "who had a whole cheering section among the pretty young girls who served as ushers."

On this same night of October 27, *The Truman Story* debuted in movie theaters across the country and was an instant hit. Jack Redding, the Democratic National Committee's publicist, would remember sitting with Tom Meade, who had supervised the making of the Universal Newsreel film, as they watched the completed version. Redding would remember Meade laughing "as I've seldom seen anyone laugh," in response to what both perceived as the brilliance of the film, which had been cobbled together using existing newsreel footage. They had shot not a single frame. The film played to Truman's authenticity; nothing about it was staged.

"It's fantastic," a delighted Meade observed. "I was told that this film would be a flop because there'd be no time to do any shooting. But this thing is the best I've ever seen." Remembered Redding: "Thus, during the last six days of the campaign no one could go to the movies anywhere in the United States without seeing the story of the President. It was probably the most important and most successful publicity break in the entire campaign."

The following morning, Truman was back on the train, making way for the finale in New York City. "We worked all through the campaign on New York," remembered Clark Clifford. "We knew that it was critical. We knew at the time that that was Wallace's major bastion of support . . . The whole Democratic organization was set to work."

Boston gave Dewey the biggest crowd he had seen yet. Still, it did not measure up to the one Truman had drawn the night before; an estimated fifty thousand fewer people came out to see the Dewey motorcade.

Here in New England, Dewey was polling far ahead, however. Gallup had him running 52 percent to Truman's 45 percent in Massachusetts. Dewey was determined to snag the state's sixteen electoral votes. Onstage, he was joined by Speaker of the House Joseph Martin—a favorite Massachusetts son. Martin sat in a chair onstage and, ignored by Dewey, listened to a speech that shocked him.

In Boston, Dewey went all out for Social Security and a higher minimum wage, ideas that were not very different from the proposals Truman had made. Martin was among those anti-Truman conservatives in Congress who refused to pass the Social Security legislation that Truman—and now Dewey himself—had called for.

Dewey said, "A social security program that leaves so many people out in the cold is not good enough for America." The "pittance" the federal government paid to the average retired worker or his widow "is not security enough," the governor continued. "We must take action to bring about an increase of these benefits to our older people and their dependents." One reporter called the speech "a GOP 'New Deal' in social security."

Sitting on the stage, Martin remained silent. At one point he glanced at a group of friends in the audience and smiled with embarrassment. In Boston, the GOP's identity crisis was on full display.

Truman's reception in New York "surpassed anything in our history," the national committee's J. Howard McGrath recorded. From the moment the president stepped out of his train in Grand Central Station, police had their hands full keeping the crowds behind ropes. A motorcade of open cars cruised down Forty-Second Street as ticker tape poured from open windows in steady streams. The police escort — 101 motorcycles — was the largest the city had ever deployed.

Meanwhile, many floors up above Grand Central at Democratic National Committee headquarters in the Biltmore Hotel, campaigners were dialing through lists of phone numbers, in a frantic effort to urge voters to make it to the polls. A day earlier, McGrath had sent out a telegram to the state chairmen of the Democratic Party in all forty-eight states. "Suggest you contact wives of all Democratic officials and committees asking them to spend as much of the day as possible telephoning friends and neighbors to get out and vote. This can be built up in an endless chain fashion."

The president made stops at an Amalgamated Clothing Workers rally in Union Square at 4:45 p.m. ("We're going to lick 'em, just as sure as you stand there!"), then at City Hall at 5:20 p.m. ("90 percent of the press is against us; 90 percent of the radio commentators are against us; and the only way you can find out the truth is for me to come out and tell you what the truth is").

By the time Truman reached the Biltmore Hotel at 6 p.m. to ready himself for the night's rally at Madison Square Garden, a police-estimated 1.4 million New Yorkers had seen him, over a nine-mile tour through the city. The moment Truman reached the Biltmore, however, he faced yet another crisis.

Oscar Ewing and Clark Clifford had been waiting for the president at the hotel, and they were obviously concerned. Ewing produced a cable he had received from a Zionist journalist named Lillie Shultz, who worked for the liberal magazine *The Nation*. Ms. Shultz claimed to have information regarding the UN negotiations in Paris. She said that Secretary of State Marshall was about to publicly announce to the United Nations his approval of the Bernadotte Plan. This was the peace proposal that would recognize statehood of both Arabs and Israelis in Palestine. The Israeli government had rejected this proposal, because it offered the new nation a smaller territory than it was fighting to obtain. Marshall, Ms. Shultz now claimed, was about to endorse the plan before the UN, without Truman's approval.

The humiliation for the president would be extreme, and it would surely cost him the Jewish vote on November 2.

Truman was set to give his biggest speech yet on the subject of Israel, in roughly two hours, at Madison Square Garden. The speech was going to go live over nationwide radio. His speechwriters had been up all night fine-tuning it, to make it align with the most up-to-date information regarding the UN negotiations in Paris. Truman had to stop Marshall from making any statement on Israel, if such a statement was in fact pending.

"What on earth can we do to prevent this?" Truman asked his aides.

Ewing suggested sending Marshall a cable straightaway, with a suggestion of a statement that Marshall *should* make, instead of Marshall making any statement of his own.

"That's a good idea," Truman answered. "Do you and Clark mind missing the speech at Madison Square Garden tonight and use the time to draft a statement for General Marshall to make?"

"Of course," came the answer. "We'd be glad to."

Sending cables to the secretary of state in Paris was no easy task, however. Clifford and Elsey drafted two cables, then Clifford called the undersecretary of state, Bob Lovett, in Washington and dictated the two cables over the phone. Lovett then had to go to the State Department coding office to encrypt the cables. The messages would then go over the wire to Marshall. "There was six hours difference in time between Washington and Paris," recalled Ewing, "so it would be nip and tuck as to whether the President's message would reach General Marshall before he had delivered his statement to the [UN] conference." The first cable read:

From: The President (in New York)

To: The Secretary of State (in Paris)

I am deeply concerned over reports here of action taken in [UN] Security Council on Palestine question. I hope that before this nation takes any position or any statement is made by our Delegation that I be advised of such contemplated action and the implications thereof.

The second cable contained a statement that Marshall should use, if he was going to make any statement on Palestine. Lovett sent it along with his own memo to Marshall, stating, "President again directs every effort be made to avoid taking position on Palestine prior to Wednesday [November 3, the day after the election]. If by any chance it appears certain vote [on the Palestine matter] would have to be taken on Monday or Tuesday he directs US Delegation to abstain."

That night, Truman ate a quick dinner at the Biltmore. Joining him was his adviser Donald Dawson, who got a phone call from an official at Madison Square Garden. Truman was hoping for a moment of rest before his MSG rally. But not tonight. The pressure was relentless. Dawson learned that the arena's seats were nearly empty, and the president was expected to arrive soon. Dawson jumped from the table and rushed down to the Garden, which was about a dozen blocks away. He recalled, "The place was half empty . . . The lights were blazing down from the highest balcony. I walked up there, ran and saw — there were no people at all . . . I saw few spectators but several photographers."

Dawson figured out the problem. The Democratic National Committee had run out of money and so a fringe group called the Liberal Party had paid for the hall that night. The Liberal Party was so small that it could not possibly fill the Garden's thousands of seats, and party officials had reserved all the tickets for party members, a relatively small number. If Truman gave one of his most important speeches to an empty hall at the climax of the campaign, the results would be disastrous. It would confirm what all the reporters and pollsters had been saying: Truman was a lost cause.

There were thousands and thousands of people outside Madison Square Garden, and Dawson arranged for the doors to be opened to the public. Soon crowds of people were filing through turnstiles and filling the seats. By the time Truman arrived, the venue was full. "We had a big motorcade and marching parade coming over from the Biltmore Hotel to the Garden with the President," Dawson recorded. "I marched the parade into Madison Square Garden, and closed the gates so they couldn't go out."

By the time Truman stepped onto the stage at the Garden, he had already given fourteen speeches on this one day, no two exactly alike. The first had been a whistle-stop at 7:30 a.m. in Quincy, Massachusetts. Now it was just after 10:30 p.m. Onstage with the president was Herbert Lehman, the former Democratic governor of New York, labor leader David Dubinsky, and Bess and Margaret, clutching bouquets of flowers. A band played "I'm Just Wild About Harry" and "Happy Days Are Here Again."

Truman approached the podium amid tremendous applause. Innumerable drafts of his speech had been written, but Truman now made a bold decision to go off script. He had a surprise for everyone.

"There is a special reason why I am glad to be here tonight," Truman said onstage at Madison Square Garden. "We have come here tonight with one mind and one purpose. We have come to pledge once more our faith in liberal government, and to place in firm control of our national affairs those who believe with all their hearts in the principles of Franklin D. Roosevelt."

Truman then began to taunt Thomas Dewey. The GOP candidate had spoken in Los Angeles, right after Truman. Dewey had spoken in Cleveland, right after Truman. He had spoken in Boston, right after Truman. Now Dewey would be coming to New York, the night after the president's speech. "Now," Truman said, "I have a confession to make to you here tonight":

> For the last two or three weeks I've had a queer feeling that I'm being followed, that someone is following me. I felt it so strongly that I went into consultation with the White House physician. And I told him that

> I kept having this feeling, that everywhere I go there's somebody following behind me. The White House physician told me not to worry. He said: "You keep right on your way. There is one place where that fellow is not going to follow you — and that's in the White House."

The crowd exploded with laughter and approval. "This brought down the house," remembered journalist Robert Nixon, in the Garden that night. "The crowd just roared and stomped and cheered."

Truman went on: "He can follow me to Cleveland . . . [Applause!] He can follow me to Chicago . . . [Applause!] He can follow me to Boston . . . [More!] He can follow me to Pittsfield and Providence . . ."

> The Republican candidate can follow me all the way from Los Angeles to Madison Square Garden, but the Republican record makes it certain that he will still be trailing along behind when the votes are counted. He is doing all he can to make you forget that record. He doesn't dare talk about it. I have never in my life been in a campaign where the opposition refused absolutely to discuss the issues of the campaign. I can't understand that sort of an approach . . .

Truman was more than halfway through his speech before he brought up the main subject of the night: Israel. Here in New York — where there were probably more Jews than there were in the Holy Land — he reiterated his support for the Democratic platform. Without committing to de jure recognition of the new Israeli government, Truman pledged his support for the success of this new nation.

"That is our objective," he said. "We shall work toward it, but we will not work toward it in a partisan and political way. I am confident that that objective will be reached."

Nearing his finish, Truman said, "I have only one request to make of you: vote on election day. Vote for yourselves. You don't have to vote for me. Vote in your own interests."

The applause resonated throughout the building, and even after Truman left the stage, it kept on coming.

Truman delivered nearly eighteen thousand words of campaign speeches on this single day, many of them off the cuff. He had one more day to make his case to New Yorkers before heading home. For over a year he had been the catalyst for a new civil rights movement, one he hoped would recast the nation's racial and political landscape forever. He was scheduled to speak on October 29 in a place no presidential candidate had ever gone: Harlem, the spiritual home of black America.

30

"I Stand by My Prediction. Dewey Is In."

FOR MONTHS, THE Republican National Committee had been holding regular meetings, meticulously planning every detail of Dewey's triumphant return to New York City. When the governor arrived at Grand Central Station, all that work paid off. There were brass bands and color guards, a torchlight parade, and even an airplane that spelled Dewey's name in the sky with its exhaust.

On the stage at Madison Square Garden, when Dewey appeared, he was flanked by a forty-by-twenty-five-foot statue of the United States Capitol. Huge portraits of Dewey and Earl Warren hung from the rafters. Every seat was filled, and the roar was the loudest Dewey had heard his entire campaign.

"It is great to be home again," Dewey said, "and you have given me a perfectly wonderful homecoming. It is all the more wonderful because it is a homecoming on the eve of victory."

In Dewey's final major campaign appearance, he stayed the course, speaking philosophically on unity, attacking the Democrats without singling out particular issues. The Democratic Party "has been divided against itself for so long that it has forgotten the meaning of unity, and it never did know the meaning of teamwork or competence," Dewey said. He punctuated his remarks by punching his open palm with his fist as he criticized his opponent's "desperate tactics" and the failure of the administration to bring peace to the world. Dewey did not mention the Jews, Israel, or Palestine. Nor did he mention what his plans were regarding taxes, immigration, or the Taft-Hartley law. He said, "We will follow strong, clear policies," without saying what those policies would be.

To end his final campaign appearance, he expressed satisfaction with what his team had accomplished: "I am very happy that we can look back over the weeks of our campaigning and say: 'This has been good for our country.' I am proud we can look ahead to our victory and say: 'America won.'"

Later that night, back on the Dewey Victory Special, the candidate headed for Albany. As the train traveled north along the Hudson River, Dewey engaged members of the press with an unexpected, impromptu talk. "On that trip . . . he came into the press car and told his plans — all off the record," recalled Raymond P. Brandt, the Washington bureau chief of the *St. Louis Post-Dispatch*. "He was positive as to whom he was going to have in his Cabinet. They were really confident. I have to admit that I thought he was going to be elected."

"He assumed in '48 that he was already President," remembered Jack Bell of the Associated Press, who was aboard the train. "And he even gave us, at one point, the makeup of his Cabinet — off the record as it were — going back to Albany."

Even before Election Day, congratulatory mail poured into the Dewey offices. Senator Vandenberg of Michigan wrote Dewey on November 1, "I am 'jumping the gun' to send you my heartiest congratulations upon your inevitable Tuesday victory. As you move into this new responsibility, I offer you every cooperation within my power . . . Again, I congratulate you upon your victory in advance."

The president of the Fitchburg Paper Company, George R. Wallace, wrote his friend on November 1, "By the time you receive this letter you will be our next President and first of all, I want to congratulate you on winning the election and for the splendid campaign you conducted." Another of Dewey's friends, Clellan Forsythe of Syracuse, wrote Dewey on November 1: "Since knowing you I have been certain that one day you would be our President and now that the time has arrived it is my earnest prayer that God will grant you in these troubled times the strength and wisdom to become our greatest president . . . Good luck—and Godspeed!"

Throughout the night of October 28, Jews filled the lobby of the Biltmore Hotel, where the president was staying. One Truman campaigner recalled that, around sunrise on the twenty-ninth, "I could hardly get through the lobby. The situation over Palestine was so tense that the Zionists were holding an overnight vigil. There were groups of Jewish war veterans and some young Zionist people that had really filled the lobby shoulder to shoulder. They were praying and singing, and at regular intervals, about fifteen minutes, calling the President's suite to demand an answer as to what he was going to do about the U.S. position before the U.N. in Paris."

Upstairs, after breakfast, Truman gathered about a dozen of his aides to go over the day's speeches, at the table in his suite's dining room. Among those present was Eddie Jacobson, Truman's former haberdashery partner and now owner of Westport Menswear in Kansas City. Jacobson had the president's ear on the Zionist issue; he had been lobbying for months in support of the Israeli cause.

Present also was Philleo Nash, Truman's special assistant for minority affairs. It had been Nash who had fought for the idea of Truman making an appearance in Harlem. He had been in Washington the night before and had gotten a call demanding his presence in New York immediately. Everyone in the Truman camp had been working on the Madison Square Garden Palestine speech for the twenty-eighth, and so no one had gotten to writing the final draft of the biggest speech of October 29—a civil rights address Truman was scheduled to give in Harlem at 3:50 p.m.

Nash arrived in New York at 5 a.m. Now he was at the table with Truman. "Mr. President," he said, "I brought up a draft of a speech on civil rights for the Harlem rally."

"Well, I've been waiting a long time to get this taken care of," Truman responded, according to Nash's account. "We should have done it sooner."

Nash handed over the speech, and Truman read the whole thing aloud

— a hard-hitting civil rights polemic. When he finished, he looked around the room and said, "Well, anybody who isn't for this ought to have his head examined."

Some at the table raised concern over the speech. Was it going too far? The race was tight in states like Tennessee and Kentucky, where many voters were against Truman's civil rights stand. Should Truman go so far out on a limb?

"Of course we have to do it," he said. "We should have been doing it all along."

Nash raised the idea of using the term *unity* in the speech, picking up on Dewey's theme and making it their own. "Unity is basically a weak concept," the president said. "It isn't only the way Mr. Dewey's been handling it and has been talking about it. We should be doing what's right even if we can't be united about it. And this speech is about what's right."

Just before noon, Truman exited the Biltmore Hotel, surrounded by Secret Service agents. He climbed into an open car and his motorcade moved down Forty-Third Street, making a left on Fifth Avenue, where the crowds were thick on either side. Truman's tour would carry him sixty-six miles on this day. According to police accounts, 1.245 million people would see the president.

At Larkin Plaza in Yonkers, New York, he blamed the Republican Congress for the current housing shortage. Congress was controlled by the real estate lobbyists, he said. In the Bronx, he taunted Dewey as his "little shadow." Then the motorcade moved over a bridge and pulled up to Dorrance Brooks Square at St. Nicholas Avenue and 136th Street, a park named for an African American soldier from Harlem who had died fighting for his country in World War I. Harlem's black newspaper, the *Amsterdam News,* estimated the crowd in the park at half a million people. Harlem had crime issues, and the Secret Service agents were concerned for the president's safety.

A speaker's platform had been built on the edge of the park, and a group of black ministers from the Ministerial Alliance welcomed Truman to the stage. Truman had been invited to Harlem to accept a humanitarian award.

People were shouting "Pour it on, Harry!" A group of students from the City College of New York led a chant of "Give 'em hell, Harry!" The *Amsterdam News* had officially endorsed Dewey, but one would never know it from the enthusiasm of this crowd.

The ministers led a lengthy prayer, and then a strange silence fell over the scene. Philleo Nash was unnerved. "All of a sudden, there was a big crowd, but a silent crowd," he recalled. "Well, this is rather ominous, rather frightening. I had my back to the crowd and I just wondered whether I'd been wrong in urging that this [Harlem speech] be done and that the people who said it wasn't safe were right." He turned around and what he saw stunned him. "I saw why they were silent . . . Almost everybody in that crowd was praying, and they were praying for the President, and they were praying for their own civil rights . . . They thought it was a religious occasion."

A minister named Dr. C. Asapansa-Johnson spoke first, followed by New York's mayor, William O'Dwyer. Truman sat listening, against a backdrop of red, white, and blue bunting, while the mayor urged the crowd to vote for Truman. This was a turnaround for O'Dwyer, who just three months earlier had been one of the many Democrats seeking to draft Dwight Eisenhower to take Truman's place at the top of the party ticket.

Harlem was not going to get Give 'Em Hell Harry. Truman was going to give this crowd something different entirely—a sober speech on an issue that touched on the very essence of Americanism. When it was his time, Truman approached the microphone and began to speak, thanking the ministers for honoring him with their invitation.

"This, in my mind, is a most solemn occasion. It's made a tremendous impression upon me," Truman said.

He recommitted himself to his civil rights platform, a plan that—if successfully put into action—would change the course of history. "Eventually, we are going to have an America in which freedom and opportunity are the same for everyone," he said. "There is only one way to accomplish that great purpose, and that is to keep working for it and never take a backward step." Truman said he was going to fight for equal rights for all races "with every ounce of strength and determination I have." In America, Truman said, everyone should have an equal chance at a job, every child should have an equal chance for an education, every person should have the right to vote and to be free of "mob violence and intimidation."

"It was the authors of the Declaration of Independence who stated the principle that all men are created equal in their rights, and that it is to secure these rights that governments are instituted among men," Truman said. "It was the authors of the Constitution who made it clear that, under our form of government, all citizens are equal before the law, and that the Federal Government has a duty to guarantee to every citizen equal protection of the laws."

The speech was the culmination of Truman's 1948 civil rights campaign. "Immediate and far-reaching repercussions were expected from the South," wrote the *New York Times*'s Anthony Leviero. "The President and his advisors apparently had weighed whatever risks were involved in his declaration."

Just hours after Truman's Harlem speech, Henry Wallace made his own address there, appearing at the Golden Gate ballroom at the corner of 142nd Street and Lenox Avenue, for the final speaking engagement of his campaign. It was perhaps his angriest. Wallace looked out from his podium and saw a predominantly black audience. He said that Truman's civil rights agenda was nothing but "shallow, hollow, worthless promises."

In the past, Truman had supported the congressional campaigns of Democrats from the South, Wallace said—men who supported white supremacy. Thus, Wallace claimed, the president had "invited the Dixiecrats, the race-haters, the lynch boys, the poll-taxers right back into the camp. And they're coming back."

When Wallace finished, he walked off the stage and headed back to his farm in upstate New York, where he would be voting two days later.

Strom Thurmond held a rally in Austin, Texas, that day, nearing the end of a sweep that had taken him throughout the state and to Louisiana. Thurmond's drumbeat had not changed. He called Truman's civil rights program "a Federal horsewhip to sting us into line." Dewey's campaign had been all about "soothing and meaningless" platitudes. While Thurmond had no chance of national victory, he still insisted that his efforts were not in vain.

"Our campaign is based on the belief that we can prevent either Truman or Dewey from winning a majority of the electoral votes," he told a crowd in Beaumont, Texas, on October 31. "In that event, the House of Representatives will choose a President who is dedicated to the preservation of local self-government."

Truman's civil rights proposals were "un-American," Thurmond said. Even if the States' Rights Democratic Party campaign failed on Tuesday, he went on, it had "accomplished our most important objective . . . to restore the Southern States to a position of respect from every political party."

On the morning of October 30, the Truman Special pulled out of Grand Central Station, bound for Missouri. Truman napped in his berth. Bess and Margaret had reached the end of their patience. They wanted the campaign to be over.

As the train barreled west, Truman's speechwriters met to put together an address for the president's final campaign appearance, at the massive Kiel Auditorium that night in St. Louis. Events had been so pressing, there had been no time to draft the speech, so it was a last-minute effort. The race in Truman's home state of Missouri was a nail-biter; this St. Louis event *had* to go well. "On the last long ride . . . ," recorded speechwriter John Franklin Carter, "all of us had picked some pieces of lovely speeches which we had composed from time to time during the campaign, and for one reason or another, hadn't been delivered. We got together a final script for St. Louis."

That afternoon, Truman was back at his table in the *Ferdinand Magellan,* reviewing the speech that his writers had prepared. By this time, his old friend John Snyder, the secretary of the Treasury, was aboard, bound for his hometown of St. Louis. Truman told Snyder that he was "considerably amazed at the lack of punch" in the speech his aides had given him.

Snyder asked, "Are you going to deliver this speech in St. Louis?"

"I am not," Truman answered.

There was no backup. Truman would speak entirely off the cuff, with no script, to the entire nation via radio.

By this time, the speech he was *not* going to use had been mimeographed and distributed to the journalists on board the train. They too were intensely weary and had already typed out their stories for the next day's papers.

"We got to St. Louis and there was a cold, nasty rain falling," recalled Carleton Kent of the *Chicago Times,* "but Kiel Auditorium was jammed to the gunnels." "There were so many people there," noted Robert Nixon of the International News Service, "that the firemen had to clear the aisles because of the regulations. There was a large overflow crowd outside the auditorium where loudspeakers had been set up so that people could listen to the President's speech." When Truman appeared, radio men hit a signal and took the broadcast nationwide.

"Thank you my friends," Truman yelled over the noise of the crowd. "I appreciate most highly this reception in St. Louis, but bear in mind that I have got to talk to the whole United States tonight . . ."

Again, the crowd roared.

"I can't tell you how very much I appreciate this reception on my return to my home State. It touches my heart—right where I live . . . I know that when Missouri feels this way, we are on the road to victory."

Truman had seen a lot of enthusiasm throughout the campaign, and the crowd in St. Louis brought it to a climax. "The country was aware of the fact that Truman had conducted a one-man battle," recalled Robert Nixon. "Americans have an affection for people who fight for what they believe in . . . [St. Louis] was his last speech of the campaign, the grand finale . . . There was a fist in almost every word and a fight in every sentence." Meanwhile the reporters began to realize that Truman was not giving the speech they expected; they would have to scramble to rewrite their stories.

> I have been in many a campaign, my friends . . . But never in my lifetime have I been in a campaign, nor seen a campaign, such as I have been through recently. I became President of the United States 3 years, 6 months, and 18 days ago, and we have been through the most mo-

> mentous period in the history of the world in that time. Twenty-six days after I became President, Germany surrendered unconditionally. Four months and 21 days after I was sworn in as President of the United States, Japan folded up and surrendered unconditionally, thus ending the greatest war in the history of the world . . .
>
> Four days after Japan surrendered on September the 2d, my first policy message went to Congress. That message contained 21 points . . . When that message went to Congress, the smear campaign on your President started in all its vile and untruthfully slanted headlines, columns, and editorials.

This was the ultimate Give 'Em Hell Harry speech. The audience "applauded for about two and a half hours," recorded John Franklin Carter. "I've never seen anything like it. It was a wild, wild reception."

Truman railed against the "saboteurs and character assassins" of the press. He attacked his old foe — the "do nothing" Eightieth Congress — for failing to pass the administration's housing bill during a housing crisis, for failing to pass health-care reform, for failing the farmers of America by taking away their grain-storage bins. After a half hour, he brought the speech to an extemporaneous end.

> People are waking up that the tide is beginning to roll, and I am here to tell you that if you do your duty as citizens of the greatest Republic the sun has ever shone on, we will have a Government that will be for your interests, that will be for peace in the world, and for the welfare of all the people, and not just a few.

With those final words, the president turned and walked off the stage. It was the last appearance Harry Truman would ever make in a campaign of his own. Later that night of October 30, he recalled, "I returned from the bedlam of the longest and hardest political campaign of my career to the restful quiet of my home in Independence."

• • •

"The campaign is all over," Margaret wrote in her diary on November 1. "Now we wait until tomorrow is done to see how the voters decide. We can take whatever comes, but I wonder if the country can."

On the night of November 1, both Truman and Dewey made final "get-out-the-vote" radio speeches — Truman from his living room in Independence, and Dewey from the Manhattan studios of NBC.

"We have come to the end of a campaign which will decide the course of our country in the four fateful years ahead," Dewey said. "The speeches have been made. The debate is ended. Tomorrow we will go to the polls."

Any number of publications and pundits offered final predictions, and while they varied in detail, they were unanimous in terms of the outcome. Radio broadcaster Walter Winchell gave the election to Dewey, with 15 to 1 odds. One St. Louis bookie gave Dewey 8 to 1 odds. One in Chicago offered 3 to 1. The final polls: Crossley had it 49.9 percent for Dewey and 44.8 for Truman, with the remainder for Wallace and Thurmond. Gallup gave 46 percent to Dewey and 40 percent to Truman. The third big pollster, Elmo Roper, gave the election to the GOP with a statement: "I stand by my prediction. Dewey is in."

The *New York Times* predicted a Dewey landslide of 345 electoral votes. *Newsweek* forecast an even bigger landslide, with 366 electoral votes. *Life* magazine had already published a photo of Dewey in a boat with the caption, "The next President travels by ferryboat over the broad waters of San Francisco Bay." Columnist Ralph McGill wrote in the *Atlanta Constitution:* "I have already made up my mind that Gov. Dewey is to be the next President of the United States. It is no new decision. It became obvious some months ago." The nation's most popular political columnist, Drew Pearson: "I would say that Governor Dewey had conducted one of the most astute and skillful campaigns in recent years . . . Undoubtedly, you'll have teamwork in the White House under Dewey." The *Wall Street Journal:* "Government will remain big, active and expensive under President Thomas E. Dewey." *Kiplinger* magazine: "What will Dewey do?"

"You've got to live with him for four years, possibly eight," *Kiplinger* stated. "He will influence your life, your thinking, your work, your business."

Even in Britain, pundits were digging Harry Truman's political grave, using boldface headlines as the shovel. The *Manchester Guardian:* "Harry S. Truman: A Study of a Failure." The *London Daily Mail:* "Dewey Gets the Votes: Truman — Admiration." The United Kingdom's most widely circulated daily paper, the *Daily Express:* "What kind of President will Tom Dewey make?"

"Most of the articles [in Britain] read like obituaries of President Truman's Administration," commented *New York Times* political writer Clifton Daniel from the paper's London office. (This story would prove especially ironic, as Daniel would later become Margaret Truman's husband and Harry Truman's son-in-law.)

In the nation's capital, the switchboards at hotels were reportedly ringing off the hook as Republicans were booking rooms for the inauguration. It was also reported that Republican families were renting homes in Washington and enrolling their kids in schools for the spring 1949 semester.

At home in Independence, the Trumans went to bed late on November 1, after the president's radio broadcast. The next day, some fifty million Americans headed to the polls.

31

"Tens of Thousands, and Hundreds of Thousands! How Can He Lose?"

The ballot is stronger than the bullet.

—**Abraham Lincoln**

AT 10 A.M. ON ELECTION DAY 1948, the door to the Truman home at 219 North Delaware Street in Independence, Missouri, opened and Harry, Bess, and Margaret emerged. North Delaware was normally a quiet street but neighbors had gotten used to crowds gathering outside the Truman home. On this day, there was a mob scene out front. The Trumans descended to the cement sidewalk, and the Secret Service escorted them along the five-minute walk to Memorial Hall.

The brick neo-Georgian building was a special place for the Truman family; as a young local politician, Truman himself had led the charge to build Memorial Hall* in honor of World War I soldiers who had lost their lives. When the building first opened, back in 1926, Truman was an obscure

*This building is now the Truman Memorial Building.

county judge. Now, twenty-two years later, he walked through these doors again, to cast his vote for himself for president.

Inside the polling station, an election judge named Emma Flowers called out the name of "Harry S. Truman, 219 North Delaware." Truman stepped forward and checked his registration card. The clerks handed him ballot #101, Bess #102, and Margaret #103. It was Margaret's first time voting in a presidential election. The Trumans filled out their ballots in booths, and after the president dropped his into the ballot box, someone in the crowd asked him, "How do you think it will go, Mr. President?"

"Why, it can't be anything but victory," Truman said.

Another voice called out, "Are you going to sit up for the returns, Mr. President?"

"I doubt it," he said. "I think I'll go to bed. You don't know anything till tomorrow. I expect to be at the Muehlebach Hotel in Kansas City at 10 o'clock tomorrow — if everything holds together."

Dewey and his wife slept late in their suite on the fifteenth floor of the Roosevelt Hotel in Manhattan, rising at 9:30 a.m. At noon, the candidate and his wife walked out of an elevator surrounded by a phalanx of police officers, who parted crowds to allow the Deweys to make it to their "NY #1" black limo out front. They motored to their polling place at the School of Industrial Art at 121 East Fifty-First Street with a police escort.

In the basement of the school, Thomas and Frances Dewey cast their votes, then stood smiling in front of the ballot box for photo and newsreel cameras.

"Well," Dewey said, "that's two votes we got anyhow."

Henry Wallace awoke early on Election Day at his farm in rural South Salem, New York. He drove his wife and a press secretary to the nearby public library in the village of Lewisboro, a 148-year-old white colonial building where there was already a small crowd lined up to vote. This district was almost entirely Republican, and at 8:05 a.m., Wallace and his wife cast two of the very few votes that would go to the Progressive Party at this polling station. Camera flashbulbs popped in their faces when they exited the polling booth.

When asked if he would estimate the total votes he thought he would earn nationwide, Wallace declined to answer, saying he would get "more votes than the pollsters say."

The Wallaces climbed back into their car and returned to the farm, where they spent the day tending to their floral gardens and their chickens. In the afternoon, they headed for the Progressive Party's headquarters in New York City, where they would await word of Wallace's fate.

Strom Thurmond traveled from Columbia, South Carolina, to the town where he grew up and where the Thurmond name had been known for generations — Edgefield — to cast his vote. With his wife and his mother, he made his way through Edgefield's familiar county courthouse and up the stairs to the second floor, shaking hands with hometown friends along the way.

His wife — who at twenty-two was voting for the first time — cast her ballot first, followed by Thurmond's mother and finally Thurmond himself. Before leaving the courthouse, the governor gave a final statement: "They said back at Philadelphia [at the Democratic National Convention in July] that southern leaders had no place to go. Well, we've gone back to the people themselves, and today they're going to let us know what they think about the matter."

All over the country, long lines formed at polling stations. In Alabama, election officials had managed to keep Truman's name off the ballot, so anyone who wanted to vote for the president had to write his name in. Thus Dewey was the only candidate on the ballot in every state. Other presidential candidates included the white nationalist Gerald L. K. Smith of the Christian Nationalist Party, John Maxwell of the Vegetarian Party, Norman Thomas of the Socialist Party, and Claude A. Watson of the Prohibition Party.

Clouds blanketed much of the country and rain was anticipated in the evening along the Eastern Seaboard. In the town where Tom Dewey was raised, and where his mother still lived — Owosso, Michigan — local businesses and small-town political leaders had a big celebration planned, for this was to be the most exciting day in the town's history. In Truman's hometown of Independence, no celebration was planned.

All over the South, voters headed for the polls hoping there would be no violence. Separate polling stations were set up for black Americans, who lined up to cast their votes while nervously watching over their shoulders. The murder of Isaiah Nixon — the twenty-eight-year-old black man killed in southern Georgia because he voted in a primary election — was fresh in their minds.

Local populations had their eyes on key special-issue referendums. In Kansas, where sales of liquor had been outlawed for sixty-eight years, voters would decide if the state would become "wet" once again (it would). In South Carolina, voters would decide if the state would remain the only one of the forty-eight that outlawed divorce (voters would decide to legalize divorce in the state).

In Independence, after the Trumans voted, Harry went to lunch at the Rockwood Country Club, where he was the guest of honor among a few dozen friends. The lunch was hosted by Truman's old friend, the mayor of Independence and a local grocer named Roger Sermon. Outside, reporters paced and littered the sidewalk with cigarette butts, unaware that they were about to fall victim to a clever ruse.

Truman excused himself from the lunch table to go to the bathroom. Three Secret Service men escorted him out the back door to a car, and together they motored out of town. The only other person along was Truman's personal doctor, Wallace Graham. Truman had informed almost no one as to where he was going. One of the people he told was his old friend Tom L. Evans, a local radio station and drugstore chain owner. Evans had helped raise money for Truman's campaign, and now on Election Day, the stress had caused him to suffer from severe abdominal pain. "Boy," he recalled, "those ulcers of mine and that day in '48 were turning over and upside down and everything." Evans would be one of the very few who would be permitted to call Truman at the place he was going — a secret hideaway.

The president's car motored over a bridge past the Missouri River and up to the Elms Hotel in Excelsior Springs, about twenty-five miles from Independence. For sixty years people had come from all around to the Elms to soothe health problems in the hotel's pools of warm natural spring water. The sprawling hotel was nearly vacant on this Tuesday night. The president checked into a room on the third floor picked out for him by the Secret Service. He had himself a Turkish bath, then ate a ham sandwich with a glass of milk in his room while he listened to the radio. He had left Independence without any baggage, so he was wearing a bathrobe and slippers borrowed from the hotel. While there is no mention of any whiskey in any surviving record, it is hard to imagine that Truman did not have a thimble of his favorite drink — bourbon and branch water.

"We didn't talk any about the election [that night]," remembered Dr. Graham. "He wasn't concerned one iota, not a bit. We talked fairly late that evening and went to bed and that's all there was to it."

In the afternoon of November 2, Dewey's black limousine cut through traffic headed north to the Ninety-Third Street apartment of Mr. and Mrs. Roger Straus. The Deweys had an election-night tradition — a lavish meal with their friends, the Strauses, and perhaps a round of cards with the radio on. Mrs. Straus served a feast: consommé, roast duck, cauliflower, peas, fried apples, and blueberry pie. Then the Deweys motored back to the Roosevelt to listen to the returns on radio and watch the first-ever election-night television broadcast.

The hallways of the Roosevelt were crawling with police officers. On the mezzanine floor, GOP campaigners busied themselves setting up for the victory party in a huge ballroom. Dewey was expected to appear at 9 p.m. in the ballroom, but for now he remained on a couch in his suite, his mother sitting on his left and his wife across from him. ABC was featuring pollster George Gallup and popular news personalities Walter Winchell and Drew Pearson on both its radio and television broadcasts. On NBC TV, pundits could be seen talking into cameras between puffs of tobacco smoke, pausing occasionally to thoughtfully toss their cigarette ashes onto the floor.

A long night awaited. The Deweys settled in—excited, expectant, and terribly nervous—not because of the outcome but because of the awesome responsibilities they believed would soon weigh on their shoulders. Sitting on a chair in the Deweys' suite, a cop was focused on a crossword puzzle. Dewey's mother, Annie Thomas Dewey, asked him, "How do you think it's going to go? What do you think his chances are?"

The cop looked up and said, "It's a hundred to one, Mrs. Dewey. He can't lose."

The first election return of November 2, 1948, came from the tiny hamlet of Hart's Location in the White Mountains of New Hampshire, where voters leaned conservative. A small group gathered at 7 a.m. in the dining room of Mr. and Mrs. Joseph Burke. Voters were handed ballots and told to fill them out on whatever surface they could find. The voting took six minutes. When it was done, the tally was announced.

Far off in Kentucky, a student named Donald P. Miller would recall sitting in a lounge at Centre College with a political science professor, hearing that New Hampshire tally over the radio: "Five votes for Dewey, two for Truman." The professor stood up and said, "That's it. Truman will win. If he can get two out of seven votes in that little town in New Hampshire, he will win the election."

Truman campaigners set up shop in the presidential suite on the eleventh floor of the Muehlebach Hotel in Kansas City. This suite with its many rooms had already seen its share of historic events. Four years earlier, Truman had played songs on the piano for crowds of drunken campaigners the night FDR won the 1944 election, the night Truman became vice president–elect. He had signed the Truman Doctrine into law in this hotel suite. Presidents Theodore Roosevelt, William Howard Taft, Woodrow Wilson, Warren G. Harding, Calvin Coolidge, Herbert Hoover, and Truman himself had used this suite as a Kansas City office space.

Downstairs in the Muehlebach's smoky lobby, exhausted Truman campaigners were loafing in chairs and on couches, catching some rest for the long night ahead. Hotel staff in white gloves and pressed uniforms darted about the place like minnows, emptying ashtrays and moving luggage. A special private elevator led up to the hotel's presidential suite, and in front of that elevator, the presidential seal had already been placed on a stand, anticipating Truman's arrival, whenever that would be.

One Truman campaigner was asked, "What do you think of the President's chances?"

"One to two weeks more and he'd be a cinch," came the answer.

Said another Truman campaigner: "I'm nearly dead, and if he doesn't win I'll want to die."

"Crowds, crowds, crowds," said another. "Tens of thousands, and hundreds of thousands! How can he lose?"

Upstairs in the presidential suite, White House press secretary Charlie Ross milled about nervously, talking to reporters who were coming in and out. Ross's deep, smokestack voice could be heard over the ringing telephones, which were being managed by White House secretaries Roberta Barrows, Grace Earle, and Louise Hachmeister. In a corner, four teletype machines had been set up next to a desk covered in typewriters.

In the early afternoon, the teletype machines began to churn and hum, pumping out paper — returns coming in from the first voting precincts on the East Coast. "It was a rather sober bunch of us that put up in the Muehlebach Hotel," recalled *Chicago Times* reporter Carleton Kent. "I think it's fair to say that those of us of the press corps who were in Kansas City were there to see the roof fall in on Mr. Truman."

Outside the hotel on West Twelfth Street, in the afternoon hours, crowds began to steadily grow.

At Democratic National Committee headquarters in the Biltmore Hotel, chairman J. Howard McGrath sat at a huge conference table that had about thirty empty seats. In front of him were three telephones, which he would be manning through the night. The hallways and offices were full not of people but of gloom. The place was virtually empty. Outside McGrath's office was a large room with teletype machines and tables with rows of silent typewriters.

When a reporter for the *New York Herald Tribune* stopped by, he found the publicist Jack Redding alone.

"Nobody here," said the reporter, who looked embarrassed. It was clear he had been sent to write a story about the losing side. Redding would remember him as a "third string" journo.

"Not yet," Redding said.

"Do you think this is the way it'll be?"

"No. It won't be this way. It's early yet. The polls are still open here in the East. Everyone's still working."

"Then you think you have a chance?"

"Look, friend." Redding was irritated. "You're here to cover what your boss thinks is a losing cause. If he's right you'll get your story as it develops. And that story will be much better than any you can get from me. If your boss is wrong, and I think he is, you've got the top assignment of the day. What more can you ask? Now let me be."

In the White House, the offices were nearly empty. Truman's special aide for minority issues, Philleo Nash, and assistant press secretary Eben Ayers were alone and had the run of the place. "We had the President's office with a TV, and the press office with a teletype, and a White House car, and the White House staff to bring us sandwiches and coffee, so we had a pretty good time," Nash recalled. Ayers wrote in his diary that morning, "Were it not for all these predictions and the unanimity of the pollsters and experts, I would say the President has an excellent chance." Ayers seized on one important factor: the economy, "the general prosperity of the country."

Was America really going to kick an administration out of office when paychecks were so high and unemployment so low?

The White House staff was all abuzz. "I had a feeling that perhaps the good Lord was not on the President's side this time," remembered head butler Alonzo Fields, "though my wife kept saying that, despite the papers, he was going to win . . . I do not recall when there was ever as much excitement and open discussion as went on around the place during this election."

Fields kept a radio tuned in, and in the Oval Office, the television was on, as the early returns began to come through.

Clark Clifford was back in Washington on Election Day. He spent much of the day in his office. At one point, his phone rang, and when he picked up, he heard the familiar voice of Robert Lovett, the State Department's second-in-command under George Marshall. Lovett wanted to know if Clifford would help him work on an orderly transition if Dewey were to win, as everyone believed would be the case. Lovett was concerned that the Soviet Union could benefit from the "terrible uncertainty" that would exist between the election and inauguration day, six weeks later.

Lovett, Clifford would later learn, was a front-runner to become secretary of defense in the Dewey administration. Clifford assured Lovett politely that he would do whatever was needed.

That night, Clifford and his wife ended up in the home of a friend, Washington correspondent Jay Hayden of the *Detroit News,* because the Hayden family was one of the first among Clifford's friends to have a television. They settled in and stared at the huge machine with its fuzzy screen.

"We had planned to stay only about an hour," Clifford remembered. "Almost everyone expected the result to be settled early."

In Moscow, the city's three major newspapers printed the exact same report on the end of Henry Wallace's election campaign, painting an inaccurate portrait of Wallace's return to New York City. From the Russian point of view, Wallace was entering the city as if he were Caesar returning to Rome.

"Police said at least half a million people greeted Wallace, who rode about 80 miles through the Brooklyn district in an automobile accompanied by 50 machines decorated with banners and posters appealing for support of the Progressive Party," read the Russian report. "Several times groups of people pushed through the police and rushed up to Wallace in order to shake his hand."

The truth was far different. Wallace headed quietly to party headquarters in the brownstone on the corner of Park Avenue and Thirty-Sixth Street. "Wallace seemed to be in good spirits," recalled campaign manager Beanie Baldwin, "and I don't think I detected how hurt he was."

As the first returns came in, the Republican National Committee's chief Herbert Brownell issued a statement from his command post on the sixth floor of the Hotel Roosevelt in New York:

"Early reports reaching us from Republican State organizations in all parts of the country indicate what may well be a record breaking popular vote, and from the indications thus far available, the Dewey-Warren Ticket will be overwhelmingly elected."

At the Muehlebach Hotel, the teletype machines continued to crank out returns while waiters carried trays with Missouri ham sandwiches and pitchers of orange juice and black coffee. Truman was ahead in New York City, but the tide was turning on him as the rural votes poured in. New York looked dubious for the Democrats. As expected, Philadelphia voters went for Truman, but not by as much as was hoped — not by enough to counter the rural Pennsylvania votes that would follow from the western part of the state. An early lead in Maryland was slipping away. It looked like Truman would carry Virginia, but South Carolina was going to go to Strom Thurmond.

By nightfall, much of the eastern vote was in. Dewey carried both New York and Maryland. It was Henry Wallace who had cost Truman those states; Wallace voters had made the difference. Both states had gone to FDR and the Democrats in four straight elections, but both went for Dewey in 1948 by slim margins. Now the Midwest would follow. Truman had an enormous lead in Chicago as expected, but the rest of the state was a mystery. Ohio was looking bright, but who knew? The Wallace vote in Ohio could be strong too.

As the Midwest votes were tallied, Truman and Dewey were running neck-and-neck in the popular vote, but not in the electoral college, where Dewey was still ahead.

All the while, some 150 to 200 reporters were milling about the hotel, flabbergasted that they had no idea of the president's whereabouts.

Where was Truman?

Bess and Margaret were at home on Delaware Street. Outside, a crowd of two hundred locals were in the street, singing "Missouri Waltz" and "Hail, Hail, the Gang's All Here." They chanted "We want Harry" — but Harry was nowhere to be found. Around 9 p.m., radio networks began to report that Truman — while still behind in the electoral college — was pulling ahead in the popular vote. Due to the strange rubric the founding fathers had built into the Constitution, Truman was winning more votes nationwide than Dewey, but losing in the official tally that would ultimately decide the outcome. Reporters outside the Truman home were growing "frantic," as Margaret later put it. "I am not using the word 'frantic' loosely either," she recalled. "It became more and more apropos as the votes began to come in. At first everyone was told there would be a Dewey victory message at nine p.m. But Harry Truman seemed to be winning at nine p.m."

Wearing her favorite black dress and ballet slippers to keep her feet comfortable for the long night ahead, Margaret came out the front door and, standing under a porch light, she announced: "Dad isn't here. I don't know where he is."

From Republican headquarters at the Roosevelt, Herbert Brownell released his next statement: "At this moment the polls have closed in 12 of the 48 states . . . On the basis of reports which I have been receiving from organizational leaders throughout the country, I am confident that the Dewey-Warren Ticket has already carried 10 of these 12 states . . . It is now apparent that we will wind up by sweeping two-thirds of the states for the Republican Ticket. This is definitely a Republican year. The people have made up their minds and have registered their decision in many of the States."

Perhaps even Brownell knew his estimates were overly optimistic. The night was young, and nothing was going as planned. In homes all over the country, Americans who had expected an early result and an early bedtime were adjusting to the idea of a long night. Truman's first cousin Mary Ethel Noland would remember sitting in a room in her modest house in Independence, not interested in hearing the election returns because she believed they would be depressing. Others in the residence were huddled around a radio; Noland wanted no part of it. She lived across the street from the Truman home and could see out the window the crowds out front.

"Along in the evening," she remembered, "the returns had begun to come in. We were sitting in the next room trying to read our paper or something because we hated to hear that everything was going against him. One of the men [at the house] said, 'Don't you want to hear this? It's getting better. You'd better come in.'"

Soon friends began to drop by the house and coffee was brewing. The excitement became tangible. Suddenly, the news over the radio was completely gripping. "That went on all night long," Noland recalled.

32

"Under No Circumstance Will I Congratulate That Son of a Bitch"

AT THE BEGINNING OF THE night, the Biltmore Hotel ballroom—the Democrats' campaign headquarters in New York—was nearly empty. "The halls leading to the Biltmore's grand ballroom, and the ballroom itself, had been bare of campaign posters and pictures early in the evening," remembered one reporter that night. "But, as optimism grew, one party worker dashed upstairs to the nineteenth floor [Democratic National Committee headquarters] and brought down several dozen pictures of Mr. Truman and Sen. Alben Barkley. They were hastily tacked up." Soon the room was "jammed with television cameras, klieg lights and radio microphones and cables."

Dewey remained secluded in suite 1527 at the Roosevelt. He had won most of New England, as expected, but lost Massachusetts. That was sixteen electoral votes predicted to go his way. He had pulled out the pivotal states of Pennsylvania, New York, and New Jersey, but Ohio was dangerously tight. Dewey had been expected to carry this critical state. Ohio had a Republican governor. Both of Ohio's senators were Republicans. One of them was John W. Bricker, the vice presidential candidate on the Republican ticket in 1944; the other was "Mr. Republican," Robert Taft. Now Dewey and Truman were running neck-and-neck in Ohio.

For Dewey, this was getting downright scary.

He left his family for the quiet of a bedroom, and shut the door so he could be alone, jotting notes on a yellow legal pad. Things were not going as planned, but elections often followed this pattern. East Coast returns tended to favor Democrats. As the farm vote of the Midwest began to roll in, the tide would turn. Midwest farmers from Ohio to Iowa were expected to vote Republican.

What was going through Dewey's mind during these solitary moments no one will ever know. Did he fear the sting of embarrassment? Was he struggling to come to terms with the idea that his entire campaign strategy might have been wrong all along?

At 11:15 p.m. Brownell issued the latest statement from campaign headquarters: "We are now getting into the stage of the election returns which permit a definite appraisal of the prospects of the respective candidates and I am convinced, as I stated earlier, the election of the Dewey-Warren Ticket is assured . . . We conclude here at Republican Headquarters that Dewey and Warren are elected."

At midnight, at the Elms Hotel in Excelsior Springs, Truman awoke from a slumber and fumbled with the knob on a radio. He heard broadcaster H. V. Kaltenborn's voice clearly over NBC radio. Kaltenborn was saying that Truman was in the lead in the popular vote by 1.2 million, but it was early; he could not possibly win.* He was "undoubtedly beaten," Kaltenborn said. Truman went back to sleep.

At 1:45 a.m. Herbert Brownell released another statement: "We now know that Governor Dewey will carry New York State by at least 50,000 votes and will be the next President of the United States."

At about 2:30 a.m. Truman was awoken by a jingling telephone. It was his friend Tom Evans, calling from the Muehlebach.

---

*The NBC microphone that H. V. Kaltenborn was speaking into that night is now in the museum collection at the Harry S. Truman Library & Museum in Independence, Missouri.

"Well, Mr. President," Evans said with excitement, "you're just about in this position that you've got to carry either Ohio, Illinois or California."

"That's good," Truman said. "Don't bother me anymore. I'm going to bed. Don't call me anymore."

"What the hell do you mean you're going to bed," Evans said. "You can't go to bed until you carry one of those states."

"Why, I'm going to carry all three," Truman said.

As the returns continued to come through, the suite at the Muehlebach became, as one present put it, "a churning madhouse of newsmen, staff workers and political friends." Hour after hour, the returns kept showing that Truman was ahead in the popular vote. The electoral vote was too close to call. Nerves began to fray; eyeballs were turning red. There was no alcohol on hand; only coffee and cigarettes.

Truman press secretary Charlie Ross took a break to escape the pressure at one point, heading down to the hotel coffee shop. Frank Holeman of the *New York Daily News* approached him and asked how the night was looking from Ross's perspective.

"We don't say that we're going to win this election," Ross said. "But it's going to be a lot closer than anybody ever thought. And win, lose or draw, there's a lot of sonsobitches we don't have to be nice to any more."

The hotel's manager Barney Allis walked in. Allis was holding telegrams, and he explained that telegram after telegram was arriving in the hotel's communications office. People wanted rooms at the Muehlebach. People were scrambling to leave Dewey headquarters in New York, wanting to head to Kansas City. Allis started reading the telegrams aloud.

"Dear Barney, I need a room."

"I need two rooms."

Ross could not believe his ears.

Twelve hundred miles away, at Democratic National Committee headquarters in the Biltmore in New York, the crowds kept getting bigger and bigger. "As the night wore on people who had never bothered to get accredited [at] our headquarters came over because the Dewey headquarters were silent," remembered the committee's assistant publicity director, Samuel

Brightman. In his office Chairman McGrath tabulated reports as they arrived, talking on the phone to Jake Arvey, a powerful Democratic political operative out of Chicago, about the action in Illinois. It was 5:40 a.m. on the East Coast. Truman was ahead in Illinois, but his lead was diminishing. Illinois was critical. The state's twenty-eight electoral votes were caught in a tug-of-war between the typically Republican farming communities and Chicago, the nation's second-most-populous city. In the state's highly competitive gubernatorial race, the rookie Democrat Adlai Stevenson was running against the virulently anti-Truman incumbent, Republican Dwight H. Green.

Standing by the teletype machines, a Democratic campaign staffer named Jim Sauter was pulling the returns out as they came in. One campaigner would remember watching him in the moment: "He was sweating, his face was flushed, his hand shook." Sauter would glance at the reports, then hand them to Chairman McGrath.

Suddenly, McGrath's face brightened. He looked at his wristwatch. Then he said to Sauter, "Jim, you can take it easy on those Illinois returns. We've got Illinois. Close, but we've got it for Truman and it's a landslide for [Paul Douglas, running for Senate] and Stevenson." (Adlai Stevenson would go on to become the Democratic presidential nominee in 1952 and 1956, losing both times to Dwight Eisenhower.)

Truman had been ahead in the popular vote. But for the first time, he was charging out front in the electoral vote too.

At the Muehlebach, reporters and campaign officials were making meals of their fingernails. Suddenly, over the radio, they heard the unmistakable voice of Drew Pearson. Truman's longtime friend and campaign official Bill Boyle stopped what he was doing and said, "What is Drew Pearson saying?"

The reply was, "He is devouring his young. He is conceding that Truman is going to win."

In the Muehlebach Hotel suite, the focus turned to Ohio, where the final tallies were imminent. The sun was rising on Kansas City. "We were all trying to pull in Ohio, definitely using a combination of prayers, pleas and profanity," remembered Truman friend Jerome Walsh, a Kansas City lawyer.

When Ohio fell into the Truman column, "there was pandemonium" at the Muehlebach, recalled journalist Carleton Kent. "The Ohio vote finally came in and finally decided the election," recalled Robert Nixon of the International News Service, who was at the president's suite in the hotel. Nixon would remember wiring his news service's bureau chief in Washington: "Bill, stop writing that Dewey is the victor. You're going to find yourself dead wrong."

In the ballroom of the Roosevelt Hotel, where campaigners had set up for the Dewey victory party, campaign staff and high-level officials could be seen with tears streaking their faces. The unthinkable had occurred. "It's awful," one sobbing twenty-two-year-old stenographer was heard saying. "It was my first vote."

In suite 1527, Dewey finally emerged from his bedroom and faced his wife and the small crowd of friends in his suite. Their expressions showed awe and heartbreak, but Dewey remained composed — ever the politician.

"What do you know?" he said. "The son of a bitch won."

At the Elms Hotel, the Secret Service men guarding Truman had stayed up all night listening to the radio. "And all of the sudden . . . ," remembered the man in charge, Jim Rowley, "comes this thing that the tide has changed. And so I figured, '*This* is important!' And so I went in and told him. 'We've won!' And he turns on the radio."

Truman was up now, in every way possible. His phone rang and it was H. Graham Morison on the line, an assistant attorney general calling from Washington. He had gotten the direct telephone number from Truman's appointments secretary Matthew Connelly.

"Mr. President," Morison said. He struggled for words. "I don't know what to say."

"Well, don't worry about that," said Truman.

"This is the greatest event that ever happened in my life."

"Well, we did skunk 'em, didn't we?"

"*We* didn't. *You* did!"

Truman told his Secret Service men, "We've got 'em beat." He asked them to get his car ready. "We're going to Kansas City."

At Wallace headquarters in Midtown Manhattan, the singer and black activist Paul Robeson had been leading Gideon's Army in a sing-along for hours. But now, the singing was over. Wallace refused to exhibit any disappointment, but his wife wore an expression of defeat. With tears running down her face, she could be heard saying, "I told him so all the time. He should never have done it."

Wallace gave his staff a pep talk. "Tonight we have had an extraordinary victory," he announced, "because nothing can beat a spirit of this kind. You cannot do the impossible at once; we have done extraordinary wonders in the last ten months . . . This crusade is going ahead with renewed vigor."

After Wallace's speech, the Progressive Party's legal counsel John Abt approached the candidate with a draft of a concession message he had written. It was not your usual concession. Wallace held the page in his hand and read it closely.

The message spoke of the moral bankruptcy that would result from Truman's leadership, "so long as the policy of the Cold War is continued and we spend increasing billions of American dollars to support reactionary regimes abroad, arm Western Europe and militarize America." It called for "one world at peace, not two hostile worlds arming for war," and for "a comprehensive program of assistance to farmers, rollback of consumer prices, public housing, social security, conservation, irrigation and public power development."

Wallace absorbed the message and noticed within it a bitter irony. His ideas on foreign policy clashed with Truman's and Dewey's. But on domestic policy, all three candidates were in the same ballpark. All three had campaigned for peace, for assistance to farmers, for anti-inflation policy, Social Security expansion, and conservation of natural resources.

Some of Wallace's campaign staff argued that the draft of the concession was too antagonistic. There was no hint of the traditional congratulatory spirit, no flavor of sportsmanship. Wallace did not want to hear it. He approved the message.

"Under no circumstance," he said, "will I congratulate that son of a bitch."

Barney Allis, manager of the Muehlebach Hotel, was awakened by his telephone. A Secret Service man was on the line. "The President is on his way," he said.

Allis glanced at a clock. "But it's only 6 o'clock and I just got into bed," he said.

The Secret Service man repeated: "The President is on his way."

Forty minutes later, press secretary Charlie Ross awoke in his bed at the Muehlebach to find Truman looking down at him through his thick, round wire-rim spectacles. Ross too had just gotten to sleep. "I looked up," he recalled, "and there was the boss at my bedside grinning."

Truman appeared crisp in a dark suit, his hair brushed and his pocket square perfectly folded. He said that he had awoken at 4:30 a.m. to hear the latest news. "I heard the broadcast," he told Ross, "and I decided I'd better drive back to town and have breakfast at the penthouse."

It was 6:40 a.m. The president retired to a room so he could call Bess at their home a dozen miles away in Independence. The door to the room was open and reporter Robert Nixon looked in. Nixon too had been quickly awakened and he was wearing a trench coat over pajamas, peering in at Truman.

"His door was wide open," Nixon recalled. "He was sitting on a sofa on the telephone . . . Tears were streaming down his eyes . . . From what he said, I knew he was talking to Bess in Independence, and he was telling her that he had won."

The party at the Muehlebach was just getting started. Truman sat on a couch, greeting people, saying, "It looks as though we have them whipped." The Associated Press's Tony Vaccaro showed up in pajamas, with his hat askew.

"Tony, straighten your hat," Truman said, cackling.

Truman also called Clark Clifford at his home in Washington. Clifford would later describe this call as "the most gratifying phone call of my life . . . With great jubilation he told me that Illinois and Ohio were going into the Democratic column. The victory was his."

All morning the teletype machines kept chattering on and the phones kept ringing. The question on everyone's lips: When would Dewey concede? Truman welcomed members of Battery D, buddies whom he had commanded in World War I, who had come to congratulate him. Also present was his former partner Eddie Jacobson, whose Westport Menswear, located nearby, would not be opening that day. Truman surprised everyone with his composure. Remembered his friend Jerome Walsh:

"He displayed neither tension nor elation. For instance someone remarked bitterly that if it hadn't been for Wallace, New York and New Jersey would have gone Democratic by good majorities. But the President dismissed this with a wave of his hand. As far as Henry was concerned, he said, Henry wasn't a bad guy; he was doing what he thought was right and he had every right in the world to pursue his course."

In states across the nation, people were reading their morning newspapers, which were noncommittal for the most part, because press time for reporters had come before a lot of the results were in. "At 6 a.m. today," noted the *New York Times*, "after a night in which his political fortunes waxed and waned with every passing hour, President Harry S. Truman took an impressive lead over his Republican opponent, Gov. Thomas E. Dewey of New York, in both the popular and electoral vote of the nation." The *New York Times* offices were deluged with twenty-five thousand phone calls between 9 a.m. and 6 p.m. on this day, from people wanting to know who had won. "Election Still in Doubt," read the *Los Angeles Times* headline on November 3. "Truman Ahead with Dewey Holding Key States."

Some other publications were even less on top of things. Columnist Fred Othman's piece the morning of November 3 in Atlanta's biggest paper, the *Constitution*, began: "The ballots haven't been counted at this writing, but there seems to be no further need for holding up an affectionate farewell to Harry Truman, who will go down in history as the President nobody hated."

The Alsop brothers' column in the *Washington Post* on November 3 began: "The first postelection question is how the Government can get through the next 10 weeks . . . Events will not wait patiently until Thomas E. Dewey officially replaces Harry S. Truman."

Other newspapers, from Chicago to as far off as Munich, incorrectly reported that Dewey had won. The Munich *Merkur* ran a banner headline on November 3: "Thomas E. Dewey Amerikas neuer Präsident." *Women's Wear Daily*'s front page featured the banner headline: "Dewey, Warren Win; Business Gain Seen." The *Washington Post* featured a gossip column with the headline: "'Persistence' Is the Dominating Trait that Carried Dewey to the Presidency."

Most famously, the early edition of the *Chicago Daily Tribune*—a newspaper that had attacked Truman as vigorously as any other—appeared that morning with the headline: "Dewey Defeats Truman; G.O.P. Sweep Indicated in State." Below the headline, an article declared that the GOP would be "back in the White House," that "Dewey won the Presidency by an overwhelming majority." (In 2007 the *Chicago Tribune* would call this "arguably the most famous headline in the newspaper's 150-year history" and "every publisher's nightmare." Roughly 150,000 copies of the paper's first edition streamed off the press, the ink barely dry, before panicked editors could change the front-page banner headline for the second edition, to "Democrats Make Sweep of State Offices.")

At Democratic National Committee headquarters in New York, where corks were popping, the phone rang, and Chairman McGrath took the call. He heard Truman's voice over the line, thanking him for all his work.

"Thank you, Mr. President," McGrath said. "Nobody deserved to win more than you did, Mr. President." McGrath held up his glass. One present remembered: "The wine shimmered effervescently in a shaft of sunlight." McGrath said into the phone, "Your staff is drinking to you, Mr. President. From the bottoms of our hearts we drink to you."

Standing next to McGrath was India Edwards, one of the only Truman campaigners who had insisted throughout that the Missourian would win. McGrath told Truman, "Now I want you to talk to the person who really had faith all the time, and who knew you were going to win." He passed the phone to Edwards.

"I burst out crying," she later recalled. "The best man won," she said into the phone, almost incoherently. "The best man won."

Minutes after McGrath hung up the phone he was handed a telegram. He called for silence. "Gentlemen," McGrath announced, speaking specifically to the press corps, "I have here a message that will make your stories conclusive. This is a message addressed to Harry S. Truman, President. I will read it slowly, for you may wish to copy it down word for word." McGrath looked down at the telegram in his hand. It was Thomas Dewey's concession statement. "'My heartiest congratulations to you on your election and every good wish for a successful administration. I urge all Americans to unite behind you in support of your efforts to keep our Nation strong and free and establish peace in the world.'"

"Signed," McGrath said, "by Thomas E. Dewey."

At the Muehlebach, Truman's arm was growing tired of handshaking. More news came through: Truman had unexpectedly won in California, against every prediction. This was the home state of the Republican vice presidential candidate Earl Warren. At 10:16 a.m. Kansas City time, a voice shouted for attention and the hum of conversation trailed off.

"Dewey has conceded!" someone shouted.

Truman was holding his hat in his left hand, and he pumped his other hand upward. In that moment, remembered one man present, "everyone was talking, yelling at once. The photographers' bulbs blazed away. The reporters crowded around for the president's first words now that his victory was confirmed . . . Radio reporters shoved microphones in the president's face. Friends grasped his hand; some of them wept."

"All I can say," Truman offered, "is that I am very, very happy."

Nearby to Truman, Eddie Jacobson stood in a daze. "I cried and I prayed for this," he said aloud.

A fuse blew out and the hotel suite turned suddenly semi-dark, but no one seemed to notice. Truman's brother Vivian, a Missouri farmer all his life, had his arms around the president, and from the crowd the words "Four more years" could be clearly heard.

The news began to spread. In New York City, lights from the Times Square Tower beacon switched to a steady beam pointing south, a declaration of Truman's victory, as Times Square below filled with revelers. One man told the *New York Times* reporter Meyer Berger, "It's something like the night President Roosevelt died. You can't quite believe it. You have to talk it over with someone—anyone—to make sure you've got it right." Many blocks south, alarm spread across Wall Street. The stock market fell into a near freefall upon news of Harry Truman's victory.

In California, the head of the Democratic state committee Harold I. McGrath rode a taxi to work that morning through San Francisco's Golden Gate Park. "It was the most exhilarating personal experience," he recalled, "an experience of personal achievement where everything felt good."

Truman had won his home state of Missouri. In Independence, after Dewey conceded, Mayor Roger Sermon declared a holiday and all the students were released from school. A sprawling crowd had come together for an impromptu celebration outside the town's Memorial Hall. By this time, enough votes had been tabulated to show that the Democrats would regain control of the House of Representatives, which was expected, but also of the Senate, which was not. So the president would begin his first full term with a friendly Congress and all hopes of success. After the sun had set, Truman made an appearance in front of Memorial Hall. He stood on the steps and looked out at thirty thousand of his hometown friends. It was the biggest gathering ever assembled in the town's history.

"It was not my victory . . . ," he said into a microphone. "It was not for me but for the whole country. I want everyone to help me in working for the welfare of the country and peace of the world."

Dewey was originally scheduled to appear at the campaign party in the Roosevelt ballroom at 9 p.m. on November 2. He did not appear until 1 p.m. the next day. Some 150 reporters were on hand for the most solemn political press conference any of them would ever recall. Dewey forced a smile for the photographers.

"Can we regard the pictures as done?" he asked them. "Will you let us go ahead without any more interruptions?"

The photographers obliged.

Dewey said, "Anything I can tell anybody here that they don't already know?"

One reporter shouted, "What happened Governor?"

"I was just as surprised as you are, Dick, and I gather that is shared by everybody in the room as I read your stories before the election."

"Looking back, was it an error of strategy or tactics?"

"No," Dewey said. "Governor Warren and I are both very happy. I talked with him — that we waged a clean and constructive campaign and I have no regrets whatsoever."

One reporter asked, "What do you think were the chief factors?"

"I think that would be impossible to answer at this date," Dewey said. "I would have to study it and get more opinions and read what you write over the next few days. I am no better able to guide you than before the election."

When asked if he would ever consider running for president a third time, Dewey responded with an emphatic syllable.

"No."

33

"Dewey Defeats Truman"

IT WAS THE GREATEST ELECTORAL upset in the nation's history, and the press had to answer for its role in calling it wrong.

The *Denver Post*: "We, and the rest of the American press, have an awful burden of explanation to offer for this refutation of our 'expert' opinion. For the fact is that we have failed abysmally in putting a finger on the real pulse of America." The *Boston Daily Globe*: "President Truman's victory in his race for election to the White House will go down in the books as one of the political miracles of all time." Marquis Childs in the *Washington Post*: "We were wrong, all of us, completely and entirely, the political editors, the politicians — except for Harry S. Truman. And no one believed him." *Newsweek* put out an "Election Special" on November 4. On the cover was Truman's smiling face and two simple words below it: "Miracle Man." "If the 1948 election proved nothing else," the magazine concluded, "it demonstrated that everyone accepted the rules but Harry S. Truman. He defied them. And he won."

That morning of November 4, the second full day after election night, Truman left Kansas City's Union Station, ensconced within the very familiar walls of the swaying *Ferdinand Magellan*. Bess and Margaret were with him. The *Magellan* had turned out to be an apt symbol for his campaign, for it was named after the sixteenth-century explorer who had risked life and limb to discover the unknown. In fact, Truman had traveled more miles on his campaign than Magellan ever did.

On the way back to Washington, Truman stopped in St. Louis. Someone gave him a copy of a November 3 issue of the *Chicago Daily Tribune*—yesterday's paper. He stood on the back platform of his train car and waved the *Tribune* at crowds who had amassed to see him. At that moment, the news photographer W. Eugene Smith snapped a photograph of a moment forever imprinted in the American consciousness. Arguably, no president in history had ever been captured with a facial expression of such unbridled joy. *Time* magazine would later comment that Smith's photo was "the greatest photograph ever made of a politician celebrating victory. Period."

Truman held up the newspaper so its headline could be clearly read: "Dewey Defeats Truman."

In Washington, DC, on the morning of November 5, Truman was greeted by some 750,000 people. The historian David McCullough would call this turnout "the biggest, most enthusiastic outpouring for a President in the history of the capital." Before Truman could even get off the train, Senator Olin Johnston of South Carolina was there to shake his hand.

Johnston had been the man behind some of the most vicious attacks on Truman's civil rights program. It had been Johnston—an outspoken white supremacist—who had publicly humiliated Truman months earlier at the Jackson-Jefferson Day Dinner by buying tickets to reserve a table right in front of the stage where Truman was to speak, and then boycotting the event so that the highly visible table remained empty. Now here Johnston was to make amends.

The well-wishers lined up in such great numbers to shake Truman's hand, it took the president twenty-two minutes to get from the *Magellan* to his automobile, at which point the motorcade began to snake through the city. Bess, Margaret, J. Howard McGrath, and others sat in the back of the open seven-seater. When they passed the *Washington Post* building, they saw a big sign waiting for them: WELCOME HOME. FROM THE CROW-EATERS. The *Post* editors had sent Truman a telegram inviting him to a "crow banquet," in which the newspapers' writers and editors would enjoy a main course of "crow en glace."

"I will never forget that ride to the White House," Margaret recorded. "Every band in the world seemed to be playing 'I'm Just Wild About Harry.'"

At the White House, a microphone had been set up on the North Portico. Truman and Barkley thanked a crowd that stretched out farther than their eyes could see, all the way down Pennsylvania Avenue. Once Truman entered the White House, however, the very moment he was out of view of all those cameras, he was cornered by a very nervous J. B. West, the White House chief usher.

"I am afraid you're going to have to move out right away," West said.

More scaffolding had been erected, and construction workers were legion. The place was not safe for inhabitation.

"Doesn't that beat hell!" Truman said. He knew he was moving out, but he did not know that—win or lose—he was moving out *now.* "Here we've worked ourselves to death trying to stay in this jailhouse," he said, "and they kick us out anyway!"

As the Trumans prepared to move across the street to Blair House—an official government home typically used to host foreign dignitaries—the congratulatory letters poured in. One arrived from the president of Israel, Chaim Weizmann, who mistakenly called Truman's victory a "re-election." Since Israel declared its independence nearly six months earlier, sixty-two thousand Jewish refugees in Europe had immigrated to the new country, Weizmann said in his letter. "We have special cause to be gratified at your re-election because we are mindful of the enlightened help which you gave to our cause in these years of our struggle."

Around the globe, State Department officials reported on the reaction to Truman's victory. In Moscow, Joseph Stalin's second-in-command, Vyacheslav Molotov, praised a rejection of a "most aggressive program of the Republican Party and Dewey." It was the closest the Soviets could come to saying something nice about Harry Truman. In Paris, the US Embassy reported, "papers of all political persuasions see Truman election as 'victory of [the] people over Wall Street,' with Gallup and bookies still being mentioned as lesser losers." In Nanking, the crumbling Chinese government of Chiang Kai-shek issued a statement: "The world looks hopefully to his [Truman's] leadership in the difficult four years which lie ahead." From Lisbon, the US Embassy reported that "opinion frequently expressed even by man in [the] street [is] that 'now there will be no war.'"

Meanwhile the condolence letters poured into Dewey's mailbox. "I think the future historians will regard your defeat as one of the most important turning points in American history," Alf Landon—the 1936 Republican nominee—wrote Dewey on November 19, 1948. An uncle of Dewey's wrote him on November 4, "Aunt Marsh and I want you to know that we are very sick over the election, all day yesterday we went around feeling as if something inside had died, and I guess it has when we realize that the voters of this great country would select such a man as a leader."

One Republican named Thomas W. Pierce wrote his friend Dorothy Bell Rackoff, who had been a delegate from New York at the Republican National Convention, five days after the election: "I have been like many other Republicans—literally picking up the pieces scattered about us by the ceiling that began crashing down on us late Tuesday night. Outside of Pearl Harbor itself I do not know of another single great event that has quite so much disturbed my mental equilibrium."

The overwhelming surprise left innumerable millions of people, at home and abroad, with a question on their lips that would baffle historians for generations to come.

How could the pollsters and the press have been so wrong?

What actually happened?

Following Election Day, the New Dealer Harold "Old Curmudgeon" Ickes wrote a friend, "It was not an 'election' but a 'revolution.'" The ballot box had revealed newly crystallizing power bases, new campaign processes showing effective results, and a renewed sense that, in America, anything could happen. The final tally had Truman with 303 electoral votes and twenty-eight states to Dewey's 189 and sixteen states, with Strom Thurmond carrying four states—Louisiana, South Carolina, Mississippi, and Alabama—and

39 electoral votes (one breakaway electoral vote in Tennessee also went in the Thurmond column). The popular vote went to Truman, 24,105,810 to 21,970,064. While Henry Wallace picked up zero electoral votes, he earned roughly 1,156,000 votes nationally, about 13,000 less than Thurmond.*

According to a postmortem statistical analysis done by the Republican National Committee, the election was the closest since 1916, and just twenty-nine thousand votes could have changed the entire outcome, if properly distributed in the states of Ohio, Illinois, and California.

The Democrats picked up seventy-five seats in the House of Representatives and nine in the Senate, regaining majority control of both. Thus the Eighty-First Congress was recast, creating what all believed would be a far more Truman-friendly Washington.

Shortly following the election, Senator Henry Cabot Lodge Jr., Republican of Massachusetts, brought a resolution to abolish the electoral college in favor of a new system. It was an antiquated algorithm that functioned clumsily, he argued, and the major example in 1948 was Tennessee. The state had given Truman eleven of its electoral votes, Strom Thurmond one rogue vote, and Thomas Dewey zero, even though Dewey had drawn well more than twice as many votes in the state than Thurmond did. How was that fair? Still, Senator Lodge's resolution to alter the system got nowhere. The highly controversial electoral college system remains in debate today.

Monday-morning quarterbacks claimed that Dewey was simply the wrong guy. "We should have known he couldn't win," Theodore Roosevelt's daughter Alice Roosevelt Longworth said. Referring to Dewey's 1944 campaign, she famously added, "A soufflé never rises twice." "My own opinion," Speaker of the House Joe Martin later wrote, "is that Taft, if nominated, could have won in 1948, and he could have won in 1952." Richard Nixon, at the time a freshman congressman, later told an interviewer that Harold Stassen was "the most interesting candidate." "Stassen, if he could have been nominated, would have been the strongest candidate," Nixon said in 1983. "I think he would have won."

---

* The numbers vary by small amounts depending on the source. The ones listed are from the American Presidency Project at the University of California, Santa Barbara.

Numerous voices called out Dewey for running a campaign that was a monument to hubris, claiming that if he had come out swinging and if he had spoken more on specific policy, the result would have been the landslide that nearly everyone expected. This was a logical conclusion, though impossible to prove.

After digesting the events and the shock of it all, Dewey himself came to a simple and poignant conclusion. "The short answer on the election was that the farmers switched and that's that and I am going to go ahead and enjoy life and live longer," he wrote his uncle George Thomas of Whittier, California, five weeks after the election. "The farmers switched in the mid-West," he wrote to Joseph Robinson of San Francisco, in January. "We carried the industrial East and lost the farm vote. That is the entire answer to the election."

According to statistical analysis, Dewey was correct that the farmers had delivered a mighty blow — particularly in Ohio and Illinois, two states that had huge weight in the ultimate outcome. Truman had effectively campaigned on the issue of the Commodity Credit Corporation's failure to supply storage bins to farmers. As the election was progressing, farmers found themselves with a bumper corn crop and record-high wheat and oat crops; they were crippled by lack of storage, and very angry about it. In the end, Truman carried the farming states of Ohio, Illinois, Wisconsin, and even Iowa, which had voted Republican in all but three presidential elections going back to 1856. "It had been taken for granted generally that this area [farmers] was still staunchly Republican," commented the columnist Thomas L. Stokes. "That is, taken for granted by all but a few which included a fellow named Harry S. Truman."

Others chalked up Truman's victory to laborers and the president's fierce opposition to the Taft-Hartley Act, which stripped away power from labor unions and was passed by the Republican Eightieth Congress over Truman's emphatic veto. Reportedly, the first words out of Truman's mouth when he entered the presidential suite at the Muehlebach on the morning of November 3 were: "Labor did it." The Taft-Hartley law provided Truman with an easy opportunity to inflame the passions of working people against Wall Street and the Republican Party.

Then there was the "Negro vote." Four days after the election, Philleo Nash sent the president a memorandum, for "some light reading on your vacation," as Truman was off for a break at his favorite vacation spot — Key West, Florida. "Over the country as a whole," Nash wrote, "your majority in the Negro districts is the highest ever. The *average* will be above 80%." In Philadelphia, nine out of ten black voters went for Truman. In Harlem, he won 65 percent of the vote, to Dewey's 19 percent (Wallace claimed 16 percent). More importantly, the black vote went heavily to Truman in two of the most decisive states: Ohio and Illinois. In both cases, Truman came out on top. His success among black voters in Los Angeles and Oakland also gave him a boost in California, which he won by the narrow margin of roughly eighteen thousand votes out of a total of over four million.

Truman would forever argue that his civil rights stance was not about politics but about morality. Nevertheless, in terms of votes, it had helped him at least as much as it may have hurt him.

Counterintuitively, the president also gained momentum due to the many crises he was facing throughout 1948. When the Berlin Blockade began, many Americans were sure it would lead to war. *Newsweek* called the blockade "the greatest diplomatic crisis in American history." The Truman administration was vastly credited with the success of the Berlin Airlift. At the time of the election, no war had started, and the airlift was working.

And what of Truman's attack on the Eightieth Congress? Was this strategy coldhearted and misleading, as the Republicans had charged throughout? After all, the Eightieth Congress had passed the Truman Doctrine and the Marshall Plan. "It always galls me to think that Harry Truman won in 1948 by attacking the Congress which gave him his place in history," the conservative Republican congressman Charlie Halleck of Indiana later said. The truth was, though Truman and the Eightieth Congress were allies in foreign policy, in domestic policy, they were far from it, and that was the root of Truman's ire. He could not attack Dewey on policy matters, but Congress was fair game. The strategy worked.

And what of economics? A huge majority of Americans were happy with their incomes in 1948. Just days before the election, the Bureau of Labor

Statistics released new numbers showing that the rise in living costs had stopped, at least momentarily, and retail food prices had actually shown a modest decline — all good news for the economy. When the war had ended, the Labor and Treasury Departments were apoplectic with fear over unemployment dangers; but in 1948 unemployment was near nonexistent. "It is almost impossible to put an administration out of power at the very peak of a prosperity boom," commented Senator Taft.

Others drew a different conclusion. Truman had, some astute observers noted, done much to win the election way back at the Democratic National Convention in July, when he called Congress back into a "Turnip Day" emergency session. The plan was to put a spotlight on the Republican schism between the conservative Congress and the more liberal politics of Thomas Dewey. After the election, Dewey refused to relinquish his fight for a more liberal GOP. In a speech three months later, he addressed straight-on the ideological split that plagued his party. Some Republican members of Congress boycotted the speech. Others praised the failed 1948 candidate for pulling the curtain off the party's dark secret, which was in fact no secret at all.

"The Republican party is split wide open," Dewey told a crowd in Washington early in 1949. "It has been split wide open for years, but we have tried to gloss over it . . . We have in our party some fine, high-minded patriotic people who honestly oppose farm price supports, unemployment insurance, old age benefits, slum clearance, and other social programs. These people consider these programs horrendous departures into paternalism . . . These people believe in a laissez-faire society and look back wistfully to the miscalled 'good old days' of the 19th century."

If the Republican Party did not start looking forward and embrace some measure of New Deal thinking, Dewey said, "you can bury the Republican party as the deadest pigeon in the country." From the perspective of many decades later, Dewey's words do not hold up, as the presidency of Donald Trump can attest.

And what of the pollsters themselves? George Gallup's first reaction was that the people who accounted for his polling numbers did not show up at the voting booths, because they assumed Dewey had it won. "Which voters stayed home?" he asked his readers, rhetorically. Elmo Roper was the pollster who stopped polling altogether weeks before the election because, he claimed, Dewey was "as good as elected," so there was no more point in taking polls. Now Roper had this to say: "I could not have been more wrong and the thing that bothers me at the moment is that I don't know why I was wrong."

One theory emerged that the pollsters erred in their sampling process, that they failed to do enough to tally the opinions of low-income voters who were less approachable and more likely to be suspicious of poll takers. In the end, these voters came out for Truman. Another, more valid theory supported Gallup's excuse: that Dewey voters were so confident, they did not bother to vote. Numbers backed up this claim; Dewey drew about forty thousand fewer total votes than he had four years earlier against FDR. The logical conclusion was that some Republican voters stayed home because they thought their vote did not matter. How many of them later regretted that decision?

"It's open season on the pollsters," Edward R. Murrow said over CBS radio. "But it ought to be pointed out that they are accused of nothing except being wrong. No one claims, so far as I know, that they were 'bought' or that they deliberately attempted to influence the outcome by contributing to despondency and alarm, or by inducing complacency in the Republican ranks. They were just wrong, and in the field of information and ideas this is no crime."

Ultimately, the story of the election — and of its outcome — centers on its main character. On November 3, Senator Vandenberg was in his Washington office chewing on a cigar when a member of his staff asked him what he thought about Truman's victory. Vandenberg stopped, pulled the cigar from his lips, and said, "You've got to give the little man credit. There he was flat on his back. Everyone had counted him out but he came up fighting and won the battle. He did it all by himself. That's the kind of courage the American people admire."

Epilogue

AFTER THE 1948 ELECTION, Thomas Dewey finished out his second and then third terms as governor of New York before retiring from public service at the end of 1954. He was highly instrumental in convincing Dwight Eisenhower to run for president in 1952, and helped Ike secure the Republican nomination over Robert Taft. During the 1948 campaign, when Dewey and Ike had famously sat together for the surprise photo op on the porch of Dewey's farmhouse in upstate New York, both men believed that one of them was going to become the first Republican president since Herbert Hoover. They were right, but ironically, wrong about which of the two of them it was going to be.

For the rest of his life, Dewey kept a cordial relationship with Truman. When, in 1950, Truman made the highly controversial decision to send US troops to fight on the Korean peninsula as part of United Nations armed forces, without the official consent of Congress, Dewey cabled the White House: "I whole-heartedly agree with and support the difficult decision you have made today to extend American assistance to the Republic of Korea in combatting armed communist aggression." When six months later Truman survived an assassination attempt that left a Secret Service man and a would-be assassin dead, Dewey sent Truman a note expressing "heart-felt gratification that no harm came to you or to your family."

Dewey had said before he ran in 1948, "I deliberately decided that I was not going to be one of those unhappy men who yearned for the Presidency and whose failure to get it scarred their lives." After retiring, he led a seemingly contented life. Nevertheless, more Americans today are likely familiar with the phrase *Dewey Defeats Truman* than they are with Thomas E. Dewey. If Americans know of Thomas Dewey, it is mostly because he lost to Harry Truman in 1948.

On March 16, 1971, Dewey was in Florida, golfing with the Boston Red Sox slugger Carl Yastrzemski. Dewey was scheduled to fly out that night to attend the engagement party of President Richard Nixon's daughter, at the White House. Instead, he died of a heart attack in his Miami hotel room. He was sixty-eight years old.

After the 1948 election, Henry Wallace left the Progressive Party, which did field a candidate in 1952, only to win less than a quarter of a percent of the national vote. After that, the party disintegrated and Henry Wallace faded into obscurity.

Throughout 1948 Wallace had led an antiwar, anti–Truman Doctrine, anti–Marshall Plan campaign that attempted to blame the Cold War not on the Soviets but on US policy. After 1948 he had an about-face. He came to the opinion that the Soviets were in fact a Cold War enemy. In 1950 he concluded, "Today, I am convinced that Russia is out to dominate the world." As for his Gideon's Army antiwar stance, that too disappeared. Wallace also endorsed Truman's decision to send troops into Korea in 1950. In an article published in 1952 called "Where I Was Wrong," he called the USSR "utterly evil."

In 1964 Wallace was diagnosed with amyotrophic lateral sclerosis — Lou Gehrig's disease. He died a year later.

Strom Thurmond won well over a million votes in the 1948 election. A month after the election, Thurmond visited his daughter Essie Mae at the college she was attending in South Carolina. They met secretly in the office of the college's president.

"How could you have said all those terrible things?" she asked him, according to her recollection of the conversation.

"What things?" he responded.

"About Negroes."

"Essie Mae," she remembered him explaining, "there is no man in the country who cares more about the Negroes than I do. I think you know that."

She kept probing him, and as she recalls, he told her, "It's the South, Essie Mae. It's the culture here. It's custom. It's the way we live. You don't go to England and tell them to get rid of the Queen and the royalty. That's not fair, either, but it's the custom. They got rid of the royalty in Russia, and what do you have? Communism! A police state. It's no different from Hitler."

Thurmond's career in government remains unprecedented. In 1954 he became a Democratic senator from South Carolina. In 1964 he mirrored his state of South Carolina and much of the South by switching from the Democratic to the Republican Party. Thurmond supported Barry Goldwater in 1964, against the Democrat Lyndon Johnson, in large part due to the civil rights issue. While Johnson supported the landmark 1964 Civil Rights Act, Goldwater was against it.

Thurmond went on to become the first and only man to remain in the Senate at the age of one hundred, and he is still one of the longest-serving senators in US history. He died in 2003, in the town where he came from —Edgefield. Six months later, seventy-eight-year-old Essie Mae Washington-Williams revealed that Strom Thurmond was her father. She published *Dear Senator: A Memoir by the Daughter of Strom Thurmond* in 2005, revealing the intimate details of her relationship with Thurmond. It was nominated for a Pulitzer Prize.

After the 1948 election the southern states that Thurmond represented —the Solid South of the Democratic Party going back to the 1870s—began to migrate to the Republican Party. Today, this region has been solidly for the GOP for half a century. Going back to 1964, South Carolina, Mississippi, and Alabama have tipped Democrat only once, for Jimmy Carter in 1976. In 2016 South Carolina, Mississippi, Alabama, Arkansas, Florida, Georgia, and Louisiana all cast their electoral votes for Donald J. Trump.

• • •

Four days after the 1948 election, Truman and an official party that included Bess, Margaret, vice president–elect Alben Barkley, and over a dozen others ventured aboard the USS *Williamsburg*, bound for the naval base at Key West, Florida. There would be volleyball and fishing trips, poker, and plenty of bourbon. The president's party numbered thirty people, in addition to more than forty reporters and fifteen members of the Secret Service. When they got to the island, according to the president's official log, "the largest crowd ever assembled at Key West" came out into the streets to welcome them.

In Key West, however, the business of running the federal government continued to press firmly on Truman's shoulders. Urgent cables came through the communications room set up at the Key West Naval Station — from Israeli president Chaim Weizmann, with an "urgent appeal" for help as Arab armies were launching a new offensive; from Chiang Kai-shek, who reported that the US-backed Chinese government was about to fall and that "the communist forces in central China are now within striking distance of Shanghai and Nanking."

Soon after Truman's return to the White House from Florida, former State Department official Alger Hiss was indicted on two counts of perjury relating to his denials of accusations that he had been a Communist spy. Cold War paranoia spread across Washington and beyond like a contagion.

But at the same time, the American people wanted to party, too. In a twist of fate that no fiction writer could have dared to write, the Republican Eightieth Congress — expecting to take control of the White House in 1948 — had voted to up the ante on the Inauguration Day festivities, with an unprecedented $80,000 budget. That money was now at Truman's disposal. A million people filled the streets for the 1949 inaugural fete, the first to be televised. One hundred million more listened via radio. There were jet-propelled bombers roaring overhead, thirty bands playing, more than forty floats motoring by in a parade, and an inauguration dinner featuring "Salad Margaret" and "Sandwiches Independence." The man who administered the thirty-five-word presidential oath to Truman was none other than

Fred Vinson, the chief justice of the Supreme Court and the focal figure of the Vinson-mission fiasco during the campaign.

That afternoon, Truman stood on a platform watching dignitaries roll by in cars in the traditional inaugural parade, smiling and waving at each of them. When Strom Thurmond's car cruised by, Truman suddenly stopped waving and turned his back on the South Carolina governor. Thurmond would later recall that Truman's voice was picked up by a microphone. According to Thurmond, Truman told the new VP, Alben Barkley, "Don't you wave to the S.O.B."

Truman's first major appearance after the election was his first speech as an elected president: the 1949 State of the Union address. In speechwriting meetings before the event, Truman explained that he was going to double down on the same liberal policies that had turned the country against him when he released his 21-Point Program to Congress in September of 1945. He would fight for universal military training, a higher minimum wage, investment in education programs, wider Social Security coverage, and a health-care system that would "enable every American to afford good medical care." He would also begin his fight to repeal the Taft-Hartley Act. Advisers asked him if he was going too far, too fast. This was what the people had voted for, Truman said, and this was what they were going to get.

In his speech on January 5, 1949, Truman packaged his policies — echoes of the New Deal era — as the "Fair Deal." The reaction was mixed, running from outright approval to stiff dissension. And so began the tug-of-war of the Democratic process, all over again.

Truman had won four more years, but they promised to be years that would put decisions on the president's desk of incalculable risk, with stakes that could not be measured. Dangers lurked in all directions, and the existence of the human race was at stake. Americans could only hope that they had made the right choice on November 2. The CBS radio man Edward R. Murrow finished his election-result broadcast in 1948 by saying: "He [the president] . . . is beset by massive problems. I do not know whether the next four years will reveal him to be a great President. But they had better."

Acknowledgments

On any number of nights during the writing and editing of this book, I awoke at 2 a.m. in a cold sweat, wondering how I was going to finish this thing, what critics might think of it, what minute fact I might get wrong, or which of the thousands of sentences was not perfectly constructed. And finally: how I could ever thank all the people who helped me, in ways maybe they don't even know.

This is my fourth book with the same publisher and agent. Thank you to all the team at Houghton Mifflin Harcourt, particularly my editors Bruce Nichols, Ivy Givens, and Jennifer Freilach. My agent Scott Waxman of the Waxman Literary Agency has been my teammate now for over ten years and I am so blessed to call him my friend. Megan Wilson at HMH is a superstar and so too is Melissa Dobson, who copyedited this book. Endless thank-yous to all of you!

I would like to thank the archivists at the Harry S. Truman Library & Museum in Independence, Missouri; at the University of Rochester library's Rare Books, Special Collections, and Preservation division; and at Columbia University's Oral History Archives. The work that archivists do is imperative to preserving and understanding our nation's history, and the fact that all these archives exist and that people can have access to them is a testament to the freedom that is at the root of our democracy.

A special thank-you goes to Lisa Sullivan and all of the team at the Truman Library Institute, from which I received a research grant. (At no time did anyone from the institute ask to see any part of my manuscript before it was published.) Particular gratitude goes to Professor Jon Taylor at the University of Central Missouri for his careful read of this manuscript.

The Baime family is a true team. We tackle the challenges of life together. Thank you to my wife, Michelle. Since the day I met you on July 19, 2000, my every day has been better, brighter, and more fulfilling. My kids, Clay and Audrey, I am proud to say, are now Truman experts. I love you both more than I ever thought possible. Keep playing guitars, clarinets, and pianos; keep skiing moguls; keep earning As; and most importantly, keep being you. Thank you to my parents, David and Denise, for so many things, not least of all reading drafts of various chapters of this book. You would have made great editors.

I would also like to thank the rest of my family, for whom I can never repay for all their love and kindness through the years: Abby Baime, Susan Baime, my Aunt Karen and Uncle Ken Segal, the late Bill Green and the late Mildred Leventhal, my "outlaws" Connie and the late Bill Burdick, Jack and Margo Ezell, my many wonderful cousins of the Crystal/Sabel/Segal clan, Peter and the late Ellen Segal, and the late Ken and Edna Wheeldon.

To paraphrase Geoffrey Chaucer, go little book!

Notes

Harry Truman once wrote, "It is my opinion that the only accurate source of information on which to make a proper historical assessment of the performances of past Presidents is in the presidential files." For this reason, for this book (and for my previous book, *The Accidental President*), I spent four weeks collecting material at the Harry S. Truman Presidential Library & Museum in Independence, Missouri. I also spent a week at the University of Rochester, researching the Thomas Dewey papers, and some time at Columbia University's library archives, researching the oral histories of members of the 1948 Progressive Party.

During the last ten-plus years, the process of historical research has changed, for the better. Today, vast amounts of important and original documentation can be found online. The Truman library has done a marvelous job of making material available. Transcripts of almost every one of Truman's whistle-stop speeches can be accessed on the library's website, along with original documents having to do with the Berlin Airlift, Truman's civil rights fight, the founding of Israel, the Truman Doctrine and the Marshall Plan, the 1948 election, and more. Many of Truman's diaries and letters, as well as numerous oral histories, were instantly available to me in my office in California as I was writing this book. A number of Henry Wallace's papers are available online, through the University of Iowa. So too is a vast database of newspaper articles via ProQuest, which enabled me to see firsthand the impressions of innumerable reporters who covered the 1948 campaign.

Still, much of the effort required traditional research and old-fashioned gumshoe reporting, including filing Freedom of Information Act requests for FBI files and hunting through dozens of boxes of documents in library archives. The original papers of Clark Clifford, George Elsey, Margaret Truman, Howard McGrath, William Boyle, and so many others; intelligence files from the National Security Council and the Central Intelligence Agency; State Department files; these documents provided the critical elements of detail and color necessary to put a book like this together.

Additionally, I used the memoirs and diaries of people who lived these experiences as firsthand accounts. The diaries of Defense Secretary James Forrestal, Senator Arthur Vandenberg, Henry Wallace, and David Lilienthal . . . the published papers of Robert Taft and General Lucius Clay . . . the memoirs of Clark Clifford, Joe Martin, Thomas Dewey, Richard Nixon,

Margaret Truman, and Harry Truman . . . all of these sources proved crucial in my attempt to make the reader feel like he or she was in the room during these historic events and historic days.

The following books also proved vital: *American Dreamer: A Life of Henry A. Wallace,* by John C. Culver and John Hyde; *Thomas E. Dewey and His Times,* by Richard Norton Smith; *Strom: The Complicated Personal and Political Life of Strom Thurmond,* by Jack Bass and Marilyn W. Thompson; and *Truman,* by David McCullough. Additionally, *Inside the Democratic Party,* by Jack Redding; *Out of the Jaws of Victory,* by Jules Abels; and *Conflict and Crisis: The Presidency of Harry S. Truman, 1945–1948,* by Robert J. Donovan, were helpful in laying the groundwork.

Introduction

page

ix *"the most colorful and astonishing"*: Robert J. Donovan, *Conflict and Crisis: The Presidency of Harry S. Truman, 1945–1948* (Columbia: University of Missouri Press, 1996), p. 395.

"a gigantic comedy": Jules Abels, *Out of the Jaws of Victory: The Astounding Election of 1948* (New York: Henry Holt, 1959), p. viii.

"the wildest campaign": Margaret Truman, *Harry S. Truman* (New York: Morrow, 1973), p. 1.

x *"the Kremlin will sponsor"*: Memorandum to Thomas Dewey dated November 15, 1947, Thomas E. Dewey Papers, Series 2, Box 28, Rare Books, Special Collections, and Preservation, River Campus Libraries, University of Rochester.

xi *"The fate of the nation and"*: "Where Politics Should End," *New York Times,* August 20, 1948.

"The history of the": Harry S. Truman, *Memoirs,* vol. 1, *1945: Year of Decisions* (New York: Konecky & Konecky, 1955), p. 120.

1. "Whither Harry S. Truman?"

3 *"All in"*: "Truman Is at Conference," *Hartford Courant,* August 15, 1945.

"I have received this afternoon": President's News Conference, August 14, 1945, Public Papers, Truman archives, https://www.trumanlibrary.gov/library/public-papers/100/presidents-news-conference.

"That is all": Ibid.

4 *"We want Harry!"*: "Truman Replies to Shouts of Crowd," *Christian Science Monitor,* August 15, 1945.

"That was Harry": David McCullough, *Truman* (New York: Simon & Schuster, 1992), p. 462.

"I told her": Harry S. Truman, *Memoirs,* vol. 1, *Year of Decisions,* p. 438.

"[Truman] was on the White House": "Truman Leads Cheering Throngs in Capitol's Wildest Celebration," *Atlanta Constitution,* August 15, 1945.

"This is a great day": "Peace at Last: Truman Accepts Jap Unconditional Surrender," *Boston Daily Globe,* August 15, 1945.

5 *"We are faced with the greatest"*: "Peace Victory: Japs Accept Allied Terms," *Los Angeles Times,* August 15, 1945.

"Everyone seemed to feel": Diary entry of Henry A. Wallace, August 7, 1945, in Wallace, *The Price of Vision: The Diary of Henry Wallace, 1942–1946*, edited by John M. Blum (Boston: Houghton Mifflin, 1973), p. 471.

6 *"we appear to be treating"*: Harry S. Truman to General Dwight Eisenhower (memorandum enclosing the Harrison Report), September 29, 1945, United States Holocaust Memorial Museum, https://www.ushmm.org/exhibition/displaced-persons/resourc2.htm.

"Secular history offers few": Edward R. Murrow, *In Search of Light: The Broadcasts of Edward R. Murrow, 1938–1961* (New York: Alfred A. Knopf, 1967), p. 102.

7 *"Whither Harry S. Truman?"*: "Right, Left? Truman Still Not Labeled," *Washington Post,* September 9, 1945.

"The President's task was": Dean Acheson, *Present at the Creation: My Years in the State Department* (New York: W. W. Norton, 1969), p. 730.

"the foundation of my administration": Harry S. Truman, *Memoirs,* vol. 1, p. 482.

8 *"Sam, one of the things"*: Ibid., pp. 482–83.

9 *"a combination of a first"*: Ibid., p. 482.

"The Congress reconvenes": "Special Message to the Congress Presenting a 21-Point Program for the Reconversion Period," September 6, 1945, Public Papers, Truman archives, https://www.trumanlibrary.gov/library/public-papers/128/special-message-congress-presenting-21-point-program-reconversion-period.

10 *"The development of atomic energy"*: Ibid.

"The President has to look": Steve Neal, ed., *HST: Memories of the Truman Years* (Carbondale: Southern Illinois University Press, 2003), p. 2.

"Not even President Roosevelt": Cabell Phillips, *The Truman Presidency: The History of a Triumphant Succession* (London: Collier-Macmillan, 1966), p. 105.

"the most far-reaching collection": Ibid.

11 *"This begins the campaign of 1946"*: Ibid.

2. *"The Buck Stops Here!"*

12 *"[Truman] said . . . he was liable"*: Diary entry of Eben Ayers, September 21, 1945, in Eben A. Ayers, *Truman in the White House: The Diary of Eben A. Ayers* (Columbia: University of Missouri Press, 1991), p. 83.

13 *"a declaration of war against"*: Harry S. Truman, *Memoirs,* vol. 1, p. 487.

"Everybody wants something": Harry S. Truman to Martha Ellen and Mary Jane Truman, September 22, 1945, Papers of Harry S. Truman Pertaining to Family, Business, and Personal Affairs, Box 19, Truman archives.

"a future war with Soviet": Gar Alperovitz, *The Decision to Use the Atomic Bomb* (New York: Vintage, 1995), p. 139.

"The atomic bomb, and the": "Cabinet Meeting Minutes, September 21, 1945," Personal Papers, Matthew J. Connelly Papers, Truman archives, https://www.trumanlibrary.gov/library/personal-papers/notes-cabinet-meetings-i-1945-1946/september-21-1945.

14 *"We do not have a secret"*: Ibid.

"If we fail to approach them now": Henry Stimson to Harry S. Truman, September 11, 1945, NuclearFiles.org, http://www.nuclearfiles.org/menu/library/correspondence/stimson-henry/corr_stimson_1945-09-11.htm.

"saving civilization not for": Ibid.

"put an end to the world": Diary entry of Henry Wallace, September 21, 1945, Wallace, *The Price of Vision*, p. 482.

15 *"should continue to carry"*: Minutes of Cabinet Meeting, September 21, 1945.
"Science . . . cannot be restrained": Ibid.
"Their attitude will make for": Diary entry of Henry A. Wallace, August 10, 1954, in Wallace, *The Price of Vision*, p. 475.
"The pressure here is becoming": Harry Truman to Martha Ellen Truman, October 13, 1945, Papers of Harry S. Truman Pertaining to Family, Business, and Personal Affairs, Box 19, Truman archives.
I'M FROM MISSOURI: "The Buck Stops Here!" desk sign, Truman archives, https://www.trumanlibrary.gov/education/trivia/buck-stops-here-sign.
"boldest, most vigorous": "Truman Makes Strong Plea for Year's Universal Training," *Christian Science Monitor*, October 23, 1945.
16 *"to maintain the power with"*: "Address Before a Joint Session of the Congress on Universal Military Training," October 23, 1945, Public Papers, Truman archives, https://www.trumanlibrary.gov/library/public-papers/174/address-joint-session-congress-universal-military-training.
"who work for a living": "Special Message to Congress Recommending a Comprehensive Health Program," November 19, 1945, Public Papers, Truman archives, https://www.trumanlibrary.gov/library/public-papers/192/special-message-congress-recommending-comprehensive-health-program.
"socialized medicine": Robert Taft, "Speech to the Wayne County Medical Society," October 7, 1946, Detroit, Michigan, in *The Papers of Robert A. Taft*, edited by Clarence E. Wunderlin Jr., vol. 3, *1945–1948* (Kent, Ohio: Kent State University Press, 2003), pp. 202–12.
"the extraordinarily dangerous situation": Donovan, *Conflict and Crisis*, p. 128.
"going to do something with": Diary entry of Eben Ayers, September 18, 1945, in Ayers, *Truman in the White House*, p. 81.
"My mind is not made up": "Powell Says He Won't Vote for Truman in '48," *Chicago Defender*, March 2, 1946.
17 *"the biggest press conference in"*: "Ickes Blowup Rocks Capital like an Atom Bomb," *Los Angeles Times*, February 14, 1946.
"un-American . . . enemy of": Alfred Steinberg, *The Man from Missouri: The Life and Times of Harry S. Truman* (New York: G. P. Putnam's Sons, 1962), p. 298.
"If I live and have my": Ibid.
"I'm just mild about Harry": William John Bennett, *America: The Last Best Hope* (Nashville, TN: Thomas Nelson, 2007), p. 286.
"If we're going to have": McCullough, *Truman*, p. 521.
"a lot of second-rate guys": "New Faces of 1946," *Smithsonian*, November 2006.
18 *"If Truman wanted to elect"*: Donovan, *Conflict and Crisis*, p. 230.
19 *"The undertaker described him"*: Walter Francis White, *A Man Called White: The Autobiography of Walter White* (Athens: University of Georgia Press, 1995), p. 324.
"The facts discovered by our": Ibid., p. 323.
20 *"My God! . . . I had no idea"*: Ibid., p. 331.
"I had as callers yesterday": Letter, Harry S. Truman to Attorney General Tom Clark, with attached memo to David Niles, September 20, 1946, Research Files, President's Committee on Civil Rights, Truman archives, https://www.trumanlibrary.gov/library/research-files/letter-harry-s-truman-attorney-general-tom-clark-attached-memo-david-niles?documentid=NA&pagenumber=2
"I am very much in earnest": Ibid.
"The main difficulty with the South": Harry S. Truman to E. W. Roberts, August 18,

1948, Research Files, President's Committee on Civil Rights, Correspondence Between Harry S. Truman and Ernie Roberts, Truman archives, https://www.trumanlibrary.gov/library/research-files/correspondence-between-harry-s-truman-and-ernie-roberts?documentid=NA&pagenumber=3.

21 *"Everything's going to be"*: Donovan, *Conflict and Crisis*, p. 33.

22 *"loaded with political dynamite"*: Diary entry of Henry Wallace, July 30, 1946, in Wallace, *The Price of Vision*, p. 606.

"You just don't understand": Ed Cray, *General of the Army: George C. Marshall, Soldier and Statesman* (New York: Cooper Square, 2000), p. 657.

23 *"The Middle East could well fall"*: "Memorandum by the Joint Chiefs of Staff to the State–War–Navy Coordinating Committee," June 21, 1946, *Foreign Relations of the United States, 1946, the Near East and Africa*, vol. 7, https://history.state.gov/historicaldocuments/frus1946v07/d489.

"After I set forth my reasons": Oral History Interview with Loy W. Henderson (transcript), 1973, Oral History Interviews, Truman archives, p. 132.

"resist at all costs": Nokrashy Pasha to Harry Truman, undated, Harry S. Truman, *Memoirs*, vol. 2, *Years of Trial and Hope, 1946–1952* (Garden City, NY: Doubleday, 1956), pp. 134–35.

"in Hitler's concentration and extermination": Robert F. Wagner, with signatures of eight other senators, to Harry Truman, June 20, 1946, President's Secretary's Files, Recognition of the State of Israel, Truman archives, https://www.trumanlibrary.gov/library/research-files/assorted-members-us-senate-harry-s-truman.

24 *"I am in a tough spot"*: Oral History Interview with Oscar R. Ewing (transcript), 1969, Oral History Interviews, Truman archives, p. 276.

"Those New York Jews!": "President Calls Pearson 'Liar' over Jewish Story," *Los Angeles Times*, March 12, 1948.

25 *"I'm sorry, gentlemen"*: Donovan, *Conflict and Crisis*, p. 322.

"It was a cruel time to put": McCullough, *Truman*, p. 482.

26 *"God damn you"*: Donovan, *Conflict and Crisis*, p. 165.

3. "Can He Swing the Job?"

27 *"Here was a man who came"*: Oral History Interview with Robert G. Nixon (transcript), 1970, Oral History Interviews, Truman archives, p. 159.

"by accident": Truman, speaking in *At Home with Harry & Bess*, introductory film at the Harry S. Truman National Historic Site visitor center, Independence, Missouri.

"When I was about six": Longhand note, May 14, 1934, Longhand Notes File ("Pickwick Papers"), Harry S. Truman Papers, President's Secretary's Files, Truman archives.

28 *"You don't want to marry"*: McCullough, *Truman*, pp. 91–92.

"He ended up being paralyzed": Oral History Interview with Mary Jane Truman (transcript), 1975, Oral History Interviews, Truman archives, p. 3.

"You have to understand how": Margaret Truman, *Harry S. Truman*, p. 6.

"Democrats were not made": Ibid., p. 50.

29 *"You may invite the entire"*: Elizabeth "Bess" Wallace to Harry Truman, March 16, 1919, Papers of Bess Truman, Box 86, Truman archives.

"my Jewish friend": A. J. Baime, *The Accidental President: Harry S. Truman and the Four Months That Changed the World* (Boston: Houghton Mifflin Harcourt, 2017), p. 61.

SHIRTS, COLLARS, HOSIERY: Ibid., p. 62.

"I am still paying on those debts": Longhand note, May 14, 1934, Longhand Notes File ("Pickwick Papers"), Harry S. Truman Papers, President's Secretary's Files, Truman archives.

30 *"How'd you like to be a county judge?"*: Jonathan Daniels, *The Man of Independence* (Port Washington, NY: Kennikat, 1971), p. 109.

"Old Tom Pendergast wanted": Oral History Interview with Harry H. Vaughan (transcript), 1963, Oral History Interviews, Truman archives, p. 12.

"Nobody knows him": Oral History Interview with James P. Aylward (transcript), 1968, Oral History Interviews, Truman archives, pp. 62–64.

"Do you mean seriously to": Ibid.

"Boss Pendergast's Errand Boy": Baime, *The Accidental President*, p. 74.

"Work hard, keep your mouth shut": McCullough, *Truman*, p. 213.

"If you had seen Harry Truman": "Uncompromising Freshman of 1934," *St. Louis Post Dispatch*, November 11, 1942.

31 *"not considered brilliant"*: "New Faces in the Senate," *Washington Post*, November 12, 1934.

"The terrible things done by the high": Harry Truman to Bess Truman, October 1, 1935, Papers of Harry S. Truman Pertaining to Family, Business, and Personal Affairs, Box 8, Truman archives.

"We didn't give him a chance": Oral History Interview with A. J. Granoff (transcript), 1969, Oral History Interviews, Truman archives, p. 86.

"I am introducing a Resolution": Harry S. Truman, speech on the Senate floor, *Congressional Record*, February 10, 1940.

32 *"To thousands, the first question"*: "Truman Report Wins Author Popularity," *Washington Post*, March 8, 1942.

"Truman just dropped into the slot": Jonathan Daniels, "How Truman Got to Be President," *Look*, August 1, 1950.

"Bob . . . have you got that fellow": Harry S. Truman, *Memoirs*, vol. 1, p. 192.

33 *"Good God! Truman will be President!"*: Baime, *The Accidental President*, p. 35.

"The gravest question mark in": Diary entry of Arthur H. Vandenberg, April 12, 1945, in Arthur H. Vandenberg Jr., ed., *The Private Papers of Senator Vandenberg* (Boston: Houghton Mifflin, 1952), p. 165.

4. *"I Was Amazed at How Calm He Seemed in the Face of Political Disaster"*

34 *"blooming chrysanthemum"*: Diary entry of Henry A. Wallace, July 9, 1946, in Wallace, *The Price of Vision*, p. 583.

"You will look toward Washington": Ibid.

35 *"was impossible under the present"*: "Stalin Sets a Huge Output Near Ours in Five Year Plan," *New York Times*, February 10, 1946.

"From Stettin in the Baltic to": Winston Churchill, Iron Curtain Speech, March 5, 1946, YouTube video, AP archive, https://www.youtube.com/watch?v=X2FM3_h33Tg.

36 *"I have been increasingly disturbed"*: Henry Wallace to Harry Truman, July 23, 1946, in Wallace, *The Price of Vision*, p. 589.

37 *"It looks as though Henry"*: Donovan, *Conflict and Crisis*, p. 221.

"That's right . . . Yes, that is": Diary entry of Henry Wallace, September 12, 1946, in Wallace, *The Price of Vision,* p. 612.

"The President apparently saw": Ibid., p. 613.

"no time to read the speech": "The Truman Memoirs: Part V," *Life,* October 24, 1955.

38 *"Mr. President . . . in a speech"*: The President's News Conference (transcript), September 12, 1946, Public Papers, Truman archives, https://www.trumanlibrary.gov/library/public-papers/216/presidents-news-conference.

"I am neither anti-British": William E. Leuchtenburg, *The American President: From Teddy Roosevelt to Bill Clinton* (New York: Oxford University Press, 2015), p. 262.

"You and I spent 15 months": James F. Byrnes, *Speaking Frankly* (New York: Harper & Brothers, 1947), pp. 241–42.

39 *"We can only cooperate with one"*: Diary of Arthur H. Vandenberg, excerpted in Arthur H. Vandenberg Jr., ed., *The Private Papers of Senator Vandenberg,* p. 301.

"has been no change in the": Margaret Truman, *Harry S. Truman,* pp. 316–17.

"worse as we go along": Harry S. Truman to Martha Ellen and Mary Jane Truman, September 18, 1946, Papers of Harry S. Truman Pertaining to Family, Business, and Personal Affairs, Box 19, Truman archives.

"The public is profoundly": Diary entry of Henry Wallace, September 18, 1946, in Wallace, *The Price of Vision,* p. 618.

"there is a school of military thinking": Ibid., Henry Wallace to Harry Truman, July 23, 1946, p. 589.

40 *"You don't want this thing out"*: John C. Culver and John Hyde, *American Dreamer: The Life and Times of Henry A. Wallace* (New York: W. W. Norton, 2000), p. 426.

"I called him and told him": Harry Truman to Bess Wallace, September 21, 1946, Papers of Harry S. Truman Pertaining to Family, Business, and Personal Affairs, Box 15, Truman archives.

"I believe he's a real Commy": Harry Truman to Bess Wallace, September 20, 1946, ibid.

"I have today asked Mr. Wallace": Transcript of the President's News Conference on Foreign Policy, September 20, 1946, Public Papers, Truman archives, https://www.trumanlibrary.gov/library/public-papers/219/presidents-news-conference-foreign-policy.

"There were audible gasps": Diary entry of Eben Ayers, September 20, 1946, in Ayers, *Truman in the White House,* p. 158.

"Well, the die is cast": Ibid., p. 159.

"The Wallace thing is getting": Harry Truman to Bess Wallace, September 17, 1946, Papers of Harry S. Truman Pertaining to Family, Business, and Personal Affairs, Box 15, Truman archives.

"To be a good President": Harry Truman to Margaret Truman, letter quoted in "HST Talked of Ethics, Scorned Snivelers," *Atlanta Constitution,* December 3, 1972.

41 *"Had enough?"*: Numerous mentions in books and in the press, such as "Had Enough?," *Los Angeles Times,* October 21, 1946.

"Well, the show's over": "Truman Votes at 9, Heads for Capital," *New York Times,* November 6, 1946.

"I was amazed at how calm": Clark Clifford, with Richard Holbrooke, *Counsel to the President: A Memoir* (New York: Random House, 1991), p. 83.

42 *"I am only suggesting that"*: "Fulbright Invites Truman to Resign," *New York Times,* November 7, 1946.

"Senator Halfbright": "New Faces of 1946," *Smithsonian,* November 2006.

"the Great White Jail": Numerous references in Truman's letters and diaries, including Harry Truman to Bess Truman, September 28, 1947, Papers of Harry S. Truman Pertaining to Family, Business, and Personal Affairs, Box 16, Truman archives.

43 *"The damn place is haunted"*: Ibid., Harry Truman to Bess Truman, September 9, 1946.

5. *"You Are Getting as Much Publicity as Hitler"*

47 *"confusion and chaos"*: "Dewey Appeals for All to Vote," *New York Times*, November 5, 1946.

48 *"Dewey for President!"*: Herbert Brownell, with John P. Burke, *Advising Ike: The Memoirs of Attorney General Herbert Brownell* (Lawrence: University of Kansas Press, 1993), p. 44.

"What has happened today": "Dewey Rides Crest of Wave Toward Nomination in 1948," *Christian Science Monitor*, November 6, 1948.

"riding the very crest of the 1946": Ibid.

49 *"Governor . . . are you ready"*: "Dewey Not in Race for '48 Nomination Now," *New York Times*, December 19, 1946.

"This didn't make him popular": Brownell, *Advising Ike*, p. 40.

"A good many people have": Scott Farris, *Almost President: The Men Who Lost the Race but Changed the Nation* (Guilford, CT: Lyons, 2012), p. 138.

50 *"The long tenure of the Democratic"*: Joe Martin, *My First Fifty Years in Politics* (New York: McGraw-Hill, 1960), p. 163.

"The greatest advantage I had": Richard Nixon, *RN: The Memoirs of Richard Nixon* (New York: Touchstone, 1990), p. 36.

"Anyone seeking to unseat an": Ibid., p. 41.

"The public's reaction to last": "Democratic Oblivion in 1948, Public's Guess," *Los Angeles Times*, December 16, 1946.

51 *"The always efficient Gov. Thomas"*: "Matter of Fact: The Dewey Jitters," *Washington Post*, December 20, 1946.

"A ten-pound Republican voter": Smith, *Thomas E. Dewey*, p. 60.

"it was one of those things": Ibid., p. 61.

"To me it seems vitally important": Henry L. Stimson, *On Active Services in Peace and War* (New York: Harper & Brothers, 1948), p. 22.

52 *"a novel idea in those days"*: Thomas E. Dewey, *Twenty Against the Underworld* (Garden City, NY: Doubleday, 1974), p. 139.

53 *"He gave you the impression"*: Smith, *Thomas E. Dewey*, p. 121.

"Gentlemen . . . there will be a lot": Ibid., p. 135.

54 *"The mobs had a tremendous"*: Dewey, *Twenty Against the Underworld*, p. 5.

"They did not look like cops": Ibid., pp. 158–59.

"Gangsters Split Girls' Tongues": Headlines from ibid., p. 219.

"the meanest poultry racketeer": Ibid. Quotes describing gangsters are from captions in photo insert.

55 *"Hines Guilty"*: Ibid.

"You made a glorious run": Arthur Vandenberg to Thomas Dewey, November 11, 1938, Thomas E. Dewey Papers, Series 10, Box 44, Rare Books, Special Collections, and Preservation, River Campus Libraries, University of Rochester.

56 *"I have confidence in the"*: "Dewey Opens Drive for Presidency on Recovery Issue," *New York Times*, December 2, 1939.

"thrown his diaper into": "Harold L. Ickes," *Washington Post*, March 8, 1948.

"You are getting as much publicity": Smith, *Thomas E. Dewey*, p. 276.

57 *"Dewey would always take on"*: Brownell, *Advising Ike*, p. 47.

"How can the Republican Party": "Thomas E. Dewey, 68, Dies," *Washington Post*, March 17, 1971.

"one of the most vitriolic speeches": "Dewey Calls F.D.R.'s Record 'Desperately Bad,'" *Boston Daily Globe*, September 26, 1944.

"I still think he's a son of a bitch": Farris, *Almost President*, p. 11.

58 *"The Truman administration is"*: "Report of Herbert Brownell Jr., Chairman to the Republican National Committee," April 1, 1946, Thomas E. Dewey Papers, Series 2, Box 38.

"It has been wickedly said": "Matter of Fact: Governor Dewey Grows," *Washington Post*, November 4, 1946.

"As long ago as Philadelphia": "Hotel Confab Picks Dewey's Veep," *Salt Lake City Tribune*, April 6, 1952.

6. "It Is a Total 'War of Nerves'"

59 *"Our nation is faced today"*: "Eisenhower, Spaatz, and Nimitz Call on the United States to Retain Strength," *New York Times*, August 30, 1947.

"I think it's one of the": David McCullough interview with Clark Clifford, quoted in McCullough, *Truman* (New York: Simon & Schuster, 1992), p. 554.

"the most disturbing statement ever": Bruce Robellet Kuniholm, *The Origins of the Cold War in the Near East* (Princeton, NJ: Princeton University Press, 1994), p. 407.

60 *"They were shockers"*: Dean Acheson, *Present at the Creation: My Years in the State Department* (New York: W. W. Norton, 1969), p. 217.

"very convinced . . . that there": Robert J. Donovan, *Conflict and Crisis: The Presidency of Harry S. Truman, 1945–1948* (Columbia: University of Missouri Press, 1996), p. 278.

"The next eighteen months look": James Forrestal to Charles Thomas, February 24, 1947, in Forrestal, *The Forrestal Diaries*, edited by Walter Millis (New York: Viking, 1951), p. 240.

"patient but deadly struggle": George F. Kennan, "Telegraphic Message from Moscow of February 22, 1946," excerpted in Kennan, *Memoirs 1925–1950* (Boston: Atlantic Monthly Press, 1967), p. 550.

61 *"Development of atomic weapons"*: Clark Clifford and George Elsey, "American Relations with the Soviet Union" ("Clifford-Elsey Report"), September 24, 1946, Truman archives, https://www.trumanlibrary.gov/library/research-files/report-american-relations-soviet-union-clark-clifford-clifford-elsey-report?documentid=NA&pagenumber=1.

"If it leaked it would blow": Clark Clifford, with Richard Holbrooke, *Counsel to the President: A Memoir* (New York: Random House, 1991), p. 123.

"This was, I believe, the turning": Harry S. Truman, *Memoirs*, vol. 2, *Years of Trial and Hope* (New York: Doubleday, 1956), p. 106.

62 *"we prepare for war"*: Harry Truman to Bess Truman, September 30, 1947, Papers of Harry S. Truman Pertaining to Family, Business, and Personal Affairs, Box 16, Truman archives.

"It is not alarmist to say": George Marshall, "Statement to Congressional Leaders, Top Secret," February 27, 1947, George C. Marshall Foundation, https://www.marshallfoundation.org/library/digital-archive/6-029-statement-congressional-leaders-february-27-1947/.

"The choice . . . is between acting": Ibid.

"Mr. President, if you will say": Acheson, *Present at the Creation*, p. 219.
"All . . . were aware": Ibid., p. 220.

63 *"the opening gun in a campaign"*: John Lewis Gaddis, *The United States and the Origins of the Cold War, 1941–1947* (New York: Columbia University Press, 2000), p. 350.
"The gravity of the situation": President Harry S. Truman's Address Before a Joint Session of Congress, March 12, 1947, Public Papers, Truman archives, https://www.trumanlibrary.gov/library/public-papers/56/special-message-congress-greece-and-turkey-truman-doctrine.

64 *"We may agree the next time"*: Ed Cray, *General of the Army: George C. Marshall, Soldier and Statesman* (New York: Cooper Square Press, 2000), p. 605.
"Europe was recovering slowly": Forrest C. Pogue, *George C. Marshall: Statesman 1945–1959* (New York: Viking, 1987), p. 196.
"Disintegrating forces are": George C. Marshall radio address, April 28, 1947, excerpted at US Department of State, Office of the Historian, https://history.state.gov/historicaldocuments/frus1947v03/d133.

65 *"without delay . . . Avoid trivia"*: McCullough, *Truman*, p. 561.
"a declaration of war on": "House Votes $400,000,000 Aid to Greece and Turkey," *Los Angeles Times*, May 10, 1947.
"The entire fabric of European": George Marshall, Marshall Plan Speech, June 5, 1947, George C. Marshall Foundation, https://www.marshallfoundation.org/marshall/the-marshall-plan/marshall-plan-speech/.

66 *"Nations, if not continents, had to"*: Harry S. Truman, *Memoirs*, vol. 2, p. 110.
"We now apparently confront the": Arthur Vandenberg to Robert Taft, excerpted in Arthur H. Vandenberg Jr., ed., *The Private Papers of Senator Vandenberg* (Boston: Houghton Mifflin, 1952), p. 374.
"no confidence whatever": Robert Taft to Grier Bartol, November 19, 1947, *The Papers of Robert Taft*, edited by Clarence E. Wunderlin Jr., vol. 3, *1945–1948* (Kent, OH: Kent State University Press, 2003), p. 333.
DON'T ARM TYRANNY: Event description from news reports, notably "Wallace Sees U.N. as Sole Peace Hope," *New York Times*, April 1, 1947.

67 *"Unconditional aid"*: Ibid

68 *"The world is devastated and hungry"*: "Wallace Suggests Britain Take Lead," *New York Times*, April 12, 1947.
"covers Wallace like a cloak": "Wallace Prosecution Asked as Congress Furor Mounts," *New York Times*, April 15, 1947.
"treasonable utterances": "Wallace Defies Critics in Senate," *New York Times*, April 14, 1947.
"only one circumstance": Ibid.
"in good standing of the Democratic": Dialogue from transcript of the President's News Conference, April 10, 1947, Public Papers, Truman archives.

69 *"I shall be campaigning in 1948"*: "U.S. Leading World to War, Wallace Says," *Washington Post*, April 12, 1947.
"filling Chicago Stadium for the first": "Report on Henry Wallace," May 22, 1947, Wallace FBI file.
"a road to ruthless imperialism": "Storm Grows over Wallace Aid Attacks," *Washington Post*, April 13, 1947.
"hatred of Russia . . . an imperialist": "Churchill Runs U.S. Policy, Says Wallace," *Washington Post*, October 11, 1948.

"crypto-Communist": "Churchill Attacks Wallace for Crypto-Communist Plot," *Christian Science Monitor,* April 18, 1947.

70 *"If it is traitorous to believe"*: John C. Culver and John Hyde, *American Dreamer: The Life and Times of Henry A. Wallace* (New York: W. W. Norton, 2000), p. 434.

7. *"The Defeat Seemed like the End of the World"*

71 *"There are 100,000 people here"*: Address by Walter White, Lincoln Memorial, June 29, 1947, President's Committee on Civil Rights file, Clark Clifford papers, Truman archives, https://www.trumanlibrary.gov/library/research-files/address-given-walter-white-lincoln-memorial.

72 *"Every man . . . should have the right"*: Address Before the National Association for the Advancement of Colored People, June 29, 1947, Public Papers, Truman archives, https://www.trumanlibrary.gov/library/public-papers/130/address-national-association-advancement-colored-people.

"I said what I did": Walter Francis White, *A Man Called White: The Autobiography of Walter White* (Athens: University of Georgia Press, 1995), p. 348.

73 *"devastating broadside at the"*: "The Watchtower," *Los Angeles Sentinel,* March 18, 1948.

"stand guard": "Southerners Plan Senate Filibuster on Rights Program," *New York Times,* March 7, 1948.

"the rule of our Government": "Convention to Succeed — Thompson," *Atlanta Constitution,* April 24, 1947.

"The world seems to be": Harry Truman to Bess Truman, September 22, 1947, Papers of Harry S. Truman Pertaining to Family, Business, and Personal Affairs, Box 16, Truman archives.

74 *MR. PRESIDENT: VETO THE:* "Mayor, at AFL Rally, Warns Bill Will Stamp Out Freedom," *New York Times,* June 5, 1947.

startling, dangerous, far-reaching: Veto of the Taft-Hartley Labor Bill, June 20, 1947, Public Papers, Truman archives, https://www.trumanlibrary.gov/library/public-papers/120/veto-taft-hartley-labor-bill.

"The defeat . . . seemed like": Jack Redding, *Inside the Democratic Party* (New York: Bobbs-Merrill, 1958), p. 79.

"maximum protection . . . be afforded": Executive Order 9835, March 21, 1947, Executive Orders, Truman archives, https://www.trumanlibrary.gov/library/executive-orders/9835/executive-order-9835.

75 *"awakened the people of North"*: Book review, "Decline and Fall of a Russian Idol . . . by Igor Guozenko," *New York Times,* July 18, 1954.

"It was a political problem": David McCullough interview with Clark Clifford, quoted in McCullough, *Truman,* p. 553.

"a campaign of terror unequaled": "Wallace Hits Denial of Civil Rights," *Gazette and Daily* (York, PA), September 20, 1947.

"Not even liberty seemed simple": Jonathan Daniels, *The Man of Independence* (New York: Kennikat, 1971), p. 346.

76 *"I think I am one of"*: Eddie Jacobson to Harry Truman, October 3, 1947, President's Secretary's Files, Truman archives, https://www.trumanlibrary.gov/library/research-files/correspondence-between-harry-s-truman-and-eddie-jacobson?documentid=NA&pagenumber=2.

77 *"Clark, I am impressed with"*: Clifford, *Counsel to the President,* pp. 5–6.
"There is no question in my": Diary entry of James Forrestal, November 12, 1947, in Forrestal, *The Forrestal Diaries,* p. 344.

8. *"Dewey's Hat Is Tossed into Ring"*

79 *"We are here to pledge our"*: "Dewey's Hat Is Tossed into Ring," *New York Times,* June 13, 1947.
"That was a charming": Ibid.
80 *"I was like a trainer with"*: "Edwin Jaeckle, 97, Lawyer and Backer of Thomas Dewey," *New York Times,* May 16, 1992.
"Reorganization of the national party": Brownell, *Advising Ike,* p. 67.
"For many voters": Ibid., p. 70.
81 *"Anti-Marshall Plan Committee"*: Robert Taft to Frank Gannett, December 26, 1947, in *The Papers of Robert Taft,* vol. 3, p. 352.
"The solution of many": Robert Taft, Address to the John Marshall Club, St. Louis, MO, December 30, 1947, ibid., p. 362.
"very clumsy Republicans": Thomas E. Dewey speech, *The Public Papers of Thomas E. Dewey* (New York: Williams, 1944), p. 774.
"The general issue [is] between people": "Taft Enters Race to Head GOP Slate," *Los Angeles Times,* October 25, 1947.
"There will be violent": Ibid.
"I think we are going to have": William Randolph Hearst to Richard Berlin, March 1948, quoted in David Pietrusza, *1948: Harry Truman's Improbable Victory and the Year That Transformed America's Role in the World* (New York: Union Square, 2011), p. 135.
82 *"The USSR does not propose"*: "Full Text of Ex-Gov. Stassen's 80-Minute Talk with Premier Stalin in Moscow," *Boston Daily Globe,* May 4, 1947.
"The document was sensational": Jack Redding, *Inside the Democratic Party* (New York: Bobbs-Merrill, 1958), p. 55.
"Among the rank and file": Pietrusza, *1948: Harry Truman's Improbable Victory,* p. 91.
"From my point of view": Thomas Dewey to John Taber, June 7, 1948, Thomas E. Dewey Papers, Series 5, Box 186.
83 *"The Kremlin will make no serious"*: Memorandum to Thomas Dewey dated November 15, 1947, ibid., Series 2, Box 28.

9. *"Wall Street and the Military Have Taken Over"*

85 *"Thousands of people all"*: Culver and Hyde, *American Dreamer,* pp. 456–57.
86 *"The lukewarm liberals sitting"*: "Text of Wallace Third Party Speech," *Washington Post,* December 30, 1947.
"Henry A. Wallace's hat-in-the-ring": Edward Folliard, "Wallace Move Overjoys GOP, White House Indifferent," *Washington Post,* December 30, 1947.
"New reinforcements": Americans for Democratic Action report, "Henry A. Wallace: The First Three Months," p. 3, Research Files, 1948 Election Campaign File, Truman archives, https://www.trumanlibrary.gov/library/research-files/henry-wallace-first-three-months?documentid=NA&pagenumber=3.

"What do the Communists": "Matter of Fact: Squeeze Play," *Washington Post*, January 2, 1948.

"If the Communists want to": "Wallace Sees End of Chiang Regime," *New York Times*, May 22, 1948.

87 *"seeing more and more of"*: Thomas W. Devine, *Henry Wallace's 1948 Presidential Campaign and the Future of Postwar Liberalism* (Chapel Hill: University of North Carolina Press, 2013), p. 44.

"stage managers": "Calling Washington: Wallace's Stage Managers," *Washington Post*, July 24, 1948.

"self-admitted espionage agent": FBI memorandum January 29, 1959, FBI file of John Abt.

"reportedly in contact with": Ibid.

"brushed aside my concerns": John J. Abt, with Michael Myerson, *Advocate and Activist: Memoirs of an American Communist Lawyer* (Chicago: University of Illinois Press, 1993), p. 144.

also named Pressman: FBI memorandums, December 28, 1954, and January 29, 1959, FBI file of John Abt.

88 *"all progressive men and women"*: Culver and Hyde, *American Dreamer*, p. 434.

"The facts . . . are": Abt, *Advocate and Activist*, p. 149.

"As you are undoubtedly": SAC, Washington Field to Director, FBI, June 3, 1947, FBI file of Henry Wallace.

"All I said . . . was that there": Reminiscences of Henry Agard Wallace: oral history, 1953 (transcript), Columbia University Libraries, Center for Oral History, p. 5080.

"I certainly told him before": Reminiscences of Calvin Benham Baldwin: oral history, 1951 (transcript), ibid., pp. 17–18.

90 *"I have been thinking of"*: Culver and Hyde, *American Dreamer*, p. 134.

"flaming one" . . . "sour one": Ibid., p. 135.

"unsigned, undated notes": Reminiscences of Henry Agard Wallace, Columbia University Center for Oral History, p. 5107.

"The gist of the whole thing": Ibid., p. 5110.

91 *"There must be no publicity"*: Culver and Hyde, *American Dreamer*, p. 143.

"It is highly essential that": Diary entry of Henry A. Wallace, June 15, 1942, *The Price of Vision: The Diary of Henry Wallace, 1942–1946* (Boston: Houghton Mifflin, 1973), p. 91.

"Some have spoken of the": "Century of the Common Man," Henry A. Wallace speech, May 8, 1942, YouTube video, https://www.youtube.com/watch?v=CAKrIdSPkHI.

92 *"the boomerang throwing mystic"*: George E. Allen, *Presidents Who Have Known Me* (New York: Simon & Schuster, 1960), p. 122.

"a job for you in world": Robert H. Ferrell, *Harry S. Truman: A Life* (Columbia: University of Missouri Press, 1994), p. 166.

"You know . . . this whole": Diary entry of Henry A. Wallace, August 3, 1944, in Wallace, *The Price of Vision*, p. 373.

"He is a small opportunistic man": Ibid., p. 374.

93 *"I had no illusions about"*: Reminiscences of Henry Agard Wallace, Columbia University Center for Oral History, p. 5115.

"We all had grandiose ideas": Abt, *Advocate and Activist*, p. 148.

"I am going to cast my lot": Dialogue from "Singing Cowboy Taylor Lines Up with Wallace," *Los Angeles Times*, February 24, 1948.

10. "There'll Be No Compromise"

95 *"Never in our history have"*: Longhand note, April 1948, President's Secretary's Files, Box 283, Truman archives.

"one of this century's most famous": "Clark Clifford Ends Mystery over Memo," *Washington Post,* May 22, 1991.

96 *"The basic premise of this"*: All quotations from this document come from Memorandum for the President, November 19, 1947, "The Politics of 1948," Research Files, 1948 Election Campaign File, Truman archives, https://www.trumanlibrary.gov/library/research-files/memo-clark-clifford-harry-s-truman.

98 *"It was clearly apparent to all"*: George M. Elsey Oral History Interview (transcript), 1964–70, Oral History Interviews, Truman archives, p. 107.

"controversial as hell": George McKee Elsey, *An Unplanned Life: A Memoir by George McKee Elsey* (Columbia: University of Missouri Press, 2005), p. 158.

"This is the most important period": Diary entry of David Lilienthal, January 2, 1948, *The Journals of David E. Lilienthal,* vol. 2, *The Atomic Energy Years 1945–1950* (New York: Harper & Row, 1964), p. 279.

99 *"the essential human rights"*: Annual Message to the Congress on the State of the Union, January 7, 1948, Public Papers, Truman archives, https://www.trumanlibrary.gov/library/public-papers/2/annual-message-congress-state-union-1.

"almost a half an hour of complete": "By the Way with Bill Henry," *Los Angeles Times,* January 11, 1948.

"success in '48!": Elsey, *An Unplanned Life,* p. 159.

"a rich present for every": Robert Taft, Address on the ABC Radio Network, January 8, 1948, in *The Papers of Robert A. Taft,* vol. 3, pp. 373–74.

100 *"Murphy and . . . Ross were nervous"*: Elsey, *An Unplanned Life,* p. 160.

"The founders of the United States": Harry S. Truman, Special Message to the Congress on Civil Rights, February 2, 1948, Public Papers, Truman archives, https://www.trumanlibrary.gov/library/public-papers?month=2&endyear=4&searchterm=&yearstart=All&yearend=All.

"We have been betrayed": "Dixie Leaders Warn Truman on Race Stand," *Washington Post,* February 8, 1948.

101 *"white supremacy"*: Ibid.

"in the strongest possible language": "Southern Governors Name PAC to Demand Supremacy Concessions," *Hartford Courant,* February 9, 1948.

"We may as well have a": Jack Bass and Marilyn W. Thompson, *Strom: The Complicated Personal and Political Life of Strom Thurmond* (New York: Public Affairs, 2005), p. 109.

"intrudes into the sacred": Ibid., p. 107.

"un-American": "S.C. House Condemns Rights Proposals," *Washington Post,* February 13, 1948.

"The South can be considered safely": Memorandum for the President, November 19, 1947, "The Politics of 1948," Truman archives.

"she might be seated next": "Southern Democrats Cancel Dinner Plans," *Washington Post,* February 19, 1948.

102 *"battalions of the press"*: Redding, *Inside the Democratic Party,* p. 135.

"Will you now": Ibid., p. 136.

"There'll be no compromise": Ibid., p. 173.

"has sent a shock throughout": Harry S. Truman, Special Message to Congress on the

Threat to the Freedom of Europe, March 17, 1948, Public Papers, Truman archives, https://www.trumanlibrary.gov/library/public-papers?month=3&endyear=4&searchterm=&yearstart=All&yearend=All.

103 *"For many months"*: General Lucius Clay to Lieutenant General Stephen J. Chamberlin, March 5, 1948, *The Papers of General Lucius D. Clay, Germany 1945–1949,* edited by Jean Edward Smith (Bloomington: Indiana University Press, 1974), p. 568.

"warmonger": "Vishinsky Screams 'War Mong' at Dulles in Turbulent UN Session," *Atlanta Constitution,* September 19, 1947.

104 *"It is the most serious situation"*: Harry Truman to Eleanor Roosevelt, March 16, 1948, *Off the Record: The Private Papers of Harry S. Truman,* edited by Robert H. Ferrell (Columbia: University of Missouri Press, 1980), p. 126.

"Since the close of hostilities": Harry S. Truman, Special Message to Congress on the Threat to the Freedom of Europe, March 17, 1948, Public Papers, Truman archives.

"It is undoubtedly the first": General Lucius Clay to General Omar Bradley, March 31, 1948, quoted in Ann Tusa and John Tusa, *The Berlin Airlift* (New York: Atheneum, 1988), p. xiii.

105 *"The possibility must be"*: Central Intelligence Agency, "Possibility of Direct Soviet Military Action During 1948," April 2, 1948, President's Secretary's Files, Box 177, Truman archives.

"People were blaming the": Oral History Interview with Eben A. Ayers (transcript), 1967, Oral History Interviews, Truman archives, p. 267.

"Unless immediate action is": Memorandum by the President's Special Counsel (Clark Clifford), "Proposed Program on the Palestine Problem," March 6, 1948, Clark Clifford papers, Box 13, Truman archives.

106 *"Unless the Palestine matter"*: Memorandum for the President, November 19, 1947, Clark Clifford to Harry S. Truman, Research Files, 1948 Election Campaign File, Truman archives, https://www.trumanlibrary.gov/library/research-files/memo-clark-clifford-harry-s-truman.

"The State Dept pulled the rug": Diary entries of Harry Truman, March 18–19, 1948, Post Presidential File, Box 643, Truman archives.

"Can you come right down?": Daniels, *The Man of Independence,* p. 318.

107 *"as disturbed as I have ever"*: McCullough, *Truman,* p. 611.

"At this time, the President's": "Prestige of President Is Vital Problem Now," *New York Times,* April 4, 1948.

"All of this is causing": Memorandum by the President's Special Counsel (Clifford) to President Truman, March 8, 1948, *Foreign Relations of the United States, 1948, The Near East, South Asia, and Africa,* vol. 5, part 2.

"Of all the meetings I ever": Clark Clifford, *Counsel to the President,* p. 3.

"the greatest living American": Ibid.

108 *"I noticed thunderclouds"*: Ibid.

"Mr. President . . . I thought this": Ibid., p. 12.

"It is obviously designed": Ibid.

"Everyone in the room was stunned": Ibid., p. 13.

"That . . . is all we need": McCullough, *Truman,* p. 618.

"Mr. President, will the United": Transcript of the President's News Conference, May 13, 1948, Public Papers, Truman archives, https://www.trumanlibrary.gov/library/public-papers/100/statement-president-announcing-recognition-state-israel.

109 *"This Government has been"*: Statement by the President Announcing Recognition of the State of Israel, May 14, 1948, Public Papers, Truman archives.

"The charge that domestic politics": Clifford, *Counsel to the President*, p. 24.
"I want to say to you that": Remarks at the Young Democrats Dinner, May 14, 1948, President's Secretary's Files, Box 74, Truman archives, https://www.trumanlibrary.gov/library/public-papers/101/remarks-young-democrats-dinner.

11. "I Will Not Accept the Political Support of Henry Wallace and His Communists"

111 *"The people have only to"*: "Dewey Announces He Is Ready to Run if Party Picks Him," *New York Times*, January 17, 1948.
"choice of cocktails, highballs": Menu, Thomas E. Dewey Papers, Series 2, Box 38.
"further evidence as to the": "The 1946 Elections: A Statistical Analysis," ibid., Series 2, Box 49.
"The outlook is exceedingly favorable": Ibid.
112 *"The organizational job"*: Thomas Dewey to Herbert Brownell, June 3, 1948, Thomas E. Dewey Papers, Series 10, Box 6.
"The Communist Party organization": "Hit Russia Harder, Stassen Proposes," *New York Times*, March 19, 1948.
113 *"There isn't any use in"*: F. N. Belgrano Jr. to Herbert Brownell, May 5, 1948, Thomas E. Dewey Papers, Series 2, Box 28.
"Dewey and Women's Rights": Oregon primary campaign literature, ibid.
"The Governor is making rapid": Clyde A. Lewis to Herbert Brownell, May 10, 1948, ibid., Series 10, Box 44.
114 *"would be a* must *pick-up"*: Fred E. Baker to Thomas Dewey, May 2, 1948, ibid., Series 2, Box 18.
"the little son of a bitch": Pietrusza, *1948: Harry Truman's Improbable Victory*, p. 135.
"I think you can take the guy": Ibid., p. 136.
115 *"Chairman Van Boskirk"*: Transcript of the complete debate reprinted in *Vital Speeches of the Day*, June 1, 1948, Thomas E. Dewey Papers, Series 5, Box 47.
"The free world looks to us": Ibid.
"Herb . . . I feel that I can": Joe Montgomery to Herbert Brownell, June 7, 1948, ibid., Series 2, Box 40.
116 *"Mister Pegler's place as"*: "The Press: Mister Pegler," *Time*, October 10, 1938.
"We have had evidence": "Wallace's Character," *Atlanta Constitution*, May 12, 1947.
"The protecting shield of the": "Did Wallace Write the Guru Letters?" *Atlanta Constitution*, March 9, 1948.
117 *"I would tell them to get ready"*: "Wallace Accuses Truman of Leading to Russian War," *New York Times*, February 25, 1948.
"laying the foundations": Ibid.
"deliberately created [a] crisis": "Wallace Accuses Truman of Scare to Get Draft, UMT," *New York Times*, March 21, 1948.
118 *"Our country's heritage means"*: "History Lesson: Red Scare in Evansville," *USA Today Courier & Press*, March 13, 2018.
"According to newspapers": "Wallace Renews His Red Vote Stand," *New York Times*, July 24, 1948.
119 *"I was very much shocked"*: Oral history of Henry A. Wallace, Columbia University Rare Book & Manuscript Library, p. 5116.

"It must be part of a communist": "Offer Rewards of $117,800 for Reuther's Foe," *Chicago Daily Tribune*, April 22, 1948.

"This is the colored entrance": "Glen Taylor Seized, Fingerprinted as He Flouts Alabama Segregation," *New York Times*, May 2, 1948.

"This is it": Culver and Hyde, *American Dreamer*, p. 470.

"They got me for pukin'": Ibid.

"I have never seen a": Ibid., p. 446.

"I'm here, I've seen it": Curtis Daniel MacDougall, *Gideon's Army*, vol. 1 (New York: Marzani & Munsell, 1965), p. 155.

120 *"Thousands of people believe"*: "Harold L. Ickes: Wallace's Popularity," *Atlanta Constitution*, June 4, 1947.

"Let the mass of American": "W. E. B. Dubois: The Winds of Time," *Chicago Defender*, March 20, 1948.

"to turn the rascals out": Frank Lloyd Wright to Henry Wallace, June 1, 1948, Henry A. Wallace Papers, Reel No. 45, University of Iowa.

"The Third Party candidate has": Americans for Democratic Action report, *Henry A. Wallace: The First Three Months*, p. 3, 1948 Election Campaign File, Truman archives, https://www.trumanlibrary.gov/library/research-files/henry-wallace-first-three-months?documentid=NA&pagenumber=3.

"test of Truman-Wallace strength": "Mayor to Support Bronx Democrat," *New York Times*, February 4, 1948.

"I do not want and I will not": Harry Truman, St. Patrick's Day Address in New York City, March 17, 1948, Public Papers, Truman archives, https://www.trumanlibrary.gov/library/public-papers/53/st-patricks-day-address-new-york-city.

121 *"There is no known method"*: "Doom of Those Near an Atomic Attack Foreseen," *Chicago Daily Tribune*, April 11, 1948.

"definite, decisive steps": "Text of Wallace Letter to Stalin Calling for Peace Program," *New York Times*, May 12, 1948.

"need of improvement": Devine, *Henry Wallace's 1948 Presidential Campaign*, p. 120.

122 *"I am humbled and grateful"*: Ibid.

"may be a possible violation": D. M. Ladd to "The Director" (J. Edgar Hoover), May 18, 1948, Wallace FBI file.

"We aren't dealing with Stalin": Devine, *Henry Wallace's 1948 Presidential Campaign*, p. 121.

12. *"For Better or Worse, the 1948 Fight Has Started"*

123 *"If people see him in person"*: Redding, *Inside the Democratic Party*, pp. 52–53.

124 *"The pretense that this"*: "Truman Tackles Congress on Cross-Country Tour," *Christian Science Monitor*, June 5, 1948.

"Rolling across the United": "Truman Looks Towards West with Both Eyes on White House," *Christian Science Monitor*, June 4, 1948.

"one of those deadly dull": Daniels, *The Man of Independence*, p. 347.

125 *"Why wasn't that on"*: Diary entry of David Lilienthal, April 18, 1948, *The Journals of David E. Lilienthal*, vol. 2, p. 317.

"A large number of reporters": Oral History Interviews with Oscar L. Chapman, 1972 (transcript), Oral History Interviews, Truman archives, p. 231.

"Truman in Omaha": "The Truman-Vandenberg Bill of Goods," *Chicago Daily Tribune,* June 9, 1948.

"It was almost a death knell": Oral History Interviews with Matthew J. Connelly, 1967–68 (transcript), Oral History Interviews, Truman archives, p. 263.

"I am honored . . . to dedicate": Numerous accounts of this event exist, including Jules Abels, *Out of the Jaws of Victory: The Astounding Election of 1948* (New York: Henry Holt, 1959), pp. 42–43, and Donovan, *Conflict and Crisis,* p. 397.

126 *"It wasn't anything to laugh at"*: Oral History Interview with Robert L. Dennison, 1971 (transcript), Oral History Interviews, Truman archives, p. 45.

"I like old Joe": "Truman Calls 'Old Joe Stalin' Nice Chap But . . . ," *Los Angeles Times,* June 12, 1948.

"The uproar caused by": Clifford, *Counsel to the President,* p. 201.

"we just have to tell you": Ibid.

"I actually cringed": Oral History Interviews with Charles S. Murphy, 1963, 1969–70 (transcript), Oral History Interviews, Truman archives, p. 18.

"At this point . . . he decided that": Ken Hechler, *Working with Truman: A Personal Memoir of the White House Years* (New York: G. P. Putnam's Sons, 1982), p. 77.

127 *"If your father knew what"*: "James Roosevelt, Son of FDR, Dies at 83," *Los Angeles Times,* August 14, 1991.

"Not even the most charitable": "Presidential Boners," *Washington Post,* June 11, 1948.

"Governors are running like deer": "McLemore: Admires the Way Truman Is Pitching," *Washington Evening Star,* June 15, 1948.

"the wrong tax cut at the wrong": Smith, *Thomas E. Dewey,* p. 477.

"was deliberately contrived": John F. Witte, *The Politics and Development of the Federal Income Tax* (Madison: University of Wisconsin Press, 1985), p. 135.

128 *"It wasn't until Butte"*: Oral History Interview with Robert G. Nixon (transcript), 1970, Oral History Interviews, Truman archives, p. 550.

"A typical reaction that you": Oral History Interviews with Charles S. Murphy, Truman archives, p. 26.

"inactivity . . . a rich man's tax": Harry Truman, Address Before the Greater Los Angeles Press Club, June 14, 1948, Public Papers, Truman archives, https://www.trumanlibrary.gov/library/public-papers/134/address-greater-los-angeles-press-club.

"If you want to continue the": Harry Truman, Informal Remarks in Washington, June 10, 1948, Public Papers, Truman archives, https://www.trumanlibrary.gov/library/public-papers/124/informal-remarks-washington.

"He is making his attack": "Truman Tackles Congress on Cross-Country Tour," *Christian Science Monitor,* June 5, 1948.

"The President is blackguarding": Redding, *Inside the Democratic Party,* p. 178.

"Please wire the Democratic": Ibid.

13. *"We Have a Dreamboat of a Ticket"*

133 *I'M ON THE DEWEY TEAM:* Campaign materials from Inter Office Correspondence, F. L. Carlisle to Herbert Brownell et al., May 11, 1948, Thomas E. Dewey Papers, Series 2, Box 39, Rare Books, Special Collections, and Preservation, River Campus Libraries, University of Rochester.

134 *"The general idea of the"*: Memorandum, Mrs. Charles W. Weis Jr. to Mrs. Carl T. Hogan, May 27, 1948, ibid.

"Cheese at Stassen's": David Pietrusza, *1948: Harry Truman's Improbable Victory and the Year That Transformed America's Role in the World* (New York: Union Square, 2011), p. 176.

"Shake his trunk": "Dewey, Taft Arrive at GOP Convention," *Washington Post,* July 21, 1948.

135 *"The great silent star of the"*: "Truman — Source of All Republican Joy," *Atlanta Constitution,* June 24, 1948.

"We are assembled in this": Joe Martin, *My First Fifty Years in Politics* (New York: McGraw-Hill, 1960), p. 163.

"What was unique about": Ibid.

"In a few minutes I began": Donald A. Ritchie, *Reporting from Washington: The History of the Washington Press Corps* (New York: Oxford University Press, 2005), p. 185.

"we were conducting our affairs": Martin, *My First Fifty Years,* p. 163.

"gone goose": "Truman 'a Gone Goose' La Luce Quips to GOP," *Boston Daily Globe,* June 22, 1948.

"Let's waste no time": Ibid.

136 *"Harold . . . you have no idea"*: Pietrusza, *1948: Harry Truman's Improbable Victory,* p. 192.

"[Dewey's] 'blitz' was a thing": Diary entry of Arthur H. Vandenberg, June 20–25, 1948, in Arthur H. Vandenberg Jr., ed., *The Private Papers of Senator Vandenberg* (Boston: Houghton Mifflin, 1952), p. 438.

"I look just awful": Pietrusza, *1948: Harry Truman's Improbable Victory,* p. 180.

137 *"It has been a difficult"*: "It's Dewey on the 3rd Ballot," *Chicago Daily Tribune,* June 25, 1948.

"Will you excuse me for": "Remarks by Governor Thomas E. Dewey on the Marquee of the Bellevue-Stratford Hotel, Philadelphia, PA, Thursday Evening, June 24," Thomas E. Dewey Papers, Series 2, Box 117.

"We were all sworn to": Diary entry of Arthur H. Vandenberg, June 20–25, 1948, in Vandenberg, *The Private Papers of Senator Vandenberg,* p. 439.

138 *"Let's not be mealy-mouthed"*: Abels, *Out of the Jaws of Victory,* p. 66.

"We should have notes": Ibid.

"Well, how about Charlie?": Pietrusza, *1948: Harry Truman's Improbable Victory,* p. 180.

"It is the unanimous opinion": "Calif. Governor's Easy Nomination Called Only Real Convention Upset," *Washington Post,* June 26, 1948.

139 *"You're running out on"*: Abels, *Out of the Jaws of Victory,* p. 67.

"If this is to be the": Diary entry of Arthur H. Vandenberg, undated, in Vandenberg, *The Private Papers of Senator Vandenberg,* p. 436.

"We have a dreamboat": Richard Norton Smith, *Thomas E. Dewey and His Times* (New York: Touchstone, 1982), p. 501.

"You will make a great": Tom Warren to Thomas Dewey, June 25, 1948, Thomas E. Dewey Papers, Series 10, Box 44.

140 *"Your victory . . . is practically"*: B. B. Hickenlooper to Thomas Dewey, June 30, 1948, ibid., Series 5, Box 84.

"in the decisive phase of": Michael Burgan, *The Berlin Airlift* (Minneapolis, MN: Compass Point, 2007), p. 25.

"not as serious as indicated": Cabinet Meeting Minutes, June 25, 1948, Matthew Connelly papers, Box 2, Truman archives.

"A very serious situation": Ibid.

141 *"improvised 'airlift'"*: Harry S. Truman, *Memoirs*, vol. 2, *Years of Trial and Hope, 1946–1952* (Garden City, NY: Doubleday, 1956), p. 123.

14. "With God's Help, You Will Win"

142 *"Nothing quite so strange"*: "Thomas L. Stokes: Will 'Ike' Come to the Rescue?," *Atlanta Constitution*, March 30, 1948.

143 *"every seasoned political leader"*: "The Washington Merry-Go-Round: Leaders See Truman Defeated," *Washington Post*, July 7, 1948.

"Doublecrossers all": Diary entry of Harry Truman, July 6, 1948, Post Presidential File, Box 643, Truman archives.

"This job gets worse every": Harry Truman to Bess Truman, July 5, 1947, Papers of Harry S. Truman Pertaining to Family, Business, and Personal Affairs, Box 15.

"I've made my decision": Diary entry of Harry Truman, July 19, 1948, Post Presidential File, Box 643, Truman archives.

"The glum resignation": "Democrats in the Dumps," *Los Angeles Times*, July 1, 1948.

"There never has been anything": "State of the Convention Operation Underdog," *Christian Science Monitor*, July 12, 1948.

144 *"a number two man"*: Diary entry of Harry Truman, July 12, 1948, Post Presidential File, Box 643, Truman archives.

"I stuck my neck all": Diary entry of Eben Ayers, July 13, 1948, in Eben A. Ayers, *Truman in the White House: The Diary of Eben A. Ayers* (Columbia: University of Missouri Press, 1991), pp. 265–66.

"Why do they hate me": "The Washington Merry-Go-Round: A Lonely Man Meditates on Hate," *Washington Post*, August 8, 1948.

"This election can only be": "Memorandum: Should the President Call Congress Back?," June 29, 1948, Clark Clifford papers, Box 33, Truman archives.

146 *"He said he had made"*: Diary entry of Eben Ayers, July 13, 1948, in Ayers, *Truman in the White House*, pp. 265–66.

"As . . . we started to": Ibid.

"you couldn't have gotten": Oral History Interview with Brigadier General Louis H. Renfrow (transcript), 1971, Oral History Interviews, Truman archives, p. 85.

"many things: politics, trivia": Alben W. Barkley, *That Reminds Me* (Garden City, NY: Doubleday, 1954), p. 203.

147 *"It seemed like almost"*: Oral History Interview with Robert G. Nixon (transcript), 1970, Oral History Interviews, Truman archives, p. 571.

"The south is no longer": "11 States Support Georgian," *Atlanta Constitution*, July 15, 1948.

"Mississippi has gone": "Truman and Barkley Nominated; Two Dixie Delegations Walk Out," *Los Angeles Times*, July 15, 1948.

"He can't win": "Truman Calls Congress in GOP Dare," *Atlanta Constitution*, July 15, 1948.

"Our fight is the fight": "Delegates Look for Spectacle and Find One," *Chicago Daily Tribune*, July 15, 1948.

"A live donkey was led": "Confederate Flag Waves as South Names Russell," *Los Angeles Times*, July 15, 1948.

148 *"We may well be watching"*: "Washington Calling: Democratic Break-up?," *Washington Post*, March 9, 1948.

"Thank you, thank you": "Acceptance Speech of the President at the Democratic National

Convention, Convention Hall, Philadelphia, Pennsylvania, July 15, 1948," Public Papers, Truman archives, https://www.trumanlibrary.gov/library/research-files/presidents-acceptance-speech. See also "1948 Truman DNC Acceptance Speech," YouTube video, https://www.youtube.com/watch?v=k-7kpqhnXHE.

"The delegates that evening": Oral History Interview with David C. Bell (transcript), 1968, Oral History Interviews, Truman archives, p. 54.

"I can't tell you how": "Acceptance Speech of the President at the Democratic National Convention, Convention Hall, Philadelphia, Pennsylvania, July 15, 1948," Truman archives.

149 *"I meant just that"*: Harry S. Truman, *Memoirs,* vol. 2, p. 207.

"It was one of the most": Oral History Interview with Max Lowenthal (transcript), 1967, Oral History Interviews, Truman archives, p. 97.

"I never in all my life": Oral History Interview with Tom L. Evans (transcript), 1963, Oral History Interviews, Truman archives, p. 512.

150 *"Everybody jumped up"*: Oral History Interview with Frank K. Kelly (transcript), 1988, Oral History Interviews, Truman archives, p. 48.

151 *"Get those goddamned"*: Zachary Karabell, *The Last Campaign: How Harry Truman Won the 1948 Election* (New York: Alfred A. Knopf, 2000), p. 151.

"I remember vividly all": Oral History Interview with Neale Roach (transcript), 1969, Oral History Interviews, Truman archives, p. 41.

"What do you want him": Joe Martin, *My First Fifty Years in Politics* (New York: McGraw-Hill, 1960), p. 188.

"Arrived in Washington at": Diary entry of Harry Truman, July 15, 1948, Post Presidential File, Box 643, Truman archives.

"Good morning, Fields": Dialogue from *Alonzo Fields: My 21 Years in the White House* (New York: Coward-McCann, 1961), p. 145.

15. "What Is at Stake Here Is the Very Survival of Western Civilization"

153 *"The president was chipper"*: Diary entry of James Forrestal, July 15, 1948, in Forrestal, *The Forrestal Diaries,* edited by Walter Millis (New York: Viking, 1951), p. 458.

"I would have done": Ibid.

154 *"serious question as to the"*: Ibid.

"to have some dashing lieutenant": Ibid.

"I don't think we ought": Diary entry of David Lilienthal, July 21, 1948, in *The Journals of David E. Lilienthal,* vol. 2, *The Atomic Energy Years 1945–1950* (New York: Harper & Row, 1964), p. 391.

"it is estimated that the": "Memorandum for the President: Estimate of the Status of the Russian Atomic Energy Project," July 6, 1948, Central Intelligence Agency, President's Secretary's Files, Box 213, Truman archives.

155 *"The position of the present"*: "The Current Situation in China," July 22, 1948, Central Intelligence Agency report, President's Secretary's Files, Box 177, Truman archives.

"We'll stay in Berlin": Diary entry of Harry Truman, July 19, 1948, Post-Presidential File, Box 643, Truman archives.

156 *"The atmosphere in Washington"*: "Prewar Atmosphere in Washington: How War Might Come," *Boston Daily Globe,* March 17, 1948.

"Bob . . . I think we ought": Dialogue is from Irwin Ross, *The Loneliest Campaign: The Truman Victory of 1948* (New York: Signet, 1968), p. 132.

157 *"It is the act of a"*: "GOP Sees Politics in Congress Call," *New York Times*, July 16, 1948.
"The Constitution says that the": Robert Taft, "Radio Address: The Special Session and Prices," July 28, 1948, in *The Papers of Robert A. Taft*, edited by Clarence E. Wunderlin Jr., vol. 3, *1945–1948* (Kent, OH: Kent State University, 2003), pp. 447–48.
"The Special Session is a": Smith, *Thomas E. Dewey*, p. 505.

158 *"In Berlin we must not"*: "Text of Press Conference with Governor Thomas E. Dewey, July 21, at Pawling, New York (During Meeting with General Eisenhower)" (Note: title seems to be dated incorrectly). Rare Books, Special Collections, and Preservation, River Campus Libraries, University of Rochester.
"I have not identified myself": Ibid.

159 *"I want to tell you, ladies"*: Jack Bass and Marilyn W. Thompson, *Strom: The Complicated Personal and Political Life of Strom Thurmond* (New York: Public Affairs, 2005), p. 117. A clip from Thurmond's States' Rights Democratic Party acceptance speech is at "Strom Thurmond's Dixiecrat Days Newsreel," YouTube video, https://www.youtube.com/watch?v=emSihCBR3XY.

160 *"If we throw the election"*: "Thurmond and Wright Head Dixie Rights Ticket," *Atlanta Constitution*, July 18, 1948.
"In Philadelphia, a definite": Ibid.
"a riotous rebel convention": Ibid.
"too moderate": "J. B. Stoner: The Symbol of a Bygone Era of Hate—Or Is He?" *Atlanta Constitution*, October 1, 1977.

161 *"declaration of principles"*: "Southern Declaration of Principles," *Hartford Courant*, July 18, 1948.
"We stand for the segregation": Ibid.
"I agree, but Truman": Abels, *Out of the Jaws of Victory*, p. 84.
"not interested one whit": Joseph Crespino, *Strom Thurmond's America* (New York: Hill and Wang, 2012), p. 72.
"All your high-flown": Alfred Steinberg, *Sam Rayburn: A Biography* (New York: Hawthorn, 1975), p. 240.
"The president has gone too": Bass and Thompson, *Strom*, p. 108.

162 *"monstrous frame-up"*: "Leading U.S. Reds Arrested," *Boston Daily Globe*, July 21, 1948.
"The American people can now": "Wallace Hits Impression He Is in Communist Grip," *Christian Science Monitor*, July 21, 1948.
"So you can save your breath": Thomas W. Devine, *Henry Wallace's 1948 Presidential Campaign and the Future of Postwar Liberalism* (Chapel Hill: University of North Carolina Press, 2013), p. 129.
"Have you ever repudiated": Abels, *Out of the Jaws of Victory*, p. 115.
"A tense, terrible silence": John C. Culver and John Hyde, *American Dreamer: The Life and Times of Henry A. Wallace* (New York: W. W. Norton, 2000), p. 483.
"I never discuss Westbrook": Dialogue is recounted in both ibid., p. 483, and Abels, *Out of the Jaws of Victory*, p. 115.

163 *"The American press had one"*: "Wallace's Gag Gives Newsmen a Shining Hour," *Chicago Daily Tribune*, July 24, 1948.
"corruption . . . betrayal . . . murder": "It's Wallace or War, Says Keynoter for New Party," *Washington Post*, July 24, 1948.

164 *"birth of a new party"*: "Wallace Party Launched in Philadelphia," *Hartford Courant*, July 24, 1948.
"Berlin did not happen": "Text of Henry Wallace's Acceptance of Presidential Nomination," *Washington Post*, July 25, 1948.

"To make that dream": Ibid.
"almost fanatical enthusiasm": "Revival Fervor Hails Nominees," *New York Times,* July 25, 1948.
"One, two, three, four": Ibid.
"I'd say they have a good": Devine, *Henry Wallace's 1948 Presidential Campaign,* p. 45.
165 *"Nobody can stop them"*: Curtis Daniel MacDougall, *Gideon's Army,* vol. 1 (New York: Marzani & Munsell, 1965), p. 504.
"It will remain a thing of awe": Culver and Hyde, *American Dreamer,* p. 488.

16. "A Profound Sense of What's Right and What's Wrong"

169 *"The prices of food products"*: The Council of Economic Advisors to the President, "The Government's Anti-Inflation Program," July 19, 1948, Truman archives, https://www.trumanlibrary.gov/library/research-files/council-economic-advisors-harry-s-truman.
170 *"stirred up the greatest biological"*: "Report on Kinsey," *Life,* August 2, 1948.
171 *"You can now summon"*: Advertisement for Otis Electronic Signal Control, *Business Week,* July 10, 1948.
"As television grows on an": "TV to Alter U.S. As Much As Model T," *Chicago Daily Tribune,* August 1, 1948.
"The political figures who": Jules Abels, *Out of the Jaws of Victory: The Astounding Election of 1948* (New York: Henry Holt, 1959), p. 82.
172 *"The lack of money in the"*: Margaret Truman, *Harry S. Truman* (New York: Morrow, 1973), p. 20.
"Our governmental house": All the quotes in this paragraph from "GOP Quotes Democrats That Truman Can't Win," *Los Angeles Times,* July 18, 1948.
"My brother Vivian": Diary entry of Harry Truman, August 2, 1948, Post Presidential File, Box 643, Truman archives.
"I would like to take this": Thomas C. Buchanan to Philip Mathews, June 24, 1948, William M. Boyle Jr. Papers, Box 3, Truman archives.
173 *"The greatest ambition Harry"*: Irwin Ross, *The Loneliest Campaign: The Truman Victory of 1948* (New York: Signet, 1968), p. 18.
"We are going to win": Margaret Truman, *Harry S. Truman,* p. 5.
"The situation isn't as bad": Jack Redding, *Inside the Democratic Party* (New York: Bobbs-Merrill, 1958), p. 263.
"It's all so futile": Harry Truman to Mary Jane Truman, July 26, 1948, Papers of Harry S. Truman Pertaining to Family, Business, and Personal Affairs, Box 20.
"I'm going to make it a": George McKee Elsey, *An Unplanned Life: A Memoir by George McKee Elsey* (Columbia: University of Missouri Press, 2005), p. 167.
174 *"We would meet at six"*: Oral History Interview with Oscar R. Ewing (transcript), 1969, Oral History Interviews, Truman archives, p. 131.
"I was their link with": Oral History Interview with Clark M. Clifford (transcript), 1971, Oral History Interviews, Truman archives, p. 190.
"White House Wonder": "White House Wonder," *Los Angeles Times,* June 22, 1947.
"Capital's Golden Boy": Ibid.
175 *"Every morning when I"*: Oral History Interview with Neale Roach (transcript), 1969, Oral History Interviews, Truman archives, p. 48.
"The pressure was increasingly": Redding, *Inside the Democratic Party,* p. 65.
"Meetings were held at the": Ibid., pp. 164–65.

176 *"I didn't come here"*: Ibid., pp. 169–70.
"Come back!": Ibid.
177 *"They asked me to go up"*: Oral History Interview with William L. Batt Jr. (transcript), 1966, Oral History Interviews, Truman archives, pp. 3–4.
"miserably noisy": Ibid., p. 4.
"We had been told right at": Oral History Interview with Dr. Johannes Hoeber (transcript), 1966, Oral History Interviews, Truman archives, p. 10.
"we lived, literally": Ibid., pp. 47–48.
"his courage, his coolness": William L. Batt Jr. to Clark Clifford, July 22, 1948, Clark M. Clifford Papers, Box 21, Truman archives.
178 *"My gosh . . . Nash is away"*: Oral History Interview with Philleo Nash (transcript), 1966, Oral History Interviews, Truman archives, p. 346.
"jumped on the night train": Ibid., p. 347.
179 *"fair employment practices"*: Executive Order 9980, Executive Orders, Truman archives, https://www.trumanlibrary.gov/library/executive-orders/9980/executive-order-9980.
"caught almost everyone off": Clark Clifford, with Richard Holbrooke, *Counsel to the President: A Memoir* (New York: Random House, 1991), p. 211.
"I believe that it is necessary": "Message to the Special Session of the 80th Congress," July 27, 1948, Public Papers, Truman archives, https://www.trumanlibrary.gov/library/public-papers/165/message-special-session-80th-congress.
"I think he was motivated by": Oral History Interviews with Charles S. Murphy, 1963, 1969–70 (transcript), Oral History Interviews, Truman archives, pp. 227–28.
"All I can say is that I'm sure": Ibid.
180 *"Would you say it was a"*: Transcript of the President's News Conference, August 12, 1948, Public Papers, Truman archives, https://www.trumanlibrary.gov/library/public-papers/174/presidents-news-conference.
"I felt justified in calling the": Harry S. Truman, *Memoirs,* vol. 2, *Years of Trial and Hope, 1946–1952* (Garden City, NY: Doubleday, 1956), p. 208.
"a petulant Ajax from": "National Affairs: Turnip Day Session," *Time,* July 26, 1948.
"the most expensive advertising": "Expensive Promotion for Turnips," *Atlanta Constitution,* August 10, 1948.
"They sure are in a stew": Harry Truman to Bess Truman, July 23, 1948, Papers of Harry S. Truman Pertaining to Family, Business, and Personal Affairs, Box 16, Truman archives.

17. *"What Exciting Times You Are Having!"*

181 *"I am having a 'holiday'"*: Thomas Dewey to Winston Churchill, July 12, 1948, Thomas E. Dewey Papers, Series 10, Box 8, Rare Books, Special Collections, and Preservation, River Campus Libraries, University of Rochester.
"principal innovations in": "Governor Dewey's Dairy Farm," ibid., Series 2, Box 117.
"What exciting times you are": Winston Churchill to Thomas Dewey, June 16, 1948, ibid., Series 10, Box 8.
182 *"Help sweep the nation clean"*: Election memorabilia and correspondence, ibid., Series 2, Box 39.
"We believe that it will": Ibid.
"Dewey Will Do It": Election memorabilia from ibid.

"Well . . . this will come as": Richard Norton Smith, *Thomas E. Dewey and His Times* (New York: Touchstone, 1982), p. 515.

183 *"which not even Goebbels would"*: "Text of Dewey Speech," *Hartford Courant*, September 26, 1944.

"That's the worst speech": Smith, *Thomas E. Dewey*, p. 515.

"This campaign will be different": Abels, *Out of the Jaws of Victory*, p. 146.

184 *"Can you tell us when you"*: Transcript of Dewey Press Conference, Thomas E. Dewey Papers, Series 2, Box 117.

"the slightest mismanagement": "Berlin Crisis a Powder Keg, Dewey Says," *Washington Post*, July 22, 1948.

"thoroughly competent grasp of": On-camera interview with Senator Arthur Vandenberg, *The Dewey Story*, YouTube video, https://www.youtube.com/watch?v=ozJFbowKWD8.

185 *"Why shouldn't we have"*: Thomas Dewey to Herbert Brownell, August 23, 1948, Thomas E. Dewey Papers, Series 10, Box 6.

186 *"Why does the Republican Committee"*: Quotes in Ben Duffy to Herbert Brownell, August 25, 1948, ibid., Series 10, Box 6.

"Why doesn't Dewey answer": Abels, *Out of the Jaws of Victory*, p. 170.

"I'm the man who beat": Ibid., p. 171.

18. "As for Me, I Intend to Fight!"

187 *"the results in civil strife"*: "Thurmond Warns of Rights Strife," *New York Times*, August 1, 1948.

"a virtual revolution in the": Ibid.

"The South's fight is not": Strom Thurmond to Thomas Dewey, April 13, 1948, Thomas E. Dewey Papers, Series 5, Box 189.

188 *"Governor Thurmond is a"*: Director, FBI, SAC, Savannah to J. Edgar Hoover, October 14, 1948, FBI file of Strom Thurmond.

189 *"The struggle in which we were"*: Jack Bass and Marilyn W. Thompson, *Strom: The Complicated Personal and Political Life of Strom Thurmond* (New York: Public Affairs, 2005), p. 15.

"Every Democrat must feel": Ibid.

190 *"He was my idol"*: Joseph Crespino, *Strom Thurmond's America* (New York: Hill and Wang, 2012), p. 18.

"What do you want?": Dialogue from Bass and Thompson, *Strom*, p. 19.

191 *"Men were stacked up"*: Bass and Thompson, *Strom*, p. 73.

192 *"The United States is a constitutional"*: Hans Kelsen, *General Theory of Law and State*, vol. 1 (New Brunswick, NJ: Transaction, 2009), p. 295n.

193 *"We will have done"*: Walter Francis White, *A Man Called White: The Autobiography of Walter White* (Athens: University of Georgia Press, 1995), p. 90.

"For too many years": Nadine Cohodas, *Strom Thurmond and the Politics of Southern Change* (Macon, GA: Mercer University Press, 1994), p. 116.

"Why I thought the world": Essie Mae Washington-Williams, with William Stadiem, *Dear Senator: A Memoir by the Daughter of Strom Thurmond* (New York: Regan Books, 2005), p. 108.

194 *"I knew they meant business"*: "Trigger Man Identified as R.C. Hurd, 45," *Atlanta Daily World*, May 15, 1947.

"Lord, you done killed me": "Statements Accuse S.C. Taxi Driver of 'Execution' in Mass Lynch Trial," *Atlanta Constitution,* May 15, 1947.

195 *"At least in that part"*: "Lynch Verdict," *Washington Post,* May 23, 1947.

19. "They Are Simply a 'Red Herring'"

197 *"Tom, when you get to the"*: Robert J. Donovan, *Conflict and Crisis: The Presidency of Harry S. Truman, 1945–1948* (Columbia: University of Missouri Press, 1996), p. 413.

198 *"Miss Bentley . . . please"*: Dialogue from *Hearings Before the Committee on Legislation of the Committee on Un-American Activities: House of Representatives, Eightieth Congress, Second Session on H.R. 4422 and H.R. 4581* (Washington, DC: Government Printing Office, 1948).

199 *"the insidious evil"*: Ibid.

"A ripple of surprise went through": Richard Nixon, *RN: The Memoirs of Richard Nixon* (New York: Touchstone, 1990), p. 53.

200 *"Smearing good people like"*: Robert W. Lee, *The United Nations Conspiracy* (Appleton, WI: Western Islands, 1981), p. 15.

"I am here at my own": *Hearings Before the Committee on Legislation of the Committee on Un-American Activities,* Second Session on H.R. 442-2 and H.R. 4581.

"High prices are not taking": Eleanor Roosevelt, "My Day," July 31, 1948, Eleanor Roosevelt Collection, Digital Edition, George Washington University, https://www2.gwu.edu/~erpapers/myday/displaydoc.cfm?_y=1948&_f=md001033.

201 *"There is still time for the"*: Dialogue from transcript of the President's News Conference, August 5, 1948, Public Papers, Truman archives, https://www.trumanlibrary.gov/library/public-papers/170/presidents-news-conference.

202 *"The President simply had"*: Oral History Interview with Robert G. Nixon (transcript), 1970, Oral History Interviews, Truman archives, p. 413.

"treasonable in spirit": "Truman's Remark Attacked by Macy," *New York Times,* August 15, 1948.

"puerile whim-wham": "Mencken Meditates on the Red Spy Hunt," *Los Angeles Times,* August 15, 1948.

"shocked . . . seeming to cover up": "Dewey Arranging Trans-US Drive," *New York Times,* August 13, 1948.

"The trend of presidential": "Impeachment of President Raised in Ferguson Speech," *New York Times,* August 8, 1948.

203 *"You have that much confidence?"*: Nixon, *RN: The Memoirs of Richard Nixon,* p. 56.

"Neither a man nor a crowd": Bertrand Russell, *Unpopular Essays* (New York: Routledge, 1995), pp. 121–22.

"In different ages there have": "Communism Is the Greatest Internal Security Threat at This Time," A Report to the National Security Council, August 6, 1948, President's Secretary's Files, Box 178, Truman archives.

204 *"If there turned out to be"*: Nixon, *RN: The Memoirs of Richard Nixon,* p. 56.

"There's no question about it": Ibid., p. 57.

"Red Activity Looms Big": "Red Activity Looms Big in Campaign," *Chicago Daily Tribune,* August 16, 1948.

205 *"Watch your step with this one"*: John J. Abt, with Michael Myerson, *Advocate and Activist: Memoirs of an American Communist Lawyer* (Chicago: University of Illinois Press, 1993), p. 152.

"It was clear that these": Ibid., p. 151.

"a shameful circus": "Think Alikes," *Chicago Daily Tribune*, August 19, 1948.

"civil rights, inflation, housing": "Pressman Sees Inquiry a 'Shameful Circus,'" *Washington Post*, August 5, 1948.

"If I had my way about": "Send Reds to Russia, Wallace at Head, Says Georgia Judge," *Boston Daily Globe*, August 8, 1948.

206 *"I don't think any person"*: Oral history of Charles "Beanie" Baldwin, Columbia University Rare Book & Manuscript Library, p. 20.

"This meant I had to stay": Oral history of Henry A. Wallace, Columbia University Rare Book & Manuscript Library, p. 5123.

"We must learn from Jesus": "Wallace Tours South; Urges Dixie Subsidies," *Chicago Daily Tribune*, August 30, 1948.

"Hey, Joe Stalin is looking . . . Why don't you go": Ibid.

SEND WALLACE BACK TO RUSSIA: "Wallace Durham Rally Protested by Vet Group," *Atlanta Constitution*, August 30, 1948.

207 *"They continually shouted"*: Oral history of Henry A. Wallace, Columbia University Rare Book & Manuscript Library, p. 5123.

"Please sit down!": "Boos Greet Wallace's Dixie Aid," *Atlanta Constitution*, August 29, 1948.

"Don't you think we ought": Oral history of Henry A. Wallace, Columbia University Rare Book & Manuscript Library, p. 5124.

"I would like to see some": "Pelt Wallace with Eggs on His Dixie Tour," *Chicago Daily Tribune*, August 31, 1947.

SELL YOUR JUNK IN MOSCOW: "Wallace Again Bombarded in Speech Making Efforts," *Los Angeles Times*, September 1, 1948.

208 *"I believe there are people"*: "Wallace Continues March Through Southern Boos," *Christian Science Monitor*, August 31, 1948.

"Get out of town!": John C. Culver and John Hyde, *American Dreamer: The Life and Times of Henry A. Wallace* (New York: W. W. Norton, 2000), p. 493.

"the greatest blow against": "When Wallace Comes a-Preaching, the Southern Sees Red," *Boston Daily Globe*, September 5, 1948.

"As the direct result of": Thomas W. Devine, *Henry Wallace's 1948 Presidential Campaign and the Future of Postwar Liberalism* (Chapel Hill: University of North Carolina Press, 2013), p. 260.

"human hate in the raw": Oral history of Henry A. Wallace, Columbia University Rare Book & Manuscript Library, p. 5123.

20. *"There Is Great Danger Ahead"*

209 *"The White House Architect and"*: Diary entry of Harry Truman, August 3, 1948, Post Presidential File, Box 643, Truman archives.

"Margaret's sitting room floor": Harry Truman to Mary Jane Truman, August 10, 1948, Papers of Harry S. Truman Pertaining to Family, Business, and Personal Affairs, Box 20, Truman archives.

"Can you imagine what": Robert Klara, *The Hidden White House: Harry Truman and the Reconstruction of America's Most Famous Residence* (New York: Thomas Dunne, 2013), p. 66.

210 *"In the intimacy of the ship"*: Elsey, *An Unplanned Life*, p. 145.

"The situation is becoming": "Memorandum for the President: Relief for Arab and Jewish Refugees in the Near East," undated, Clark Clifford papers, Box 13, Truman archives.

211 *"We have said 'no' and we"*: Ann Tusa and John Tusa, *The Berlin Airlift* (New York: Atheneum, 1988), pp. 222–23.

"immediate use": James Forrestal, *The Forrestal Diaries*, edited by Walter Millis (New York: Viking, 1951), p. 478.

212 *"Do you think so?"*: Abels, *Out of the Jaws of Victory*, p. 163.

"I'd be much better off": Harry Truman to Mary Jane Truman, September 2, 1948, Papers of Harry S. Truman Pertaining to Family, Business, and Personal Affairs, Box 20, Truman archives.

The Ferdinand Magellan *was the only:* Much of the description of this train car comes from photographs on the Harry S. Truman Library & Museum website, such as this one, of the dining compartment: https://www.trumanlibrary.gov/photograph-records/68-1588.

213 *"I lived in a little tiny"*: Oral History Interview with Clark M. Clifford (transcript), 1971, Oral History Interviews, Truman archives, p. 272.

"I was armed with briefcases": Elsey, *An Unplanned Life*, p. 166.

"I worked at it night and": Oral History Interview with Charles S. Murphy, Truman archives, pp. 133–40.

214 *"He was on his own five-yard"*: Oral History Interview with Clark M. Clifford, Truman archives, p. 246.

"My, what a wonderful crowd": Rear Platform and Other Informal Remarks in Michigan and Ohio, September 6, 1948, Public Papers, Truman archives, https://www.trumanlibrary.gov/library/public-papers/183/rear-platform-and-other-informal-remarks-michigan-and-ohio.

"The record proves conclusively": Ibid.

215 *Truman was ushered into a special:* Detailed schedules and arrangements for Truman's campaign stops can be found in the Truman archives; the descriptions of the Grand Rapids campaign stop come from "Trip of the President to Grand Rapids, Lansing, Detroit, Pontiac, and Flint, Michigan," Clark Clifford Papers, Box 33.

"the first major crisis": Margaret Truman, *Harry S. Truman* (New York: Morrow, 1973), p. 20.

"Well, that broadcast is": Oral History Interview with Matthew J. Connelly, Truman archives, p. 287.

216 *"As you know . . . I speak"*: Labor Day Address in Cadillac Square, Detroit, September 6, 1948, Public Papers, Truman archives, https://www.trumanlibrary.gov/library/public-papers/184/labor-day-address-cadillac-square-detroit.

"Along the highway from": Oral History Interview with Matthew J. Connelly, Truman archives, p. 287.

"A President can always bring": Oral History Interview with Jack L. Bell (transcript), 1971, Oral History Interviews, Truman archives, p. 55.

21. *"The All-Time Georgia Champion of 'White Supremacy'"*

218 *"Yesterday in Detroit . . . the American"*: "Test of Stassen's Reply to Truman," *Los Angeles Times*, September 8, 1948.

"the inflationary spiral": Ibid.

219 *"He said he listened to the speech"*: "Dewey Compliments Stassen," *New York Times*, September 8, 1948.

"the all-time Georgia champion": "The Southeast: Klan Openly Backs Talmadge in Georgia Campaign," *New York Times,* August 15, 1948.
"Wise Negroes . . . will stay away": "FBI Probes Georgia Primary As Talmadge 'Warns' Negroes," *Christian Science Monitor,* July 15, 1946.
220 *"We're going to have white"*: "White Supremacy In Peace or By Force—Talmadge," *Chicago Defender,* August 14, 1948.
"I guess I voted for": "Bullets and Ballot Boxes: The Isaiah Nixon Story," Georgia Civil Rights Cold Cases Project at Emory University (Note: this article cites FBI documents), https://coldcases.emory.edu/bullets-and-ballot-boxes-the-isaiah-nixon-story/#_ftn23.
221 *"Fall, Isaiah, fall!"*: Ibid.
"Herman Talmadge's victory in": "Talmadge Victory Boost for Dixiecrats," *Atlanta Constitution,* September 12, 1948.
"My mama ain't going": "Election Highlights," *Atlanta Daily World,* November 3, 1948.
"a weird combination of the": "Rally Combines Revival, Song-Fest," *New York Times,* September 11, 1948.
222 *SAFEGUARD FREEDOM:* Ibid.
"I can tell you a lot of things": Ibid.
"They can call us Reds": "48,000 Hear Wallace Assert Prejudice Will Fail in South," *New York Times,* September 11, 1948.
"This is a great American": "Text of Wallace's Speech at Yankee Stadium," *New York Times,* September 11, 1948.
"We must work": Ibid.

22. *"We're Going to Give 'Em Hell"*

223 *"that he prayed that he would never"*: Diary entry of James Forrestal, September 13, 1948, in *The Forrestal Diaries,* p. 487.
"The situation in Berlin is bad": Diary entry of David Lilienthal, September 13, 1948, *The Journals of David E. Lilienthal,* vol. 2, *The Atomic Energy Years 1945–1950* (New York: Harper & Row, 1964), p. 406.
224 *"I am appealing to you for"*: "Washington Merry-Go-Round: Democrats Hunt Down Money," *Washington Post,* September 18, 1948.
"Mr. Truman looked pathetic": Ibid.
"I have a terrible feeling": Diary entry of Harry Truman, September 13, 1948, Post Presidential File, Box 643, Truman archives.
"I think I am going to mow 'em": Numerous accounts of this conversation have the wording slightly different. See "Truman Gay as He Starts Western Trip," *Washington Post,* September 18, 1948; Alben W. Barkley, *That Reminds Me* (Garden City, NY: Doubleday, 1954), p. 203; David Pietrusza, *1948: Harry Truman's Improbable Victory and the Year That Transformed America's Role in the World* (New York: Union Square, 2011), p. 344.
"Daddy, you shouldn't say": Barkley, *That Reminds Me,* p. 203.
225 *"I don't think I have ever seen"*: Rear Platform and Other Informal Remarks in Illinois, Iowa, and Missouri, September 18, 1948, Public Papers, Truman archives, https://www.trumanlibrary.gov/library/public-papers/194/rear-platform-and-other-informal-remarks-illinois-iowa-and-missouri.
"Well, those people had to": William Bray, "Recollections of the 1948 Campaign," Clark Clifford papers, Box 22, Truman archives. Also: Research Files, 1948 Election Campaign

Collection, Truman archives, https://www.trumanlibrary.gov/library/research-files/recollections-1948-campaign-william-j-bray.

"It is fascinating": Diary entry of Margaret Truman, September 17, 1948, Margaret Truman Daniel and E. Clifton Daniel Papers, Box 14, Truman archives.

"Going across the country": Oral History Interviews with John P. McEnery (transcript), 1970, Oral History Interviews, Truman archives, p. 94.

226 *"It was like a traveling circus"*: Oral History Interview with Richard L. Strout (transcript), 1971, Oral History Interviews, Truman archives, p. 7.

"Nothing in the world is": "Calling Washington: Strange Ritual," *Washington Post,* October 2, 1948.

"The most important function": Oral History Interview with Clark M. Clifford (transcript), Truman archives, p. 275.

"As an advance man": Oral History Interview with Oscar L. Chapman (transcript), 1972, Oral History Interviews, Truman archives, p. 113.

"They worked like dogs and": Oral History Interview with George M. Elsey, Truman archives, p. 63.

227 *"When [Truman] would come into"*: Oral History Interview with Clark M. Clifford, Truman archives, p. 274.

"He didn't have time between": Oral History Interview with Charles S. Murphy, Truman archives, p. 9.

"we developed a pattern for": Clifford, *Counsel to the President,* p. 227.

"We'd bring the rope up and": Oral History Interview with Floyd M. Boring (transcript), 1988, Oral History Interviews, Truman archives, p. 50.

228 *"You guys let me down"*: Oral History Interview with George Tames (transcript), 1980, Oral History Interviews, Truman archives, p. 12.

"Come on, boys . . . you have": Ibid.

"Despite Mrs. Truman's reserve": Elsey, *An Unplanned Life,* p. 169.

"If it had been left to your": Margaret Truman, *Bess W. Truman* (New York: Macmillan, 1986), p. 298.

229 *"wasn't trying to run the world"*: Oral History Interview with Oscar L. Chapman, Truman archives, p. 121.

"The interest the public takes": "Margaret Truman, Career Girl," *New York Times,* September 8, 1946.

"Now don't get scared": David McCullough, *Truman* (New York: Simon & Schuster, 1992), p. 567.

230 Pepsodent Hour with Bob Hope: Correspondence regarding Ms. Truman's singing invitations are in Margaret Truman Papers, Box 5, Truman archives.

"my greatest asset": Ken Hechler, *Working with Truman: A Personal Memoir of the White House Years* (New York: G. P. Putnam's Sons, 1982), p. 266.

"Where is Margaret?": "Truman Gay as He Starts Western Trip," *Washington Post,* September 18, 1948.

"the Odyssey of the 'everyday'": Jonathan Daniels, *The Man of Independence* (Port Washington, NY: Kennikat, 1971), p. 9.

"Hardly any other President": Ibid., p. 19.

"Judging by his appearance": Donovan, *Conflict and Crisis,* p. 4. (Note: Donovan was a political reporter on the campaign trail in 1948.)

"He had a tremendous veneration": Oral History Interview with George M. Elsey (transcript), Truman archives, p. 33.

"You know the issues in": Rear Platform and Other Informal Remarks in Illinois, Iowa, and Missouri, September 18, 1948, Public Papers, Truman archives, https://www.trumanlibrary.gov/library/public-papers/194/rear-platform-and-other-informal-remarks-illinois-iowa-and-missouri.

231 *"While I knew that the"*: Harry S. Truman, *Memoirs,* vol. 2, p. 209.

"This was another blistering": Oral History Interview with Robert G. Nixon (transcript), 1970, Oral History Interviews, Truman archives, p. 624.

232 *"You know farmers tend"*: Oral History Interview with Leonard Miall (transcript), 1964, Oral History Interviews, Truman archives, p. 47.

"I have my own airplane": Oral History Interview with Robert G. Nixon (transcript), Truman archives, p. 626.

"Now the farmers need such": Address at Dexter, Iowa, on the Occasion of the National Plowing Contest, September 18, 1948, Public Papers, Truman archives, https://www.trumanlibrary.gov/library/public-papers/195/address-dexter-iowa-occasion-national-plowing-match.

233 *"There was not much of a"*: Oral History Interview with James J. Rowley (transcript), 1988, Oral History Interviews, Truman archives, p. 50.

23. *"The Presidency of the United States Is Not for Sale!"*

234 *"the most intensive in the modern"*: "Intensive Tour Set for Dewey," *Boston Daily Globe,* September 16, 1948.

"The FBI helped Dewey during": McCullough, *Truman,* p. 673.

235 *"the most news-covered"*: "State of the Nation Dewey Train Doesn't Muffle Its Whistle," *Christian Science Monitor,* September 21, 1948.

"as momentous as any which": "Matter of Fact: Nothing Succeeds Like Success," *Hartford Courant,* September 22, 1948.

"spoke with special": "Dewey and Truman: The Contrast in Iowa," *Los Angeles Times,* September 23, 1948.

"Caravans from out in the state": "Nothing Succeeds like Success," *Washington Post,* September 22, 1948.

236 *"Tonight we enter upon"*: "Dewey's Opening Speech: Republican Candidate Expounds Philosophy and Aims," *Washington Post,* September 21, 1948.

"the unity that binds us together": "Dewey Urges Firm Foreign Policy by U.S.," *Boston Daily Globe,* September 22, 1948.

"unity among our people": "Text of Dewey Speech," *Boston Daily Globe,* September 23, 1948.

"spoke the language of Robespierre": "Dewey and Truman — Contrast in Iowa," *Los Angeles Times,* September 23, 1948.

237 *"You really have to get to know"*: Robert Schnakenberg, *Distory: A Treasury of Historical Insults* (New York: St. Martin's Press, 2004), p. 70.

"The Truman show was threadbare": "Matter of Fact: Nothing Succeeds Like Success," *Hartford Courant,* September 22, 1948.

"Life begins at nine o'clock": Frank McNaughton to Don Bermingham, "Dewey XXI — Campaign Train," October 1, 1948, 1948 Election Campaign Collection, Truman archives, https://www.trumanlibrary.gov/library/research-files/frank-mcnaughton-don-bermingham-dewey-xxi-campaign-train.

238 *"And now, I want to introduce"*: Numerous examples found in Series 2, Box 117, Thomas E. Dewey Papers, Rare Books, Special Collections, and Preservation, River Campus Libraries, University of Rochester.

"Things are looking good": Barak Mattingly to Thomas Dewey, April 26, 1948, Thomas E. Dewey Papers, Series 10, Box 28.

"I had hoped": "Thurmond Headed Here for Press Talk," *Washington Post*, September 29, 1948.

"the white man's party": Joseph Crespino, *Strom Thurmond's America* (New York: Hill and Wang, 2012), p. 73.

"The Democratic South finally": "Truman Hit in Tennessee: Nashville Paper Comes Out for States Rights Ticket," *New York Times*, September 18, 1948.

239 *"the Southern Democratic Revolt"*: "Analysis of the Southern Democratic Bolt," undated, Research Files, 1948 Election Campaign collection, Truman archives, https://www.trumanlibrary.gov/library/research-files/memo-analysis-southern-democratic-revolt.

"the Republicans [have] an excellent": Ibid.

"A grass roots sentiment against": Ibid.

240 *"spreading like wildfire . . . dishonest"*: "Rivals Branded as 'Traitorous' by Thurmond," *Washington Post*, October 2, 1948.

"In their traitorous bids": Ibid.

"All agree that the Russians": "False War Scares Seen by Wallace," *New York Times*, September 18, 1948.

WHY NOT CONDEMN RUSSIAN: Photographs in "Old Parties Leading Us to War, Wallace Says," *Boston Daily Globe*, September 19, 1948.

241 *"enemies"*: "Wallace Marks 60th Birthday with Attack on Administration for Activities Outside U.S.," *Washington Post*, October 8, 1948.

"Their real intention is to": Ibid.

"live in history as the worst": "Progressives Plan to Boost Radio Speeches by Wallace," *Christian Science Monitor*, October 12, 1948.

"Wallace did not come without": Abt, *Advocate and Activist*, p. 147.

"to talk about the emanations": Ibid.

"Of course. Didn't you": Ibid.

242 *"It could reasonably be"*: Devine, *Henry Wallace's 1948 Presidential Campaign*, p. 154.

"There was no secret about": Abt, *Advocate and Activist*, p. 165.

"Why shouldn't the Communists": Ibid.

"She has always been very": Oral History of Henry A. Wallace, Columbia University Rare Book & Manuscript Library, p. 5142.

"Mrs. Wallace was particularly": Abt, *Advocate and Activist*, p. 154.

243 *"I am now ready . . . to take"*: "A Couple More of the Guru Letters," *Atlanta Constitution*, September 21, 1948.

"I have hard fighting ahead": Ibid.

24. *"You Will Be Choosing a Way of Life for Years to Come"*

244 *"It was a typical Truman family"*: Dialogue from Margaret Truman, *Harry S. Truman* (New York: Morrow, 1973), pp. 1–2.

245 *"We arrived in Denver"*: Diary entry of Margaret Truman, September 20, 1948, Margaret Truman Daniel and E. Clifton Daniel Papers, Box 14, Truman archives.

"Election day this year": Address at the State Capitol in Denver, September 20, 1948, Public Papers, Truman archives, https://www.trumanlibrary.gov/library/public-papers/199/address-state-capitol-denver.

"Today . . . I want to talk": Ibid.

246 *"We shall have to fight"*: Ibid.

"It is difficult to see": "Taking the Campaign to the Lowest Level," *Los Angeles Times*, September 21, 1948.

"Thomas E. Dewey is almost": "Poll Reveals Dewey Holds Wide Lead," *Hartford Courant*, September 9, 1948.

"Nowhere is there any": "The South, Dewey and Truman," *Atlanta Constitution*, September 14, 1948.

"President Harry S. Truman will get": "Big Labor Vote for President Will Not Win Larger States," *New York Times*, October 11, 1948.

"One can reasonably deduce": "Senate Seat Fight Big Worry," *Atlanta Constitution*, September 13, 1948.

247 *"famous divorce city"*: Diary entry of Margaret Truman, September 22, 1948, Margaret Truman Daniel and E. Clifton Daniel Papers, Box 14, Truman archives.

"I was besieged by an attack": Oral History Interview with Clark M. Clifford (transcript), Truman archives, pp. 272–73.

"What weeks of travel can": Margaret Truman, *Souvenir: Margaret Truman's Own Story* (New York: McGraw-Hill, 1956), p. 236.

"When to get our laundry done": Clifford, *Counsel to the President*, p. 227.

"My mother and I love to": Margaret Truman, *Harry S. Truman* (New York: Morrow, 1973), p. 3.

248 *"The thing I remember most"*: Oral History Interview with Jack L. Bell (transcript), Truman archives, p. 67.

"Many of the reporters who": Alfred Steinberg, *The Man from Missouri: The Life and Times of Harry S. Truman* (New York: G. P. Putnam's Sons, 1962), p. 328.

"I'm just telling the truth": George McKee Elsey, *An Unplanned Life: A Memoir by George McKee Elsey* (Columbia: University of Missouri Press, 2005), p. 170.

"We had tremendous crowds": Harry Truman to Mary Jane Truman, October 5, 1948, Papers of Harry S. Truman Pertaining to Family, Business, and Personal Affairs, Box 20, Truman archives.

"I never saw anything in my": Oral History Interview with Robert L. Dennison, 1971 (transcript), Oral History Interviews, Truman archives, pp. 43–44.

"Even after twenty-five years": Oral History Interview with Robert G. Nixon (transcript), Truman archives, p. 948.

249 *"He fought, and fought"*: Oral History Interview with Clark M. Clifford (transcript), Truman archives, p. 327.

"You know, sometimes India": Oral History Interviews with India Edwards (transcript), 1969 and 1975, Oral History Interviews, Truman archives, pp. 48–49.

250 *"It will be extremely difficult"*: "Strategy on Warren," George Elsey Papers, Box 24, Truman archives.

"We were startled when": Oral History Interview with Howard I. McGrath (transcript), Truman archives, p. 23.

"The most significant thing": "Address at Lakeside Park, Oakland, California," September 22, 1948, Public Papers, Truman archives, https://www.trumanlibrary.gov/library/public-papers/203/address-lakeside-park-oakland-california.

251 *"You have got a terrible"*: Rear Platform Remarks in California, (Fresno), September 23, 1948, Public Papers, Truman archives, https://www.trumanlibrary.gov/library/public-papers/204/rear-platform-remarks-california.

"you couldn't put any more in": Oral History Interview with Judge Oliver J. Carter (transcript), 1970, Oral History Interviews, Truman archives, p. 105.

"We want Bogey!": "Searchlight Spectacle Lights Gilmore Stadium," *Los Angeles Times,* September 24, 1948.

"This is a championship fight": "Address at the Gilmore Stadium in Los Angeles," September 23, 1948, Public Papers, Truman archives, https://www.trumanlibrary.gov/library/public-papers/205/address-gilmore-stadium-los-angeles.

252 *"The fact that the Communists"*: Ibid.

"I just have never seen anything": Oral History Interview with Judge Oliver J. Carter (transcript), Truman archives, p. 106.

"It was at that point": Oral History Interview with Howard I. McGrath (transcript), Truman archives, p. 23.

"A grim, new struggle is on": "Text of Dewey's Address at Bowl," *Los Angeles Times,* September 25, 1948.

253 *"It would be foolish to make"*: "Dewey Renews Stand Against Communism at Home and Abroad," *Christian Science Monitor,* September 25, 1948.

25. *"The Democratic Party Was Down to Its Last Cent"*

254 *"It is surprising to me that"*: Albert Z. Carr to Matthew Connelly, September 22, 1948, Clark Clifford Papers, Box 34, Truman archives.

"The railroad station was at the": Oral History Interview with Donald S. Dawson (transcript), 1977, Oral History Interviews, Truman archives, pp. 31–32.

255 *"He hadn't had any sleep"*: Oral History Interview with Jonathan Daniels (transcript), 1963, Oral History Interviews, Truman archives, p. 162.

"I remember we stopped at": Oral History Interview with Donald S. Dawson (transcript), Truman archives, p. 32.

"Your horse is eight years": Ibid.

"In some towns . . . they didn't even": Margaret Truman, *Harry S. Truman* (New York: Morrow, 1973), p. 33.

256 *"the most tremendous breakfast"*: Ibid., p. 34.

"only to be used in case of": Ibid.

"That question is too deep": "U.S. Moscow Envoy Sees Truman; Takes Grave View but Doubts War," *New York Times,* September 28, 1948.

"If we did have unity": "Address at Bonham, Texas," September 27, 1948, Public Papers, Truman archives, https://www.trumanlibrary.gov/library/public-papers/213/address-bonham-texas.

"We were headed for Oklahoma": Oral History Interview with Robert G. Nixon (transcript), Truman archives, pp. 599–600.

257 *"the hostest with the mostest"*: "For Perle Mesta, Postage Is Overdue," *Washington Post,* March 1, 1987.

"And to keep this from": Oral History Interview with Robert G. Nixon (transcript), Truman archives, p. 600.

"The President and everybody else": Ibid., p. 603.

"I should like the American": "Address in Oklahoma City," September 28, 1948, Public

Papers, Truman archives, https://www.trumanlibrary.gov/library/public-papers/215/address-oklahoma-city.

258 *"We ran out of money"*: "Why Truman's Campaign Train Lingered in Oklahoma City," *New York Times,* October 25, 1992.

"ready to crawl into a hole": Diary entry of David Lilienthal, September 28, 1948, *The Journals of David E. Lilienthal,* vol. 2, p. 413.

"more dead than alive": George M. Elsey to William L. Batt Jr., October 1, 1948, George Elsey Papers, Box 23, Truman archives.

259 *"It's all over"*: Diary entry of Margaret Truman, October 1, 1948, Margaret Truman Daniel and E. Clifton Daniel Papers, Box 14, Truman archives.

26. "This Was the Worst Mistake of the Truman Campaign"

263 *"Beyond any election in the"*: "The Difference: Dewey Confident, Truman Hopeful," *Boston Daily Globe,* October 31, 1948.

265 *"Our government is made up"*: "Informal Remarks in San Antonio, Texas," Gunter Hotel, September 26, 1948, Public Papers, Truman archives, https://www.trumanlibrary.gov/library/public-papers/210/informal-remarks-san-antonio-texas.

"structural nerves": Robert Klara, *The Hidden White House: Harry Truman and the Reconstruction of America's Most Famous Residence* (New York: Thomas Dunne, 2013), p. 68.

266 *"Vitamin C stands for"*: Dialogue is from "Washington Merry-Go-Round: Truman-Ickes Relations Oiled Up," *Washington Post,* October 7, 1948.

"On election day . . . we'll all": Oral History Interview with Dr. Johannes Hoeber (transcript), 1966, Oral History Interviews, Truman archives, p. 42.

"I remember catching the": Ibid., pp. 42–43.

"What was most urgently needed": Harry S. Truman, *Memoirs,* vol. 2, *Years of Trial and Hope, 1946–1952* (Garden City, NY: Doubleday, 1956), p. 213.

267 *"We were pretty desperate"*: Oral History Interview with Jonathan Daniels (transcript), 1963, Oral History Interviews, Truman archives, p. 150.

"to use diplomatic language or a": Robert H. Ferrell, *Off the Record: The Private Papers of Harry S. Truman* (Columbia: University of Missouri Press, 1980), p. 31.

"I outlined to him what": Harry S. Truman, *Memoirs,* vol. 2, p. 213.

268 *"as Chief Justice"*: Dialogue from ibid., p. 214.

"a public statement of major": Ibid., p. 216.

"You don't know any Russian": Tom Connally, as told to Alfred Steinberg, *My Name Is Tom Connally* (New York: Crowell, 1954), p. 331.

269 *"He must be feeling desperate"*: Ibid.

"I have heard enough": Jonathan Daniels, *The Man of Independence* (Port Washington, NY: Kennikat, 1971), p. 29.

"[Truman] got up and went out of": Ibid.

"The capital was alive with": "President Reported Planning to Send Vinson to Moscow," *Hartford Courant,* October 9, 1948.

"It is dangerous to the peace": "The Incredible Harry Truman," *Los Angeles Times,* October 12, 1948.

"a resounding blunder": "Blundering Diplomacy," *Wall Street Journal,* October 18, 1948.

270 *"further confirmation of the"*: "Thurmond's View Caustic: Says Vinson Plan Was 'Hatched Up' for Political End," *New York Times,* October 11, 1948.

"This was the worst mistake": Clark Clifford, with Richard Holbrooke, *Counsel to the President: A Memoir* (New York: Random House, 1991), p. 233.
"But the damage was done": Harry S. Truman, *Memoirs,* vol. 2, p. 216.
"The Republicans have the": "Address at the Armory, Akron, Ohio," October 11, 1948, Public Papers, Truman archives, https://www.trumanlibrary.gov/library/public-papers/232/address-armory-akron-ohio.
"Election Forecast: 50 Political": "Election Forecast: 50 Political Experts Predict a GOP Sweep," *Newsweek,* October 11, 1948.
"That Dewey would be": Clifford, *Counsel to the President,* p. 235.
"What have you got under": Dialogue from ibid.
271 *"The greatest danger that could"*: J. E. Broyhill to Governor Dewey, July 27, 1948, Thomas E. Dewey Papers, Series 5, Box 24, Rare Books, Special Collections, and Preservation, River Campus Libraries, University of Rochester.
"If you don't open up on": Earle S. Clayton to Thomas E. Dewey, undated, ibid., Series 2, Box 28.
"No, I won't do it": Jules Abels, *Out of the Jaws of Victory: The Astounding Election of 1948* (New York: Henry Holt, 1959), p. 203.
272 *"our friends of the free world"*: "Governor Seeks to Offset Damage of Peace Project, Called 'Blunder,'" *Washington Post,* October 11, 1948.
"The people of America": Ibid.
"perhaps without precedent in": Ibid.
"Certainly": Ibid.
273 *"We need the money and"*: "Republicans Lag on Campaign Gifts," *New York Times,* October 14, 1948.

27. *"Could We Be Wrong?"*

274 *"Again renew my challenge to"*: Strom Thurmond to Harry Truman, October 10, 1948, Research Files, President's Committee on Civil Rights, Truman archives.
275 *"The oil men's generous"*: "Strange Mixture of Southerners Among Dixiecrats," *Boston Daily Globe,* October 20, 1948.
"understandable mistake": "Explains Big to Hastie," *New York Times,* October 26, 1948.
"pro-Truman": Ibid.
"I would not have written": David Pietrusza, *1948: Harry Truman's Improbable Victory and the Year That Transformed America's Role in the World* (New York: Union Square, 2011), p. 310.
"an inefficient and confused": "Thurmond Pledges to Cleanse Party," *Washington Post,* October 22, 1948.
276 *"His endless attacks on"*: Essie Mae Washington-Williams, with William Stadiem, *Dear Senator: A Memoir by the Daughter of Strom Thurmond* (New York: Regan Books, 2005), p. 136.
"On the question of social": Ibid., p. 137.
"I don't like that man": Ibid.
"brainwashed . . . if not by": Ibid., p. 133.
"If the South had been stabbed": Ibid., p. 135.
"We went through Illinois": Oral History Interview with Robert G. Nixon (transcript), 1970, Oral History Interviews, Truman archives, pp. 628–29.

277 *"There is something happening"*: Oral History Interview with Eben A. Ayers (transcript), 1967, Oral History Interviews, Truman archives, p. 153.

"The Truman crowds had just": Oral History Interview with Richard L. Strout (transcript), 1971, Oral History Interviews, Truman archives, p. 18.

"This correspondent's inquiries": "Looks Now as if Republicans Will Carry Senate," *Boston Daily Globe,* October 15, 1948.

"about 75 percent of the newspapers": "Merry-Go-Round: Gov. Dewey Is Picked as Sure Victor," *Washington Post,* October 14, 1948.

"13 Oct 1948 between": "Handwritten estimated tally of electoral votes, October 13, 1948," Research Files, 1948 Election Campaign collection, Truman archives, https://www.trumanlibrary.gov/library/research-files/handwritten-estimated-tally-electoral-votes.

"George, how many do I have?": Dialogue from George McKee Elsey, *An Unplanned Life: A Memoir by George McKee Elsey* (Columbia: University of Missouri Press, 2005), p. 170.

278 *"Farm boy, Soldier, Statesman"*: *The Story of Harry S. Truman,* Research Files, 1948 Election Campaign collection, Truman archives, https://www.trumanlibrary.gov/library/research-files/story-harry-s-truman.

"Workers at the precinct level": Jack Redding, *Inside the Democratic Party* (New York: Bobbs-Merrill, 1958), p. 238.

"The 'Democratic Record' show is": Ibid., p. 239.

"I think, Mrs. Roosevelt, that": Dialogue from ibid., p. 228.

279 *"The country is going to be in"*: "Rear Platform and Other Informal Remarks in Wisconsin and Minnesota," Adams, Wisconsin, October 13, 1948, Public Papers, Truman archives, https://www.trumanlibrary.gov/library/public-papers/235/rear-platform-and-other-informal-remarks-wisconsin-and-minnesota.

"On November 2 . . . you are going": Ibid., Spooner, Wisconsin.

280 *"Could we be wrong?"*: "Truman's Mostly Making Neighbors," *Washington Post,* October 17, 1948.

28. *"The Campaign Special Train Stopped with a Jerk"*

281 *"That's the first lunatic I've"*: Richard Norton Smith, *Thomas E. Dewey and His Times* (New York: Touchstone, 1982), p. 532.

"The campaign special train": Ibid.

"I think as much of Dewey as": "Dewey Engineer Resents Being Called Lunatic," *Chicago Daily Tribune,* October 14, 1948.

282 *"wonderful train crews"*: "Rear Platform and Other Informal Remarks in Indiana," October 15, 1948, Public Papers, Truman archives, https://www.trumanlibrary.gov/library/public-papers/240/rear-platform-and-other-informal-remarks-indiana.

LUNATICS FOR TRUMAN: "When Harry Gave 'em Hell," *U.S. News & World Report,* January 28, 2008.

"Johnny . . . we are slipping": Smith, *Thomas E. Dewey,* p. 533.

"He didn't really like handshaking": Ibid., pp. 348–49.

283 *"as certain as anything can"*: "A Reporter Looks Back: A 'Sure' Defeat for Truman," *Christian Science Monitor,* August 20, 1980.

"I am worried": Helen Brigham to Herbert Brownell, October 9, 1948, Thomas E. Dewey Papers, Series 2, Box 21.

"Don't float in, fight your": Grace Burdick to Herbert Brownell, October 21, 1948, ibid.

"I tell you": "Fire Gen. Marshall, Wallace Demands of Truman in Speech," *Chicago Daily Tribune,* October 20, 1948.

"Harry S. Truman has abdicated": "Wallace Asserts Truman Abdicated," *New York Times,* October 20, 1948.

284 *"He's going to take the worst"*: "Party to Stay, Wallace Says," *Washington Post,* October 21, 1948.

"I see a lot of faces that": "Wallace Attacks Truman in St. Louis," *New York Times,* September 26, 1948.

"I'm not tired": Ibid.

"I can't help feeling that": Thomas W. Devine, *Henry Wallace's 1948 Presidential Campaign and the Future of Postwar Liberalism* (Chapel Hill: University of North Carolina Press, 2013), p. 278.

285 *"There was a parade through Miami"*: Diary entry of Margaret Truman, October 18, 1948, Margaret Truman Daniel and E. Clifton Daniel Papers, Box 14, Truman archives.

"Let me say here again": "Address in Miami at the American Legion Convention," October 18, 1948, Public Papers, Truman archives, https://www.trumanlibrary.gov/library/public-papers/244/address-miami-american-legion-convention.

286 *"You can win the south without"*: E. R. Roberts to Harry Truman, undated, Research Files, President's Committee on Civil Rights, Truman archives, https://trumanlibrary.gov/library/research-files/correspondence-between-harry-s-truman-and-ernie-roberts?documentid=NA&pagenumber=5.

"I can't approve of such": Harry Truman to E. R. Roberts, August 18, 1948, ibid.

287 *"At almost any point in Berlin"*: Oral History Interview with William H. Draper Jr. (transcript), 1972, Oral History Interviews, Truman archives, pp. 68–69.

"the extraordinary demands of the": Harry Truman to Executive Secretary, National Security Council, October 22, 1948, Harry S. Truman Papers, President's Secretary's Files, Box 178, Truman archives.

288 *"It must be assumed that"*: "Prospects for Survival of the Republic of Korea," October 28, 1948, Harry S. Truman Papers, Central Intelligence Agency, President's Secretary's Files, Box 177, Truman archives.

"Rhee's government would be": Harry S. Truman, *Memoirs,* vol. 2, p. 330.

"Arab refugee tragedy is rapidly": John McDonald to the President and Acting Secretary of State, October 17, 1948, Clark M. Clifford Papers, Box 14, Truman archives.

289 *"fully acceptable to the State of"*: "Text of Platform as Drafted by Resolutions Committee," *New York Times,* July 14, 1948.

"Like you and everyone else who": Chester Bowles to Clark Clifford, September 23, 1948, Clifford Papers, Box 13, Truman archives.

"any parliamentary procedures": John B. Judis, *Genesis: Truman, American Jews, and the Origins of the Arab/Israeli Conflict* (New York: Farrar, Straus and Giroux, 2014), p. 333.

"use every effort to avoid": Ibid.

"every effort [should] be made to": Ibid., p. 337.

"unity to our country to meet": "Dewey Tells Rally He Expects Abuse," *Los Angeles Times,* October 23, 1948.

"the vacillation of the Democratic": "Dewey Asks Backers Not to Use Abuse," *Washington Post,* October 23, 1948.

290 *"I am working on a statement"*: Clark Clifford to Harry Truman, Telegram, October 23, 1948, President's Secretary's Files, Recognition of the State of Israel, Truman archives, https://www.trumanlibrary.gov/library/research-files/telegram-clark-clifford-harry-s-truman.

304 *"This brought down the"*: Oral History Interview with Robert G. Nixon (transcript), Truman archives, p. 652.
"He can follow me to Cleveland": "Address in Madison Square Garden, New York City," October 28, 1948.

30. "I Stand by My Prediction. Dewey Is In."

306 *"It is great to be home again"*: Press release, "Text of the Address by Governor Thomas E. Dewey, Republican Nominee for President, Delivered at Madison Square Garden," October 30, 1948, Thomas E. Dewey Papers, Series 2, Box 117.
"has been divided against": Ibid.
307 *"On that trip . . . he came"*: Oral History Interview with Raymond P. Brandt (transcript), 1970, Oral History Interviews, Truman archives, p. 46.
"He assumed in '48 that": Oral History Interview with Jack L. Bell (transcript), 1971, Oral History Interviews, Truman archives, p. 53.
"I am 'jumping the gun'": Arthur Vandenberg to Thomas Dewey, October 30, 1948, Thomas E. Dewey Papers, Series 1, Box 195.
"By the time you receive": George R. Wallace to Thomas Dewey, November 1, 1948, ibid., Series 5, Box 198.
"Since knowing you I have": Clellan S. Forsythe to Thomas Dewey, November 1, 1948, ibid., Series 5, Box 66.
308 *"I could hardly get through"*: Oral History Interview with Philleo Nash (transcript), Truman archives, p. 391.
"I brought up a draft": Dialogue from ibid., p. 393.
309 *"Unity is basically a weak concept"*: Ibid., p. 394.
"little shadow": "Informal Remarks in New York," October 29, 1948, Public Papers, Truman archives, https://www.trumanlibrary.gov/library/public-papers/264/informal-remarks-new-york.
310 *"Pour it on, Harry!"*: "President Renews Civil Rights Plea," *New York Times,* October 30, 1948.
"All of a sudden, there": Oral History Interview with Philleo Nash (transcript), Truman archives, pp. 399–400.
"This, in my mind, is a most": "Address in Harlem, New York, Upon Receiving the Franklin Roosevelt Award," October 29, 1948, Public Papers, Truman archives, https://www.trumanlibrary.gov/library/public-papers/265/address-harlem-new-york-upon-receiving-franklin-roosevelt-award.
"Eventually, we are going to have": Ibid.
311 *"Immediate and far-reaching"*: "President Renews Civil Rights Plea," *New York Times,* October 30, 1948.
"shallow, hollow, worthless promises": "Wallace Calls Truman Vows 'Worthless,'" *Washington Post,* October 30, 1948.
"invited the Dixiecrats": Ibid.
"a Federal horsewhip to": "Thurmond Assails Rivals," *New York Times,* October 30, 1948.
312 *"Our campaign is based on"*: "Address by Governor Thurmond, States' Rights Candidate, in Texas," *New York Times,* October 31, 1948.
"un-American": Ibid.
"On the last long ride": Oral History Interview with John Franklin Carter (transcript), Truman archives, p. 26.

"Are you going to deliver": Dialogue from Oral History Interview with John W. Snyder (transcript), Truman archives, p. 936.

313 *"We got to St. Louis and"*: Oral History Interview with Carleton Kent (transcript), 1970, Oral History Interviews, Truman archives, p. 74.

"There were so many people": Oral History Interview with Robert G. Nixon (transcript), Truman archives, p. 660.

"Thank you my friends": "Address at the Kiel Auditorium, St. Louis, Missouri," October 30, 1948, Public Papers, Truman archives, https://www.trumanlibrary.gov/library/public-papers/268/address-kiel-auditorium-st-louis-missouri.

"The country was aware": Oral History Interview with Robert G. Nixon (transcript), Truman archives, p. 669.

"I have been in many a": "Address at the Kiel Auditorium, St. Louis, Missouri," October 30, 1948.

314 *"applauded for about"*: Oral History Interview with John Franklin Carter (transcript), Truman archives, p. 26.

"saboteurs and character assassins": "Address at the Kiel Auditorium, St. Louis, Missouri," October 30, 1948.

"I returned from the bedlam": Harry S. Truman, *Memoirs,* vol. 2, p. 220.

315 *"The campaign is all over"*: Diary entry of Margaret Truman, November 1, 1948, Margaret Truman Daniel and E. Clifton Daniel Papers, Box 14, Truman archives.

"We have come to the end": "Dewey Text," *Boston Daily Globe,* November 2, 1948.

"I stand by my prediction": "Poll Shows Dewey Still Leads Race," *Hartford Courant,* November 1, 1948.

"The next President travels by": Robert J. Donovan, *Conflict and Crisis: The Presidency of Harry S. Truman, 1945–1948* (Columbia: University of Missouri Press, 1996), p. 429.

"I have already made up": "Dewey to Win: But the People Fret," *Atlanta Constitution,* November 1, 1948.

"I would say that Governor": "The Washington Merry-Go-Round: Dewey Unscathed in Gantlet Run," *Washington Post,* November 1, 1948.

"Government will remain big": "Dewey As President," *Wall Street Journal,* November 2, 1948.

"What will Dewey do?": Abels, *Out of the Jaws of Victory,* p. 261.

316 *"Harry S. Truman: A Study"*: David McCullough, *Truman* (New York: Simon & Schuster, 1992), p. 703.

"Dewey Gets the Votes": "London Press Sees Dewey Victory, But Shows No Warmth for Him," *New York Times,* November 2, 1948.

"What kind of President": Ibid.

"Most of the articles [in Britain]": Ibid.

31. "Tens of Thousands, and Hundreds of Thousands! How Can He Lose?"

317 *"The ballot is stronger"*: Carl Sandburg, *Abraham Lincoln: The Prairie Years and the War Years* (New York: Sterling, 2007), p. 78.

318 *"Harry S. Truman, 219 North"*: "3 Trumans Go to the Polls," *New York Times,* November 3, 1948.

"How do you think it will": Dialogue from ibid.

"Well . . . that's two votes we": "Gov. Dewey, Family Sit Up to Scan Election Returns," *Boston Daily Globe,* November 3, 1948.

319 *"more votes than the pollsters say"*: "Wallace Votes, Then Tends Farm," *New York Times*, November 3, 1948.

"They said back at Philadelphia": "Thurmond and His Wife Vote States' Rights," *Los Angeles Times*, November 3, 1948.

320 *"Boy, those ulcers of mine"*: Oral History Interview with Tom L. Evans (transcript), 1963, Oral History Interviews, Truman archives, p. 526.

321 *"We didn't talk any about"*: Oral History Interview with Wallace H. Graham (transcript), 1989, Oral History Interviews, Truman archives, p. 23.

322 *"How do you think it's"*: Smith, *Thomas E. Dewey*, p. 23.

"Five votes for Dewey, two": Donald P. Miller, "A Remembrance of November 2, 1948," Harry S. Truman Papers, President's Secretary's Files, Truman archives.

323 *"What do you think of the"*: Dialogue from "When Hotel Muehlebach Becomes the White House," George Elsey papers, Truman archives. Also published in book form: Barney L. Allis, *When Hotel Muehlebach Becomes the White House*, privately printed, 1949.

"It was a rather sober bunch": Oral history of Carleton Kent (transcript), Truman archives, pp. 67–68.

324 *"Nobody here"*: Dialogue from Redding, *Inside the Democratic Party*, pp. 11–12.

"We had the President's office": Oral History Interview with Philleo Nash (transcript), Truman archives, p. 405.

"Were it not for all these": Diary entry of Eben Ayers, November 2, 1948, in Eben A. Ayers, *Truman in the White House: The Diary of Eben A. Ayers* (Columbia: University of Missouri Press, 1991), p. 83.

"I had a feeling that perhaps": Alonzo Fields, *My 21 Years in the White House* (New York: Coward-McCann, 1961), p. 148.

325 *"terrible uncertainty"*: Clifford, *Counsel to the President*, p. 238.

"We had planned to stay": Ibid., p. 239.

"Police said at least half": "Soviet Press Takes Note of Election," *Hartford Courant*, November 3, 1948.

326 *"Wallace seemed to be in"*: Oral history of Calvin "Beanie" Baldwin, Columbia University Rare Book & Manuscript Library, p. 36.

"Early reports reaching us": "Statement by Herbert Brownell Jr.," Thomas E. Dewey Papers, Series 2, Box 117.

327 *"We want Harry"*: "Truman Gets Out of Sight During Count," *Los Angeles Times*, November 3, 1948.

"frantic . . . I am not using": Margaret Truman, *Harry S. Truman* (New York: Morrow, 1973), p. 40.

"Dad isn't here": McCullough, *Truman*, p. 706.

"At this moment the polls": "Text of 7:30 Statement by Brownell," Thomas E. Dewey Papers, Series 2, Box 117.

328 *"Along in the evening"*: Oral History Interview with Mary Ethel Noland (transcript), 1965, Oral History Interviews, Truman archives, p. 200.

"That went on all night long": Ibid.

32. "Under No Circumstance Will I Congratulate That Son of a Bitch"

329 *"The halls leading to the"*: "Vote Peps Up Surprised Democrats," *Los Angeles Times*, November 3, 1948.

330 *"We are now getting into"*: "Statement by Herbert Brownell Jr., at 11:15 pm," Thomas E. Dewey Papers, Series 2, Box 117.
"undoubtedly beaten": McCullough, *Truman*, p. 707.
"We now know that Governor Dewey": "Statement by Herbert Brownell Jr. at 1:45 am," Thomas E. Dewey Papers, Series 2, Box 117.
331 *"Well, Mr. President . . . you're"*: Dialogue from Oral History Interview with Tom L. Evans (transcript), Truman archives, p. 534.
"a churning madhouse": "When Hotel Muehlebach Becomes the White House," George Elsey papers, Truman archives. Also published in pamphlet form under byline Barney L. Allis (Kansas City, MO: Hotel Muehlebach, 1949).
"We don't say that we're": Oral History Interview with Frank Holeman (transcript), 1987, Oral History Interviews, Truman archives, p. 22.
"Dear Barney, I need a room": Ibid.
"As the night wore on": Oral History Interview with Samuel C. Brightman (transcript), 1966, Oral History Interviews, Truman archives, p. 115.
332 *"He was sweating"*: Redding, *Inside the Democratic Party*, pp. 20–21.
"Jim, you can take it": Ibid., p. 21.
"What is Drew Pearson saying?": Dialogue from Oral History Interview with John Franklin Carter (transcript), Truman archives, pp. 48–49.
"We were all trying to": Letters to the Editor, *Life*, November 22, 1948, p. 12.
333 *"there was pandemonium"*: Oral History Interview with John Franklin Carter (transcript), Truman archives, p. 69.
"The Ohio vote finally came": Oral History Interview with Carleton Kent (transcript), Truman archives, p. 684.
"Bill, stop writing that": Ibid., pp. 684–85.
"It's awful": Smith, *Thomas E. Dewey*, p. 49.
"What do you know?": Ed Cray, *Chief Justice: A Biography of Earl Warren* (New York: Simon & Schuster, 1997), p. 193.
"And all of the sudden": McCullough, *Truman*, p. 707.
"Mr. President . . . I don't": Dialogue from Oral History Interview with H. Graham Morison (transcript), 1972, Truman archives, pp. 248–49.
334 *"We've got 'em beat"*: McCullough, *Truman*, p. 707.
"I told him so all the time": John C. Culver and John Hyde, *American Dreamer: The Life and Times of Henry A. Wallace* (New York: W. W. Norton, 2000), p. 502.
"Tonight we have had an": "Wallace Vote Is Far Short of His Party's Expectations," *New York Times*, November 3, 1948.
"so long as the policy of": John J. Abt, with Michael Myerson, *Advocate and Activist: Memoirs of an American Communist Lawyer* (Chicago: University of Illinois Press, 1993), pp. 163–64.
335 *"Under no circumstance"*: Ibid., p. 164.
"The President is on his way": Dialogue from "When Hotel Muehlebach Becomes the White House," George Elsey papers, Truman archives.
"I looked up": Ibid.
"I heard the broadcast": Ibid.
"His door was wide open": Oral History Interview with Robert G. Nixon (transcript), Truman archives, p. 687.
"It looks as though we": Dialogue from "When Hotel Muehlebach Becomes the White House."
336 *"the most gratifying phone"*: Clifford, *Counsel to the President*, p. 239.

"He displayed neither tension": Letters to the Editor, *Life*, November 22, 1948, p. 12.
"At 6 a.m. today": "Forecasts Upset: President Surprises by Taking Early Popular Vote Lead," *New York Times*, November 3, 1948.
"Election Still in Doubt": "Election Still in Doubt," *Los Angeles Times*, November 3, 1948.
"The ballots haven't been": "An Affectionate Farewell to Harry," *Atlanta Constitution*, November 3, 1948.
337 *"The first postelection question"*: "Matter of Fact: Flying Dual Control," *Washington Post*, November 3, 1948.
"Thomas E. Dewey Amerikas": "Thomas E. Dewey Amerikas neuer Präsident," *Muenchen Merkur*, November 3, 1948.
"Dewey, Warren Win; Business Gain": "Dewey, Warren Win; Business Gain Seen," *Women's Wear Daily*, November 3, 1948.
"'Persistence' Is the Dominating": "'Persistence' Is the Dominating Trait that Carried Dewey to the Presidency," *Washington Post*, November 3, 1948.
"Dewey Defeats Truman": "Dewey Defeats Truman; G.O.P. Sweep Indicated in State," *Chicago Daily Tribune*, November 3, 1948.
"arguably the most famous": "Dewey Defeats Truman," *Chicago Tribune*, December 19, 2007.
"Thank you, Mr. President": Redding, *Inside the Democratic Party*, p. 23.
"The wine shimmered effervescently": Ibid.
"Now I want you to talk to": Oral History Interviews with India Edwards (transcript), 1969 and 1975, Oral History Interviews, Truman archives, p. 81.
338 *"I burst out crying"*: Ibid.
"Gentlemen . . . I have here a message": Jack Redding, *Inside the Democratic Party*, p. 23.
"Dewey has conceded!": "When Hotel Muehlebach Becomes the White House," George Elsey papers, Truman archives.
"everyone was talking, yelling": Ibid.
"All I can say . . . is that": Ibid.
"I cried and I prayed for": "Home Town Turns Out for Truman Victory Celebration," *Chicago Daily Tribune*, November 4, 1948.
339 *"Four more years"*: Ibid.
"It's something like the night": "Common Man Dazed by Election," *New York Times*, November 4, 1948.
"It was the most exhilarating": Oral History Interview with Harold I. McGrath (transcript), 1970, Oral History Interviews, Truman archives, p. 98.
"It was not my victory": "Home Town Turns Out for Truman Victory Celebration," *Chicago Daily Tribune*, November 4, 1948.
340 *"Can we regard the pictures as"*: Dialogue from "Text of Press Conference by Governor Thomas E. Dewey, November 3, 1948, at the Hotel Roosevelt, New York City," Thomas E. Dewey Papers, Series 2, Box 117.

33. *"Dewey Defeats Truman"*

341 *"We, and the rest of"*: "He Asked for a Miracle and, Lo, He Got It," *Denver Post*, November 3, 1948.
"President Truman's victory in his": "Truman Aimed at Voters' Hearts, Dewey at Heads, Roberts Explains," *Boston Daily Globe*, November 5, 1948.

"We were wrong, all of": "Washington Calling: Truman's Sweep," *Washington Post*, November 5, 1948.

"Miracle Man": *Newsweek*, November 8, 1948.

342 *"the greatest photograph ever"*: "Behind the Picture: 'Dewey Defeats Truman' and the Politics of Memory," *Time*, May 4, 2014.

"the biggest, most enthusiastic": McCullough, *Truman*, p. 723.

WELCOME HOME: James K. Libbey, *Dear Alben: Mr. Barkley of Kentucky* (Lexington: University of Kentucky Press, 2009), p. 98.

343 *"I will never forget that ride"*: Margaret Truman, *Harry S. Truman*, p. 43.

"I'm afraid you're going": Robert Klara, *The Hidden White House: Harry Truman and the Reconstruction of America's Most Famous Residence* (New York: Thomas Dunne, 2013), p. 72.

"Doesn't that beat hell!": Ibid., pp. 72–73.

"We have special cause to be": Provisional Government of Israel (Weizmann) to Truman, November 5, 1948, Research Files, Recognition of the State of Israel, Truman archives, https://www.trumanlibrary.gov/library/research-files/correspondence-between-eliahu-epstein-chaim-weizmann-and-harry-s-truman?documentid=NA&pagenumber=4.

"most aggressive program": U.S. Department of State, Moscow to Secretary of State, November 13, 1948, Clark Clifford papers, Box 21, Truman archives.

"papers of all political persuasions": U.S. Department of State, Paris to Secretary of State, November 5, 1948, Clark Clifford papers, Box 22, Truman archives.

344 *"The world looks hopefully to"*: U.S. Department of State, Nanking to Secretary of State, November 5, 1948, Clark Clifford papers, Box 22, Truman archives.

"opinion frequently expressed even": U.S. Department of State, Lisbon to Secretary of State, November 5, 1948, Clark Clifford papers, Box 22, Truman archives.

"I think the future historians": Alf M. Landon to Thomas E. Dewey, November 19, 1948, Thomas E. Dewey Papers, Series 10, Box 24.

"Aunt Marsh and I want you": Aunt Marsh and Uncle Peter to Tom and Frances Dewey, November 4, 1948, ibid., Series 10, Box 44.

"I have been like many other": Thomas W. Pierce to Dorothy Bell Rakoff, November 8, 1948, ibid., Series 10, Box 44.

"It was not an 'election' but a 'revolution'": Harold L. Ickes to Judge William J. Campbell, November 5, 1948, Campaign Collection, Box 1, Truman archives.

345 *"We should have known he couldn't"*: "Thomas E. Dewey," *Chicago Daily Tribune*, March 18, 1971.

"My own opinion": Joe Martin, *My First Fifty Years in Politics* (New York: McGraw-Hill, 1960), p. 169.

"the most interesting candidate": Frank Gannon, "Minnesota's Boy Wonder Was RN's Pick for POTUS," September 2, 2008, Richard Nixon Foundation, https://www.nixonfoundation.org/2008/09/minnesotas-boy-wonder-was-rns-pick-for-potus/.

346 *"The short answer on the election"*: Thomas Dewey to Geo. I. Thomas, December 15, 1948, Thomas E. Dewey Papers, Series 10, Box 44.

"The farmers switched in the mid-West": Thomas Dewey to Joseph Robinson, January 13, 1949, ibid., Series 10, Box 38.

"It had been taken for granted": "The Farmers Wanted to Know," *Atlanta Constitution*, November 8, 1948.

"Labor did it": Robert H. Ferrell, *Harry S. Truman: A Life* (Columbia: University of Missouri Press, 1994), p. 282.

347 *"some light reading on your"*: Philleo Nash to Harry Truman, November 6, 1948, 1948

Election Campaign Collection, Truman archives, https://www.trumanlibrary.gov/library/research-files/philleo-nash-harry-s-truman.

"the greatest diplomatic crisis": Robert A. Divine, *Foreign Policy and U.S. Presidential Elections, 1940–1948* (New York: New Viewpoints, 1974), p. 266.

"It always galls me to think": Abels, *Out of the Jaws of Victory,* p. 139.

348 *"It is almost impossible to put"*: "Taft Makes Comment," *New York Times,* November 4, 1948.

"The Republican Party is split": "GOP Is Split 'Wide Open,' Dewey Says," *Washington Post,* February 9, 1949.

"Which voters stayed home?": "Gallup Sees Close Election A 'Nightmare,'" *Washington Post,* November 4, 1948.

349 *"I could not have been more"*: "Election Prophets Ponder in Dismay," *New York Times,* November 4, 1948.

"It's open season on the pollsters": Broadcast of Edward R. Murrow, November 5, 1948, in *In Search of Light: The Broadcasts of Edward R. Murrow, 1938–1961,* edited by Edward Bliss Jr. (New York: Alfred A. Knopf, 1967), p. 138.

"You've got to give the little man": Arthur H. Vandenberg Jr., ed., *The Private Papers of Senator Vandenberg* (Boston: Houghton Mifflin, 1952), p. 460.

Epilogue

350 *"I whole-heartedly agree with"*: Thomas E. Dewey to Harry S. Truman, June 27, 1950, Thomas E. Dewey Papers, Series 10, Box 44.

"heart-felt gratification that no harm": Thomas E. Dewey to Harry S. Truman, November 1, 1950, ibid., Series 10, Box 44.

351 *"I deliberately decided that I was"*: "Hotel Confab Picks Dewey's Veep," *Salt Lake City Tribune,* April 6, 1952.

"Today, I am convinced that": "World Domination Now Russia's Aim, Says Henry Wallace," *Boston Daily Globe,* December 4, 1950.

"utterly evil": "Where I Was Wrong," *Los Angeles Times,* September 7, 1952.

352 *"How could you have said"*: Dialogue from Essie Mae Washington-Williams, with William Stadiem, *Dear Senator: A Memoir by the Daughter of Strom Thurmond* (New York: Regan Books, 2005), p. 145.

353 *"the largest crowd ever assembled"*: "The President's Party," undated, President's Permanent File, Box 4, Truman archives.

"urgent appeal": Chaim Weizmann (via Myra Phillips, the White House) to Clark Clifford, November 9, 1948, Clark Clifford papers, Box 14, Truman archives.

"the communist forces in central": V. K. Wellington Koo, Chinese Embassy, Washington, to the President of the United States, November 9, 1948, Clark Clifford papers, Box 2, Truman archives.

354 *"Don't you wave to the S.O.B."*: Joseph Crespino, *Strom Thurmond's America* (New York: Hill and Wang, 2012), p. 83.

"enable every American to": "Annual Message to the Congress on the State of the Union," January 5, 1949, Sound Recordings, Truman archives, https://www.trumanlibrary.gov/soundrecording-records/sr62-62-annual-message-congress-state-union-president-truman.

"He [the president] . . . is": Murrow, *In Search of Light,* p. 137.

Index

Abt, John
background/communism and, 87
HUAC and, 199, 205
Marion (sister), 87
Wallace/presidential campaign and, 87, 93, 199, 205, 241, 242, 334
Acheson, Dean, 34–35, 60, 61, 62
Agg, T. R., Mrs., 231
Aiken, Conrad, 296
Air Force and reorganization, 75
Albright, Robert, 235, 261
Alexander, Perry, 182
Allen, George, 92
Allis, Barney, 331
Allwright, Smith v. (1944), 192, 220
Allwright, S. S., 192
Alsop, Joseph, 237, 277
Alsop, Joseph/Stewart, 51, 58, 86, 143, 235, 246, 275, 337
American Anti-Communist Association, 79
American Medical Association, 16
Amsterdam News, 309, 310
Arab-Israeli War (1948), 109, 210, 288, 353
Arvey, Jacob ("Jake"), 142, 332
Asapansa-Johnson, C., 310
Associated Press, 41, 163, 216, 235, 307
Atlanta Constitution, 42, 180, 221, 246, 315, 336
atomic weapons/bombs
Bikini Atoll test, 35–36
description/future bombs and, 14
detecting use (US) and, 154, 155–56n
Lilienthal on, 154
Operation Sandstone, 121, 154
responsibility discussions, 154, 211, 223
significance of, 5, 33
Soviet using, 154, 154–55n
US bombings of Hiroshima/Nagasaki, 5, 14, 15, 34
as US secret/sharing with Soviets and, 13–15
White House lunch/watching test, 34–35
Auschwitz, 5–6
Austin, Warren, 106
Ayers, Eben, 12, 105, 146, 277, 324

Bacall, Lauren, 210, 251
Balance, Elayne, 215
Baldwin, Calvin Benham ("Beanie")
background/description, 88
Wallace/presidential campaign and, 88, 118, 164, 206, 207, 241, 242
Ball, Joseph H., 283
Barkley, Alben
at Democratic National Convention, 144, 146, 148
vacation and, 353

as VP candidate/election and, 144, 146, 224, 343, 354
Barrows, Roberta, 12, 323
Baruch, Bernard, 24, 64
Batt, William ("Bill"), 176–77, 213, 226, 266
Begin, Menachem, 21–22
Behrens, Earl, 184
Belgrano, F. N., 113
Bell, David C., 148
Bell, Elliott, 182
Bell, Jack, 216, 235, 248, 307
Bentley, Elizabeth, 197–99
Berger, Meyer, 339
Berlin. *See* Germany, Berlin
Bernadotte, Folke/Plan, 210, 288, 301
Biffle, Leslie, 211–12
bikini bathing suit, 170
Blaine, Anita McCormick, 165
Blair House, 343
Bloch, Charles J., 147
Bogart, Humphrey, 55, 210
Bohlen, Charles, 64
Boring, Floyd, 227–28, 228n
Boston Daily Globe, 263, 297, 298
Bowles, Chester, 289
Boyle, Bill, 332
Boyle, Hal, 165
Bradley, Omar, 104, 155
Brandt, Raymond P., 307
Bray, William, 225
Bricker, John W., 329
Bridges, Styles, 180
Brigham, Helen, 283
Britain postwar, 59–60
British Mandate for Palestine, 22, 76, 105, 107, 108–9
Brotherhood of Railroad Trainmen, 17
Brownell, Herbert, Jr.
  Dewey and, 49, 57, 58, 79–80, 82, 111, 112, 113, 115, 182, 186, 234, 326, 327, 330
  Republican National Committee/rebuilding party and, 57, 58, 80
  Republican National Convention/Dewey and, 133, 136, 137
  on Truman, 58
Brown, Thomas W., 194
Broyhill, J. E., 271
Buchalter, Louis "Lepke," 54
Buchanan, Thomas, 172
Buchenwald, 5–6, 191–92
Burdick, Grace, 283
Burke, Joseph, Mr./Mrs., 322
Burton, John, 282
Business Week, 171
Butler, Carrie, 119
Byrd, Harry, 73
Byrnes, James, 37, 38–39

Canham, Erwin, 143
Capote, Truman, 297
Carr, Albert, 254
Carroll, James J., 258
Carter, Jimmy, 352
Carter, John Franklin, 296, 312, 314
Carter, Oliver J., 251, 252
Central Intelligence Agency creation, 75
Chambers, Whittaker
  background, 87, 199
  as former communist/spy, 87, 199
  Hiss/family and, 199, 203, 204
  HUAC/naming names, 199, 203, 222
Chaplin, Charlie, 120
Chapman, Oscar, 125, 171, 226, 229, 296
Charleston News and Courier, 238
Chiang Kai-shek, 344, 353
Chicago Daily News, 119, 331
Chicago Daily Tribune, 125, 134, 204, 293, 294, 337, 342
Chicago Sun, 42
Chicago Times, 313, 323
Childs, Marquis, 31, 148, 226, 341
China and communism, 155
Christian Science Monitor, 48, 143
Chrysler, Walter, 273
Churchill, Winston
  Dewey and, 112, 181
  "Iron Curtain" speech, 35
  losing power (1945), 7
  Potsdam Conference and, 7
  Wallace and, 69–70
civil rights
  DNC platform and, 178
  federal employment and, 179
  McGrath and, 101–2
  military desegregation, 178–80
  southern white Democrats reaction/revolt and, 72, 73, 100–102, 147–48, 149–50, 179–80

civil rights (*cont.*)
  State of the Union (1948) and, 99, 195
  Truman and, 72–73, 99, 100, 195, 286, 305, 308–11, 347
  Truman speech/Harlem, 308–11
Civil Rights Act (1964), 352
Civil War (US), 28, 179, 188–89
Clark, Tom, 15, 20, 68, 171, 255
Clay, Lucius, 102–3, 104–5, 141, 155
Clayton, Earle S., 271
Cleveland, Grover, 47
Clifford, Clark
  background/description, 77, 174
  election day/night and, 325
  exhaustion/skin rash and tour, 247, 258
  Jewish homeland/Palestine and, 23, 77, 105, 106–8, 109, 289, 290–91
  Truman and, 23, 41, 59, 61, 75, 77, 95, 105, 106–8, 109, 126, 173, 174, 177, 178, 213, 214, 224, 226, 227, 247, 267, 270–71, 296, 299, 300, 336
  wife, 325
  See also "Politics of 1948, The" memo (Rowe)
Clifford-Elsey Report, 61
Cold War
  beginnings, 25
  Dewey on, 83, 296
  "Iron Curtain" speech, 35
  military action fears (1948), 105
  naming, 64
  Truman speech on (1948), 104
  in US following Hiss indictment, 353
  Wallace and, 86, 91, 93
  Washington elite and, 86
  See also Germany/Berlin
comic book as Truman biography, 278
Commodity Credit Corporation (CCC), 232–33, 346
communism
  arrests/Communist Party USA members, 162, 198
  China and, 155
  Isacson/passport and, 120
  "loyalty" board creation, 74–75
  National Security Council memo on, 203–4
  postwar expansion fears, 59–66
  spy scandal, Canada and, 75
  See also HUAC hearings; Red Scare; *specific countries; specific groups/individuals*
Communist Party USA
  arrests of leaders and, 162, 198
  HUAC hearings and, 198
  Wallace group connections, 87, 88
  See also specific individuals
Congress. *See* Eightieth Congress
Connally, Tom, 74, 268–69
Connelly, Matthew, 12, 171, 216, 254
Coolidge, Calvin, 52, 80, 89, 145, 322
Crosby, Bing, 210
Crouch, Jean, 188
Currie, Lauchlin, 198, 200

Daily Express, 316
Daniel, Clifton, 316
Daniels, Jonathan, 255, 269
Darwin, 170
Dawson, Donald, 254–55, 302
Dear Senator: A Memoir by the Daughter of Strom Thurmond (Washington-Williams), 352
De Gasperi, Alcide, 112
Democratic National Committee (1948 campaign), 175–77, 178
Democratic National Convention (1944/Chicago), 36
Democratic National Convention (1948)
  Liberty Bell/pigeons and, 150–51
  mood/conditions, 143, 146
  southern Democrats protests and, 147–48, 149–50
  television and, 143, 146, 148
  Truman acceptance speech, 148–50, 177
Democratic Record (radio show), 278
Dennis, Eugene, 88, 162, 198
Dennison, Robert, 126
Denver Post, 341
Department of Defense reorganization, 75
Depression, 8–9, 11, 52, 53–54, 169, 191, 232
de Rochemont, Louis, 185
Detroit News, 162
"Dewey Defeats Truman" headline, 337, 342
Dewey, Frances
  home (late 1920s/early 1930s), 52
  husband's presidential campaign and, 183, 234, 238, 283, 293, 318, 333

midterm elections (1946) and, 47
Republican National Convention and, 136, 137
Dewey Story, The, 185, 279
Dewey, Thomas
after 1948 election/death, 350–51
Annie (mother), 137, 157, 319–20, 322
description/personality traits, 48, 49, 51, 53, 56, 139, 197, 235, 236, 281–82
FDR and, 183
on GOP split, 348
midterm elections (1946) and, 42, 47–48
presidential campaign (1939/1940), 55–56
presidential campaign (1944), 57
on presidential hopefuls, 58, 351
presidential talk around (1946), 48–49, 50–51
residences/offices, 49
Robert Taft and, 18
Roosevelt, Theodore and, 48, 56–57
social programs and, 81
on Truman/presidency, 57–58
views, 49, 50, 81
winning election/reelection (New York governor), 48, 56
Dewey, Thomas childhood/background
Brownell's campaign and, 52–53
coming-of-age era, 52
family and, 51–52
as hero/celebrity, 54, 55
law/as prosecutor, 52, 53, 54–55
music and, 52
Republican Party significance and, 50–51
Roosevelt, Theodore and, 51, 52
run for New York governor (1938), 55
Young Republican Club and, 52
Dewey, Thomas presidential run/general election
advertising agency, 185–86
on Berlin, 157–58, 184
black vote and, 195
California and, 249, 251, 252–53
campaign beginnings/Stassen rebuttal speech and, 186, 218–19
celebrities/*The Dewey Story*, 185
congratulations and, 307–8
contrasts with Truman campaign, 236–37
dairy farm vacation and, 181–82
data/polls use and, 182, 183–84, 185
Eisenhower's visit to dairy farm and, 157–58
election day, 317–18, 321–22
expectations/endorsements, 183, 184, 185, 197, 212, 235–36, 246, 258, 264, 270, 272–73, 277, 282–83, 294, 297, 307–8, 320, 321–22, 325, 326, 327, 348, 349
fans and, 181–82
final itinerary/following Truman, 283, 292, 293–94, 295–96, 299–300
handshaking and, 282
Idlewild Airport dedication/Truman and, 196–97
in-house polling unit, 186
on Israel/foreign affairs, 289, 290, 291
mail from angry voters, 271
making no commitments, 237–38
managing New York/successes and, 185
money/donors and, 272–73
platform schism/Republican Party, 139, 145, 263, 299–300
platform/views similar to Truman, 231, 264, 299
pollsters/interviews and, 185–86
public appearances and, 184
staff worries and, 283
strategy/discussions on, 182–84, 236, 264, 283, 293
stumping for other Republicans, 237
team worries on Truman crowd size, 272, 282–83
train lurch/Dewey comment and, 281–82
train tours, 234–38, 252, 272, 281, 283, 292, 293–94, 295–96, 299–300
on Truman, 253, 295–96
Truman win/concession speech, 333, 338, 340
"unity" and, 236, 237, 253, 256, 283, 289, 290, 293, 306, 309
Vinson mission/foreign policy statement and, 271–72, 274
See also election (1948)
Dewey, Thomas presidential run/GOP nomination
advertising agency/activities, 111
black vote and, 97
congratulations on becoming candidate, 139–40

Dewey, Thomas presidential run/GOP nomination (*cont.*)
expectations, 111–12, 120
global leaders visiting, 112
Jewish vote and, 106
launching, 79, 110–11
as liberal Republican, 80, 81
luncheons/donations, 111
Marshall Plan and, 80–81, 83
Oregon and, 113–15
policy views, 80–81
poll on GOP candidates, 110
primary results and, 112, 113–14
Stassen debate/consequences, 114–16
western states tour (1947), 110
See also Republican National Convention (1948)
Dixiecrats
as anti-civil rights/anti-Truman, 158, 159–61, 238, 239, 246
campaign strategy, 160
consequences of southern revolt, 230
name, 158–59
platform/segregation, 159, 160–61
as political party, 158
as States' Rights Democratic Party, 161
Wallace on, 311
See also specific individuals
Dixon, Frank, 160
Donnelly, Phil, 148
Donovan, Robert, 230
Douglas, William O., 144
Draper, William H., Jr., 287
Drummond, Roscoe, 15, 119, 235, 253
Dubinsky, David, 24, 303
Du Bois, W.E.B., 120, 163
Dulles, John Foster, 137, 138, 184, 204, 272

Earle, Grace, 323
Earle, Willie
accusation against, 194
mob killing and, 194–95
economy under Truman, 144, 169–70, 347–48
Edison, Charles, 172
Edwards, India, 249, 278, 337–38
Edwards, Willard, 293
Egan, Leo, 235
Eightieth Congress
description, 139, 145
"do-nothing Congress" and, 180, 227, 245, 290, 314
elections (1948) predictions and, 246–47
overriding Truman vetoes and, 127, 128
schism with Dewey-Warren platform, 139, 145
Truman and, 62–63, 73–74, 98–100, 128, 149, 178–80, 200–201, 227, 231, 232–33, 245–46, 250, 283, 290, 314, 347
See also specific individuals/legislation
Eightieth Congress, emergency session (1948)
Democratic strategy, 145
Dewey-Warren platform schism and, 139, 145
"do-nothing Congress," 180
GOP meetings on/response to, 156–57
rumors/memo on, 144–45
Truman acceptance speech and, 150, 349
"Turnip Day" and, 150, 151, 180, 348
Eisenhower, Dwight
background/description, 142, 158
campaign to draft, 127, 142–43
Dewey and, 157–58, 350
Mamie (wife), 157
on national situation (1947), 59
election (1948)
background events/communication and, 263–64
candidates/parties (summary), 165
Democrats/Congress changes and, 339, 345
Dewey family/GOP headquarters, 321–22, 326, 327, 329–30, 333, 339–40
Dewey family voting, 318
DNC headquarters, Biltmore Hotel, 323–24, 329, 331–32, 337–38
final predictions, 315–16
Hart's Location, New Hampshire, 322
Moscow misinformation on Wallace, 325
newspapers and, 336–37
"other" candidates, 319
returns and, 322, 326, 327–28, 329, 330–33
Roper analysis on, 143
television and, 321, 324, 325, 329
Thurmond family voting, 319
Truman 1948 State of the Union/significance, 98–99

Truman and Alabama ballot, 319
Truman campaign headquarters, Kansas City, 322–23
Truman family voting, 317–18
Truman "missing" and, 320–21, 326–27
Wallace family voting, 318
Wallace run consequences, 326, 336
warning on Soviet/Russian interference, 83–84, 96–97
White House scene, 324–25
See also "Politics of 1948, The" memo (Rowe); *specific aspects/events*; *specific individuals/groups*
election (1948) and Truman win
aftermath, 333–40
analysis of, 345–49
black vote and, 346–47
crowds/welcome back to Washington, 342–43
Dewey and, 344
media and, 336–37, 341, 342–43
pollster/mistakes and, 344, 348–49
Truman family/group vacation, 353
world leaders' congratulations/communications, 343–44
election, presidential (1876)
candidates/results and, 189–90
Compromise of 1877 and, 189–90
elections, midterm (1946), 41–42
electoral college/abolishing resolution, 345
elevators, 170–71
Elmore, George/case, 192, 193
Elsey, George
on Bess Truman, 228
Truman/Truman administration and, 61, 95, 98, 99, 100, 178, 210, 213, 226–27, 230, 258, 267, 277, 301
Emperor Waltz, The (movie), 210
Esquire, 36
Europe, postwar overview, 5–6
Evans, Tom, 330–31
Ewing, Oscar, 24, 171, 172, 176, 178, 300
executive mansion, Albany New York, 47

fake news, 295
Ferdinand Magellan (railcar)
description/accommodations, 123, 212–13, 247
name and, 341–42
Truman tours/speeches and, 123, 200, 212, 214, 224–25, 244–45
Ferguson, Homer, 98, 202–3
Fields, Alonzo/wife, 151–52, 324–25
Flynn, Ed, 32
Folliard, Edward, 86
Folsom, James, 101
Fontaine, Joan, 210
Foreman, Clark, 208
Forrestal, James
atomic bombs and, 153, 154, 211, 223
background/description, 153–54
Berlin/Blockade and, 140, 155, 211
on Jewish homeland debate, 22
military/intelligence establishments reorganization and, 75
postwar communism and, 60
suicide of, 75–76
Truman running for election and, 77–78
Forsythe, Clellan, 307–8
Foster, William Z., 162, 198
France, "Big Bill," 170
Franks, Oliver, Sir, 258–59
Frisino, Woody, 182
Fulbright, J. William, 42

Gallop, George, 50, 186, 321, 348, 349
Gallop polls, 50–51, 77, 92, 110, 134, 238–39, 272, 282–83, 299, 315
"Gangbuster," 55
Garner, John Nance, 255–56
Gathering Storm, The (Churchill), 181
Gearhart, Bertrand W., 251
Georgia
political crisis/governor-elect (1946), 219
racism in, 219–21
Germany and Allied powers postwar control, 103
Germany, Berlin
Berlin Blockade/Berlin Airlift, 140–41, 155, 210, 287, 347
Berlin city council and, 211
fears of war, 143, 155, 156, 223, 224, 256, 287
postwar control and, 103–5
Soviets raiding US sector, 210–11
Germany, West Germany, 103
Gilda (film/atomic bomb), 36

Goldwater, Barry, 352
Gordon, Waxey, 53
Graham, Wallace, 42, 210, 320, 321
"grand jury squad," 54
Grant, Ulysses S., 23
Great Depression, 8–9, 11, 52, 53–54, 169, 191, 232
Greathouse, Pat, 119
Greek-Turkish aid, 59–64, 65–66, 67
Green, Dwight H., 332
Green, Samuel, 220
Greenville Piedmont, 194
Grew, Joseph, 13

Hachmeister, Louise, 323
Hagerty, James, 164, 246, 293
Hague, Frank, 142
Hale, William Harlan, 87
Halleck, Charles
  background/description, 137, 138
  Dewey campaign and, 283
  on midterm elections (1946), 11
  as possible Dewey VP candidate, 137, 138–39
  on Truman, 347
Hall, John H., 113
Hannegan, Robert, 32, 40
Harding, Warren G., 52, 80, 89, 322
Harris, John G., 263
Harrison, Earl G., 6
Harris, Willie, 190
Hartford Courant, 269, 296
Hartley, Fred, 73–74
Hastie, William, 275
Hayden, Martin, 162
Hayes, Rutherford B., 47, 189–90
Hayworth, Rita, 36
Hazard, Tom R., 182
health insurance program (Truman), 16
Hearst, William Randolph/organization, 81–82, 297
Heck, Oswald, 111
Hellman, Lillian, 93, 163
Henderson, Leon, 172
Henderson, Loy, 23
Hepburn, Katharine, 119–20
Herbert, "Tootsie," 54
Hickenlooper, B. B., 140
Hines, James J., 54–55
Hiss, Alger
  description/status, 199–200
  espionage and, 253
  HUAC and, 199, 200, 203, 222
Hitler, Adolf/comparisons, 23–24, 56, 75, 91, 160, 292
Hoeber, Johannes, 177, 266
Holeman, Frank, 331
Hoover, Herbert, 52, 53, 58, 80, 99, 322
Hoover, J. Edgar, 69, 88, 122, 188, 234–35
Hopkins, Harry, 267
House Un-American Activities Committee. *See* HUAC hearings
Howard, Charles P., 163
HUAC hearings
  Bentley and, 197–98
  descriptions, 197–200
  names given, 198–99
  Truman/"red herring" comment and, 201–3, 253, 257, 298
  See also Red Scare; *specific individuals*
Hume, Paul, 229–30
Humphrey, Hubert H., 283
Hurd, R. Carlos, Sr., 194

Ickes, Harold
  Dewey and, 56, 120
  Eisenhower and, 142
  FDR administration, 56
  Truman administration/resignation, 17, 37
  Truman presidential run/election and, 171, 297, 344
impeachment, 202–3
Iowa and politics, 225
Irgun, 21
Isacson, Leo, 120
Israel. *See* Jewish homeland/Israel

Jackson, Andrew, 101
Jacobson, Eddie
  Jewish homeland and, 76, 308
  Truman and, 29, 76, 308, 336, 338
Jaeckle, Edwin, 182, 293
Japan
  Korea and, 287
  Potsdam Declaration and, 3
  surrender and, 3, 4–5, 33
  US bombings of Hiroshima/Nagasaki, 5, 14, 15, 34

Jefferson-Jackson Day Dinner, Mayflower Hotel, Washington DC (1948), 101
Jefferson, Thomas, 101
Jessel, George, 251
Jester, Beauford, 256
Jewish homeland/Israel
  Arab-Israeli War (1948), 109, 210, 288, 353
  Arab refugees and, 288
  assassination of Bernadotte, 288
  Austin incident and, 106–7
  complications during presidential campaign and, 288–91, 300–302, 308
  Israelis wanting US loan, 155
  Jewish declaration of nation, 109
  Palestinian violence and, 155
  State Department views, 23, 25
  Stern Gang and, 105, 288
  support/opposition for establishing, 22–25, 76–77
  Truman administration discussions on, 22–25
  Truman views/recognizing, 10, 77, 109, 304
  UN and, 76–77, 106
  US public opinion/Gallop poll, 76–77
  See also Palestine/"Palestine problem"
Jews
  concentration camps and, 5–6, 23–24
  post-World War II situation, 5–6
  US electorate statistics/influence, 24
  See also Jewish homeland/Israel
Johnson brothers killing black voter, 220–21
Johnson, Louis, 175, 223
Johnson, Lyndon B., 255, 283, 352
Johnston, Olin D., 192–93, 342
Johnston, Vic, 186
Jones, John C., 18–19
Jones, Joseph M., 62–63

Kaltenborn, H. V., 330
Kansas City Star, 294, 341
Kelly, Ed, 292
Kelly, Frank, 150, 297
Kennan, George, 60
Kennedy, John F., 41–42
Kent, Carleton, 313, 323, 333
Kent, Frank R., 246
Key Largo (movie), 210, 251
King David Hotel bombing, 21–22
Kinsey, Alfred, 170
Kiplinger (magazine), 315
Knous, William Lee, 245
Korean War, 287–88, 350, 351
Ku Klux Klan (KKK), 160, 220, 276

Land, Edwin H., 170
Landon, Alf, 57, 97, 344
Lane Act (1795), 122
Laney, Benjamin Travis, 100
Lansky, Meyer, 53
Lee, Robert E., 240
Lehman, Herbert, 55, 303
Leviero, Anthony, 311
Lewis, Clyde, 113
Lewis, Fulton Jr., 183
Lewis, Sinclair, 296
Liberal Party hall mix-up, 302–3
Life (magazine), 125, 170, 315
Lilienthal, David, 98, 125, 223, 258
Lincoln, Abraham, 50, 97, 188–89, 317
Lockwood, Paul, 114, 293
Lodge, Henry Cabot, Jr., 345
Logan Act (1799), 68
London Daily Mail, 316
London *Times*, 59
Longworth, Alice Roosevelt, 345
Los Angeles Times, 50, 246, 269, 294, 336
Lovett, Robert, 107, 108, 289, 291, 325
Lowenthal, Max, 24
Luce, Clare Boothe, 57, 135–36
Luciano, Lucky, 53, 54

MacArthur, Douglas, 16, 81–82, 113
McCarthy, Joseph, 41–42
McCullers, Carson, 297
McCullough, David, 342
McDonald, John, 288
McEnery, John P., 225–26
McGill, Ralph, 315
McGovern, George, 163
McGrath, Howard I., 250, 253, 339
McGrath, J. Howard
  civil rights and, 101–2
  Democratic National Committee/Truman and, 102, 175–76, 177, 224, 323, 331–32, 337, 338, 342
McKim, Eddie, 125
MacLeish, Archibald, 297

McLemore, Henry, 127
McNaughton, Frank, 237
Macy, Kingsland, 202
Madison Square Garden
  history, 66, 66n
  Taft-Hartley bill and, 74
  Wallace and, 66–67
Mailer, Norman, 93, 163
Manchester Guardian, 316
Manhattan Project, 14, 91
  See also atomic weapons/bombs
Mann, Thomas, 93
Marcantonio, Vito, 222
Marked Woman (movie), 55
Marshall, George C.
  Berlin/war possibility and, 155
  China/communism and, 61
  commencement address/Marshall Plan, 65, 66
  Greek/Turkish aid and, 60, 61, 62
  Jewish homeland and, 77, 107–8, 291, 301–2
  Stalin meeting/aftermath, 64–65
  Truman and, 60, 98, 269
Marshall Plan
  description, 65–66
  Soviets and, 102, 103
  support/opposition, 80–81, 347
  US House passage, 104
  Wallace and, 67, 117, 206, 207, 264, 284
Marshall, Thurgood, 192
Martin, Joe
  background/description, 50, 231
  Dewey and, 299–300
  on election (1948), 345
  Greek/Turkish aid and, 62, 63
  Republican National Convention (1948) and, 134, 135
  Truman and, 10, 151
Masaryk, Jan, 102
Mason, George, 240
Maxwell, John, 319
Maybank, Burnet, 21
Mead, James M., 48
Mellett, Lowell, 131
Memorial Hall (Truman Memorial Building), 317–18, 317n
Mencken, H. L., 135, 163, 202
Merkur (Munich newspaper), 337
Mesta, Perle, 257
Meuse-Argonne Offensive, 29
Miall, Leonard, 232
Middle East
  bombing Arab office building, Jaffa, 105
  postwar situation, 6
  See also Jewish homeland/Israel; *specific events/locations*; *specific individuals/groups*
Miller, Arthur, 93
Miller, Donald P., 322
Miller, Emma Guffey, 150
Millikin, Eugene, 127, 156
Molotov, Vyacheslav, 210, 343
Morin, Relman, 163
Morison, H. Graham, 333–34
Morse, David, 176–77
Mostel, Zero, 67
Mundt, Karl, 197, 198
Murphy, Charlie, 100, 126, 128, 179, 213–14, 227
Murrow, Edward R., 6, 349, 354

NAACP
  description, 192
  Elmore case, 192
  helping blacks vote, 220
  Truman's speech to members/aftermath, 71–73
  White meeting with Truman, 18–20
  See also specific individuals
NASCAR beginnings, 170
Nash, Philleo, 178, 308, 309, 310, 324, 346–47
Nashville Banner, 238
National Association for the Advancement of Colored People. *See* NAACP
National Security Act (1947), 75
National Security Council, 75
Nation, The, 300–301
New Republic, 87
Newsweek (magazine), 270–71, 315, 341, 347
New Yorker, 134, 235
New York Daily News, 331
New York Herald Times, 324
New York Post, 24
New York Star, 208
New York Times/polls, 5, 75, 107, 120, 134, 164, 182, 194, 195, 202, 219, 229, 235, 242, 246, 258, 282, 293, 294, 311, 315, 316, 336, 339

Nicholson, Henry J., 26, 233
Niles, David, 20, 23, 24
1948 summer (US)
  cars/NASCAR and, 170
  cigarettes and, 170
  consumerism/products, 169–71
  offices/office buildings and, 170–71
  situation/inventions (overview), 169–71
  See also specific events
Nixon, Isaiah voting/murder, 220–21, 320
Nixon, Richard
  daughter's engagement party/Dewey and, 351
  on election (1948), 345
  HUAC/Hiss and, 197, 199, 203, 204, 205
  midterm elections (1946) and, 41–42
  Republican trend and, 50
Nixon, Robert, 128, 147, 201–2, 297, 304, 313, 333, 335
Nokrashy Pasha, 23
Noland, Mary Ethel, 327–28
Noyes, David, 293

Odets, Clifford, 93
O'Dwyer, William, 310
Operation Sandstone, 121, 154
Othman, Fred, 180

Palestine/"Palestine problem"
  British Mandate for Palestine, 22, 76, 105, 107, 108–9
  oil and, 22, 25
  Truman administration discussions, 22–24
  See also Jewish homeland/Israel
Parker, George F., 118
Pearson, Drew, 25–26, 142–43, 224, 315, 321, 332
Pegler, Westbrook, 116, 162–63, 165, 242–43, 295–96
Pendergast, Jim, 29
Pendergast, Mike, 29–30
Pendergast, Tom ("Big Boss"), 30, 31
Pepper, Claude, 142
Pierce, Thomas W., 344
"Politics of 1948, The" memo (Rowe), 95–98, 101, 106
polls. *See* Gallop polls; Roper, Elmo/polls
Potsdam Conference/Declaration, 3, 7, 13
Powell, Adam Clayton, Jr., 16–17
presidential airplane nickname, 65
Presidential Succession Act (1947), 42n
President's Committee on Civil Rights, 20
Pressman, Lee, 87, 199, 205, 222
Progressive Citizens of America (PCA), 88
Progressive Party. *See* Wallace, Henry campaign for presidency
Prohibition, 53
Propper, Karl, 120

racism
  against black veterans, 18–20
  black vote suppression, 189, 192–93, 195, 219, 220–21, 255
  federal law against lynching and, 100
  following Truman's NAACP/civil rights speech, 72, 73
  in Georgia, 219–21
  lynchings/stories, 18–20, 194, 208, 286
  segregation and, 16–17, 20–21, 72, 73, 101, 188, 193, 205–8, 220, 238
  Truman opposing, 20–21, 71–73
  Wakulla Springs, Florida and, 100
  "white supremacy" and, 71, 72, 73, 100–101, 160, 161, 187–88, 189, 190, 191, 193, 219, 220, 311, 342
  See also Dixiecrats; southern Democrats; *specific individuals/groups*
Racket Busters (movie), 55
Rackoff, Dorothy Bell, 344
Ravensbrück, 5–6
Rayburn, Sam, 151, 162, 255, 256
Reconstruction, 189
Redding, Jack
  on Stassen, 82
  Truman/DNC and, 74, 102, 123, 175, 278–79, 298–99, 324
"red herring" comment (Truman), 201–3, 253, 257, 298
"red herring" meaning, 201
Red Scare
  beginnings, 201, 203–4
  Hollywood and, 251
  See also HUAC hearings
Red Shirts/movement, 189
Reece, B. Carroll, 136

Republican National Committee (1948 campaign) headquarters, 175
Republican National Convention (1948)
balloting and, 136
Dewey and, 133, 134, 136–37
GOP candidate selection and, 81, 133
Little Eva (elephant) and, 134, 135
official plank, 139
polls/media predictions, 134
schism between Dewey-Warren platform/ Eightieth Congress, 139, 145
speeches, 135–36
television and, 135, 140
Truman and, 139, 140
VP candidate/possibilities and, 137–39
Reuter, Ernst, 211
Reuther, Wallace, 119
Revenue Act (1948), 127
Rhee, Syngman, 287, 288
Rickard, Tex, 66
Rivers, Mendel, 172
Roach, Neale, 151, 175
Roberts, Ernest, 286
Robeson, Paul, 163–64, 222, 334
Robinson, Edward G., 120
Robinson, Jackie, 134
Roerich, Nicholas
background/description, 89–91
Wallace letters ("guru letters"), 90, 116, 162–63, 164, 242–43
Romagna, Jack, 227
Roosevelt, Eleanor
on HUAC, 200
on Jewish homeland, 24
Truman and, 4, 71, 104, 179, 278–79, 296–97
Roosevelt, Elliot, 67, 93
Roosevelt, Franklin
death/Truman becoming president, 4, 6, 33
description, 56
on Dewey, 57, 271
New Deal/other policies and, 7, 8–9, 31, 50, 83, 161
presidential elections and, 53, 55, 191
time as president, 7
Truman supporting, 31
vice president and, 32–33
Roosevelt, James, II, 127, 142
Roosevelt, Theodore
becoming/as president, 9, 145, 234, 322
Dewey/Dewey's family and, 51, 52
liberalism and, 52
New York governor mansion and, 47
Roper, Elmo/polls, 143, 172, 212, 246, 315, 348–49
Rose, Billy, 17
Rosenman, Samuel, 7–8, 9, 171
Ross, Charlie
background/description, 12, 245
Truman and, 9, 12, 39, 41, 42, 126, 268, 323, 331, 335
Rovere, Richard, 25, 235
Rowe, James H., Jr./memo, 95–98
Rowley, James J., 233, 333
Royall, Kenneth, 140, 153
"rubber" capital of US, 270
Russell, Bertrand, 203
Russell, Richard B., 73, 147
Ruth, Babe, 184

St. Louis Post-Dispatch, 294, 307
San Francisco Chronicle, 184
Sarnoff, David, 171
Sauter, Jim, 332
Scott, Hugh, 139, 156, 157, 182, 183, 273
Seeger, Pete, 163, 222
Sermon, Roger, 320, 339
Sexual Behavior in the Human Male (Kinsey), 170
Shahn, Ben, 93
Shapiro, Jacob "Gurrah," 54
Shapley, Harlow, 67
Shultz, Lillie, 300–301
Sims, Byrd, 147
Sloan, Alfred, 272–73
Smith, Al, 58
Smith, Gerald L. K., 160, 319
Smith, Lonnie E., 192
Smith, Merriman, 41
Smith v. Allwright (1944), 192, 220
Smith, Walter Bedell, 210, 256
Smith, W. Eugene, 342
Snyder, John, 312
southern Democrats
civil rights and, 72, 73, 100–102, 147–48, 149–50, 179–80
historical alignments, 72, 96

military desegregation and, 178, 179–80
protests at convention (1948) and, 147–48, 149–50
racism of, 72, 73, 97, 100–102, 147–48, 178, 179–80
Rowe-Clifford memo and, 96, 97, 101
segregation and, 72, 73, 101
Wakulla Springs, Florida and, 100
See also Dixiecrats
Soviet Union
atomic weapons/bombs use, 154, 154–55n
communism expansion and, 59–65, 102–5
Czechoslovakia control and, 102–3
"Long Telegram" (Kennan) and, 60
Marshall Plan and, 102, 103
postwar US relationship, 6, 13, 102–5
See also Cold War; Germany, Berlin; Stalin, Joseph
Sprague, J. Russell, 79, 80, 182
Stalin, Joseph
atomic weapons and, 35
Berlin and, 210
Marshall meeting and, 64
Moscow speech/Five-Year Plan, 35
open letter from Wallace/response, 121–22
Potsdam Conference and, 7
Stassen and, 82
See also Soviet Union; Vinson mission
Stassen, Harold
background/description, 51, 82, 113
Dewey campaign/Truman rebuttal speech and, 186, 218–19
Stassen, Harold presidential run (1948)
on communism, 112, 114, 115
Dewey debate/consequences, 114–16
polls and, 110
primaries and, 112, 113
Republican National Convention (1948) and, 134, 136
State of the Union (1948)
civil rights and, 99, 195
description/significance, 98–99
response, 99
States' Rights Democratic Party. *See* Dixiecrats
Steelman, John, 60
Stennis, John C., 179–80
Stern Gang, 105, 288
Stevenson, Adlai, 332
Stimson, Henry, 14, 51–52
Stokes, Thomas, 142
Stone, I. F., 24
Stoner, J. B., 160
Straus, Roger, Mr./Mrs., 321
Stripling, Robert, 198, 199
Strout, Richard, 124, 128, 226, 277, 282–83
Sunday Evening Hour, 229

Taber, John, Dewey and, 82–83
Taft-Hartley bill/Act, 73–74, 98, 205, 216, 238, 264, 290, 307, 346, 354
Taft, Robert
background/description, 16, 80, 231, 329, 350
emergency session and, 156, 157
Marshall Plan and, 66
presidential run (1948), 81, 110, 134, 137
Truman and, 16, 18, 66, 98, 99
"whistle stop" use and, 128–29
Taft, William H., 14, 134, 322
Talmadge, Eugene, 73, 219
Talmadge, Herman, 219–20
"Talmadge White Supremacy Clubs," 73
Taylor, Glen H.
background/description, 93
as Wallace running mate, 93–94, 119, 163, 164, 165, 242
television
election (1948) and, 171, 321, 324, 325, 329
inauguration (1949), 353
national convention (1948) and, 135, 140, 143, 146, 148
predictions on/effects, 171, 263
Terkel, Studs, 93
Thackrey, Ted, 24
Thomas, J. Parnell, 68, 197, 205
Thompson, Melvin E., 220
Thurmond, John
background, 188, 190–91
killing a man, 190
Tillman and, 190–91
Thurmond, Strom
after 1948 election, 351–52, 354
becoming/as South Carolina governor, 192, 193, 194–95, 205
changing parties, 240
description/personality traits, 101, 159, 188
Jean (wife) and, 188, 240, 319

Thurmond, Strom (*cont.*)
party realignment and, 239–40, 352
protesting Democratic National Convention, 147
racism of, 101–2, 147, 158, 159–60, 187–88, 190–91, 192, 193, 195, 238, 275, 276
Willie Earle murder and, 194–95
See also Dixiecrats
Thurmond, Strom background
childhood/youth, 188, 190–91
Essie Mae (child/secrecy) and, 191, 195, 276–77, 351–52
father relationship/admiration, 191
racism and, 190–91
Tillman and, 190–91, 276
World War II and, 101, 191–92
Thurmond, Strom presidential run
debate request (Truman) and, 274
Dixiecrats/States' Rights Party and, 158, 159–60, 161, 187–88, 238–40
election day, 319
expectations/results, 285, 353–54
invitations to governors/African American governor, 275
oil money and, 274–75
polls on, 238–39, 254, 274
Texas and, 254, 311–12
on Truman/civil rights, 270, 275, 311–12
on Vinson mission, 270
Tilden, Samuel, 47, 189–90
Tillman, Benjamin ("Pitchfork"), 189, 190–91
Time (magazine), 82, 116, 164, 199, 237, 342
Tindle, Lee, 281
train tours
laundry/showers and, 217, 236, 237, 247
life/routine descriptions, 237, 244–45, 247–48
speeds, 245
Truman, Bess
communication/relationship with husband, 25–26, 31, 40, 62, 73, 180, 227
description/views, 228–29, 286
expectations on presidential election, 249, 266
husband's presidential duties and, 3, 33
husband's presidential run/election and, 123, 212, 225, 229, 244, 247, 249, 259, 292, 303, 312, 317, 318, 327, 335, 341, 342
Pearson criticism and, 25–26
segregated theater event and, 16–17
vacation, 353
visiting family, 212, 224
White House deterioration and, 42–43
See also Wallace, Elizabeth "Bess"
Truman Doctrine
beginnings/description, 63–64
controversy over, 65
passing/support for, 157, 264, 347
signing, 322
Soviets and, 103
Wallace and, 67, 69, 264, 351
Truman, Harry
communication/relationship with mother, 4, 13, 15, 65
communication with sister, 13, 209
FDR/Hopkins and, 267
First Family as curiosity to Americans, 228, 229
inauguration (1949) and, 353–54
speaking abilities and, 4, 98, 124–25
Truman, Harry childhood/background
becoming/as judge, 29–30, 317–318
becoming vice president/FDR, 32–33, 92, 322
"Bess" and, 27–28, 29
family background/Civil War, 28, 179
family home of Bess and, 29
locations/description, 27
parents/siblings, 27, 28
politics/Democrats and, 28
reading/diphtheria and, 28
segregation and, 20–21
Truman & Jacobson haberdashery and, 29
World War I and, 29
Truman, Harry presidency
approval ratings, 15, 25, 33, 144, 148, 160
assassination attempt, 228n, 350
becoming president, 4, 6, 33
criticism of/jokes about, 16–18, 62
descriptions/personal traits, 4, 98, 197, 230, 249, 266, 282
Fair Deal/views and, 354
Greek-Turkish aid and, 60–64, 65–66
issues facing (overview) and, 25–26
military/intelligence establishments reorganization, 75

on national situation, 95
as New Deal Democrat president, 10
obscurity of, 6
Pearson criticizing wife/daughter and, 25–26
press/bad news overview, 12–13
questions about future presidency, 6–7, 33
sign on desk, 15
successes, 144
See also specific aspects/events

Truman, Harry presidential run
attacking Dewey/Dewey response, 292–96
attack on media, 294–95
black vote and, 97, 195
California/supporters and, 247, 248–51, 252
campaign beginning/train tour, 186, 200, 212–17
comedy routine, Pittsburgh, 290
communism, 251–52, 257–58
confidence in winning, 152, 173, 177, 249, 266, 277, 295, 318, 331
contrasts with Dewey campaign, 236–37
crowd sizes/reception and, 248–49, 276–77, 282, 292, 297–98, 300, 303, 309, 313, 314
decision to run, 77–78
Detroit/Michigan appearances and, 186, 200, 214–17
"Draft Eisenhower" campaign and, 127, 143
election and, 317–18, 320–21, 330–31, 333–34, 335–36, 337–39
Ewing adviser group/advice and, 171, 174, 176–77
expectations, 124, 127, 142–43, 144, 147, 148, 160, 171–73, 212, 214, 216–17, 225, 232, 233, 246, 248, 258, 264, 270–71, 279, 320, 323–24, 327
farmers and, 225, 231–33, 277
final itinerary/Dewey "following," 283, 292–93, 294–95, 296–99, 300–305
in Florida, 285–86
global issues (overview) and, 154–56
Harlem/civil-rights and, 305, 308–11
identifying his opponent, 230–31
Idlewild Airport dedication/Dewey and, 196–97
money/donors and, 124, 171–72, 211, 215, 223–24, 250, 251, 256–57, 258, 266, 277–78, 285, 320
mood leading up to convention, 145–46
organized labor and, 186, 215–16, 217
platform/views similar to Dewey, 231, 264, 299
plowing demonstration/stunt and, 233
"Politics of 1948, The" memo and, 95–98
St. Louis/final appearance, 312–14
speaking tour/problems (June), 124–29
statement on Wallace/Communists and, 120–21, 122
State of the Union address and, 98–99
strategy/populism, 264–65
Texas and, 254–56, 265
tour west (September), 224–28, 230–33, 244–52
train kitchen food, 226
train tour (October-November), 270–71, 276–77, 279–80
University of California, Berkeley commencement and, 124, 126
vacation/presidential yacht, 210
on Wallace/communism, 251–52
"whistle-stop"/speeches use, 129, 173, 212, 213, 214, 226, 227, 227n, 230, 231, 244, 248–49, 254, 255, 277, 292, 303
See also Democratic National Convention (1948); election (1948); *specific aspects*; *specific groups/individuals*

Truman, Harry Senator
becoming senator/controversy, 30–31
investigating National Defense Program and, 31–32
reelection as senator, 31
as senator, 30–32

Truman, Margaret
background, 286
correspondence/relationship with father, 25–26, 33, 40, 41, 180, 227, 229, 230
Daniel and, 316
on Democrats/Independence, 28
election day/night and, 317, 318, 327
music/career and, 229–30
Pearson criticism and, 25–26

Truman, Margaret (*cont.*)
presidential run/election and, 123, 172, 212, 215, 216, 224, 225, 230, 244–45, 247–48, 256, 259, 266, 270–71, 290, 292, 303, 312, 315, 319, 341, 342–43
public interest in, 229
vacation, 353
White House deteriorating and, 200
Truman, Mary Jane, 13, 27, 167, 173, 209
Truman Presidential Library, 330n
Truman Story, The (documentary), 279, 298–99
Truman, Vivian, 27, 172, 339
Trump, Donald J., 348, 352
Turkish-Greek aid, 59–64, 65–66, 67
Turner, Roy J., 215
Tweed, "Boss," 55
21-Point Plan for the Reconversion Period (Truman), 9–11

United Nations negotiations, Paris (1948), 269, 271, 272, 278, 301–2, 308
United Press, 41, 147, 297
USS *Augusta*, 8
USS *Williamsburg*, 210, 353

Vaccaro, Tony, 41, 335
Van Boskirk, Donald, 115
Vandenberg, Arthur
Dewey and, 55, 58, 184, 296, 307
emergency session and, 156
Greek/Turkish aid and, 62, 63
Marshall Plan and, 66
Republican National Convention (1948) and, 134, 137–38
on Truman, 33
Vinson mission and, 268, 269
Wallace and, 38–39, 68
Vardaman, James K., 174
Vaughan, Harry, 30
veterans
black soldiers/violence against, 18–20
homelessness and, 13
vice presidency poll (1944), 92
Vinson, Fred, 267–68, 353–54
Vinson mission
debate on, 267, 268–69
Dewey and, 271–72, 274
leak/criticism of, 269–70
Truman canceling, 269
Truman idea on, 266–67, 268
Voorhis, Jerry, 50
Vyshinsky, Andrey, 103

Wallace, Elizabeth "Bess"
family social status and, 28
Truman and, 27–28
See also Truman, Bess
Wallace, George R., 307
Wallace, Henry
after 1948 election/death, 351
atomic weapons/Soviets and, 15, 34–35, 36–40, 91
"Century of the Common Man, The" speech, 91
childhood/education, 89
Cold War and, 86, 91, 93
description/lifestyle, 89
on differences between communism/himself, 88
eccentricity of, 89–91, 92
European tour, 67–68
father's work and, 89
FDR vice presidency/dropping and, 32, 91, 92
Hi-Bred Corn and, 89
Ilo (wife), 85, 89, 242, 318–19, 334
letter to Truman/consequences, 39–40
on "loyalty boards," 75
New Deal and, 40, 68, 85–86, 89, 92
positions (Truman administration), 5, 34
Roerich and, 89–91
"speech"/reactions and, 36–39
suspicions on, 68–69, 70
Truman firing, 40
Truman relationship (summary), 36, 92
Wallace, Henry campaign for presidency
American divisions and, 117
on Berlin crisis, 164
black vote and, 117, 195, 206–8
communism/support and, 69–70, 86–88, 94, 96, 117, 118–19, 120–21, 162, 164–65, 199, 205, 206–7, 222, 240–42, 285
election day/night and, 318–19, 325–26, 334–35
expectations/results, 212, 274, 345
final speech, 311

"Gideon's Army" and, 85, 163, 164, 165, 207, 221, 285, 334, 351
HUAC and, 199, 205
Isacson election and, 120
launching/speech, 85–86
lawsuit/Supreme Court and, 242
Marshall Plan and, 67, 117, 206, 207, 264, 284
Moscow misinformation, 325
New York City rally (1948), 221–22
open letter to Stalin/response, 121–22
peace and, 85, 86–87, 91, 93, 117, 118–19, 121, 122, 164, 240
platform comparisons with Truman/ Dewey, 334
political fallout from launch, 86
Progressive Party/convention, 86, 161–16585
Roerich (guru) letters and, 116, 162–63, 164, 242–43
running mate, 93–94
southern tour/showing discrimination, 205–8, 266
supporters and, 91, 93, 117, 119–20, 163–64, 165, 221–22, 284–85
tone changing/eccentricities, 241
on tour/fighting Truman's foreign policy, 67–70, 71
on Truman, 283–84, 311, 335
Truman win/concession speech and, 334–35
views/platform, 92–93, 94, 164–65, 221–22, 351
vitriol/violence towards, 119, 205–8, 240–41
Wallace, Henry Cantwell, 89
Wallaces' Farmer, 89
Wall Street Journal, 269, 294
Walsh, Jerome, 336
Waring, J. Waties, 193
Warren, Earl
background/California and, 249–50, 338
Dewey/as VP candidate, 110, 138, 139, 184, 231, 249, 340
Warren, Tom, 140
Washington Evening Star, 127
Washington Post, 1, 10, 30–40, 86, 95, 127, 148, 195, 202, 224, 229–30, 235, 261, 277, 337, 341
Washington Star, 294
Watson, Claude A., 319
Watt, Sam, 194
Weizmann, Chaim, 106, 343, 353
Welles, Orson, 24
West, J. B., 343
Wheeler, Al, 266
White, Harry Dexter, 198
White House deterioration/repairing, 42–43, 209, 258, 265, 343
White House press corps, 41
White, Walter Francis
background/description, 18
Truman's speech to NAACP and, 71–72
undercover investigations/stories to Truman, 18–20
Whitney, Alexander, 17
Williams, Gladstone, 135
Williams, Julius, 276
Willkie, Wendell, 56, 58, 119
Wilson, Charles G., Reverend, 284
Wilson, Woodrow, 106, 322
Winchell, Walter, 315, 321
Winslow, Lorenzo, 265
Women's Wear Daily, 337
Woodard, Isaac, 19–20
World War I, 29, 52, 317
World War II
Nazi triumphs and, 31
rationing, 169
Truman Committee/military spending investigation, 31–32
See also specific events/individuals
World War III fears, 143, 155, 156, 169, 173, 184, 223, 224, 256, 287
Wright, Fielding, 161
Wright, Frank Lloyd, 93, 120
Wyatt, Lee B., 205

Yalta Conference, 13
Yastrzemski, Carl, 351
Yeager, Chuck, 170